SHELDON NORD

INVOLVING COLLEGES

George D. Kuh

John H. Schuh

Elizabeth J. Whitt

Rosalind E. Andreas

James W. Lyons

C. Carney Strange

Lee E. Krehbiel

Kathleen A. MacKay

INVOLVING COLLEGES

Successful Approaches to
Fostering Student Learning
and Development
Outside the Classroom

Jossey-Bass Publishers

San Francisco • Oxford • 1991

INVOLVING COLLEGES

Successful Approaches to Fostering Student Learning and Development Outside the Classroom
by George D. Kuh, John H. Schuh, Elizabeth J. Whitt, and Associates

Copyright © 1991 by: Jossey-Bass Inc., Publishers
350 Sansome Street
San Francisco, California 94104
&
Jossey-Bass Limited
Headington Hill Hall
Oxford OX3 0BW

Library of Congress Cataloging-in-Publication Data

Involving colleges : successful approaches to fostering student
   learning and development outside the classroom / George D. Kuh . . .
   [et al.].
      p.   cm. — (The Jossey-Bass higher and adult education series)
   Includes bibliographical references (p.   ) and index.
   ISBN 1-55542-305-1
   1. College students — United States.   2. Universities and colleges —
United States.   3. Student activities — United States.   4. Learning.
5. Personality development.   I. Kuh, George D.   II. Series.
LA229.I58   1991
378.1'98'0973 — dc20   90-46106
                                                                           CIP

Manufactured in the United States of America

The paper in this book meets the guidelines for
permanence and durability of the Committee on
Production Guidelines for Book Longevity of
the Council on Library Resources.

JACKET DESIGN BY WILLI BAUM

FIRST EDITION

Code 9106

The Jossey-Bass
Higher and Adult Education Series

Contents

Preface

In a given week, about two-thirds of a college student's waking hours are devoted to activities other than attending class and studying. What do students do when they are not in the classroom? Interest in the answer to this question has increased in recent years for several reasons. Student behavior antithetical to the educational aims and purposes of higher education has received attention in the popular media. Substance abuse, racial incidents, and violence on campus are seen by some as symptomatic of an erosion of the sense of community on campus.

Because students spend more time out of class than in class, it would seem that learning could be enhanced if students were involved in such educationally purposeful out-of-class activities as institutional governance, leadership roles in student organizations, community service activities, and independent research projects. In fact, when asked about what they learned in college, graduates frequently mention that participation in activities outside class increased their confidence, competence, and self-assurance (Marchese, 1990). The research is unequivocal: students who are actively involved in both academic and out-of-class activities gain more from the college experience than those who are not so involved. *Involvement in Learning* (Study Group on the Conditions of Excellence in American Higher Education, 1984) underscored the importance of creating institutional conditions that encourage students to take advantage of learning opportunities.

Assessment of student learning has focused largely on

classroom activities, emphasizing the effectiveness of formal teaching-learning processes in classrooms or laboratories and essentially ignoring what students learn outside class. Few efforts have been undertaken to assess the contributions of out-of-class experiences to the overall quality of the undergraduate experience, perhaps because little is known about institutions where the out-of-class experience is a positive educational force and extracurricular opportunities complement classroom goals. Indeed, in *College: The Undergraduate Experience in America,* Boyer (1987) observed that the educational role of out-of-class experiences was often misunderstood and underemphasized. Moreover, the literature is silent on the institutional factors and conditions that encourage students to take advantage of learning opportunities outside the classroom.

Taken together, these themes provide a clear warrant for discovering what institutions can do to encourage student learning outside class. In addition, a study of such learning opportunities may provide insights into how undergraduate learning environments can be assessed.

Purpose

The assumption on which this book is based is that there are colleges and universities that provide undergraduate students with unusually rich opportunities for out-of-class learning and personal development — that complement the institution's educational goals. Our purpose is to describe the factors and conditions that characterize such institutions. The information on which *Involving Colleges* is based was collected under the auspices of the College Experiences Study, a yearlong investigation of fourteen four-year colleges and universities. We hope that the findings from this project will stimulate thinking about the relationship between out-of-class experiences and student involvement in learning both inside and outside the classroom.

This book is not a blueprint for ensuring a high-quality undergraduate experience for every student, nor does it present "one best model" that should be adopted by every college or university for promoting student learning and personal development outside the classroom. Institutions of higher education and the students who attend them are too diverse and complex for such simple products to be useful. However, we believe that the policies and practices of the "Involving Colleges" described here can be adapted and used on campuses with different missions, environments, and cultures. The book provides a framework that can be used by administrators, faculty members, and others to examine their own campuses and identify ways in which their practices can be modified to enhance student learning.

Audience

College and university presidents, academic and student affairs administrators, and faculty members will find examples of ways they can encourage students to take advantage of learning opportunities outside class. Chief academic officers and student life officers can use the ideas presented here in planning professional development opportunities for faculty and staff, new student and new faculty orientation, and leadership development activities for students. Particular attention has been given to the ways in which faculty members can use out-of-class contacts with students to encourage learning, and to the ways in which the institutional culture shapes behavior. State legislators and university trustees should find the information useful for policy development and resource allocation.

The book will also be a valuable resource for higher education scholars and students preparing for teaching and administrative roles in colleges and universities because it illustrates how students' experiences outside the classroom can complement educational goals and what institutional agents can do to enhance student learning. Graduate students in higher education and student affairs preparation programs will find material pertinent to their work and suggestions for what they can do to enhance the quality of student learning opportunities out of class.

Scope and Treatment

The fourteen institutions that participated in the College Experiences Study are described in this book in very positive terms. Because the purpose of the study was, in essence, to discover and describe the best practices, accentuating the positive is certainly appropriate. We do not claim, however, that these colleges and universities are *the* best in the United States. Nor do all these institutions manifest every one of the properties described. Every institution has problems, unmet challenges, critics, and programs and services that could be improved.

Some readers may be disappointed that we have not addressed the perennial issues associated with student life outside the classroom that occasionally paralyze a college or university community, such as athletics overshadowing academics, fraternity hazing, violence, and alcohol or other drug abuse. The primary reason these issues receive relatively little attention in the book is that they were not galvanizing forces in the colleges we studied, at least during the time our study was conducted. That is not to say, of course, that no students at these institutions abuse drugs or indulge in behavior inconsistent with the mission and educational purposes of the institution. We are satisfied, however, that the quality of student life at the institutions we describe is high, in part because of the productive ways students spend their time out of class. On balance, a good deal can be learned from Involving Colleges about promoting student involvement in educationally purposeful out-of-class activities.

Overview of the Contents

The book is divided into three parts. In the chapters in Part One, the warrant for the study is discussed in more detail. Chapter One examines the contributions of out-of-class experiences to student learning and personal development — for example, satisfaction, achievement, and development of leadership skills. Chapter Two describes how we selected the institutions and discusses the questions that guided our study of how institutions promote student learning outside the classroom.

The material in Part Two describes the five sets of factors and conditions shared to varying degrees by Involving Colleges: mission and philosophy (Chapter Three), campus culture

(Chapter Four), campus environment (Chapter Five), institutional policies and practices (Chapter Six), and the role of administrators, faculty, and students in promoting students' out-of-class learning and personal development (Chapter Seven). In Chapters Eight through Ten, we describe selected policies and practices to illustrate how the factors and conditions work in different types of institutions.

In the chapters in Part Three, we discuss the implications of these factors and conditions and offer recommendations for administrators, faculty, and others committed to enhancing the quality of out-of-class learning opportunities at their institutions. Before an institution can take action, someone must discover what students do with their time outside class and what the institution does to encourage (or discourage) student learning and personal development. Chapter Eleven presents principles for conducting a campus audit, an institutional self-study process designed to determine the out-of-class learning and personal development opportunities available at the institution. Chapters Twelve through Fourteen discuss how institutional mission and philosophy, campus environments, and policies and practices can be used to promote student learning and personal development out of class. These chapters are based on what we saw and heard taking place at Involving Colleges, not on a review of the literature. Where appropriate, however, we cite published works the findings of which are consistent with Involving College policies and practices. In Chapter Fifteen, we present the conclusions from the study and offer recommendations for institutions interested in enhancing out-of-class learning opportunities for their students. We also consider some unresolved issues related to student involvement and conditions that seem to be associated with a sense of community on campus.

We have tried to be sensitive to the differences in language used at the fourteen institutions to describe various groups on their campuses. As we discuss in Chapter Fourteen, terms of respect for students of color vary by region of the country. For example, we have used the terms *Mexican American* or *Chicano* and *Chicana* when discussing students of Mexican descent at the University of California, Davis, or at Stanford University. However, when referring to students of Mexican descent at Iowa State University, the term *Hispanic* is used because that is the term of respect on that campus. Similarly, black students are referred to variously as black, African American, or black American, depending on the campus being discussed.

Acknowledgments

A project such as this is costly and requires the assistance and good will of many people. We are indebted to three organizations that provided funds to conduct the study: the Lilly Endowment, Inc., the Institute for Research and Development of the National Association of Student Personnel Administrators, and the Education Division of the Marriott Corporation. Without the interest and support of these organizations, we simply could not have undertaken a project of this magnitude. Also, a sabbatical leave from Indiana University afforded a large block of uninterrupted time for George Kuh to write and edit without distraction. Bowling Green State University provided a professional development leave for Carney Strange, part of which was spent visiting campuses and writing institutional case summaries. Special thanks to our colleagues at the University of Arizona, Stanford University, and Wichita State University for taking care of business while Rosalind Andreas, James Lyons, and John Schuh were conducting site visits to other institutions. We hope this book reflects favorably on the investment these groups made in our work.

We sought the counsel of many colleagues at various points in the project. Elaine El-Khawas, vice-president of the American Council on Education, Theodore Marchese, vice-president of the American Association for Higher Education, and Elizabeth Nuss, executive director of the National Association of Student Personnel Administrators, deserve special mention for their help. In addition, forty-five other members of the higher education community assisted us in identifying colleges and universities that offer unusually rich out-of-class learning opportunities for their students (Resource A). With their advice, we were able to winnow the approximately 2,100 four-year colleges and universities for a reasonable number to consider for inclusion in the study.

In a project such as this, the information obtained is only as good as the people involved — those who provide the information and those who collect and make sense of what they have heard and seen. As the "Authors" section indicates, the members of the project team have extensive experience in various positions in different types of institutions (see also Resource D). Although he is not listed among the authors, J. Herman Blake played a significant role in conceptualizing the project and gathering data. As a member of the College Experiences Study team, Herman participated in the selection of institutions and visited five of them. During the course of the study, he accepted his present position as vice-chancellor of Indiana University–Purdue University at Indianapolis. The demands of his new job reduced the amount of time he was able to devote to this project. Blake's ideas, support, and encouragement have been invaluable to us throughout the project.

Jeffrey McCollough, a master's student at Indiana University, assisted in the data collection at Stanford University and the University of California, Davis. Nicholas Vesper, a doctoral candidate in higher education at Indiana, was very helpful in analyzing the results of the College Student Experiences Questionnaire presented in Resource B.

When selecting the institutions to be studied, we were sensitive to the fact that several project team members were employed by institutions that received multiple nominations by the panel of experts. After considerable discussion, we concluded that it would be irresponsible to eliminate an institution from consideration for this reason. Ultimately, two such institutions (Stanford University and Wichita State University) were included. The team members from these institutions did not participate in the data collection at their universities.

At the time of writing, two additional members of the College Experiences Study team have taken positions at institutions represented in the study. Lee Krehbiel and Elizabeth Whitt joined their respective institutions, Berea College and Iowa State University, *after* the study was completed.

We owe a special debt of gratitude to the people who served as the institutional contacts. They coordinated our visits to their institutions and devoted many hours to compiling materials, gathering documents, arranging interviews, and handling other details related to the study. The following individuals, and their assistants, were instrumental in making our campus visits productive, informative, and enjoyable: Ruth Butwell, Berea College; Anne Wright, Earlham College; Gail Martin, The Evergreen State College; Thomas Crady and Oda Callison, Grinnell College; Thomas Thielen and Ardys Ulrichson, Iowa State University; Robert Etheridge and Derrell Hart, Miami University; Sheila Murphy and Laura Gauthier, Mount Holyoke College; Nadine O'Leary, Stanford University; John Jones, University of Alabama, Birmingham; Thomas Dutton and David Haggerty, University of California, Davis; Dennis Golden and Dale Adams, University of Louisville; Charles Lynch, University of North Carolina, Charlotte; James Rhatigan, Wichita State University; and Ann Harvey and Barbara Franklin, Xavier University.

Conducting a research project on multiple campuses and preparing a manuscript such as this required the assistance of people with exceptional organizational and clerical skills. In addition to regular duties, Connie Riggins did her usual superb job in preparing materials during the start-up phase of the project. Joyce Regester joined the project as a clerk-typist but by the end of the study had emerged as the project manager. In addition, she typed drafts of most chapters. Cheryl Wolff was very helpful in preparing institutional case reports and several chapters.

Finally, we wish to thank the hundreds of students, faculty members, administrators, staff, and others at these fourteen institutions, many of whom spoke with us more than once, for sharing their insights into their colleges and universities.

January 1991

Rosalind E. Andreas
Burlington, Vermont

Lee E. Krehbiel
Berea, Kentucky

George D. Kuh
Bloomington, Indiana

James W. Lyons
Stanford, California

Kathleen A. MacKay
Bloomington, Indiana

John H. Schuh
Wichita, Kansas

C. Carney Strange
Bowling Green, Ohio

Elizabeth J. Whitt
Ames, Iowa

The Authors

Rosalind E. Andreas is vice-president for student affairs at the University of Vermont. She received her B.A. degree (1963) in English from Bethel College in Kansas, her M.A. degree (1973) in speech communication from the University of Kansas, and her Ph.D. degree (1984) in higher education from the University of Michigan.

Andreas previously served as dean of students at the University of Arizona and at Oakland University, where she directed offices of student activities and commuter affairs. Before becoming a college administrator, Andreas taught an interdisciplinary secondary school curriculum and was a consulting teacher in both staff and curriculum development. She was the founding chairperson of the Commuter Programs Commission (XVII) of the American College Personnel Association (ACPA) and currently serves on the editorial board of the *NASPA Journal*. Andreas has written on student leadership programs, commuter students, and institutional planning. She is a member of the board of directors of Bethel College.

Lee E. Krehbiel is director of campus activities and of the Alumni Building at Berea College in Kentucky. He received his B.A. degree (1981) in history from Wichita State University, his B.S. degree (1984) in secondary education from the University of Kansas, and his M.S. degree (1989) in college student personnel administration from Indiana University, Bloomington.

Previously, Krehbiel taught high school social studies and

xxi

coached track. Krehbiel has given presentations at regional and national conferences of the National Association of Student Personnel Administrators (NASPA) and has coauthored an ERIC digest on voluntarism and a technical report on personal development during the college years for the New Jersey Department of Higher Education.

George D. Kuh is professor of higher education in the School of Education and graduate school at Indiana University, Bloomington. He received his B.A. degree (1968) in English and history from Luther College in Iowa, his M.S. degree (1971) in counseling from St. Cloud State University in Minnesota, and his Ph.D. degree (1975) in counselor education and higher education from the University of Iowa.

Author of more than 100 books, monographs, and articles, Kuh received the Contribution to Knowledge Award from ACPA in 1986 and NASPA's Outstanding Contribution to Literature and Research Award in 1987. In 1989 he was named an ACPA Senior Scholar. Kuh is active in the Association for the Study of Higher Education (ASHE) and the American Educational Research Association (AERA), in addition to ACPA and NASPA. He currently serves on the advisory board for *Higher Education Abstracts* and is a member of the National Review Panel for the ASHE-ERIC Higher Education Report series. Kuh has worked in admissions and placement, taught at a community college, and served as associate dean for academic affairs and chair of the Department of Educational Leadership and Policy Studies in the Indiana University School of Education. Along with John H. Schuh, he was principal investigator and director of the College Experiences Study.

James W. Lyons is a senior fellow at the Stanford University Institute for Higher Education Research. Lyons received his B.A. degree (1954) in history and economics from Allegheny College, his M.S. degree (1956) in counseling and guidance from Indiana University, and his Ed.D. degree (1963) in higher education and the history and philosophy of education from Indiana University.

Lyons was a chief student affairs officer for twenty-seven years, first at Haverford College (1963–1972), then at Stanford University (1972–1990). He has held leadership positions in NASPA, been a consultant to numerous colleges and universities and the U.S. Office of Education, and served as a member of accreditation teams for the Western Association of Schools and Colleges and Middle States Association of Colleges and Secondary Schools. In 1988 he received the Scott Goodnight Award from NASPA for outstanding service as a dean.

Kathleen A. MacKay is a doctoral candidate in higher education and sociology at Indiana University. She received her B.A. degree (1978) in journalism from Colorado State University and her M.S. degree (1980) in college student personnel administration from the University of Vermont.

Before beginning her doctoral studies, MacKay was the director of student affairs for Lyman Briggs School at Michigan State University and associate dean of students at Mills College. Active in ACPA, MacKay served as the national membership co-chairperson (1989–1991) and is currently the graduate student representative. She has written about college student development, cultural pluralism, and voluntarism.

John H. Schuh is associate vice-president for student affairs and professor of counseling and school psychology at The Wichita State University. He received his B.A. degree (1969) in history from the University of Wisconsin, Oshkosh, and both his Master of Counseling degree (1972) and his Ph.D. degree (1974) in higher education from Arizona State University.

Schuh has held administrative assignments in student affairs and faculty appointments at Arizona State University and Indiana University. He is the author, coauthor, or editor of over eighty-five books, monographs, chapters, articles, and technical reports. In 1989 he received the Contribution to Knowledge Award from ACPA and the Leadership and Service Award from the Association of College and University Housing Officers-International (ACUHO-I). Named a Senior Scholar by ACPA in 1990, Schuh has served two terms as a member of the executive board of ACUHO-I and is currently editor and chairperson of the ACPA Media Board and a member of the editorial board of the *Journal of College and University Student Housing.* He has made more than fifty-five presentations at regional and national meetings and been a consultant to ten colleges and universities. Along with George D. Kuh, he was principal investigator for the College Experiences Study.

C. Carney Strange is associate professor and chairperson of the department of college student personnel administration at Bowling Green State University. Strange received his B.A. degree (1969) in French literature from Saint Meinrad College in Indiana and both his M.A. degree (1976) in college student personnel and drug counseling and his Ph.D. degree (1978) in college student personnel and higher education from the University of Iowa.

Strange's teaching and research have focused on student development, the impact of educational environments on student behavior, needs and characteristics of returning adult learners, and factors that encourage student involvement. Active in several professional organizations, Strange has served on the editorial boards of the *NASPA Journal* and the *Journal of College Student Development.* He is a member of the board of overseers of the Saint Meinrad School of Theology and College of Liberal Arts.

Elizabeth J. Whitt is assistant professor of higher education in the College of Education at Iowa State University. She received her B.A. degree (1973) in history from Drake University, her M.A. degree (1977) in college student personnel administration from Michigan State University, and her Ph.D. degree (1988) in higher education and sociology from Indiana University.

Whitt was previously on the higher education faculty at Oklahoma State University and has worked in residence life and student affairs administration, including as the chief student affairs officer at Doane College in Nebraska (1980–1984). She served on the board of directors of ASHE (1986–1988) and is a member of the Monograph Board of NASPA.

INVOLVING COLLEGES

PART ONE

===============

What Is
an Involving College?

If you overheard the following comments by students, what conclusions would you draw about their college or university?

> This college expects you to excel academically and perform outside the classroom . . . . By accepting me, they showed confidence in me and I was prepared to work very hard. . . . But along with that there is an incredibly strong support system. There's not a sense of competition — the students are here for each other [Mount Holyoke College student].

> The first semester here was really scary . . . . Every time my adviser would see me he'd ask, "Mary, how you doing?" "Putrid," I'd say, "thank you. I'm killing myself, spending hours and hours studying and not feeling like I'm getting anything." He says, "Mary, what you need to do is get involved, maybe with something like Hippodrome." I had never seen Hippodrome, didn't know what it was — skits or something. But I went through with the interviews . . . I learned not to be afraid to jump in even though you don't know exactly where to start, organizational skills, working with people who are very different than me. The main point is that I learned that the

1

only way for me to be successful here is to be involved so I feel I belong here, that I'm a part of this place [Wichita State University student].

I didn't do well my freshman year. I came out of high school with a 3.5-3.6 GPA and got a 2.3 here. A couple of upperclass friends got me involved in some things and kept me motivated. I learned a lot about how the university worked, how to use the system. I got to know a couple of administrators in Minority Affairs and Affirmative Action who took an interest in me as a student and as a person. They always asked me, "How are you doing?," not just how are your grades, but "how are you doing overall, do you need any help?" That kind of thing really makes a difference [Miami University student].

They said the best way to adjust to college was to get involved, that students who got involved in campus activities usually perform better academically . . . I'm now the president of my fraternity. I became active in the Black Student Association because I realized how important it is for minority students to remain close. . . . The leadership roles on the basketball team and in the fraternity forced me to conduct meetings and express myself. I had to come out of that shell [Iowa State University student].

Some people say that the extracurricular is extraneous to the real goals of higher education. Actually I think they complement one another; what you learn outside the classroom is just as important as what you learn in class. And what you learn in the classroom can be applied outside the classroom. The ability to talk in front of groups [of peers] helps you become more confident about speaking out in class [Earlham College student].

When you apply for a job, people say, "Well, great, you went to UC Davis. What else did you do?" If you haven't done things in addition to your studies, you aren't as attractive compared to people who had other experiences on and off the campus. Grades show that you can read a book and pass a test. The real world is more than reading and passing tests. Don't get me wrong, faculty here have high expectations for us, but they also encourage us to do these other things [University of California, Davis student].

I did two summer internships with an insurance company in New York City. Those were fantastic! I learned that I loved auditing work, could leave home and find places that suited me, get involved in a new community, learn different things about different places outside of New Orleans. That was very important because I knew that to be successful in my career, a big part of my life would be traveling and living in different cities. In fact, I've accepted a job in Atlanta after I graduate [Xavier University student].

Talking about what we learn in or out of class here doesn't make sense. It seems I learn things from everybody wherever I am. Everybody gets ideas from everybody else here. And we share ideas. Collaborative learning is so much a part of this place it's almost taken for granted [The Evergreen State College student].

The themes that run throughout these comments suggest blurred, fuzzy lines between what, where, and how students learn in college. The reasons these students participate in out-of-class learning activities differ, as do their personally relevant benefits. Although they attend different types of institutions, they have one thing in common — all are actively engaged in their education and the life of their college.

Taken together, these snippets of conversation indicate that some institutions provide environments that seem to encourage student out-of-class learning. The following themes are just a few that surfaced: faculty members and staff take time for students; the blending of curricular and out-of-class learning experiences is acknowledged and valued; everyone is held to high, clearly communicated standards; institutions value undergraduate learning wherever it occurs.

The purpose of this book is to describe how these and other institutional factors and conditions work together in different colleges and universities to promote learning and personal development through out-of-class experiences. In Chapter One, the importance of student learning out of the classroom is discussed. The study on which this book is based is described in Chapter Two.

1

The Importance of
Out-of-Class Life
to the College Experience

Higher education is supposed to effect desirable changes in students' values, intellectual capacities, and esthetic sensibilities (Bowen, 1977; Clark and others, 1972). The impact of the college experience on students is increased when they are more actively engaged in various aspects of college life. "The attainment of a broad range of personal and social benefits, of liberal viewpoints on important social issues, and of subsequent involvement in the civic and artistic life of the community seems to be related to the extent to which the college experience itself provided a rich opportunity for personal and social relationships, involvement in campus activities, and in associations with the faculty" (Pace, 1974, p. 129).

As Astin (1985, pp. 60–61) points out, "True excellence lies in the institution's ability to affect its students and faculty favorably, to enhance their intellectual and scholarly development, and to make a positive difference in their lives. The most excellent institutions are, in this view, those that have the greatest impact — 'add the most value,' as economists would say — on the student's knowledge and personal development." Boyer (1987, p. 180) concluded that "the effectiveness of the undergraduate experience relates to the quality of campus life and is directly linked to the time students spend on campus and the quality of their involvement in activities." Yet, on many campuses, few efforts are made to connect extracurricular events to classroom goals, an unfortunate state of affairs (Heller, 1988).

Studies of learning in college usually focus on academic aspects of the undergraduate experience — the classroom, laboratory, and library. Academic rituals and routines, including the courses that students must take to earn a degree, are relatively easy to document. No one questions whether classroom learning activities are related to the institution's educational purposes. Less is known about the contribution of the out-of-class experience to the desired ends of college. Indeed, the out-of-class experience is often taken for granted or lightly regarded as a positive educational force. Many faculty pay little attention or give minimal support to extracurricular activities (Boyer, 1987). Out-of-class environments, however, are rarely neutral with regard to student learning. It seems reasonable to assume that when out-of-class experiences complement the institution's educational purposes, they contribute significantly to student learning and personal development.

Defining Learning and Personal Development

Because our goal was to understand institutional environments that promote student learning and personal development, rather than the learning processes or outcomes of individual students, we did not attempt to measure how, or how much, students learn. Also, because we were interested in student learning beyond the boundaries of cognitive or intellectual domains and beyond the parameters of the classroom, we adopted a broad definition of learning. For the purposes of this study, learning was defined as the acquisition by students of any lasting knowledge or skill consistent with the educational purposes of the institution.

Our definition of personal development was similarly comprehensive:

Personal development includes those attitudes, skills, and values that enable one: to understand

and reflect on one's thoughts and feelings; to recognize and appreciate the differences between oneself and others; to manage one's personal affairs successfully; to care for those less fortunate; to relate
meaningfully with others through friendships, marriage, and civic and political entities; to determine
personally and socially acceptable responses in various situations; and to be economically self-sufficient. These qualities are usually associated with
satisfaction, physical and psychological well-being,
and a balanced, productive life of work and leisure
[Kuh, Krehbiel, and MacKay, 1988, pp. 13–14].

Implicit in this definition is the assumption that successful accomplishment of a wide variety of personal development
tasks is integral to achievement, success, and satisfaction both
during and after college (Bowen, 1977). We also assume that
college environments can encourage or hinder the personal development of students, both in and out of the classroom.

Contribution of the Out-of-Class Experience

Classroom work is usually distinguished from out-of-class
life by the award of academic credit. The accumulation of academic credits is used to account for student progress and to award
degrees. However, neither credits nor grades accurately represent all of what students learn during college. Indeed, it is
difficult to determine what students learn in classes and what
they learn through out-of-class experiences. In fact, the demar-
cation between activities undertaken in the classroom, laboratory, library, residence hall, or on-campus job that promote
learning and personal development is not always clear, as will
become evident.

A high-quality out-of-class experience is active participation in activities and events that are not part of the curriculum
but nevertheless complement the institution's educational purposes. Out-of-class experiences include, but are not limited to,
interactions with faculty after class — in the hallway, laboratory,

library, residence hall, or union — as well as collaboration on research and teaching projects. Learning and personal development opportunities are also present in traditional settings, activities, and events, such as student residences, social organizations and clubs, recreational sports, off-campus work opportunities, internships, and public service.

Although the benefits from involvement in out-of-class activities are considerable, they are not widely discussed. Wilson (1966) estimated that more than 70 percent of what a student learns during college results from out-of-class experiences. About 80 percent of traditional-age undergraduate students participate in one or more of seven kinds of out-of-class activities: cultural, social, political, communication, religious, academic, athletic. About a third are involved in three or more of these kinds of activities (Kapp, 1979). With so many students devoting so much of their discretionary time to out-of-class activities, what could possibly be the benefit other than relaxation and fun? What do students learn, if anything, from these activities?

Research on college students and their experiences has shown that:

1. Participation in orientation activities, including first-semester activities such as freshman seminars, positively influences both social integration and institutional commitment and thus has indirect positive effects on satisfaction and persistence (Pascarella, Terenzini, and Wolfle, 1986). A student's initial commitment to college is associated with his or her degree of participation in high school activities and the anticipated level of involvement in college activities (Wilder and Kellams, 1987).

2. Students involved in out-of-class activities are more positive about their college experience, are more satisfied with their social life, living environment, academic major (Kegan, 1978), and contacts with faculty, and are more likely to graduate (Astin, 1977; Kapp, 1979; Pascarella, 1980) than students who are not involved. In addition, students who were involved in college attribute some of their job success after college to participation in out-of-class activities (Kapp, 1979).

3. Out-of-class activities provide opportunities for development of leadership skills, such as teamwork, decision mak-

ing, and planning (Schuh and Laverty, 1983), which are increasingly important for effective participation in civic and community affairs (Gardner, 1990). Similar benefits, such as self-esteem, accrue for both men and women who have held leadership positions (Astin and Kent, 1983; Hanks and Eckland, 1976; Schuh and Laverty, 1983). Also, "extra-curricular activities and leadership responsibilities are good indicators of managerial performance. . . . Since every college experience is limited in terms of the many skills needed in organizations, a well-rounded curriculum and campus life is the most appropriate preparation for future executives and leaders" (AT&T, 1984, p. 34).

4. The ability of students to establish the capacity for mature, intimate interpersonal relationships is positively related to participation in campus organizations and recreational activities (Hood, 1984).

5. The single most important variable associated with gains during college in social concern or altruistic values is participation in leadership activities (Pascarella, Ethington, and Smart, 1988). Humanitarian values accentuated by college attendance are manifested after college in involvement in civic activities such as voting (Pace, 1979), interest in political affairs (Hyman, Wright, and Reed, 1975), participation in public service (Kapp, 1979; Pace, 1974; Solmon, 1973), and financial support of one's alma mater (Nelson, 1984).

6. The *only* factor predictive of adult success—however defined, and including post-college income (Pace, 1979)—is participation in out-of-class activities (Krumboltz, 1957; Munday, Davis, and Wallach cited in Power-Ross, 1980).

7. The relationship between involvement in out-of-class activities, learning, and personal growth is probably curvilinear. That is, students who devote the majority of their time to out-of-class activities, or are not involved at all, benefit less than students who are involved at moderate levels (Whitla, 1981). Too much involvement in out-of-class activities is sometimes associated with lower academic performance (Hartnett, 1965).

Given the positive benefits of active participation in college life, a closer look at the importance of "involvement" to learning and personal development is warranted.

Involvement: The Key to Learning

The importance of involvement to learning and personal development was emphasized by The Study Group on the Conditions of Excellence in American Higher Education (1984, p. 17): "Perhaps the most important [condition] for improving undergraduate education is student involvement . . . the more time and effort students invest in the learning process and the more intensely they engage in their own education, the greater will be their growth and achievement, their satisfaction with their educational experiences, and their persistence in college, and the more likely they are to continue their learning."

Involvement encompasses two elements: the investment of psychological energy or commitment to an activity or project, and the time devoted to an activity (Astin, 1984). In some ways, attending college is like joining a fitness center. Membership does not guarantee physical well-being. Unless one exercises regularly, the benefits of physical fitness will not accrue (Kuh and Wallman, 1986). Similarly, the impact of college depends on the degree to which students take advantage of the institution's resources.

Astin (1984, 1985) explicated the relationship between student involvement and learning through five postulates:

1. Involvement is the investment of psychological and physical energy in some kind of activity, whether it is specific, such as organizing a blood drive or singing in the choir, or more general, such as attending a concert or occasionally using the campus recreation facilities.

2. Students invest varying amounts of energy in activities. For example, some students hold an elected office in student government and are significantly involved; other students may be satisfied to attend a residence hall social event. A varsity athlete may spend more time on athletics during the season of the sport and be involved in other activities the rest of the time.

3. Involvement has quantitative and qualitative features. Estimating involvement could be as simple as counting the number of clubs to which a student belongs or the number of times

he or she has used the library. But involvement also has more subtle dimensions, such as a state of mind that results in being committed to an endeavor.

4. The benefits derived from involvement are a function of the quality and quantity of effort expended. For example, to outline required readings or interpret major points to another student requires that students put forth more effort, and is probably a more powerful learning experience, than merely underlining passages in a textbook. It is not surprising that the greater the amount of intellectual effort put into studying, the higher the grades (Pace, 1980). Students in the humanities devote effort to personal and social activities and benefit more; engineering, business, and physical science majors expend less effort in personal and social activities and benefit less (Pace, 1984a, 1986). In general, "student quality of effort in scholarly/intellectual activities and informal interpersonal activities is positively related to reported gains in intellectual skills and personal/social development" (Ory and Braskamp, 1988, p. 127).

Pace (1987) concluded that "good things go together" (p. 1); that is, those who benefit the most intellectually also seem to benefit more in the personal development domain. The direction of this relationship is not known. That is, it is possible that being involved in out-of-class activities may enhance classroom and laboratory learning or vice versa. Time on task is a necessary, but not sufficient, condition for encouraging learning and personal development. "What counts most is not who they are or where they are but what they do" (Pace, 1984b, p. 1).

5. The effectiveness of any educational policy or practice is related to the extent to which it encourages students to take initiative and become actively engaged in appropriate activities (Astin, 1985).

Focusing on the Out-of-Class Experience

Attention to the out-of-class experience is warranted for at least four reasons: college students spend the majority of their time out of class; a student's peer group exerts considerable influence on how a student spends discretionary time and, thus, on how much time is devoted to study and other educationally purposeful activities; out-of-class experiences provide opportunities to acquire important skills that are not often addressed in the classroom; and participation in out-of-class activities contributes to a sense of community, a valued constellation of feelings and beliefs in need of attention on many campuses (Carnegie Foundation for the Advancement of Teaching, 1990).

Only about forty-eight hours of a typical college student's week are devoted to attending class and studying (Boyer, 1987). About two-thirds of the time in a given week is spent on other activities. If as many as fifty hours are devoted to sleeping, at least seventy hours in a student's week remain. What do students do when they are not in class or the laboratory? Of the many who work, most are employed part-time, about ten to twelve hours per week. Some devote considerable time to children and spouses. Traditional-age students (eighteen to twenty-three years), however, continue to spend a substantial portion of their time engaged in noncurricular activities such as public service, student government, cooperative education, and social events. Given the substantial amount of time students spend out of class, perhaps learning and personal development during college could be maximized by focusing on institutional factors and conditions that either promote or inhibit these outcomes.

Influence of Peers

Much of the time traditional-age students spend out of class is with peers. "Once a person identifies himself with a group, that group becomes an anchor and a reference point. The values and behaviors approved by the group provide a background for developing individual attitudes and behaviors" (Chickering, 1974, p. 88). The quality of peer relationships is also related to persistence and self-reported gains in intellectual and personal development (Bean, 1985; Pascarella, 1984, 1985; Pascarella, Duby, Terenzini, and Iverson, 1983).

However, certain groups of peers may have a negative influence on learning and personal development. For example, spending time with friends whose orientation to learning is incompatible with the educational purposes of the institution may reinforce inappropriate behaviors. The peer group, rather than challenging old attitudes and behaviors, may allow a student to rely on comfortable, perhaps anti-intellectual behavior patterns. The differences in personal development outcomes exhibited by resident and commuting students (Astin, 1977; Chickering, 1974; Pascarella, 1985) have been attributed in part to the limited number of opportunities commuting students have to interact with new acquaintances who have different attitudes and values. Peer groups of precollege acquaintances or new friends who resist adapting to challenges inherent in the college environment can inhibit a student's academic and social integration into the college community, a situation that is often associated with dissatisfaction, poor academic performance, and departure from the institution (Tinto, 1987).

Learning Opportunities Outside the Classroom

The changing demographics in the United States (Hodgkinson, 1985), an interrelated world economy, an influx of persons for whom English is a second language, and other factors (Naisbitt, 1982; Toffler, 1981) will place a premium on college-educated persons who can work collaboratively and communicate effectively. Some of the skills related to success and quality of life after college are developed by working with different types of people, an experience that is not usually acquired through often passive, noninteractive classroom learning situations. The "personality" of the future will be one that can successfully cope with ambiguous and complex work tasks and interact with co-workers and clients who are increasingly diverse in terms of backgrounds and cultures. Indeed, the ability to get along with persons different from oneself will be at least as important as information or technical skills (Toffler, 1981).

Leadership, possibly an underdeveloped commodity in American society at present, requires maturity, vision, commitment, persuasion, energy, intuition, and common sense (Gardner, 1990). Consensus seeking, compromise, and negotiation are indispensable skills for working with people from culturally diverse groups and are outcomes often associated with participation in student government, newspaper or yearbook editing, clubs, and so on.

Other important issues that are more likely to be addressed outside of class than in academic courses include moral and ethical conflicts, sexuality, and issues related to wellness, such as the use of controlled substances and learning to cope with stress.

The Campus As a Community

In a recent survey, college presidents indicated that strengthening a sense of "community" on campus was a major concern (Boyer, 1990). These perceptions are not surprising, given the changes that have occurred over the past twenty-five years in American higher education. Consider only three: institutional size, student characteristics, and faculty roles.

Size. Many colleges and universities have become larger and more complex. "Since 1950 alone, enrollment in higher education has increased by almost 400 percent, while the number of institutions has increased by almost 60 percent to nearly 3,300" (The Study Group . . . , 1984, p. 7). Attention to individual needs and interests of students is increasingly difficult to provide. Large institutions offer fewer opportunities for students to become meaningfully involved in leadership and other positions that contribute to feelings of being connected to the campus community. As Chickering (1969) pointed out, many students on large campuses are "redundant" because there are not enough positions of responsibility to go around. On many university campuses, students can be detached, uninvolved, and anonymous. While some students select their college expecting anonymity, anonymity does not engender feelings of belongingness and can be a barrier to productive involvement.

In small colleges, and in large institutions that have created smaller "subcommunities" of students, a higher proportion of students must become involved for the institution to maintain necessary services and functions: residence hall government and advising, athletic teams, musical ensembles, student government, and so on. In this sense, small colleges are "undermanned [sic] environments" (Barker, 1968) where "an inverse relationship exists between the number of people on the campus and the frequency and intensity of opportunities" (Hawley and Kuh, 1986, p. 13). In environments that offer numerous opportunities for participation and leadership (Astin, 1984; Barker and Gump, 1964; Chickering, 1969), "people tend to be busier, more vigorous, more versatile, and more involved" (Walsh, 1978, p. 7). Such environments also tend to instill loyalty among students, ostensibly because students are involved in the life of the community (Clark and Trow, 1966; Heath, 1968).

Student Characteristics. Only about half of today's undergraduates are of traditional age, eighteen to twenty-three years; more students live off campus than on. More than two-fifths of today's undergraduates are enrolled part-time (National Association of Student Personnel Administrators, 1987), and even full-time students are likely to have jobs. Traditional-age first-year students say that it is more important for them to be financially well off than to develop a meaningful philosophy of life (Astin, 1985). For many students who have families, work full-time, and own their own homes, attending college is not the top priority in their lives. Finally, the presence of increasing numbers of students from historically underrepresented racial and ethnic groups emphasizes the need for students to communicate effectively and to learn about, acknowledge, and celebrate differences in cultural heritage, aspirations, and expectations for higher education and personal achievement. Racial incidents on campuses are one manifestation of the significant challenges presented by student diversity, and the difficulties institutions face in helping students acknowledge, accept, and appreciate diversity. Balancing the need to reestablish a sense of community on campus with a commitment to appreciating differences is a major challenge for administrators, faculty members, students, and others.

Faculty Roles. Changing expectations for roles of faculty members, particularly with regard to scholarship and research, are well documented (Austin and Gamson, 1983; Bowen and Schuster, 1986). Although research is not always a solitary endeavor, the more time faculty devote to research, the less time they have for teaching and consulting, advising, and interacting with colleagues. As a consequence, faculty, particularly junior faculty, spend little time with undergraduate students and in university service, direct avenues to maintaining a sense of campus community. Without spending time together, people cannot develop the relationships and understanding needed to establish and maintain a sense of community.

Summary

Clearly, active engagement in classroom, laboratory, and out-of-class activities is integral to learning and personal development. Patterns of student involvement in learning experiences — in and out of class — are as diverse as American higher education. Single-purpose liberal arts colleges, large public research universities, and institutions with a metropolitan or urban mission have different purposes, histories and traditions, organizational structures, and policies and practices. They attract students from different backgrounds who have different educational and vocational aspirations and who devote varying amounts of time and effort to the learning enterprise. These characteristics surely influence an institution's ability to attain its goals, and may require that an institution redefine itself. Student characteristics also shape the means (policies and programs) that colleges and universities develop to pursue their aspirations.

Both student effort and institutional effort are required to promote student involvement. More is known about the former than the latter. By identifying the factors and conditions shared to varying degrees by colleges and universities reputed to provide unusually rich out-of-class learning environments, policymakers could gain a better understanding of ways to promote student learning and personal development. In the next chapter, we describe a study designed to learn more about how some colleges have succeeded in this regard.

2

=====

Institutions with Rich Out-of-Class Learning Opportunities

In this chapter, we describe the processes used to discover institutional factors and conditions that promote student learning and personal development. Before describing the selection process for identifying institutions to participate in the study and the data-gathering methods, several assumptions that guided the study are discussed.

Guiding Assumptions

To identify institutional factors that promote student involvement, one must assume that, at some colleges and universities, the ways in which students spend their time out of class complements, and is integrated with, the educational purposes of the institution. Typically, the term *academic* is used to describe the mission and purposes of a college or university. We use the term *educational* to connote a broader set of ideas that embrace moral and social development in addition to development of intellect and reason. In other words, we were interested in studying institutions that encouraged the development of "the whole person through the cultivation not only of the intellect and practical competence but also of the affective dispositions, including the moral, religious, emotional, social, and esthetic aspects of the personality" (Bowen, 1977, p. 33).

17

Identification of relevant institutional factors and conditions demanded open minds about the policies, practices, and other institutional properties that promote student learning and personal development. Until recently, most estimates of quality in higher education were based on indexes such as institutional resources and student characteristics. For example, students' rank in high school class or scores on entrance examinations have typically been used as indicators of quality (Astin, 1985; Kuh, 1981). Reputation and prestige shape public perceptions of the colleges that provide rich learning and personal development opportunities for undergraduates. Such indicators, however, are less relevant for student involvement than some other factors, such as a clear institutional purpose (Kuh, 1981), opportunities for students to participate in and influence institutional governance processes, residential honors programs, and cooperative education-work programs (Astin, 1977, 1985; Boyer, 1987; National Association . . . , 1987).

> Virtually every institutional policy and practice —
> from class schedules, attendance regulations, and
> research participation to work-study, faculty office
> hours, student orientation, and parking — affects the
> way students use their time and the amount of effort
> they devote to academic pursuits. . . . The physi-
> cal campus itself can attract or alienate stu-
> dents. . . . Administrators' attitudes toward stu-
> dents, the degree of collegiality among faculty, the
> number and diversity of cultural events, the degree
> to which the college interacts with its surrounding
> community — all of these factors, and others, deter-
> mine the tone of the environment [The Study
> Group . . . , 1984, pp. 23-24].

To be sure, formal administrative structures, resources, policies, and programs influence behavior (Morgan, 1986). But colleges and universities are not simply educational bureaucracies; they are social communities as well. A stroll across a college campus suggests that faculty and students have a form of

life all their own, a culture (Kuh and Whitt, 1988). To understand why students and faculty think and behave the way they
do, "we must first be able to both appreciate and describe their
culture" (Van Maanen, 1979a, p. 522).

Culture is a complex set of properties which has been
defined in many different ways (Kroeber and Kluckhohn, 1952;
Peterson and others, 1986). Each college or university has a culture that differs from those of other institutions. These differences are expressed through institution-specific language, symbols, ceremonies, stories, rituals, and traditions (Kuh and Whitt,
1988). For example, the language used by groups on one college campus differs from the language of similar groups on other
college campuses (Becker, Geer, Hughes, and Strauss, 1961;
Louis, 1985). For the purposes of this project, culture was
defined as "the collective, mutually shaping patterns of norms,
values, practices, beliefs, and assumptions which guide the behavior of individuals and groups in an institution of higher education and provide a frame of reference within which to interpret the meaning of events and actions on and off the campus"
(Kuh and Whitt, 1988, pp. 12–13).

The organizational structure of colleges and universities,
the significance and meaning of behavior, and the influence of
policies and practices are context-bound. That is, some policies and practices that seem to work in a given setting may not
work or even make sense at another institution. Thus, we needed
conceptual frameworks and data collection methods that would
accommodate institutional differences and distinctiveness while
aiding us in the search for properties shared to varying degrees
by the institutions we studied. Also, we needed an approach
that would be sensitive to the various factors and conditions that
encourage student involvement. Quantitative indicators, such
as data from the Higher Education General Information Survey (HEGIS), were judged inappropriate for our purposes. The
gross expenditure categories used to aggregate HEGIS information obscure the amount an institution invests in various out-
of-class programs and activities. Further, institutions are organized differently; such functions as academic advising are administratively assigned to student affairs in some institutions

and to academic affairs in others. Because the funding levels reported in various categories sometimes reflect support for different activities, errors can result when comparisons are made across institutions. We therefore decided to use qualitative research methods, which are discussed in more detail later in this chapter.

Guiding Questions

We did not develop a priori hypotheses about the institutional factors and conditions associated with student involvement in out-of-class experiences because we wanted to avoid the "believing is seeing" trap (Weick, 1979). We could not afford to focus only on information that might either confirm or disconfirm hypotheses. Rather, we wished to remain open to information that institutional participants considered important to understanding how students were encouraged to take advantage of high-quality out-of-class learning opportunities.

Drawing on the work of Astin (1985), Boyer (1987), the National Association of Student Personnel Administrators (1987), and the Study Group on Conditions of Excellence in Higher Education (1984), we used the following questions to guide our search for institutional factors and conditions related to high-quality out-of-class learning opportunities for undergraduates.

1. What is the guiding institutional philosophy or ideology expressed by institutional leaders and others concerning out-of-class experiences?
    *   How does the president, as the symbolic leader of the institution, communicate the importance of the out-of-class life of students to the institutional mission and student learning?
    *   How is commitment to the out-of-class experience demonstrated by the chief academic officer, the chief student affairs officer, faculty leaders, and others?
2. What is the nature of the institution's culture?
    *   How does the culture of the institution suggest to students, faculty, and others that participation in certain out-of-class activities is important?

- What rituals, traditions, language, stories, and other artifacts communicate expectations to students and encourage involvement on the part of students? How did these cultural elements evolve?
- What are the norms and values that foster high-quality out-of-class learning experiences?
- What is the nature of the dominant faculty subculture(s)?
- What is the nature of the dominant student subculture(s)?
- Who are the heroes and heroines in the faculty and student subcultures?

3. What are the characteristics of students who attend "involving colleges"?
    - What is the ability level of students who matriculate?
    - What are the educational and vocational aspirations of students who matriculate?
    - To what degree were students actively involved in out-of-class learning and personal development opportunities in high school?
    - What proportions of students are full-time, part-time, traditional age, working off campus, and so forth?

4. What proportion of faculty are involved with students out of class either formally, such as serving as student organization advisor, or informally, such as meeting with students in the union or in the residence hall?
    - What are the characteristics of faculty members who interact with students outside the classroom?
    - How does the institution encourage faculty members to become involved with students out of class?
    - What kinds of contact between students and faculty members after class contribute to student learning and personal development?

5. What resources are allocated to out-of-class activities?
    - What are the sources and amount of financial support for out-of-class activities?
    - How are resources for out-of-class activities allocated? Who participates in the allocation process?

6. What is the nature of institutional policy related to out-of-class activities?

- Who is responsible for monitoring the quality of out-of-class experiences (chief student affairs officer, academic affairs, other institutional agents)?
- How are student life and academic policies developed?
- How is appropriate behavior for students communicated and how does the institution respond to inappropriate behavior?

7. In what institutional functions and programs, such as student government, work-study programs, recreational sports programs, and public service activities, are students involved?
    - What are the distinguishing physical and organizational features of facilities in which students live?
    - Are there public places on campus where students and faculty members routinely come together for informal discussions?
    - How many and what kinds of leadership roles and other opportunities for participation are available to students?
    - How are students recognized for their participation and achievement in academic and out-of-class programs and activities?
    - How are academic programs, student support services, and extracurricular activities coordinated?

8. To what degree are opportunities for student employment on and off the campus available and integrated with the academic program?
    - Is an attempt made to match student jobs with academic and vocational interests?
    - How do out-of-class experiences complement students' vocational aspirations and post-college plans?
    - Do students who work also participate in other out-of-class activities?

9. What other factors and conditions seem related to student involvement in learning and personal development opportunities?

While these questions were useful for getting started, after a few campus visits we began to rely more on what we were learning from the participating institutions to guide subsequent interviews and data collection. That is, as we acquired more knowledge about the institutions and became more experienced with the data collection methods, our questions became more focused, our sense of potentially fruitful areas of inquiry was heightened, and our understanding about important factors and conditions became richer.

Selecting the Institutions

Identifying the institutions to be visited was a critical step in the research process. Because of the diversity of American higher education, we decided to visit institutions of different types and sizes so that our findings would be of use to the greatest number of people. The process of institutional discovery, however, is time consuming and challenging. Because of time and resource limitations, some choices had to be made. One difficult decision was to limit the study to four-year colleges and universities. Even though the number of students served by community colleges approaches about half of those participating in higher education (including more than half of the students who are historically underrepresented, such as racial and ethnic minority students), two-year institutions were not included because we determined that the differences between two-year and four-year colleges would make the task of understanding how institutions promote involvement very difficult to ascertain, given the resources available to conduct the study. Hence we decided to err in the direction of describing in depth how some types of institutions promote student out-of-class learning rather than risk the possibility of a superficial understanding of how all types of institutions promote involvement. Two-year colleges must be included in subsequent investigations, an issue to which we return in the final chapter.

We cast a wide net for advice. In May and June 1988, an expert nomination process was used to begin to identify colleges and universities reputed to provide high-quality out-of-class experiences for undergraduates. Fifty-eight experts were identified to represent a variety of constituencies and viewpoints in American higher education. Forty-eight participated in one or both rounds of the nomination process (Resource A).

The experts were asked to identify institutions noted for the high quality out-of-class experiences they provided for undergraduates. They were invited to nominate as many as five institutions in each of the following categories devised to ensure some diversity in institutional size and mission: (1) residential colleges with fewer than 5,000 students; (2) residential colleges and universities with 5,000 or more students; (3) urban institutions — those with high proportions of commuting and part-time students; (4) single-sex colleges, and (5) historically black colleges.

The research team met for three days in early August 1988 in order to select, from among those institutions nominated by the expert panel members, the colleges and universities to be included in the study. Five decision rules emerged during the discussions. First, we decided that, because widely known studies had been done on some of the institutions that received many nominations, such as Haverford (Heath, 1968) and Swarthmore (Clark, 1970), the study would be more likely to enrich understanding of the undergraduate experience by visiting some colleges and universities about which less had been written. Second, some institutions where students are highly involved were excluded because of policies and programs resulting from anomalous conditions, such as unusually plentiful resources, and program characteristics, such as military academies; we felt that such policies and practices would be impossible for other institutions to adopt. Third, an effort was made to include institutions from different geographical regions of the United States; we assumed that the regional context influences, in some ways, both the student body and the institution and, hence, the student experience (Kuh and Whitt, 1988). Fourth, we attempted to achieve a balance between public and private institutions to account for the possibility that form of control may affect student experiences (Astin, 1977). Finally, we decided to visit four urban institutions even though some expert panel members suggested that we probably would not find students at those institutions, many of whom are over the age of twenty-five and have family and work obligations, to be involved to the same degree as students at residential colleges and universities. As we shall see, involvement on the part of students at urban universities, although rarely the quantitative or qualitative equivalent of that of students at residential institutions, takes different forms which can be quite challenging and rich in learning opportunities.

No scientific sampling process is claimed. However, through the advice of experts, and the development and review of the final list of nominations by the research team, we were satisfied that this set of colleges and universities could offer useful information about high-quality out-of-class learning and personal development experiences for undergraduate students.

Fourteen institutions participated in the study. The small residential colleges were Berea College in Kentucky, Earlham College in Indiana, Grinnell College in Iowa, and The Evergreen State College in Washington. Four large residential institutions participated: the University of California, Davis, Iowa State University, Miami University in Ohio, and Stanford University. The institutions with urban missions were the University of Alabama, Birmingham, the University of Louisville in Kentucky, the University of North Carolina, Charlotte, and The Wichita State University in Kansas. Mount Holyoke College in Massachusetts was the single-sex college in the study. The historically black institution was Xavier University of New Orleans. While some of these institutions are resource rich and attract more than their share of the most highly sought undergraduates, the resource base of others is average at best and they serve student populations with very diverse characteristics.

A post hoc verification of our selections was conducted. In the spring of 1989, near the conclusion of our campus visits, the College Student Experience Questionnaire was administered to students at thirteen of the institutions. The results indicated that, on average, students at these colleges and universities tend to exert more effort and report greater gains on learning and personal development measures than students at similar types of institutions (Pace, 1987). These data are explained in more detail in Resource B.

We make no claim that these fourteen colleges are the "most involving" in the country. There are without doubt many other institutions from which valuable lessons can be learned about promoting student learning and personal development.

However, after twenty-six visits to the fourteen institutions, we are convinced that, in many respects, these colleges and universities can serve as exemplars for institutions that are similar in size and mission.

Visiting the Campuses

Prior to the campus visits, we reviewed numerous documents, including institutional histories, catalogues, admissions information, and data about student characteristics (Resource D). Further, a list was provided of persons to be interviewed, including the president, chief academic affairs officer, chief student affairs officer, faculty members, and students (Resource D).

The first round of site visits was conducted by teams of two to four investigators from September 1988 through January 1989. The teams typically spent two to four days at each institution. After the first round of visits, the research team met to begin to identify themes common to the institutions and to decide which institutions warranted a second visit in order to better understand the factors and conditions that seemed to promote student involvement. Between January and May 1989, second visits were made to twelve institutions.

Collecting the Data

Traditional social science survey methods, such as questionnaires and checklists, were judged inappropriate for our purposes because they impose predetermined limits on what can be discovered (Lincoln and Guba, 1985). We decided instead to use qualitative research methods, including interviews, observations, and document analysis, because they are particularly effective for identifying and understanding complex organizational elements such as values, assumptions, expectations, and behaviors that may influence the out-of-class experiences of students (Goetz and LeCompte, 1984). These methods produced data in the form of words, and inductive data analyses were conducted by the researchers (Lincoln and Guba, 1985). Additional information about the selection of institutions, data collection, and data analysis is provided in Resource C.

A total of 1,295 individuals were interviewed at the fourteen institutions: 175 faculty, 83 academic administrators, including presidents, chief academic officers, and registrars, 305 student affairs staff, 644 students, and 73 others, including trustees, librarians, campus ministers, graduates, and support staff. Many of these participants were interviewed two or more times.

Reporting the Results

Fortunately, in reporting the results of this study we have permission to use the real names of institutions and many individuals. Identifying the institutions promotes two helpful outcomes:

> First, the reader is able to recall any other previous information he or she may have learned about the same case — from previous research or other sources — in reading and interpreting the case report. . . . Second, the entire case can be reviewed more readily, so that footnotes and citations can be checked, if necessary, and appropriate criticisms can be raised about the published case [Yin, 1984, p. 136].

Furthermore, the institutions were selected because they were perceived to provide unusually rich out-of-class learning environments for students. Thus, most of the information gathered was not controversial but rather was affirming and complimentary to the institution.

In the chapters in Part Two, the factors and conditions shared to varying degrees by these fourteen Involving Colleges are described.

PART TWO

How Involving Colleges Promote Student Learning and Development

Imagine a college where students and faculty are actively engaged in the life of the campus community and with one another in teaching and learning. Imagine an institution where students are expected to take, and do assume, responsibility for their learning and personal development. What would such a college look like? What might be some of that institution's characteristics?

Heartland College, Small Town, U.S.A.

When Heartland College (HC) was founded, its mission was to prepare young men and women for a life of leadership and community service. Over the years, the mission has been reinterpreted in the context of the times, but the college's fundamental purposes, and the means used to attain these purposes, have remained consistent. For example, expectations for student performance have always been high. However, the founder, it is told, encouraged students to teach and learn from one another and to take care of one another. Some observers wonder how Heartland is able to maintain high expectations for academic performance and yet encourage the cooperation and mutual respect that characterize relationships among HC students.

Most students, faculty members, and administrators are on a first-name basis. Administrative and professorial titles, when used, are used out of respect, not to acknowledge status differences. Newcomers are neither advantaged nor disadvantaged by institutional policies with regard to where they live, study, or work. If anything, Heartland seems to go to extraordinary lengths to make certain that members of all groups, particularly groups that have historically been mistreated, such as women and members of racial and ethnic minorities, enjoy the same rights, privileges, and social and educational comfort as white men.

Recognizing that some students who share a cultural heritage often desire to live together, the college has designated cross-cultural living arrangements and centers for group activities for persons from traditionally underrepresented groups. Comfortable indoor space — in residence halls, the union, and the library — is available for small group meetings and encourages informal, spontaneous discussions. However, to use public space on campus, students and others must demonstrate that the activity is related to one or more of the institution's educational purposes. In this sense, Heartland intentionally attempts to blur any perceived distinctions between the goals of the classroom and out-of-class experiences.

As with many colleges, Heartland was intentionally established some distance from a major metropolitan area. This creates both advantages and disadvantages in attaining the college's purposes. Most of the students who attend HC are full-time students for whom college life is their primary role commitment. Also, because virtually all students live on or near the campus, the college uses students' physical proximity to one another and campus facilities to promote learning about and understanding of individual and cultural differences.

Both in-class and out-of-class learning opportunities are plentiful. Indeed, the institution has devoted considerable energy and resources over the past few decades to create opportunities for students to spend time off campus. For example, foreign study opportunities are available through consortia with other colleges with missions similar to that of HC. Internships have been developed in the closest major cities, one of which is the state capital, and at other locations ranging from Washington, D.C., to a nearby American Indian reservation. Most important, a long-standing commitment to public service motivates almost every HC student to spend a summer or part of a semester working in a community agency or a comparable activity.

The well-kept campus seems to blend with its natural surroundings. Plantings include trees and shrubs indigenous to the region as well as some from a Far Eastern country where the college has developed a special relationship with a university. Several outdoor "natural courtyards," carved out of stands of trees, and the nearby college farm allow students to get away for solitary moments of reflection. Campus buildings are not overpowering; no structure stands more than three stories above ground, except for the clock tower on "Old Main." This building has been rebuilt twice, first after a fire in the early years of the college and again following a tornado several decades ago. Almost everyone knows the stories about how the Heartland community rallied and refused to falter after these devastating events.

A high level of interaction occurs among students and faculty members. College policies and practices keep students from being anonymous or unconnected. The routines of campus life and staffing patterns in residence halls keep students in touch with one another. It seems as though every student is involved in at least one of the numerous campus clubs and organizations. Every new year brings several new groups as students organize to pursue their interests.

Heartland is both simple and complicated. Some attribute the college's success to its good fortune in attracting good students and faculty and in creating a physical plant that takes advantage of its rural, but no longer remote, physical setting. Heartland is also a state of mind shaped by decades of history and tradition. Indeed, it has been said that HC works as well

as it does because administrators and faculty members do not
have to expend a lot of energy monitoring how students spend
their time. Student cultures socialize new students about appropriate behaviors and expectations for performance. Perhaps
that is why so much effort is devoted to creating opportunities
for current students and alumni and alumnae to meet and talk
with prospective students about life at Heartland.

Students, faculty, and staff describe Heartland in similar terms. Although they are sometimes critical of certain policies and practices, they are nonetheless animated when talking
about "their college." However, their words do not necessarily
flow easily. Sooner or later, most say something like, "there's
just something about the place."

A cornucopia of events, actions, and beliefs contribute
to this shared observation. Heartland's president and senior
faculty and administrators often tell stories about the college
and link historical incidents to current issues on campus. The
values represented in those stories come through clearly in all-
campus events such as the opening convocation and commencement. And while the words used by faculty members, staff, and
students to describe the college are not unique, they are used
in patterns that make interpretation and meaning distinctive
to Heartland. It is almost as if you have to be a member of the
community to fully understand and appreciate what is going
on. In that sense, members of the Heartland family seem to share
similar views of teaching and learning and campus life.

Because community members understand what is important and valued at HC, one might expect that the institution
has developed a rather lengthy, comprehensive list of policies
and procedures to guide faculty, staff, and student behavior.
However, just the opposite is the case. Heartland relies on formal and informal socialization activities to teach newcomers —
students, faculty, and staff — what is desirable and worthwhile.
For students, the introduction to life at Heartland begins with
the first admissions brochure, which sets forth in plain language
the institution's mission, purposes, and expectations for student
life. Most prospective students visit the campus; many spend
a night or two in a student residence. Once a student is admit-

ted, HC periodically sends information that introduces the newcomer to campus life, including the demands of the academic program and what is expected of members of the HC community. One message in particular is reiterated over and over: students are expected to take responsibility for their learning. Yet the message is conveyed with a tone of caring and a deep, sincere interest in the welfare of the individual. In addition, students receive the message that they are expected to participate fully in the life of the community.

Institutional values and the ways in which Heartland policies and practices reinforce its educational priorities are also emphasized to new faculty. Another persistent message is that learning takes place in many forms and forums; students learn from other students as well as faculty members and staff, and faculty members and staff learn from students. Equally important, all groups acknowledge that learning can occur everywhere, both in and out of the classroom.

As with other institutions, Heartland receives more requests from faculty members, students, graduates, and others to develop programs, services, and activities than its resources can support. This sometimes fuels debate and creates tensions. In general, decisions about where and how resources are used adhere to two fundamental principles: the program, service, or activity must contribute to Heartland's mission, and the manner and forums in which decisions are made must allow the views of students and others with a stake in the college to be heard. Taken together, these two principles ensure that the college's educational purposes and philosophy drive the use of finite, precious resources and that the process permits open discussion and debate about institutional values and priorities.

As with any productive enterprise, people are at the heart of Heartland College. Commitment to the ideals and core values of the college runs deep through key members of the administration, faculty, and staff. The caretakers of the HC culture, particularly the president, trustees, and senior faculty and administrators, understand that values decay over time and that if the founding beliefs are to continue to be useful in guiding the college, the institution's values and purposes must periodically be revisited. After all, over a quarter of the students are new to the community each year, and in some years, new tenure track faculty members have made up as much as 15 percent of the faculty.

Because the college takes seriously every admission and employment decision, once an offer is accepted, one immediately becomes, and is expected to act like, a full member of the HC community. But the only way to really learn and understand "the Heartland way" is by being a member of the community. To summarize how well Heartland works, consider the words of a senior just weeks before graduation: "When I visited this place four years ago it felt like home even though I had never been here before and didn't know anybody here. I can't imagine a school that would have been better for me."

In many ways, Heartland is similar to dozens of colleges and universities. Although it is not clear from this description whether Heartland is a small college or a university with many thousands of students, Heartland certainly "feels" small. Heartland is also special because many complementary properties work together to produce a "resonance" between the institution and students as well as among faculty members, administrators, and others. Resonance connotes something qualitatively different from the concept of student-institution fit described in the enrollment management literature (Hossler, 1984). Certainly, a sense of "fitting in" is important. But Heartland College and others with similar characteristics have fashioned more than just a match. Resonance means that mutually enhancing elements are present that stimulate both the institution and the student to peak performance. Students find peers, faculty members, and staff with whom to work, to challenge and to learn. Student and institution contribute to the growth and development of each other. Students not only feel comfortable at the institution but also are challenged to take advantage of as many learning opportunities as possible. Similarly, the presence of students who seem to belong there makes the institution stretch to be more than it is and to provide greater challenges and opportunities for student participation as full members of the community. Both the student and institution are stronger, more confident, and more vibrant for their coming together. Thus, resonance connotes a developmentally appropriate — even powerful — relationship between the institution and its students.

Some will assert that places like Heartland College, a composite description of some of the fourteen colleges and universities that participated in this study, are the dinosaurs of American higher education, evolving toward extinction because of the increasing numbers of part-time and older students for whom college is but one, and often not the primary, life role. But many of the characteristics of a Heartland College can be found in different forms in other types of institutions. Consider Metro University.

Metro University, Downtown, U.S.A.

Metro University was founded after World War II when the need to educate returning veterans became obvious to city leaders. In the early years, Metro was essentially a night school offering classes in several high schools in different parts of the city. As enrollments increased, city leaders and state legislators agreed that the university's resources had to be consolidated in one place to provide a broader array of academic programs. The site ultimately selected was in a decaying area of the city.

The development of the Metro campus was met with a fair amount of skepticism and, in some quarters, substantial opposition. Representatives from the other state universities were concerned that Metro would siphon resources and, perhaps, enrollments. To a degree, these concerns were justified. However, Metro is now unlike any other institutions of higher education in the state.

The Metro campus is well kept. Although the campus is surrounded by the city, the boundaries of the campus, while permeable, clearly distinguish the university from the town. At the same time, Metro belongs to the city. Citizens frequently use the term "our" when describing Metro's successful athletic teams. Because the mission of Metro is to respond to the needs of the urban area, city leaders regularly consult with university representatives as economic development plans are made. Faculty members frequently consult with business, industry, and educational groups. Graduate programs are developed to address the economic, social, and health concerns in the city. The university considers itself an integral part of the city, "a citizen of downtown," rather than simply being located there.

For Metro students, attendance at the university is just one, and perhaps not the most important, priority in their lives. Some high school students take advanced mathematics and science classes not available in their curriculum. Most of Metro's students are the first in their family to go to college; many are from economically disadvantaged backgrounds. Other Metro students are teachers, business people, artists, and practicing professionals seeking graduate degrees or technical competence; many take courses at night while pursuing their careers during the day. Any degree the university offers can be earned through evening classes; some classes are also available on weekends and in other parts of the city when the demand is great.

The average age of Metro students is twenty-nine and rising. A substantial proportion have families, homes, and full-time jobs in the city. Indeed, it is difficult to differentiate students from the faculty on the Metro campus. Many of the faculty and students are about the same age, wear the same style of clothes, drive the same kinds of cars, and compete for the best parking places on or near the campus.

Many of the students who attend Metro are at risk; some have academic needs that can be attributed in part to their economic background. It is not surprising, therefore, that many students are insecure about starting classes; they often have low self-concepts and think of themselves as academically disadvantaged. Adult learners, many of whom have been away from academic work for some time, are concerned about keeping up with traditional-age students. Some traditional-age students, conversely, fear that their lack of life experience will put them at a disadvantage in classes with older learners. Faculty know this and intentionally draw on the strengths of all students. Hence, class discussions are often very stimulating and result in rich learning experiences for both older and younger students.

Metro provides a variety of services and resources to help

students enroll and stay in college. For example, Metro has scholarships for returning adult learners, mentors for education-ally underprepared students, special academic advising for students with poor high school records, tutoring assistance for students who encounter problems in math and science, and child-care programs. Admission standards tend to be flexible and most student services are available in the evening.

Because many Metro students are not well prepared for college, every possible effort is made by staff and faculty members to help them succeed. For example, if a Metro student has a disastrous first semester, she or he can, with the approval of an advisor, wipe the record clean and start over. Metro is not a university without standards, however. Academic adminis-trators are quick to point out that much is expected of Metro students; academic standards are not compromised.

Most Metro students have jobs; some work on campus, others off campus. Most work part-time although a substantial number work full-time, particularly those taking evening classes. At any given time, more than a quarter of Metro students par-ticipate in cooperative education or internship activities. Strong but hard-won ties between university administrators and faculty members and representatives from local businesses, industries, and service organizations have led to the development of a va-riety of programs that use the work experience to educational advantage. Indeed, Metro does everything it can to make cer-tain that students' jobs complement their academic and occupa-tional goals. Students receive a quarterly newsletter that includes information and advice about how to apply what they learn in the classroom or laboratory to practical situations.

Most Metro students live at home; in fact, many own their own home! Available residence hall space serves the growing international student population and traditional-age students whose homes are well beyond the city limits. Because of the de-mands of class and work, it is unusual for students to partici-pate in more than one activity on campus; this activity is often an organization based in an academic department. Students have other important commitments, however. For example, many students are active in civic and religious organizations. Because of students' study and work schedules and family commitments, the biggest challenge for student organizations is to find a time to meet. As a result, it is not uncommon for groups to meet on the weekend or on Friday night. Organizations tend to be small, typically numbering only a dozen or so students, but those members have a keen interest in the activity.

Meeting spaces for faculty members and students and for student organizations were part of the design of campus buildings. For example, space for group study, which is encouraged, is available in virtually all the academic departments and the library. The noon hour is a busy time at Metro; student organization meetings and major events, such as guest speakers, are often scheduled at this time.

Metro administrators and faculty members also realize that, without family support, many students simply could not be successful. Thus, family members are always welcome at Metro events. Metro hosts a "family weekend" to celebrate the contributions of family members—parents, spouses, children—to the success of Metro students. The union frequently sponsors outdoor picnics so that students can get together and visit with one another and faculty members.

Recreational programs cater to the diversity in the Metro student body. While some traditional intramural activities, such as basketball tournaments, are offered, individual and small group recreation are emphasized. Metro students use the recreation building from early morning to late night, lifting weights, using exercise machines, jogging, and taking exercise classes.

Keeping students and faculty members informed is a university priority. The student newspaper cannot compete with the local press, however, so it is published just twice a week. Instead, Metro relies on electronic media such as the campus radio station and its cable television channel. An electronic bulletin board outside the union advertises upcoming activities and events and provides academic information. The word seems to get out, and events are usually quite well attended.

For many students, Metro was their only college option. Indeed, the critical decision for most graduates of the city's high schools is whether to get a job or attend Metro. For most students, a Metro degree will make a significant difference in their lives — in their ability to enjoy life, to be economically productive, and to appreciate the fruits of their labors.

Characteristics Common to Heartland and Metro

Heartland and Metro are very different institutions, but they are similar in some respects. Both have clear institutional missions and educational purposes; campus environments that are compatible with the institution's mission and philosophy; opportunities for meaningful student involvement in learning and personal development activities; an institutional culture (history, traditions, rituals, language) that reinforces the importance of student involvement; and policies and practices consistent with institutional aspirations, mission, and culture. In Chapters Three through Seven, the factors and conditions that characterize Heartland College and Metro University are discussed, drawing on examples from fourteen institutions with different missions, purposes, philosophies, student characteristics, resource bases, and locations. In Chapters Eight through Ten, selected policies and practices are described in some detail in order to understand why and how these policies and practices promote student involvement in out-of-class learning opportunities in large, small, and urban institutions. The term *learning* will be used throughout the remaining chapters to represent the benefits that accrue from student involvement in out-of-class experiences.

A caveat is appropriate. The properties that make up an Involving College cannot be easily separated or isolated. That is, the factors and conditions common to involving institutions work together, in different combinations, toward different purposes, depending on the institutional context and mission, expectations for student and faculty behavior, and desired educational purposes and outcomes. In addition, none of the fourteen institutions exhibited all of the factors and conditions exactly as they are described here. To be useful, these factors and conditions must be interpreted and adapted to the particular purposes, culture, and context of a specific institution. Toward that end, we challenge the reader to think about how the institutional qualities described in the next five chapters are, or could be, manifested in her or his institution.

3

========

Mission and Philosophy

The literature on academic strategy suggests that the success, even the survival, of a college or university is dependent on its ability to project a clear, forceful image (Keller, 1983). In this way, a college or university fulfills its "organizational charter" (Kamens, 1971), the tacit understanding that faculty, staff, students, graduates, parents, and the public have about what the institution should do and be (Thelin, 1986).

For Involving Colleges, no factor is more powerful in promoting student involvement in learning than the institution's mission and philosophy. Mission refers to the "broad, overall, long-term purpose of the institution" (Welzenbach, 1982, p. 15) that guides institutional priorities and practices. An institutional mission establishes the tone of a college and conveys its educational purposes. The mission may be based on religious, ideological, or philosophical beliefs (Davies, 1986; Keeton, 1971), as will be illustrated later in this chapter. An institution's philosophy is made up of values, assumptions, and beliefs about human potential, teaching, and learning. In this way, an institutional philosophy is similar to Schein's (1985) "hidden" layer of culture, beliefs, and assumptions that are represented in artifacts such as language and behavioral norms as well as in policies and practices—"how we do things here."

Together, mission and philosophy provide a rationale for the institution's educational programs, policies, and practices. For example, the assumption that every person has the potential to learn could be reflected in a mission that dedicates the college to expanding educational opportunity for students who, by traditional measures, are not likely to succeed in higher education. Values that are supported by this mission might include quality teaching, support (in all forms) for students, commitment to multiculturalism, and social responsibility. Programs, policies, and practices that put these values into action include open-door admissions, rewards for teaching, orientation courses that help new students acquire study skills and self-confidence, and a low faculty-student ratio. We shall return to the role of assumptions and values in the next chapter and to policies and practices in Chapter Six.

Although the missions and philosophies of Involving Colleges are diverse, they have five characteristics in common: (1) they are relatively clear and coherent; (2) they support high, but reasonable, expectations for student achievement undergirded by an ethic of care; (3) they determine and legitimate distinctions among individuals and groups; (4) they enable multicultural and multiracial student subcommunities; and (5) they provide a unifying focus for all members of their communities. A description of each of these characteristics of the missions of Involving Colleges follows.

Clarity and Coherence

Missions of Involving Colleges are clear, coherent, and often distinctive; the institution is "one thing to all people." The institution's purposes and values, as well as the means (policies and practices) used to attain its purposes and implement its values, set an Involving College apart from other similar institutions and make what goes on there understandable, definable, and educationally purposeful. Although many of the values espoused by Involving Colleges are similar to those of other colleges, the *means* by which an Involving College implements its values and aspirations complements the academic program and student characteristics. That is, while a meritocratic ethic dictates how students are expected to behave at Miami University and Xavier University, the manner in which this ethic is implemented at each institution differs, as we shall see shortly.

Although Involving Colleges may not always explicitly articulate their missions in catalogues or other publications, faculty, administrators and external audiences (alumni and alumnae, prospective students, state legislators, higher education scholars) can accurately describe the institution's guiding values and aspirations by pointing to a variety of symbols and traditions. Students can talk about, in their own words, the mission(s) of their institution, although they often do not understand how important a clear, coherent mission is to institutional stability in terms of resources and image or perhaps the distinctiveness of the institution's mission in the broader context of higher education.

The power of a salient institutional mission to educational quality has been discussed often (Keeton, 1971; Pace, 1974). At Involving Colleges, the mission serves as a touchstone, influencing the actions and behaviors of all members of the community, and helps students differentiate between right and wrong, what is valued and what is not. Administrators, faculty, and students use the mission as a yardstick against which to measure the appropriateness of the curriculum and out-of-class experiences.

Space does not permit reference to the missions of all fourteen institutions. The following are illustrative of the variation in the missions and philosophies at this group of Involving Colleges and how mission and philosophy encourage student involvement.

Earlham College. At Earlham College, founded in Richmond, Indiana, in 1847 by the Society of Friends (Quakers), Quaker values and ways of doing business define many aspects of institutional life, from how to greet a professor or administrator (on a first-name basis) to how to determine the expectations for student behavior in residences (through group consensus). To understand the Quaker tradition is to understand the mission of Earlham College; the Quaker ethos runs deep in the life of the college. The importance of community is described in the college's statement of purpose: "The network of human relationships is sustained by a sense of common purpose, mutual caring and respect. . . . In such a community, the teaching and learning roles are merged, and the curricular and experiential are combined. Earlham is both a sanctuary for reflection and a stimulus to practical action."

Three core assumptions and values emanate from the Quaker traditions. First, it is assumed that the "light of truth" can be found in each individual, and so value is placed on consensual ways of learning and knowing. People are expected to participate in discussions without a firmly held position and to be prepared to hear the words and insights spoken by all members of the community. The conditions valuing the person and active listening will enable the light of truth to arise, yielding a solution that takes into account the views of all involved ("a sense of the meeting"). For the same reasons, consensus building (rather than majority rule) is used at Earlham to develop policies and practices. Typically, a period of silence is used to initiate and to conclude campus meetings; silence insulates the experience from the outside world and encourages active listening on the part of participants.

Among Quakers, no single individual (or discipline) is expected to hold the light of truth or raise all the appropriate questions. At Earlham this belief is reflected in a strong emphasis on interdisciplinary coursework and collaborative learning techniques. New faculty learn quickly that to make a contribution to the Earlham community, one must learn the form and syntax of other disciplines. One way this is accomplished is through the freshman Humanities seminar, where faculty from a variety of disciplines discuss major themes from an interdisciplinary perspective and "reinvent" the course each year, complete with new reading lists and assignments. Collaboration rather than competition is the norm. Ideas are not criticized or discarded because they do not "sound right"; rather, people are more likely to build on and pick out what is useful in an idea, and are very careful not to put down the person who put forth the idea. A balance between individual rights and community values is sought by making decisions by consensus.

The second assumption expressed by Earlham's mission is contained in the phrase "Let your lives speak"; knowledge is not only to be appreciated but, more important, it is also to be lived. Quakers traditionally have been skeptical of learning for its own sake; knowledge must be applied to be of value. Students not only read about the causes of illiteracy, for example, but are also urged to identify ways to eliminate this problem.

Finally, Earlham is committed to the responsibility of the individual in a global community. This value, in combination with the Quaker tenet, "let your lives speak," results in an emphasis on global awareness and social action throughout the student's experience at Earlham College. For example, Earlham is a charter member of both Campus Compact and Campus Outreach Opportunity League (COOL). Cooperative programs with a sister institution in Japan have existed for more than 100 years. Over 70 percent of the student body will participate in an off-campus program in the course of their studies, the majority in an international setting. Earlham students also support a very active Service Learning Program (outreach to the Richmond community) and a host of other activities that reflect a collective sense of responsibility to improve the human condition. Earlham's commitment to preparing educated women and men for a lifetime of service is manifested in its graduates in many ways; perhaps the most compelling evidence of the college's success in living its mission in this regard is the number of graduates who hold positions in government, teaching, and other service-related professions.

Berea College. Like many other small, isolated residential institutions, Berea College in Berea, Kentucky (population 10,000), is ideally situated for reflective learning and personal development. Yet Berea's location is as much a function of its commitment to the peoples of Appalachia as of any desire on the part of the institutional founders to establish, in 1855, an isolated and protected oasis of scholarship. Through the Seven Great Commitments and a celebrated Labor Program, Berea College provides a Christian, interracial educational experience emphasizing the liberal arts and service to students from Appalachia whose educational and financial backgrounds would otherwise preclude college attendance.

The history of Berea is important to understanding and appreciating its mission in the present. The college was founded during a time of social reform, including a strong antislavery sentiment. Prominently displayed on the edge of campus is a sign describing the founding and mission of the college:

For Mountain Youth
Berea College, founded 1855 by John G. Fee with the support of Cassius M. Clay, in a one-room school built by the community. Its constitution, 1858, made it Christian, non-sectarian, and anti-slavery. Compelled to close 1859 by pro-slavery factions, re-opened 1865. Dedicated to the service of mountain areas. Berea is a historic monument to equality.

During the time that the Kentucky Day Law, which prohibited black students from attending integrated colleges, was in effect, Berea founded the Lincoln Institute, a separate school for blacks. The college continues to hold firm to The Seven Great Commitments which were formulated during Berea's early years and serve as its mission today:

1.   To provide an educational opportunity primarily for students from Appalachia who have high ability but limited economic resources
2.   To provide an education of high quality with a liberal arts foundation and outlook
3.   To stimulate understanding of the Christian faith and to emphasize the Christian ethic and the motive of service to mankind
4.   To demonstrate through the student labor program that labor, mental and manual, has dignity as well as utility
5.   To promote the ideals of brotherhood, equality, and democracy, with particular emphasis on interracial education
6.   To maintain on our campus and to encourage in our students a way of life characterized by plain living, pride in labor well done, zest for learning, high personal standards, and concern for the welfare of others

7. To serve the Appalachian region primarily through education but also by other appropriate services.

A healthy tension characterizes the college: faculty and administrators continually question whether institutional programs and practices are appropriate to its mission. Of course, the expectation that all students work in the Labor Program, which is described in more detail in Chapter Nine, has played an important, central role in integrating general education with the practical arts, thus making Berea's mission quite distinctive.

Mount Holyoke College. Members of the Mount Holyoke community share a clear sense of mission — there may be disagreement about implementation, but about the mission, "we're consistent." According to one administrator, this consistency can be attributed to the will and vision of the founder, Mary Lyon; "there's just something in the woodwork here" that generates shared basic understandings. The acting provost asserted that in the forefront of the institutional mission is commitment to the individual development of students. Also central to the mission is a commitment to excellent liberal arts education for women.

The message that this consistency of mission communicates to students is that "you're uncommon women — by coming to Mount Holyoke, you've accepted the challenge to excel." Mount Holyoke challenges students to be anything they want to be, uninhibited by traditional expectations and supported by a "community of women empowering women." The Mount Holyoke challenge to be uncommon women is reflected not only in academic rigor but also in the expectation that students will excel out of class in leadership and service and will push themselves and one another to develop understanding and appreciation for important current issues, including racism, sexism, classism, and heterosexism. These challenges are met in an environment of support and encouragement, and with a willingness to ask difficult questions and face struggles openly.

Mary Lyon founded Mount Holyoke to provide quality education for women in an atmosphere of nontraditional expectations. Her aspirations have long been realized, although her vision still guides the college. Today, Mount Holyoke is a place where women experience themselves in ways that they have not before — in scholarly endeavors, in leadership positions, and in meeting robust academic challenges. Most important, perhaps, is that women are taken very seriously there and their opinions are valued to an extent that women at Mount Holyoke believe is not possible at an institution with a different mission.

Xavier University. Xavier University of Louisiana (New Orleans) is a historically black, Catholic institution whose students regularly exceed their own expectations and whose graduates have distinguished themselves in the fields of pharmacy, education, and government service. Xavier's educational purposes are clearly and firmly rooted in, and reinforce, its black heritage and Catholic character. Fundamental to the Xavier mission is an unwavering commitment to opportunity, achievement, and excellence within the context of social responsibility. Each student receives a liberal and professional education for the purpose of helping to create a more just and humane society for all people, with a particular emphasis on service to the black community. For example, the student body president told us that the purpose of knowledge is to help those less fortunate and explained his plans to attend medical school and open a clinic in rural Mississippi.

The director of volunteer student programs noted that the institution's mission is practiced "from the president on down." Norman Francis, Xavier's president, spoke about administering "in the Catholic way — what is just and right is what we should be doing. . . . A society is judged by how it treats its young and its old. . . . If we are true to our mission, then they [the students] will be motivated to be concerned." This sentiment was the focus of Francis's message to the Xavier community in his 1988 Founder's Day convocation address.

The vice-president for academic affairs, Sister Rosemarie Kleinhaus, talked about Xavier's special quality — "our founding and our mission of commitment to excellence, dedication to blacks . . . that all may be one." Sister Rosemarie described as "mission-driven" the practice of admitting 100 students a year who do not meet the regular admission criteria. Students allude to the mission when speaking of Xavier as an excellent college that teaches black students the value of their heritage and prepares them for service.

Stanford University. Leland Stanford, Junior, University was founded and built on farmland and additional extensive acreage donated by Leland and Jane Stanford in memory of their son. Construction began in 1887 and classes began in 1891. In its early years, Stanford was a tuition-free university, apparently one of the roots of Stanford's egalitarian traditions; charging tuition did not begin until the 1920s.

At the time Stanford was founded, higher education in the United States was being redefined. The liberal arts tradition, emphasized by undergraduate colleges influenced by English traditions, began to be modified by an emphasis on research and graduate training imported from German universities. Out of this confluence, flavored with the uniquely American aim of using knowledge to address practical problems, emerged the research university.

At the undergraduate level, Stanford's mission is to bring knowledge and understanding to each new generation of young people; to instill in them an appreciation of scholarship and of health and physical vitality; and to provide the basis for ethical and responsible lives, productive careers, and contributions to the public welfare. To attain this mission, Stanford provides instruction in analysis, reasoning, and expression; in human and self-understanding; in a student's own and other cultures; in the fundamental skills and methods needed in a rapidly changing world; and in preparation for professional life and studies. Stanford's purposes are also pursued by providing a campus environment and activities through which students develop attitudes and values in the midst of a diverse population.

The Stanford community is a complicated collage of subcommunities. Indeed, there are many Stanfords. The most obvious is Stanford the research university, which encompasses — and in some ways dominates — a second Stanford, the undergraduate college. To outside observers and to many Stanford faculty members, Stanford *is* a research university that values entrepreneurial behavior on the part of faculty members and students — primarily, but not exclusively, graduate students. The prestige and resources Stanford attracts are the result of its international stature as one of the premier research universities in the world.

But Stanford also offers a rich collegiate experience for undergraduates. While academic endeavors are obviously very important to Stanford students, virtually every student with whom we spoke mentioned the powerful learning distilled from living with, getting to know, comparing oneself to, and learning from others.

Stanford's educational mission is reflected in the guiding rule for the Stanford community, the Fundamental Standard outlined by David Starr Jordan, Stanford's first president. It states: "Students are expected to show both within and without the university such respect for order, morality, personal honor, and the rights of others as is demanded of good citizens. Failure to observe this will be sufficient cause for removal from the university." Thus, Stanford students are expected to be responsible for their own behavior and in making choices. To reciprocate, university administrators, faculty members, and staff members state, in various policies and in public forums, that they trust students. The Honor Code, which applies to both students and faculty, constitutes a statement of trust, student responsibility, and dedication to academic integrity.

Stanford's mission is not as distinctive as that of Berea or Earlham or Mount Holyoke. Of course, Stanford (or the two Stanfords) is large in comparison to those institutions. But the undergraduate academic program and residential education are powerful, complementary influences and make their own distinctive imprints on the Stanford collegiate experience.

Iowa State University. The Iowa State University of Science and Technology was created as the Iowa Agricultural College and Model Farm by the Iowa General Assembly in 1858 and became a land-grant college in 1864 under terms of the Morrill Act. One of the first land-grant institutions, Iowa State emphasizes service to all Iowa citizens through the application of knowledge and scientific research to practical problems, particularly those related to agriculture and engineering. Today this mission is reflected in county extension agents who work with farmers and young people, economic development partnerships, nonelitist admissions standards (top half of high school graduating class, 24 ACT composite score, or attendance at summer programs), and research focused on agriculture, veterinary medicine, biotechnology, economics, and engineering.

Approximately 78 percent of Iowa State's 21,500 undergraduates come from the state of Iowa; a high proportion are from within a 100-mile radius of the university. To understand the rituals and traditions of rural, small-town Iowa life is to understand why Iowa State students are so involved in campus life. Over two-thirds of the Iowa State undergraduates come from high schools where there are fewer than 200 students. One student with whom we talked graduated in a class of 39, was a member of the high school track team and marching band, had a role in the school play, and was active in her 4-H group. Multiple commitments are the norm, if not the expectation, of students from small rural communities. By necessity, many high school activities cannot be maintained without many members playing several roles at once. As a consequence, a "pitch in and help" ethic is very familiar to these students, who arrive at Iowa State ready and willing to become involved in the life of the institution. The land-grant mission of the institution — to serve the needs of the state — is reflected in a willingness to provide numerous opportunities for involvement.

A key to the university's success in encouraging student involvement in out-of-class activities has been its ability to make the institution "feel small," a characteristic that is attractive to the type of student who enrolls at Iowa State. We will describe in more detail later (Chapters Six and Eight) what Iowa State does to create this perception.

University of Louisville. Just off the Eastern Parkway exit from Interstate 65 in Louisville, Kentucky, stands the new $24 million University of Louisville Student Activities Center, featuring a nine-story clock tower and 250,000 square feet of space dedicated to the athletic, recreational, food service, student activity, governance and organizational needs of the 21,000 University of Louisville students. This building represents a significant commitment of the institution to enhancing the quality of student life in the urban environment. This development also parallels the renaissance taking place in downtown Louisville, where new and imaginative designs are reshaping the skyline and rejuvenating the waterfront.

Embracing its recently differentiated niche in the Kentucky system as the state's urban institution, the university's mission of service and responsiveness to the local community has led to the development of vibrant centers of teaching and research in the fields of health, law, engineering, business, education, and the performing arts. In 1983 the College of Urban and Public Affairs consolidated several existing schools and programs to add coherence to, and further emphasize, the emerging urban mission of the institution. The university is closely tied to the economy of Louisville, as it is the eighth largest employer in the city (4,000 faculty and staff). Seventy-seven percent of the university's students now come from Jefferson County and almost half of all its graduates live in the Louisville metropolitan area.

Miami University. Miami University of Ohio, founded in 1809, is also a state-supported university that has evolved over the years into an institution that looks and feels very much like a private, selective college — one of the "public ivys." In fact, four of the five "roots" of Miami are private. These include two seminaries and two women's colleges, Western College (founded as the Mount Holyoke of the West) and Oxford College. The single public "root" comes from the original site for Miami, which was a parcel of land in a nearby township, designated by President George Washington's administration (the university continues to receive $7,500 annually from the township). The first seven Miami University presidents were Presbyterian ministers. Thus, the "feel" of a private college has always been a part of Miami, which was patterned after a traditional English college.

Oxford, Ohio, was founded and named *after* the college was established, and High Street is the main street of both Oxford, Ohio, and Oxford, England.

The mission of Miami—to provide high-quality state-assisted liberal arts education with an emphasis on undergraduate teaching—is frequently cited in Miami literature and speeches. Administrators strive to make the mission even more clear. According to both the president and former provost, Miami aspires to be the best public institution in the country emphasizing undergraduate education. Toward this end, Miami University hopes to become a "third kind of institution"—one that values both scholarship and teaching of undergraduates.

Some faculty members believe that because the institution's mission continues to be scrutinized, Miami has a self-concept problem: "we aren't settled yet because we are forever talking about what we are about." However, as with other Involving Colleges, such as Mount Holyoke and Berea, examination by faculty and administrators of the appropriate role of the institution in a changing society may well be a sign of healthy self-assessment.

From its inception, Miami's mission emphasized student learning from out-of-class experiences. The first president of the university stated in unequivocal terms the importance of the total learning experience and the need for students to become involved in teaching other students. This statement was precipitated by an increase in the number of students from 9 to about 120 in one year, even though the number of faculty (3) stayed the same. In the words of one Miami student, "student activities encourage us to use what we learn in class—to integrate what's in class with real experience." Thus, from the earliest days, students were expected to make important contributions to the life of the Miami community and to learn from one another. These and other factors have resulted in many rich traditions, some of which are described in the next chapter.

The Evergreen State College. The Evergreen State College (TESC) was founded as, and remains, a state-supported alternative school on the outskirts of Olympia, Washington.

Although dissimilar from Miami in most respects, TESC also feels like a private or independent college; there is a sturdy independence of philosophy and spirit that sets it apart from most public institutions. Data from the American Council on Education/UCLA Cooperative Education Research Program (internal memorandum, September 13, 1988) suggest that, although TESC is public and nonselective, the attitudes of TESC first-year students were very similar to those of freshmen entering highly selective, private, liberal arts colleges. TESC students tend to be liberal in their political and social views and hold the value of a liberal arts education above the value of landing a well-paying job.

While TESC is younger than most four-year colleges in the United States, it has a very distinctive character and is laden with traditions that support its mission. Chartered in 1967 by the Washington state legislature, TESC opened in 1971 with the dual mission of a liberal arts college and regional public institution. Recently, the regional mission was removed by the state because it conflicted with the liberal arts mission and created curricular expectations that a liberal arts college could and should not meet.

Evergreen's first president, Charles McCann, rejected "standardization" and the usual academic routines in favor of working collegially, of helping students take responsibility for their own education, and of affording students the freedom to grow with a minimum of intellectual prescription or restraint. Instead, TESC faculty members have developed an effective pedagogy marked by individual attention and The Program, the interdisciplinary core of the academic experience described in Chapter Nine. They believe that any student can learn anything, given the proper circumstances. Consistent with the institution's mission, all aspects of the Evergreen experience — academic, social, extracurricular — are seen as interconnected. Moreover, Evergreen emphasizes the importance of working collectively; a strong egalitarian ethic and a caring community encourage collaborative learning that is unique yet highly supportive of the spirit of its institutional participants.

Challenge, Support, and Great Expectations

The values and aspirations expressed in the missions and philosophies of Involving Colleges serve as the basis for clear, high, but reasonable expectations for student achievement. For some students, these "great expectations" are compatible with the prevailing cultural values they know and share; for others, the expectations may stretch their aspirations and challenge perceptions of their abilities. In most cases, institutional expectations seem to diminish stereotypes, and almost always push students to perform in ways that exceed them.

Expectations for Achievement. All Involving Colleges have high expectations for their students. How the institution holds students accountable for academic achievement and the types of support the institution provides vary consistent with the characteristics of students the college attracts and the institutional mission. For example, the vast majority of students at Earlham, Grinnell, Miami, Mount Holyoke, Stanford, and the University of California, Davis, possess well-developed academic skills. Other Involving Colleges, particularly the urban universities, attract a high proportion of first-generation college students whose academic skills need to be sharpened. In the *Selective Guide to Colleges* (Fiske, 1988), Xavier University was described as "a school where achievement has been the rule, and beating the odds against success a routine occurrence." Students are constantly challenged to succeed in spite of the conditions of, and limited support many of them experienced in, their economically depressed neighborhoods. The Xavier yearbook proclaims that "Xavier is a no excuse school. You take what you have, do the best with it, and don't make any excuses." Students are continually exposed to models of achievement and aspiration. For example, halls and entryways to academic buildings are lined with display cases featuring pictures and brief biographies of recent graduates who have been admitted to graduate and professional schools.

Ethic of Care. Expectations for achievement at Involving Colleges are almost always buttressed by a system of support, an institutionalized ethic of care that assists students to
succeed. At Involving Colleges, students "matter" (Schlossberg,
Lynch, and Chickering, 1989). Institutional agents (faculty, student affairs staff, and others such as clerical and maintenance
personnel) care about students. As students sense this ethic of
care, they begin to care for one another. For example, Earlham and Grinnell faculty members model involvement in the
life of the community and share the excitement of participation
with students both in and out of the classroom. The Xavier student newspaper editor said "faculty care about us"; another
Xavier student said "professors take time for us and they believe in us." One student noted that when alumni and alumnae
return to the New Orleans area, "they leave their kids on campus," implying that the Xavier "family" cares for offspring of
graduates as well. Xavier students are expected to share their
good fortune through service to the black community; it is important to "bring others along." Thus, Xavier's institutional mission
and values translate into programs (such as SOAR, ChemStar,
Biostar, Mathstar, SOAR II, EXCEL, MARC, GRADSTAR,
University 1010) that expect and inspire success, and provide
the skills and support necessary to succeed. Some of these programs are described in more detail in Chapter Nine.

At Involving Colleges, educational Darwinism — survival
of the most fit — is not the guiding philosophy. Students are appreciated for what they bring to the institution, and institutional
resources are devoted to helping each student further develop
his or her potential. At the same time, most Involving Colleges
promote inclusion as an institutional goal through an "ethic of
membership."

Ethic of Membership. The ethic of membership that oper-
ates in many Involving Colleges is the assumption that, once
a student chooses the institution, she or he is immediately a fully
participating member of its community. This ethic, called a "theory of membership" at Stanford, goes something like this: "Because you have chosen us, and we have chosen you, we will do

everything we can to help you succeed. This is your place now, your home, and we are happy to have you here. You belong here and you are, by the very act of choosing us, a full member of the community." Throughout pre-matriculation contacts with the institution, such as literature sent by the admissions office or distributed at orientation activities and induction events, prospective students are sent the message that "you have a claim on us."

Many Stanford students, for example, sense that they are empowered just by virtue of being admitted. Another way of thinking about this is that students get a sense of "being a Stanford person as opposed to being a student at Stanford." The degree to which students share this feeling varies; some students of color, for example, would take issue with this statement, a matter understandably of concern to all. Nevertheless, the institution aspires to make members of all groups feel that they belong. Thus, the ethic of membership at Stanford is compatible with its aspirations toward egalitarianism — of free access and inclusion in all aspects of community life.

Interpersonal Distinctions

Involving Colleges make distinctions among their members according to the values expressed in their missions and philosophies. Some Involving Colleges are democratic communities with egalitarian aspirations. Egalitarianism in this context suggests equal rights free from the influence of political, social, and economic differences. Other institutions, including Xavier and Miami, can be described as meritocracies, with hierarchical structures for status and achievement.

Egalitarian Aspirations. Earlham, Grinnell, Stanford, and TESC are collegial and heterarchical institutions; information is shared freely and decision making is a collective responsibility. Distinctions based on race, gender, family background, rank, or title are unwelcome. Formal titles, such as Doctor, President, or Professor, are eschewed on the assumption that they make people seem more different from one another than they really are, and that someone is usually placed in a dependent, secondary role and, in the process, is viewed as of lower status.

For example, at Stanford, institutional memoranda do not carry the titles of individuals, and a need-blind admission policy is another illustration of efforts on the part of the institution to stamp out inappropriate practices. Once students matriculate, they all look very much the same. The campus dress norm is unpretentious and informal, which also serves as a leveler of sorts. Also at Stanford, undergraduate students have access to any course or any major. If students can get into small advanced seminars and succeed, they may do so. No failing grades are given. Further, there are no policies to regulate the flow of students, such as differential grade point averages for admission to popular majors such as human biology. All on-campus housing, regardless of how old or new, plush or worn, costs the same.

At TESC, faculty members are often referred to as "senior learners" and students are "junior learners," signifying that all participate in and benefit from the learning process. In addition, although Evergreen is a state-supported college, initiatives and decisions come from all parts of the organization and the people of the college community feel that they, not the legislature, are in charge of the institution. The clear, coherent institutional mission described earlier encourages interactions across all categories of institutional agents and students and actively discourages class, race, and other distinctions among groups.

Egalitarian aspirations and practices also permeate policies and practices at Berea College. By institutional charter, at least 80 percent of Berea students are from Appalachia; almost all come from socioeconomic backgrounds that ordinarily would preclude college attendance. Particularly powerful institutional levelers (programs, policies, or practices that establish equality among students) are found in Berea's Labor Program, an important aspect of the college's mission, and its free tuition. Every student is assigned to one of the 130 different types of labor positions, from general custodial service to skilled crafts, all of which contribute directly to the various programs and industries of the college. The net effect is that everyone at Berea starts from the same point: no one has any money; everybody labors. Such practices are further underscored by the absence of formal social groups on campus, such as fraternities or sororities, that might draw attention to distinctions inconsistent with the institution's mission.

Another example of levelers can be found in the omnipresent bicycles at the University of California, Davis. Students, faculty, and administrators share a common means of transportation, riding together to class or offices and parking their bikes side by side.

Earlham College challenges the prevailing Western ethic of competition with an ethic of collaboration. Although expectations for academic performance at Earlham are high, students find that eighteen years of socialization to traditional notions of success through competition are inconsistent with the Earlham way of doing things — of emphasizing individual worth and collective responsibility. Through admissions materials and campus visits, Earlham's expectations are made very clear to prospective students, so they are not surprised when, during New Student Week, they begin to experiment with the guiding values of Earlham — consensus decision making, simplicity, equality, nonviolence, and social justice.

At some Involving Colleges, commitment to egalitarianism encourages involvement. Students are recognized as full and equal partners in community life, and their activities reflect that recognition. For example, the value placed on empowering women at Mount Holyoke College is reflected in a high level of student participation in college leadership, including residence hall administration (Chapter Nine), planning college events such as Fall and Spring Convocation, and working toward institutional change with regard to relationships between cultural and ethnic groups and men and women.

Despite the egalitarian aspirations of some Involving Colleges, elements of their mission and philosophies — the inherent meritocracy of selective admissions, the competition characteristic of research universities — also send a message to students and faculty that "you are the best and the brightest." This message

can exacerbate for some the sense of being imposters; in the
words of a Stanford student, "maybe I'm the admissions director's first mistake." Some of the Involving Colleges have addressed this problem by reinforcing to students that they are
able to succeed and by minimizing the importance of past performance and family or educational background through the
"ethic of membership" described earlier.

Meritocracies. Xavier's "ladder" of achievement—programs and workshops emphasizing study skills—is consistent
with the institution's mission and values. These programs and
workshops in academic and career skills, and the means by which
these programs are implemented (a top-down management style
marked by the formal use of titles, addressing students by family names, and professional dress), are deliberate efforts to raise
the hopes, expectations, and confidence of students whose backgrounds do not predict success in college. Xavier's ladders and
"guided control," illustrated in Chapters Six and Nine, mark
the Xavier way, are consistent with the mission and philosophy
of the institution, and tell students exactly what to do to be academically successful.

Sometimes involvement is motivated by a desire to improve one's status—such as climbing a ladder of student achievement and recognition. At Miami University, competition is particularly intense for membership and leadership positions in the
most prestigious groups. Within most organizations there are
hierarchies of involvement—from follower to leader to senior adviser to the leader, a position achieved after long and significant
service to the organization. Students interview for appointments
to student committees and other activities, such as homecoming planning committees and Laws, Hall & Associates (an advertising agency described in Chapter Eight), and Greek organizations.

In summary, Involving Colleges tend to be egalitarian
or meritocratic in ways that are consistent with the mission and
philosophy of the institution and that establish the tone for student interaction with one another and with faculty members and
administrators. Any distinctions made between individuals and

groups at Involving Colleges are consistent with the institutional mission and value system. The commitment to egalitarianism or meritocracy also defines achievement and success. Distinctions, when they exist, help students discern appropriate behavior, how to succeed academically and socially, and empower students to take advantage of institutional resources.

Multiple Subcommunities

Involving Colleges acknowledge the importance of developing and sustaining multiple subcommunities — separate and distinctive living units and subcultures that coexist within the campus culture. In a sense, an Involving College is "one house with many rooms." The small colleges seem to reflect the "great room" concept, where the living room, kitchen, study, and recreation room all are, essentially, one large space that encourages contact among those who live there no matter in what activity they may be engaged. Large institutions are like quad-level houses, where many discrete rooms exist, allowing people to move to rooms or other levels of the "house" to seek privacy or to pursue specific tasks. The subdivisions tend to reduce the opportunities for spontaneous interaction among residents.

Subcommunities may be formal, such as living units organized according to cultural or ethnic background or by academic interest — as in the theme houses at Earlham, Stanford, and the University of California, Davis — or student organizations based on gender, race, ethnicity, or lifestyle, such as the Lesbian-Bisexual-Gay Persons Union at Earlham. Subcommunities may also be informal, such as older adult students at Wichita State, international students at Iowa State, and students of color at any of the predominantly white institutions.

One example of intentionally created subcommunities is the more than 70 houses and dorms at Stanford, some of which are theme or ethnic houses. Each can be thought of as a community (Chapter Eight). Members of these subcommunities are, of course, expected to conform to institutional norms and mores. However, each unit establishes its own governing policies and practices, determines its own social and educational program-

ming, and sets its own fees and — where the students operate
their own food service — board rates. Other institutions, such
a TESC, Iowa State, and Mount Holyoke, also provide examples of how multiple subcommunities can coexist, enrich the
quality of community life, and increase the possibility that the
collegiate experience is empowering for all students. Several subcommunities at TESC are described in the following section.

   Subcommunities at The Evergreen State College. Evergreen
students, known as "Greeners," are politically active and socially
conscious, more liberal than conservative, more casual than formal, and clearly not interested in mainstream careers such as
business, engineering, or medicine. Nevertheless, one senior who
sought to distance himself from the larger group of political activists noted, "They play the part but don't actually do it!" This
was an older student with a long record of social and political
activism — mostly concerned with environmental issues — for
which he had been arrested repeatedly.

   To some extent, the students housed in on-campus dorms
at TESC are a subcommunity. Their regular interactions with
each other in the residences and in their cooperative dining room
tend to set them apart. They also tend to be underclass students.

   Evergreen students in off-campus housing also make up
subcommunities. There are no fraternities or sororities at Evergreen; the idea would be inconsistent with the institution's
egalitarian mission and philosophy. But on the country roads
that surround the campus, roads that are bounded by dense evergreen forest on both sides, one encounters occasional clearings
with a house or two on them. These houses have a run-down
look, in part because of the woodsy, rain forest quality of their
surroundings, but also because they are, indeed, run down! Students have lived in most of them for twenty years, as long as the
college has existed. The houses are passed down from one student generation to another and, like many student residences,
have developed personalities of their own. To a large extent,
all offer students a challenge in cooperative and self-sustained
living. Each has its own "culture," which may range from par-
tying to introspection, to environmentalism, to political action

of one sort or another, to the known location of one "fringe element" or another. Some of the better-established of these houses include: Yogurt Farm, Whitehouse, Pinkhouse, 7 Cedars, Turquoise House, Evergreen Shack, Sunny Muffin, Emma Goldman, Red House, and Brandywine Forest.

Another identifiable group is the environmentalists, whose concern for the environment is evident in the Organic Farm and in the Programs, individual study projects, and internships that are focused on environmental issues. Aluminum and glass are routinely recycled. Plates and cups in the food service are paper and not plastic. The main lobby area (three stories high) in the campus Activities Building is full of posters, some of which hang at least two stories; environmental matters are a dominant theme. Examples of posters hanging in March 1989 included: "Help Blockade a Logging Operation," "Our Nevada Test Site Action: Train for Non-Violent Action," "Adopt-A-Forest Program: Workshops on 'Quality Wood and Sustainable Forestry,'" and "Help Save the Ancient Forest."

Nine percent of TESC students are of Native American, African, Asian, or Mexican/Latino heritage. Nearly all at the college are aware that the relatively low minority population in Washington makes Evergreen's efforts to recruit more students of color a special challenge; yet these students speak highly of Evergreen. TESC also has institutionalized its diversity by sponsoring activities, events, and organizations that enable students of color to help each other, discover and celebrate their cultural heritages and to guarantee full membership in the school. Subcommunities of students of color also take part in a wide array of social and service activities—big sibling programs, social and political action, and community outreach and service programs.

Students of color at TESC have also formed a very effective coalition: The First People's Coalition, a support group where both individuals and groups can find friendship, common cause, and mutual support. They also see themselves as having a role in helping the college understand issues associated with racism, such as lack of respect, and ethnic matters with which other students tend to be unfamiliar. The absence of stridency or anger in this group was striking. The First People's Coalition expressed a refreshing faith in the mission of the college and in its unusual forms of learning. They liked the absence of competition and were acutely aware of one of the underlying (and founding) assumptions of the college: that all students, regardless of ability or background, can and will learn, given an encouraging, supportive environment.

Seniors point to the positive effects of TESC's ethnic subcommunities. Students are at once challenged and supported, work collaboratively, and learn in an environment in which there are unusually high levels of respect for the worth and dignity of the individual. They report that the faculty are accessible and helpful. Students talked freely about how they had come to TESC with many self-doubts but had soon learned to trust themselves and be confident.

From Tolerance to Pluralism — Another Aspiration. The commitment to foster multiple subcommunities reflects more than an institution's acknowledgment of the importance of recognizing and tolerating differences represented by groups of people on campus. Involving Colleges expect students to do more than merely tolerate differences. These colleges and universities advocate pluralism, a state in which cultural, ethnic, sexual orientation, and other differences are encouraged, understood, protected, respected, and celebrated throughout the community.

Pluralism enriches campus life by valuing the traditions, lifestyles, and values of diverse groups. For example, Wichita State is a more vibrant, interesting place for the presence of students who have full-time jobs, extensive life experience, families, and mortgages; traditional-age students at WSU value the presence of older students above all other aspects of campus life.

A multicultural learning community also allows students to learn about themselves by exploring their racial or ethnic heritage and experimenting with different lifestyles. An Asian student at the University of California, Davis, can say that she has learned about being an Asian American by being part of the

Asian student community, learned about being a female by being part of a women's organization, and learned about leadership by being treasurer of her sorority.

Multiculturalism also serves as a basis for involvement by expecting and empowering all students to contribute to the campus community as they contribute to their own group. Involvement in a subcommunity, such as the Lesbian-Bisexual-Gay Persons Union at Earlham, can make involvement in the broader college community less threatening because the gay, lesbian, or bisexual student feels part of a smaller supportive community.

The multicultural theme in these institutions' missions represents an aspiration rather than something that they have attained. And these institutions have become multicultural learning communities to a greater or lesser extent. What is important to note is that an Involving College *aspires* to pluralism and manifests its commitment in the creation of supportive structures, such as the learning subcommunities at TESC, and adherence to ideas such as the ethic of membership.

A multicultural learning community made up of multiple subcommunities is not without risks or tensions. Involving Colleges work very hard to maintain the delicate balance between inclusion and separation. While diversity is cherished, community is also valued. In this way, the culture allows for the inclusion of all individuals and groups in the community — in decision making, activities, traditions, educational benefits, and access to resources. At the same time, the needs of the community — for shared values and experiences, for a sense of wholeness — can threaten to overwhelm the needs of its subcommunities. On many campuses, white students question the desirability of black student organizations, perceiving them as contradictory to the ideals of the academic community and an integrated society. Black students assert a need for a place to go to "learn to be myself" and to escape the pressures of being black in a predominantly white institution. Conflicts can (and often do) arise from these different viewpoints and the conflictual values they represent.

Involving Colleges do not ignore these conflicts but attempt to use them to educational advantage. Students, faculty, and administrators are forced to face the tensions inherent in

confronting "isms"; as one administrator at Mount Holyoke said,
if sustaining a multicultural community is a goal for the institution, "someone will finally have to say 'Professor X is a racist' . . . but we're willing to struggle and talk about things and
talk about our mistakes in a very public way." Such struggles
can be particularly painful at small colleges where there is little
anonymity and, perhaps, a stronger press to conform to the
dominant culture. These are complicated issues to which we will
return in Part Three.

Unifying Focus

　　Snyder (1971) described the problems that can occur on
a campus when the institution's espoused expectations for learning are in conflict with the "hidden curriculum," what students
really need to know about how the institution works to be academically and socially successful. Students, faculty, administrators, and others at Involving Colleges have similar views of
how the institution works and how to get things done in their
context. It is as if "we're all headed in the same direction." For
example, some institutions, such as Miami and Xavier, typically operate as hierarchical organizations; in such settings, students learn how to use the system to get things done. Other institutions seem more like "organized anarchies" (Cohen and
March, 1974). For example, decision making at Stanford, compared with Miami, is decentralized; students learn that they often
must visit several offices to acquire resources for activities. The
strong notion of entrepreneurship at Stanford is fed by the expectation that students will take the initiative to get to know
faculty members, create organizations, and find meaningful ways
to participate in the life of the community.
　　Earlham, Grinnell, and TESC are collegial organizations
(Baldridge, Curtis, Ecker, and Riley, 1977), although consensus
seeking takes different forms and uses different forums on each
campus. Nevertheless, students learn to work within a consensus
model. In each of these environments, students learn how to play
the game the same way (more or less): decisions are made by

the group, with significant participation by all members of the community.

Decision makers in Involving Colleges tend to act in the interest of a common educational goal rather than the aggrandizement of any particular subunit. This is not to say, however, that disagreements or controversies are avoided, or that difficult choices do not have to be made about the use of institutional resources. In Chapter Six, we discuss the importance of making choices to eliminate some programs so that others can be initiated or enhanced. In the end, though, the compelling focus of the institution's mission is preserved. As President Donald Swain of the University of Louisville explained, "when we come together to make decisions, we put on our university hat" (rather than our "student services hat" or "faculty hat").

Many examples of a compelling institutional focus are found in the collaborative administrative structures and programs in these institutions. The legacy of former chancellors Emil Mrak and James Meyer to the University of California, Davis, was a system of thirty administrative advisory committees that fosters broad campus involvement. Every fall a general application form for participation in these committees, with an accompanying letter of invitation by the current chancellor, is circulated widely throughout the campus to solicit the participation of faculty, staff, and students. Although criticized at times for being too cumbersome, this system has been successful in channeling input into the affairs of the campus and in providing an arena for assessing the institution's mission in the context of many different issues. Collaboration further supports a sense of community and common purpose among institutional constituencies.

The relationship between academic and student affairs at these institutions is, more often than not, seamless. A shared vision of the enterprise and an appreciation for the other's contribution to the institution's educational purposes guide a host of programs and practices. At Iowa State University, for example, a 30-member university orientation committee is chaired by a faculty member and charged with the task of designing

and coordinating decentralized college-level orientation programs. Again, the communication and cross-fertilization of ideas
in this collaborative process allow the institution to reassert its
values and to bring the larger agenda of institutional mission
and image into sharper focus.

Another illustration of the complementary relationship
between academic and student affairs is found at Grinnell College, where highly talented and self-directed student cultures
are served by a residence system that expects them to construct
their own living communities and by an academic curriculum
that challenges them to bring their own meaning, coherence,
and application to a broad range of courses. In like manner,
the spirit of the Quaker values that undergirds the Earlham mission is supported by teaching-learning processes that are collaborative through a required interdisciplinary Humanities Program, and by the use of consensus in the conduct of campus
affairs.

The consistency of focus at Involving Colleges lies, in part,
in the knowledge institutional agents have about both the institution and their students. This knowledge—who we are, whom
we serve—guides the development of policy and practice consistent with the institution's mission and educational purposes.

Summary

Mission and philosophy guide an Involving College through
transitions and turbulent times. Equally important, decisions
about out-of-class activities and events emanate from the mission. This is not to say that the mission is never challenged;
it is. These institutions test and challenge themselves, and the
mission is reinterpreted in light of current challenges and issues with which the institution must deal. In this sense, the mission of an Involving college is similar to Peters's (1987, p. 488)
description of an effective corporate vision: "[The vision] must
be stable, be consistently challenged—and changed at the margin."

Involving Colleges use different means to promote student learning and personal development, means that are compatible with institutional missions and student characteristics.

The means employed, manifested as policies and practices (Chapter Six) and cultural properties (Chapter Four), create environments in which students can be successful. Most striking is that, at each institution, the foundational values, institutional mission and philosophy, and campus policies, practices, and procedures are in harmony and are carefully communicated to prospective students. Consequently, there is a strong resonance between the type of student each institution attracts and the type of experience that institution offers. In the next chapter, the impact of the cultures of Involving Colleges on student experiences is explored.

4

Institutional Culture

The nature of an institution of higher education is as much a matter of its culture as its organizational structures, policies, and practices (Morgan, 1986). Thus, in order to understand Involving Colleges, one must understand their cultures. In this chapter, we briefly discuss some of the complexities encountered in attempting to "discover" the cultures of colleges and universities and identify some cultural aspects of Involving Colleges that seem to foster student involvement.

Understanding Colleges as Cultures

Cultural perspectives provide a powerful interpretive and analytical framework for institutional analysis. But cultural perspectives are also complicated to use. Because an institution's culture is unique and holistic, composed of subjective values, assumptions, and beliefs, the meanings of institutional behavior and events cannot be interpreted or understood outside of the context in which they occur (Kuh and Whitt, 1988). As a consequence, what might appear to be similar behavior and events mean different things in different institutional settings, and what is effective in one culture is not necessarily effective in another. Moreover, "attempts to determine whether one institutional culture is better than another seem wrongheaded" (Kuh and Whitt, 1988, p. 15). The lessons of Involving Colleges, then, must be considered in light of their unique cultures, as well as the cultural context of the reader.

Although institutional culture is a source of security and continuity for its members (Kuh and Whitt, 1988), culture is constantly evolving, incorporating changes in the values, beliefs, and attitudes of the external environment as well as those of institutional members (Morgan, 1986). The culture of an institution is likely to be invisible to its participants as their shared values and beliefs become taken-for-granted threads in the fabric of their daily lives (Chaffee and Tierney, 1988; Morgan, 1986). The tacit nature of an institution's culture complicates attempts to identify its elements (Kuh and Whitt, 1988). Our descriptions of the cultures of Involving Colleges have been affirmed by their participants as mostly accurate, but the reader must keep in mind that these descriptions are the interpretations of outsiders.

Finally, rarely is there a singular institutional culture (Kuh and Whitt, 1988; Morgan, 1986). Colleges and universities encompass many groups (faculty, students, administrators, and staff members) with different, and often competing, value systems, creating "a mosaic of organizational realities rather than a uniform corporate culture" (Morgan, 1986, p. 127). Our descriptions of the cultures of Involving Colleges are, for the most part, descriptions of *dominant* institutional cultures.

In an effort to make something so complicated seem, at least temporarily, simple, Schein (1985) has described culture as encompassing three levels, arranged hierarchically from most visible to most tacit: artifacts, values, and assumptions. Artifacts are what we can "see" about the cultures of an institution and what we are most likely to attend to and identify when we talk about culture (Kuh and Whitt, 1988). Cultural artifacts include history, traditions, stories, heroes and heroines, norms, symbols, and interaction patterns.

The operating philosophy of the institution is based on values and assumptions. Values are widely held beliefs — what the members of a culture assert to be most important to them. These values may be spoken ("We're a teaching institution") or unspoken, manifested in actions (teaching is rewarded more than other faculty activities). Values may be espoused but not lived, as in the case of an institution that claims teaching as a primary value but gives the most rewards to faculty who publish. Valued behavior, such as teaching and research, may also conflict and create tension and uncertainty as community members try to determine which behavior is valued over others.

Assumptions make up the "core of culture" (Kuh and Whitt, 1988, p. 25), "a much deeper and all-pervasive system of meaning" (Morgan, 1986, p. 133). Assumptions undergird values and artifacts, and exert a powerful influence on what people in the culture think about, what they perceive to be important, how they feel about things, and how they spend their time. At the same time, a culture's beliefs and assumptions are largely tacit, implicit in the life of the institution and, therefore, difficult to identify both by outsiders and insiders.

In the following sections, we offer some insights into the cultures of Involving Colleges. Adopting Schein's (1985) framework, we have focused primarily on cultural artifacts in this chapter for two reasons: they are visible and therefore somewhat easier to ascertain, and many of the values and assumptions — the hidden or tacit dimensions of culture — were identified in Chapter Three in the discussions of mission and philosophy. When relevant, examples of some assumptions introduced in Chapter Three are used as illustrations.

Artifacts

Seven categories of cultural artifacts of Involving Colleges warrant attention: history, traditions, language, heroes and heroines, sagas, the physical setting, and symbols and symbolic action. The role that each plays in promoting student learning is also examined.

History. The evolutionary nature of an institution's culture is reflected in its history, the institution's lifetime of personalities, values, and interactions among people (Kuh and Whitt, 1988). Internal and external forces at work now and at the time of an institution's founding, and the ways in which the institution has dealt with crises and change, influence institutional assumptions. These assumptions are reflected in mission and philosophy (Clark, 1970; Jencks and Riesman, 1962) and underscore expectations for student involvement.

As mentioned in Chapter Three, The Evergreen State College (TESC) was founded in the late 1960s as an alternative college, roots that are a source of great pride to students and faculty. A continuing commitment to the original academic purposes — including sharing decision making, expecting students to be responsible for their own education, and believing that any student can learn, given the proper circumstances — is evidenced twenty years after TESC's founding. Students at TESC have the freedom to grow with minimal intellectual prescription or restraint, giving life to the founding ideal that "anyone can learn anything."

Because of the collegial nature of the Coordinated Study Programs (Chapter Nine), TESC faculty deal with "the whole student" as a person who is growing and learning all of the time, not just someone who attends class for a period of time each week; concern for personal development is not viewed by faculty as the purview of nonacademic specialists. Thus, the TESC faculty behave in some ways like student affairs staff at other institutions; the seamlessness of student and academic life at Evergreen is thus reinforced.

A Mount Holyoke alumna who is now a staff member said that "to understand Mount Holyoke, you need to understand its history, its founding — what we feel here is the progression of the historical moment." At Mount Holyoke, there is a strong sense of the continuity of shared experience, symbolized in the laurel chain carried by graduates at commencement, stretching back in time to the founder, Mary Lyon. Mary Lyon's purpose for founding Mount Holyoke was to provide quality education for daughters of farmers, women who could not otherwise afford to go to college, and to prepare them for nontraditional (for the time) lives as teachers. This historical commitment to the education of women continues to the present as an underlying spirit — "It's a community of women empowering women" — as well as an explicit mission. Women students are taken very seriously and, as a consequence, come to believe in their own abilities to an extent that has not been possible in their pasts.

Risk taking is encouraged and students and alumnae speak often of the experience of being stretched beyond their assumed limits to accept the challenge of being, in Mary Lyon's words, "uncommon women."

The history of Berea is also important to an understanding of the college in the present. As noted in Chapter Three, a sign displayed at the edge of the Berea campus describes the founding and mission of the college. Berea's founder, John Fee, came from Oberlin College and established several educational institutions that were open to persons of all races and poor backgrounds. The college's commitment to the youth of Appalachia is still firm and, although black students were prohibited from attending Berea for a time because of the Kentucky Day Law (passed in the early 1900s), blacks were warmly received by the Berea College community as soon as the law was repealed in the early 1950s.

The University of California, Davis (UC Davis), was founded in 1905 as the "University Farm" for the University of California. The agricultural tradition is also strong at Iowa State. Life in small towns and on farms is characterized by citizen involvement in schools, churches, or other forms of neighborly interaction; involvement is part of the rural lifestyle. The hands-on heritage of these agricultural roots is reflected in the long history of involvement in governance, recreational activities, and residence life shown by students at UC Davis and Iowa State.

The history of the founding of Xavier University by Mother Katharine Drexel and the Sisters of the Blessed Sacrament in 1915 permeates the institutional culture. Xavier is the only black Catholic university in the Western hemisphere, and was founded to serve blacks and persons of color who were denied educational opportunities. The preparation of black professionals in a tradition of excellence and service continues to be the primary mission of the institution; the College of Pharmacy has trained over 25 percent of the nation's black pharmacists. Pictures of Mother Katharine are found in almost all Xavier buildings and often on every floor. Celebration of religious holidays, the continuing presence of sisters, and an active campus ministry program keep the Catholic mission alive.

The unique character of Earlham is a product of its foundation on Quaker traditions. The life of the college is infused with the Quaker values and beliefs described in Chapter Three, the core assumptions being that the light of truth can be found in each individual, the responsibility of each individual is to the betterment of the global community, and consensus and silence are the means for conducting the affairs of the institution.

Unlike the institutions discussed thus far, Wichita State University (WSU) is not at all as it was in its original form, and its history is characterized by numerous changes in form of control and mission. Nevertheless, some spirit of the past remains. Wichita State began life in the nineteenth century as Fairmont College, a Congregational liberal arts college. In the 1920s, Fairmont's financial problems led to its transformation into the University of Wichita, a municipal university with a strong liberal arts mission. After World War II, the institution began to identify a mission that went beyond providing degrees for local students. In 1964, the University of Wichita became Wichita State University, a member of the Kansas Regents Institutions. The municipal history continues to influence WSU's mission in that it is still very much the "city's university." In addition, the liberal arts remain a living part of the university's heritage.

The University of Louisville was chartered as a municipal institution in 1798 when the city was only twenty years old. The history of the university is the history of the city itself. City fathers promoted a number of civic improvements during the 1830s, including the establishment of the Louisville Medical Institute (1837) and the Louisville Collegiate Institute (1838) which, in 1846, merged to form the University of Louisville, including a law school. The medical school was founded shortly thereafter. In 1910 the university began to receive regular appropriations from the city. Despite the economic depression of the 1930s, the period was marked by academic expansion and dedication to high educational ideals. The Louisville Municipal College, a black undergraduate division, opened in 1931; the School of Music in 1932; and the Graduate Division of Social Administration in 1936, which later became the Kent School of Social Work.

By the early 1960s, however, the University of Louisville faced serious financial problems. As it was a "semiprivate," semi-municipal institution, income from the city was reduced over time while tuition skyrocketed. The city was unwilling (perhaps unable) to provide the needed additional support. After several years of difficult negotiations, the university joined the state system of higher education in 1970. In 1977 the Kentucky Council on Higher Education made the University of Louisville the state's "urban university," which affirmed its municipal heritage and the long-standing educational and cultural traditions in Louisville and Jefferson County, Kentucky's largest urban area.

Traditions. Traditions communicate important institutional values to their members, constituents, and external audiences. Traditions also maintain and renew the community by binding past and present lives with shared meanings and actions (Kuh and Whitt, 1988). Involving Colleges are rich in traditions that remind their members of the importance of students' learning and development.

The traditions of Earlham reflect the institution's Quaker beliefs and values. One of the powerful symbolic features of Earlham, the "heart," is not obvious to visitors. The heart is an oval area of grass, trees, and shrubs near the center of the campus, surrounded by a sidewalk. The heart is significant for two reasons. First, it is the area where an Earlham tradition, vigils on the heart, is perpetuated. Students stand inside or around the heart to demonstrate their interest in and support for concerns, such as stock divestiture in corporations with holdings in South Africa, women's right to abortion, and sexual-preference issues. It is said that a vigil at Earlham is successful if enough people participate so that, while standing on the sidewalk holding hands, they can form a complete circle. The vigils are uniquely Quaker in that they provide a way to "let your lives speak" — a public demonstration of beliefs, conducted in silence. Second, campus buildings have been positioned to surround the heart. That is, symbolically the heart stands for the center of life at Earlham, including the physical plant.

Earlham's "Big May Day" is a medieval festival held every

four years. Students assume roles such as Queen, Robin Hood, Queen's Court, and Jesters and participate in puppet plays, costume horse jousting, sword fights, and "romping around." An annual "Little May Day" is also held. This tradition goes back at least to the 1920s, and it gives students the opportunity for make-believe fun, something that may be hard to find in a community that is as intense, academic, and issue-oriented as Earlham.

Another Earlham tradition is Winter Carnival, established unintentionally in 1978 when a blizzard forced the cancellation of classes. Each winter, following a snowfall, classes are canceled and Winter Carnival begins. Some students use the day for relaxation, others catch up on their studies. Students told us that in planning winter term classes, faculty say "now if it snows on Tuesday, then Tuesday's work will be due on Thursday, and on the following Thursday we'll do X." However, because the winter of 1989 was mild, with little snow, there was no Winter Carnival. This created some consternation among students who were looking forward to a free day.

Although The Evergreen State College is relatively young, it boasts a set of traditions as distinctive as its history. Students and alums describe with affection the potlucks, a time when a Program's students and faculty get acquainted. Potlucks are often held in the homes of faculty and provide the initial "glue" for the bonding that is so much a part of the Evergreen Program experience. Retreats serve much the same function as potlucks, and are typically held at the Farmhouse (really a small lodge) at the Organic Farm. Super Saturday at TESC occurs annually just after the end of the academic year. Initiated by a former dean of students, it is a celebration designed for fun and to thank everyone for another year. Super Saturday now draws nearly 25,000 people for a street fair, three stages of entertainment, two beer gardens, barbecues, and a "Friends of the Library" book sale. The event has created a strong feeling of goodwill between the college and its community (Olympia and environs), students, and graduates.

At Mount Holyoke we were told that "we have a tradition here for everything." Traditions are handed down by students, although current students do not tend to look at what they do as traditional — it has relevance for them in the present. Elfing, Big Sisters, and Disorientation are all ways in which first-year students are introduced to upper-class students (sophomores, juniors, and seniors, respectively). Gifts and notes are exchanged, and the upper-class women share advice about being Mount Holyoke students, while new students are quickly made to feel a part of the college.

Other Mount Holyoke traditions include Mountain Day, when classes are canceled so that students can enjoy a fall day outdoors. In the distant past, students actually climbed Mount Holyoke Mountain, located east of the campus, and spent the night in a lodge on the mountaintop. Founder's Day is celebrated in November by eating ice cream at 6:00 in the morning on Mary Lyon's grave — the reasons for which no one is able to articulate. A more frequent tradition is "m & c's": ten o'clock each evening finds Mount Holyoke students gathering in their dorm lounges for milk and crackers. A faculty member told us of a recent alum who, on a return visit to campus, spoke of an obstacle she had encountered in the "real world": "there are no naps and no m & c's." It is a study break and more — a time for talking about what happened that day and renewing feelings of togetherness within the residences.

Reunion and Commencement are Mount Holyoke traditions that explicitly link past and present generations of students, evoking a timeless sense of sisterhood. Graduating seniors, all dressed in white, march to the amphitheater bearing chains of laurel leaves that symbolize achievement and continuity. They are preceded by scores of alumnae (some from as far back as sixty years), also wearing white with touches of their class colors, carrying signs with statements about their student adventures and their lives after graduation. The effect is a human chain of history — each woman and each class unique, yet all having shared the experience of Mount Holyoke, the experience of being "uncommon women."

Institution-wide traditions at Berea include Scholarship Day, an opportunity to acknowledge outstanding academic performance, Mountain Day, and Labor Day. On Mountain Day, which is similar to the Mount Holyoke event, classes are canceled and students and faculty climb a nearby mountain. The purpose of the event is to celebrate the Appalachian culture and the affection many Appalachian people have for the outdoors. In some years, students and faculty camp overnight prior to starting their climb. One student estimated that perhaps as much as half of the student body took part in the most recent Mountain Day, although fewer faculty participate now than a decade ago.

Labor Day is held in the spring and is a celebration of the intrinsic value of work. Berea's student workers, dressed in their work uniforms (farm clothes, machine shop clothes, and so on), march in a parade. Awards are given for extraordinary performance on the job during the past year. One student described Labor Day as a time when students are relieved of their work duties and faculty, administrators, and other staff have to do the students' jobs; this is an indication of how people within an institution can have very different interpretations of cultural traditions.

As with many other institutions, Xavier has a Founder's Day convocation in the early fall. Such convocations at Xavier and elsewhere are opportunities to reiterate and emphasize the institution's values and expectations for students. For example, President Norman Francis challenges students to excel and overcome the overwhelming odds many of them have had to face prior to college. At Founder's Day in October 1988, a new freshman talked about the obligation of an educated person to give back to the community. The institution's mission, to serve blacks and others who have been denied educational opportunities and to reach out into the community to help others, is underscored during this campus celebration. The Founder's Day convocation also includes ceremonies to honor outstanding faculty and students, welcome new students, acknowledge seniors who are spending their last year at Xavier, install new student leaders, and give service awards for faculty and staff. Thus, after a few weeks of class, the Xavier community meets as a family to affirm the reasons for its existence.

Xavier also has special emphasis weeks, such as Martin

Luther King, Junior, Week for Peace, and special convocations, including a Mass of the Holy Spirit and Black History Convocation, all of which serve to emphasize the black and Catholic values of the university. Homecoming and Celebration in Black are also cited by students as important traditions. When asked about traditions at Xavier, students added "individuality and high standards," affirming that the respect for the individual that is a part of the university's mission is also communicated clearly to students.

The Grinnell Relays were once a major spring activity, a parody of the Drake Relays (a major collegiate track event held each spring at Drake University in Des Moines). The purpose of the Grinnell Relays was to tell "academics to jump in the lake for a day." All rules were ignored during the course of the event, which was instigated in the early 1970s by a new faculty member from Yale. On Wednesday evening a ceremony would be held and the first keg of beer tapped. Thursday was relatively quiet, but on Friday classes were skipped, bands performed, students sunbathed, and a talent show was held. The winner of the talent show became the titular head of the Relays. On Saturday the Grinnell Relays were held, events that consisted mostly of drinking games, parodies of the Drake Relays, and picnic games. As many as fifty kegs of beer were available, according to one student, but as much beer was thrown and spilled as was consumed.

The specter of liability and a change in the drinking age in Iowa prompted college officials and students to rethink the propriety of the Relays. Within one year, the focus of the weekend changed. Peace Day has now replaced the Relays. Peace Day is an outdoor festival aimed at actively engaging participants in their personal commitment to peace and justice. From 10:30 A.M. to 9:30 P.M. on a Saturday, special-interest sessions are held, interspersed with musical events. In 1988 about 400 noncollege visitors took part in the event. Thus, Grinnell used its mission, embracing global awareness and service to others, and the altruistic values of its students, to substitute an educationally purposeful event for a tradition that competed with, rather than complemented, the institution's educational purposes.

Miami University students are quick to point to their traditions as being a special part of the Miami experience; as at Mount Holyoke, Miami students stated that "we have traditions here for everything." Student groups keep the most prominent traditions alive. Homecoming is a very important Miami tradition and, as mentioned in Chapter Three, being a member of the homecoming committee is a highly sought-after appointment among Miami students. A special aspect of homecoming at Miami is the fact that so many Miami students are sons and daughters of graduates. Participation in homecoming is, then, a family affair and an opportunity for youngsters to learn early about what life at Miami is like and what is expected of Miami students. One message they receive is that Miami students play a pivotal role in planning and implementing community-wide events.

"Little Sibs" is a weekend during which current Miami students entertain their younger sisters and brothers on campus. The "little sibs" get a first-hand look at student life and the students enjoy playing the role of guide to their community and culture; for siblings, this is part of the anticipatory socialization experience, which will be described in more detail in Chapter Six. Other popular traditions include the Miami bike race, alumni and alumnae weekend, avoiding "stepping on the seal" (or you will fail your next exam), kissing in the Upham Arches, and the Western College "Shore to Slimy Shore Boat Race," in which teams design and race paper boats. These stories and traditions are passed on to students from their alumni or alumnae parents, during the initial tour of campus, at orientation activities, and other freshman activities. The message they convey is clear: "there are so many things to do here, so do them."

Continuity of traditions at Stanford seems to be as much a function of administrative interest as student culture. There are some traditions of short duration, such as the Mark Twain Dance hosted by the Twain House, the EAST FEST (a celebration of Asian culture and arts), Ujamaa's "Club Ujamaa" (with dancing, food, and casino-like games), and the Oxford and Viennese Balls. Of course, there is "Full Moon on the Quad" — a kiss from a senior (some students even check IDs to verify senior

status) under a full moon at midnight in the quad makes one
a Stanford man or woman—which is now a formal event sponsored by one of the fraternities.

The Big Game (University of California, Berkeley, versus
Stanford in football) tradition is alive and well. Cardinal and
White Night includes a dance in White Plaza after Gaieties, a
spoof of faculty, administrators, and students. Happily (as far
as most undergraduates are concerned), the bonfire and "bear-
ial" (disposing of the University of California, Berkeley, mascot) persist. We heard of a less "traditional" (yet very much in
keeping with Stanford values) way to celebrate the Big Game
from a senior Resident Assistant. She helped her floor plan a
Chinese dinner to honor the memory of the Chinese laborers
who built the railroads that helped Leland Stanford, Senior, the
university's founder, amass his fortune.

Because of their relative youth and absence of a large undergraduate "collegiate corps" (full-time students eighteen to
twenty-three years of age), urban Involving Colleges have fewer
distinctive traditions than their residential counterparts. For example, students and faculty at Wichita State could identify few
community-wide traditions, perhaps because of the dramatic
changes in structure and mission the university has undergone
in the last seventy years. Over the years, WSU's "natural rival-
ries," such as in intercollegiate sports, have changed and some
historically meaningful traditions have disappeared. At one time,
an important tradition was the passing of the lamp of knowledge from the senior class president to the junior, but there are
now no class presidents; as one student stated, "we don't even
have a yearbook anymore." Although some vestiges of the original liberal arts college remain, such as a liberal arts focus for
the undergraduate curriculum, the only "traditions" that WSU
people mentioned were basketball (football was also important
until it was discontinued several years ago), Homecoming, and
Hippodrome, a student-run variety and talent show.

Homecoming is viewed as a celebration for the city of
Wichita, many of whom are WSU graduates, as much as it is
for the campus community. The elimination of WSU's football
program removed much of the spirit—as well as the central

focus — from homecoming, although the event seems to be undergoing a renaissance. Recent homecoming celebrations have included concerts and other activities.

Another Wichita campus-city tradition is the annual Fourth of July celebration held in the football stadium. The 1989 event, the fourteenth, included a performance by "Up with People," recognition of people who have made significant contributions to the community, an aircraft fly-over, and a fireworks display. These traditions underscore the important relationship between WSU and the city of Wichita. Thus, it may be the case that while urban-commuter universities have few traditions that one "traditionally" associates with college life, they do have traditions that demonstrate and affirm values unique to that type of institution.

Some traditions at the University of Louisville are maintained by the colleges and professional schools. On Engineer's Day, the Speed Scientific School (Engineering and Applied Science) invites high school students to tour the campus. While many institutions provide programs to bring high school students to their campus, this event has an academic focus: students make bridges out of balsa and the best bridges receive awards. Professional school traditions include the Law School Ball, the Cadaver Ball (the medical school), and the Dental School Gong Show.

Cultural traditions of Involving Colleges, no matter what their form, serve to remind community members of values they hold in common: student initiative, ties with the past, student development, equality, individual responsibility and respect, academic achievement, positive relationships with the surrounding community, time for recreation, pluralism, religious ideals, work, and communal bonding. This is not to say that traditions always serve positive purposes, an issue to which we return in Part Three.

Language. Language is more than just words; the language of a culture — words and expressions, the ways in which they are used, their context-bound meanings — encourages feelings of belonging in its members (Kuh and Whitt, 1988). The language of Involving Colleges, what we call "terms of endearment," conveys membership in the institution and, like traditions, gives expression to institutional values and beliefs.

Miami has an extensive cultural vocabulary. The phrases "Mother Miami," "cradle of coaches," and "mother of fraternities" connote nurturance and sense of family; the university is a source of life (of the mind) and nourishment (for the spirit), and a sheltering home for all her "children." Similarly, the "Miami bubble" implies that the university is a safe place, a protected seat from which to observe, and occasionally experience, the real world. "Miami mergers" are marriages between Miami students; these couples annually receive valentines from the university, commemorating their symbolic affirmation of the Miami family. "Miami memos" are the calendars that students keep in order to organize their time "by the hour." The message of Miami memos is "we are so busy" — students are so involved in so many activities that they must live by precise schedules in order to get everything done.

The language of Evergreen speaks of a place that refuses to take itself too seriously, yet is very serious about the qualities that set it apart from traditional institutions. The college's motto is *Omnia Extares,* a Latin phrase which roughly translated means, "Let it all hang out!" — the perfect motto for a place that is fervently committed to personal freedom. Students are known, and refer to one another, as "Greeners," a title that has come to stand for political activism, social consciousness, and liberalism. The collegiality that is part of the college's mission is reflected in the language used to describe the roles of students and faculty: "At Evergreen many of the things that separate students and faculty [at other institutions] just don't exist. Here there are only younger learners and older learners."

Quaker beliefs are reflected in the language of Earlham. Interpersonal distinctions based on superficial criteria, such as appearance, material wealth, and title, are inappropriate. For example, hierarchical relationships among students, administrators, and faculty are discouraged. As mentioned earlier, it is customary to use first names for all community members (students refer to the current college president as "Dick"). In fact, attaching last names to faculty confuses students. They are more likely to recognize a reference to "Bob in political science" than to "Bob Jones." Faculty members with the same first names are identified by their department, that is, "Sue in economics" and "Sue in English."

The result of successful socialization to Earlham, becoming "Earlhamized", makes one "politically correct" or "PC." An "Earlhamized" student, in one person's words, "has a bumper sticker that says 'Farms Not Arms,' at least one tie-dye shirt, a closet full of good clothes never worn, a Grateful Dead album, espouses a '60s-type liberalism, and is an outsider to the system." Another defined "PC" as liberal, sensitive to social values, sensitive to the oppressed, seeking social change, and rejecting capitalist ideas of individualism and material consumption. The message that these phrases communicate is ironic: although Earlham students are vocal in their liberalism and openness to diverse opinions (recall the Quaker principle of finding truth in every person), there is a "right" way to think and a "correct" set of beliefs.

As mentioned in the preceding chapter, strong egalitarian forces are at work at Earlham, Grinnell, Mount Holyoke, Stanford, and TESC to minimize differences within and among groups. Thus, first-year students are referred to by the student affairs staff, as well as a growing number of faculty and students, as "frosh" or first-year students rather than the masculine term "freshmen."

Stanford University is referred to by many students, faculty, and administrators as "the Farm" because it was built on farmland owned by Leland Stanford, Senior. The use of such a homely term for a world-class research university and undergraduate college seems, at first glance, to be inappropriate. In fact, "the Farm," like the Leland Stanford Junior University Marching Band and the Frosh Book (described in Chapter Six), reminds Stanford people not to take themselves too seriously — an important, if surprising, community value.

Unlike Earlham and Stanford, Xavier is a community in which last names and titles are used conscientiously. At Xavier, a title, such as "doctor" or "professor" or "sister," acknowledges effort and achievement. The message to students is that, although everyone in the institution is deserving of respect, respect must be earned through hard work.

For Mount Holyoke students, the phrase "uncommon women" describes not only the expectations held for them by the institution but also an ideal toward which to strive. Student involvement, even excellence, in in-class and out-of-class experiences is, according to a faculty member, "expected, it's part of the Mount Holyoke tradition of 'uncommon women.'" A senior told us that "the message" students receive about involvement is that "you're uncommon women, you've accepted the challenge to excel" by coming to Mount Holyoke.

One term of endearment common across Involving Colleges is "dorm." Many student affairs professionals prefer "residence hall" because the term "dormitory" historically connoted a place where students simply slept and, perhaps, took their meals. The phrase "residence hall" is intended to connote a living environment rich in out-of-class learning opportunities. Yet, at Involving Colleges almost all of those who used the word "residence hall" were residence hall advisers and counselors, not students, or even other student affairs staff. In the case of Stanford and Iowa State students, the term "house" was often used.

Two matters are worthy of note: at Involving colleges, the term "dorm" was almost always used with affection — in no way did students or others view the word as pejorative; and the dorms and houses at Involving Colleges were very rich living-learning environments where students often took responsibility for themselves and the welfare of members of their living unit. Student affairs professionals have discouraged use of the word "dorm" and championed the phrase "residence hall" with the hope that the symbolism of the term would encourage responsible behavior and high levels of learning and development. Such efforts seem to be irrelevant to administrators, students, and faculty at Involving Colleges. While we readily acknowledge the symbolic power of language, a symbol must have meaning to people if the symbol is to shape behavior. Apparently at Involving Colleges, what is most important is not what student residences are called but what goes on there.

Institutional language can be limiting or even debilitating for some groups. We have already mentioned the potential implications of being "politically correct" at Earlham. Some members of the Mount Holyoke community expressed concern that the expectation for "uncommon women" and the pressures to achieve that it implies might be a "double-edged sword." The pursuit of excellence can create debilitating levels of stress. Students speak of having no time to do anything but study, and we were told that eating disorders are not uncommon. Also, there are alumnae who feel that, by making what some would see as traditional women's choices to marry and have children and work in the home, they have failed to live up to the college's expectations for them.

The "Miami bubble" is viewed by some at the university as implying detachment from the concerns of the real world. Miami students can, if they choose, avoid encounters with people whose backgrounds, views, lifestyles, and problems are very different from their own and so may become complacent about issues such as poverty, political oppression, hunger, and racism.

Another example of how language can be limiting is the reference by some people to Wichita State as "Hillside High." At least two interpretations were offered as to the genesis and influence of this term. Some use it to refer to the university's state-mandated open admissions policy, which suggests to a shrinking number of local people that WSU is a place to go if one cannot get into, or cannot afford to go to, another institution in Kansas or elsewhere. Others use the term to describe an institution where students mistakenly assume that opportunities for involvement and out-of-class learning are limited. In both cases, the term "Hillside High" works to discourage some students from getting as much out of their WSU experience as they can because they incorrectly assume that opportunities for involvement and learning outside of class do not exist.

Heroines and Heroes. Individual actors within institutions can "often loom larger than life in the making of an organizational saga and sustaining a campus culture" (Kuh and Whitt, 1988, p. 72). Institutional leaders such as founders, presidents, and senior faculty, and the stories and legends that are told about them, shape interpretations of the mission, values, and practices. The heroes and heroines of Involving Colleges play a role in forging institutional commitment to student learning and development.

The founder of Mount Holyoke was Mary Lyon, a teacher and feminist whose impact continues to be felt on the campus, almost as if she were alive. The use of her words and ideas in daily conversation enhances the impression that she is a living presence. During a campus visit at the height of the New England "tree season," we were told that "the blue of the October sky over Mount Holyoke" was Mary Lyon's choice for the school color. More important, however, is the persistence of her commitment to the higher education of women for service to society; she expected that students would leave Mount Holyoke prepared to share their valuable experiences with the world. During Mary Lyon's time at the college and for many years thereafter, students were responsible for keeping their residences clean and preparing and serving their own meals. Although that is no longer the practice, Mount Holyoke students still feel that "you owe something," that what is learned there must be shared. They also hear "loud and clear" that "you can do anything," that they must not be inhibited by traditions and fears. This creates a "can do" feeling about the place that flows directly from Mary Lyon's commitment to an enhanced role for women in society.

Many distinctive elements of the culture of Stanford can be traced to the influence of its first president, David Starr Jordan, formerly president and professor of biology of Indiana University. Jordan's vision was to build a world-class university, and he immediately began to recruit high-quality faculty members; Stanford thus began with a national faculty. This was not easy; at that time California was still the Wild West and attracting people from eastern institutions such as Cornell, Harvard, and Yale took some convincing. Jordan is also credited with outlining the Fundamental Standard, described in Chapter Three, which continues to be the guiding rule for the Stanford community.

One of the key figures in sustaining the hands-on and involving heritage of the University of California, Davis, was former chancellor Emil Mrak, the university's second chancellor and the man for whom the UC Davis administration building is named. Mrak was instrumental in setting a participatory tone for the Davis campus. His philosophy, "helping students to help themselves," is evident in a number of administrative systems, including the peer advisory program and administrative advising committees. Many current staff and administrators never met Emil Mrak, but they know what he stood for; his legacy of commitment to students is carefully and affectionately communicated from one UC Davis generation to the next.

James H. Meyer, chancellor at UC Davis from 1969 to 1987, also left his mark on the institution. When Meyer began his tenure as chancellor, UC Davis had 12,320 students and 2,215 faculty; by 1987 the enrollment was 20,230 and the number of faculty had more than doubled to 5,016. Chancellor Meyer's style was characterized as low key, consultative, and process oriented, an approach that made for widespread involvement in decision making and significant student input. Meyer also encouraged the development of career-related internships, an experience in which about 4,000 students per year participate.

Some of the rich tradition of Miami's out-of-class life and the importance of out-of-class life to the undergraduate experience can be attributed to former president Phillip Shriver. Shriver was described by several faculty as "the best dean of students Miami University ever had." He is still very student oriented, appears in the residence halls at least once a week, and continues to be one of the most popular professors on campus.

Involving College heroes and heroines are not always presidents or founders. The chief student affairs officer at Wichita State, James Rhatigan, has been at the institution for nearly twenty-five years. Rhatigan emphasizes the pastoral rather than the executive functions of the CSAO, "pastoral" implying a spiritual concern for students' welfare. Many individuals at WSU refer to him in glowing terms; one called him a "beloved buffer" between the students and the university. He is seen as available, helpful, wise, nonjudgmental, and an advocate for students. He also seems to be a personification of student services for WSU students, and his "halo effect" is far-reaching. In his role as "the good dean," Rhatigan's personal ethic of care permeates the Student Affairs Division and has also influenced many faculty members and some aspects of academic administration, such as notifying students by phone about class cancellations — "a very important service" for WSU's commuting student population.

Sagas. A saga is a story that has become institutionalized over time and that describes significant individuals and events in an institution's history (Clark, 1970, 1972; Masland, 1985) and can be invoked as needed to give credibility or legitimacy to a decision or policy change (Kuh and Whitt, 1988). The saga is part of an institution's memory, that "connective tissue" (Kuh and Whitt, 1988, p. 45) linking past and present and shaping the future. Sagas of Involving Colleges focus primarily on the founding of the institution and the ways in which it has weathered crises and survived.

Mount Holyoke was originally founded as a women's seminary (or secondary school) in 1837, and served as a model for other female seminaries and female departments at coeducational institutions. Unique to Mount Holyoke was its commitment to a rigorous academic experience (unusual as well as controversial at the time) combined with a system of discipline (enforced hours for work and sleep, assigned duties) which "propelled its students outward into the world. Mary Lyon created Mount Holyoke to turn daughters who were acted upon into women capable of self-propelled action" (Horowitz, 1984, p. 12). Today's Mount Holyoke is similarly rigorous and equally committed to the education of highly capable women.

Xavier was founded in 1915 by Mother Katharine Drexel and the Sisters of the Blessed Sacrament. Mother Katharine was an heiress to the Drexel furniture fortune who obtained an audience with the pope to discuss how best to use her wealth in serving the Church. Xavier University was the result of that meeting, and Mother Katharine's belief that if opportunities were provided to persons who faced overwhelming odds, they would excel, is still being implemented there today.

It is clear from the description of the founding of Berea on the sign quoted in Chapter Three that the college faced many crises early in its history. Berea opened in 1855 and its 1858 constitution committed the college to an antislavery stance. Proslavery factions forced the college to close one year later, but it reopened after the end of the Civil War. Another setback occurred in the early 1900s with the passage of the Kentucky Day Law when Berea was required to refuse to admit black students, but the repeal of the law in the 1950s brought blacks back to the campus. Today, the Berea student body is thoroughly integrated, with students of all races mixing freely in and out of class. Despite the obstacles it has faced in living its mission, Berea is, indeed, "a historic monument to equality."

Evergreen has also faced crises in its short life. During the past twenty years, seven bills have been introduced in the Washington state legislature to close the college. Although TESC has survived, a siege mentality lingers. Evergreen both thrives (internally) and suffers (externally) for its reputation as a school with different ideas and different students. Some residents of nearby Olympia, the state capital, also feed the siege mentality. The "shaggy, baggy, unkempt, '60s" appearance of the Greeners invites some ridicule, occasional caustic comment, and some anger. These perceptions seem to be changing, however, especially since *U.S. News and World Report* (1987) identified Evergreen as being among the best schools in the nation. Soon thereafter, a reporter from the Olympia newspaper commented: "When that came out attitudes changed almost overnight. It was as though many realized that maybe there was something actually good happening there!"

Physical Setting. The physical environment of an institution reflects the values and beliefs of its participants (Kuh and Whitt, 1988; Sturner, 1972). Where buildings are placed, what they look like and how they are maintained, the amount of open space provided, the care taken to provide places for large and small groups to interact, the priority given to space for students, and the amount of control students have for their setting can be viewed as demonstrating the institution's commitment to community and student life.

The Red Barn, located on the edge of the University of Louisville campus, is celebrating its twentieth anniversary as the locus of many U of L activities. During that period of time, the Red Barn has sponsored approximately 10,000 programs involving over one million students, faculty, and staff, and has generated more than two million dollars in revenue. Perhaps the best illustration of the degree to which U of L students are encouraged to become involved and take responsibility for their own behavior is Red Barn programming. Students, including older nontraditional students, design and implement innovative activities and programs with minimal supervision. Staff members demonstrate an obvious caring attitude and communicate to students that they are trusted to try new things on their own.

Although the Red Barn is a center for U of L programming, its events are also attractive to Louisville residents of all ages. The university is becoming known as a fun place to be, largely because of the Red Barn activities; the Red Barn, then, plays an important role in maintaining positive ties between the university and the city of Louisville.

The Red Square at TESC is a place to meet friends, hang out, and celebrate life. Evergreen students speak fondly of Red Square on sunny days: music, dancing, political talks, and soapbox oration. The Forum (Grinnell's Union) is the location of public discussions and presentations about issues of student and societal concern. The Earlham "heart" is the site of vigils, in which Earlham students show their support for various issues. Each of these areas is, in effect, the crossroads of the campus and symbolizes the social consciousness that is characteristic of the institutions. Discussions of political and social issues and current events are very much a part of the social life at these colleges, a practice that is enabled and reinforced by the presence of public gathering places.

Earlham's dining hall also plays an important role in maintaining student activism as well as an active on-campus social life. Dining hall tables are covered with handouts about campus activities and descriptions of political action issues and concerns. One handout listed facts about the Middle East, including official positions of parties within the Israeli parliament. Large banners are hung around the room to announce campus events. For example, Pink Triangle Week (to show support for the gay, lesbian and bisexual communities at Earlham and elsewhere) was being observed during one of our visits.

The Opinion Board in the Runyan Center (the union) is a forum for students to exchange views on a variety of issues. The board is always full, demonstrating the value placed on open, free exchange of ideas. Also, the presence of the board reminds members of the community that everyone's opinion is important, that everyone's opinions are open to criticism with respect, and that speaking out demands owning one's thoughts.

A walk around Wichita State will reveal an intentional effort to create the "feel" of a college campus despite its urban setting. Trees, spacious grassy areas, and sculptures evoke images of an academic retreat from the fast pace of the surrounding city. There are many convenient places for students to gather, very important for a largely commuter population — they need to know how to find one another. The entrance to the Campus Activities Center (CAC) is a place to run into friends and watch lunchtime entertainment. Inside, CAC lounges and dining areas are divided into small niches for conversation and study. The Heskett Center — "more a focal point for campus life than the CAC" — is a recreational facility that includes a swimming pool, racketball courts, basketball courts, weight rooms, aerobics and other fitness classes, and health evaluations and wellness programs. The Heskett Center is open from early in the morning to late at night, a response to the widely varying schedules of WSU students; students and community people can work out before or after work, classes, or library time.

Symbols and Symbolic Action. Cultural "meanings are 'stored' in symbols" (Geertz, 1973, p. 127). Institutional symbols call attention to important values and elicit feelings of pride and identification. Symbolic action is an effort on the part of groups and individuals (often leaders) to bring institutional symbols into focus for members of the community, reminding them of the ideals for which they exist. Involving Colleges are characterized by symbols and symbolic actions that promote involvement.

At Iowa State's university and college orientation sessions, the deans of academic units make a point of urging new students to participate in out-of-class activities. This is an important symbolic action in that students are given the message that involvement by students is expected, is important to the university, and is related—even in the deans' eyes—to the academic experience.

Intercollegiate basketball seems to be an important symbol at all four urban-commuter Involving Colleges. Basketball is certainly an urban game—a street game that brings people together under a hoop to share a community experience. The communities in which these universities are located take great pride in the teams' success. There are no more adamant supporters of Wichita State basketball than the residents of Wichita, and the team reinforces the feeling that WSU is the city's university.

At Earlham and Evergreen, the absence, or diminution of the importance, of major sporting events elicits pride. Parents Day at Earlham in 1988 was scheduled for a weekend when the football team was scheduled to play an *away* game! "At what other college," the TESC director of recreation and athletics reported, "would the athletic director occasionally have to call an intercollegiate competitor to report that the Evergreen team decided to forfeit because 'they were too busy [with academic projects] to play' that game, match, or meet?"

In keeping with the unique character of Evergreen, its mascot is the geoduck (pronounced "gooeyduck"), a giant clam native to Puget Sound. Evergreen's intercollegiate teams—men's and women's soccer, swimming, and diving—call themselves the "Fighting Geoducks." The film shown to prospective students and visitors was made by students and begins with a scene of a young man rowing a small dory across Puget Sound toward the Evergreen Beach where he is met and given a campus tour by an eight-foot-tall geoduck. The film and the mascot symbolize the Greeners' pride in being different, as well as their sense of humor.

One of the most interesting symbols of TESC is the Freebox, across from the entrance to the cafeteria on the bottom floor of the Campus Activities Building (CAB). The Freebox is the place where students discard clothes they no longer want or need, and miscellaneous items such as ski wax, frying pans, walking sticks, belts, and shoes. Not all items in the Freebox are old, but most are. At the Freebox, passersby were asked whether the box was used. Almost to a person, they answered, "Of course!" and pointed to something they were wearing at the time. There is no doubt that the Freebox accounts for much of the wild array of colors, sizes, and styles of clothing worn by students which are, by ordinary standards, ill-fitting and clashing. But that is part of living the role of a Greener: people share what they have, conservation is important, and egalitarianism runs deep.

Clothing also symbolizes attitudes at other Involving Colleges. The mode of attire for Earlham students has an "Annie Hall" look: loose-fitting, larger-size-than-needed, and no two articles seem to match. This is in stark contrast to their southern neighbors, Miami University students, who favor button-down shirts, khaki slacks or skirts, crewneck sweaters, and penny loafers. The style of dress of Miami students and administrators reflects the community's conventional attitudes, just as the clothing of Earlham students is an expression of their liberal, nonconformist, and cosmopolitan viewpoints as well as their commitment to underplay status differences.

Commitment to the environment and egalitarianism is symbolized at UC Davis by the ever-present bicycle. The Davis campus is virtually free of automobile traffic. A network of bike paths and roads forms the principal conduits by which students, faculty, and staff move about the campus. Bicycles are both an expression of a California "thing to do" and a symbol of the belief that "we're all in this together"—even the chancellor rides a bike.

The whimsy that is a part of Stanford is best characterized by the Leland Stanford Junior University Marching Band. "The Band" is open to any student who can play a musical instrument, and, occasionally, some who cannot. They do not wear the uniforms typical of marching bands and are determined never to march in traditional formation. However, on rare occasions (no more than once a decade), they have been known to square up, form lines, and march well. In any case, their fans (all students and some graduates) find "The Band"'s parody of "real" marching bands to be hilarious, and a reminder not to take themselves too seriously.

The academic and social honor codes at Stanford, Mount Holyoke, and Grinnell, described in Chapters Six and Fourteen, and the social contract at TESC are symbols of the value those institutions place on treating students as adults. At the same time, students are expected to take responsibility for their own actions and respect the rights of others.

Mount Holyoke's founder, Mary Lyon, is buried on the campus in South Hadley. The presence of her gravesite conveys the message that she is still part of the community, that her spirit lives on in everyday events and activities. The University of Louisville is the location of the grave of Supreme Court Justice Louis Brandeis, a symbol of the social conscience of the institution and its historical commitment to individual and human rights. The U of L was integrated in 1954 and was the first institution in the state to admit black athletes. This liberal stance has not always been popular. Because the U of L teams had black players, the Louisville Cardinals were sometimes referred to as the "Blackbirds." Nevertheless, the university has been willing to confront controversial issues on campus and take actions that may be out-of-step with the rest of the state.

Values and Assumptions

Values are what the members of a culture assert to be most important. The artifacts described above represent many of the values of Involving Colleges, such as egalitarianism, activism, community, and (of course) involvement or active participation in the life of the institution. The "ethic of membership" discussed in Chapter Three describes institutional values about who belongs, who can take part in community affairs, and who has an impact on student learning and development. This value is not implemented by catering to students' whims or asking little of them in return. To the contrary, students are expected to be full participants in the life of the institution. They play significant roles in institutional decisions and have a lot of freedom to regulate their own activities. Students at Earlham decide by consensus the rules by which their hall community will live. At Mount Holyoke, student hall presidents and resident assistants (all of whom volunteer their time) are largely responsible for the quality of life in student residences. At the same time, extensive systems of support are available should students need them (Chapter Nine). Other sources of support, including "invisible safety nets," are discussed in Chapter Six.

The assumptions underlying cultural artifacts and values are often difficult to identify because they are for the most part tacit, in the minds of the members of the culture, and so are rarely discussed. Nevertheless, we think that we have identified some of the basic assumptions that undergird the cultures of Involving Colleges.

At Evergreen, the assumption is that "anyone can learn anything." This is manifested in the policy that some spots in each incoming class are held for students who have had difficulty in traditional educational settings. From the freshman year, students are involved in seminar experiences in the Programs; they do not spend two years in introductory-level classes, as is the case at many institutions. Also, students are given freedom to participate in the planning of Programs (described in Chapter Nine) and may pursue any Program that interests them; if they have difficulty with the work, they can get assistance—but no prior constraints exist for admission to the Programs. Students and faculty are viewed as partners in learning, implying that faculty can learn from students as much as students can learn from faculty.

A similar assumption can be found at the urban institutions: every student should have the opportunity to pursue a college degree, and with hard work, anyone can succeed. At Xavier, a basic assumption is that anyone, if given the opportunity, can overcome overwhelming odds and achieve. Of course, the manner in which these beliefs are played out and how they are manifested in policies and practices differs depending on other ethics and values that are operating. As with values, institutional assumptions are inextricably linked with institutional missions; other assumptions of Involving Colleges were discussed in Chapter Three.

Summary

"Organizations end up being what they think and say, as their ideas and visions realize themselves" (Morgan, 1986, p. 133). In general, the institutional culture and dominant subcultures at Involving Colleges promote student involvement as well as feelings of pride and ownership of the institution. When asked to describe what is special about their institution, students, faculty, and administrators at Involving Colleges said, "there's just something about the place." There is an ineffable "something in the woodwork" that is the essence of these places, not describable except through examples, yet felt by and familiar to all who come to know and love them.

Using a cultural lens to look at Involving Colleges illuminates a number of lessons about their quality of student life. Despite their differences, these institutions have something in common. A high-quality out-of-class experience for students, an active valuing of student learning and development, are guiding cultural values. These values usually have persisted through time and are given life in institutional traditions, heroes and heroines, symbols, language, and the physical setting.

In the following chapter, the environments of Involving Colleges are examined for the ways in which they encourage student involvement.

5

Campus Environment

Although students' biographical, intellectual, and psychosocial characteristics determine in part what and how much they learn, institutional resources and facilities also contribute to outcomes of the undergraduate experience. The campus environment includes all the conditions and influences, such as physical, chemical, biological and social stimuli, that affect the growth and development of living things (Western Interstate Commission for Higher Education, 1973). A campus environment can be described in terms of physical properties such as the size and location of campus facilities and the use of open space (Gerber, 1989); the environmental "press" (Stern, 1970) or norms and expectations established by dominant student subcultures (Clark and Trow, 1966) or faculty groups; the ambience created by the personalities of students (Astin and Holland, 1961); and the perceptions of students (Pace, 1984a). These descriptions are encompassed by the concept of campus ecology: the mutually shaping interactions between individuals and the environments of a college. In this sense, student behavior is a product of students interacting with the institution's various subenvironments made up of physical spaces, policies, and people (Huebner, 1979).

An institution's physical, social, and organizational environments can be discouraging, confusing, and alienating, or orderly, predictable, coherent, and encouraging (Corbally, 1989; Snyder, 1971). For example, an institution that allows students to choose from among 700 courses to fulfill general education requirements may appear confusing and overwhelming to many students. Some environmental elements that affect students can be influenced by administrators, faculty members, and students, and some cannot. But all are important to learning and personal development, and any attempt to study an institution's environment should embrace as many environmental elements as possible.

Environments can be assessed in different ways. Baird (1988) identified four approaches to studying college environments: demographic, perceptual, behavioral, and multimethod. Demographic approaches use data such as student characteristics and distribution of majors. The perceptual approach relies on responses to survey items presenting varied perceptions of the institution. The behavioral approach assesses observable actions of students, faculty, and staff. The multimethod approach, the method used in this study, uses a combination of the other three.

In this chapter, four categories of environmental characteristics shared to varying degrees by Involving Colleges are described: location, physical properties, psychological properties, and organizational properties. Cultural properties, which could arguably be included in a broad definition of campus environments, were discussed in the preceding chapter.

Location

Whether surrounded by a city, nestled in a suburb, or seemingly isolated in a rural setting, Involving Colleges take advantage of their setting in enacting their mission, philosophy, policies, and practices. Indeed, all fourteen of the institutions in this study would assert with pride and confidence that where they are located is "a good place for a college." Institutional leaders are sensitive to the qualities of the location and how these qualities promote or detract from attaining the institution's educational purposes. Over time, institutional policies and practices have been developed to use the qualities of the location to educational advantage.

Isolated or Surrounded

Locations of colleges and universities can be arranged on a continuum. At one end is an institution that is geographically distant from any major population center. At the other is an institution that is ensconced in a metropolitan area.

Isolated. The historical precedents for selecting an isolated location when establishing a college are well known. One reason was purely pragmatic. As metropolitan areas expanded around colleges, institutions had little choice for their own growth but to move to a more spacious setting, as was the case of Columbia University, which was founded as King's College on the outskirts of New York City in 1754. By 1859 the city had expanded and closed in around the college, which compelled the institution to relocate (Stern, 1986).

Educational philosophy and religious interests also promoted the desirability of a pastoral setting for colleges. In 1817 Thomas Jefferson chose a location a mile away from the village of Charlottesville for his "academical village," the University of Virginia. Jefferson wanted a new kind of university, an alternative to the College of William and Mary that would be a nearly self-sufficient, coherent social and cultural learning community, "a place apart from the bustle, temptations, and conflicts of the city" (Stern, 1986, p. 41). The University of Georgia was established among the pine trees in Athens to get away from the evils of Atlanta (Brubacher and Rudy, 1976). To isolate their young charges from the temptations of the secular world, religious groups often selected remote locations for their colleges. Catholics founded St. John's University in Collegeville, Minnesota, the Norwegian Lutherans finally placed Luther College in Decorah, Iowa, and the Presbyterians founded Hanover College in Hanover, Indiana. These are but a few of the hundreds of colleges established with the purpose of isolation in mind (Tewksbury, 1965).

Today, isolation from a metropolitan area is justified more with educational arguments than religious or social preferences.

Students who attend isolated colleges are presumably shielded from competing interests or distractions indigenous to metropolitan areas that may compete for their energy, time, and attention. Because students who attend colleges like Grinnell or Berea or Earlham are first and foremost full-time students — that is their primary role orientation — they can be fully immersed in the student role. They can enjoy the benefits of the traditional collegiate experience, including living away from home and being free, usually for the first time, from parental guidance.

Isolated colleges tend to attract the largest proportion of their students from the traditional-age cohort for obvious reasons. There is no older, non-traditional-age cohort nearby, and students as well as their parents prefer a residential college experience. Because of its isolation, the institution must provide virtually all the necessary resources to promote student learning and personal development, such as housing, jobs, and social activities.

For students at Involving Colleges, their isolation is either real or perceived.

Real Isolation. Grinnell College is located in a place known to very few people outside of Iowa. The issue of isolation is addressed by the College in a forthright manner in bold letters on the first page of the Grinnell viewbook: "Grinnell WHERE?" Located seventy-five miles from the state capital, the campus is in a town of about 8,500 people. To get to Grinnell from any direction requires travel on roads cut through miles of cornfields.

Because they are geographically isolated, Grinnell students, 85 percent of whom are from communities more than 500 miles away, are forced to turn to one another for social activities and relationships. Isolation forces Grinnell students to come together in activities in which they have mutual interest and create interesting activities with which to experiment and learn more about one another. Isolation also means that students have few externally imposed distractions. According to George Drake, the president of Grinnell: "One of the things that sets us apart from our peer institutions is the quality of our residential experience. We do not put the residential program above the academic program but because our program is so strong, it makes the Grinnell experience special." Thus, isolation contributes to Grinnell's top priority, cultivation of the mind and full participation in the life of the college community.

Isolation is not without limitations. For example, students and faculty members at Berea, Grinnell, and Earlham are very sensitive to the potential for isolation from issues and concerns that dominate the "outside" world. To ameliorate this situation, isolated Involving Colleges tend to emphasize off-campus programs such as internships and study abroad. For example, more than 40 percent of Grinnell students study overseas.

Perceived Isolation. Miami University is located in Oxford, Ohio, a community of about 17,000 people. The city of Oxford was founded and named after the institution was established in what was then considered a remote area of southwestern Ohio. People continue to think of Miami and Oxford as being isolated, a perception that is due in part to the fact that Oxford is seventeen miles from the nearest four-lane highway. Thus, it is difficult to get to Miami and (students believe) even more difficult to leave. Even though people think Miami is isolated, Oxford lies within a corridor stretching from Dayton to Cincinnati, Ohio. Indeed, some Cincinnati shopping malls are within a forty-minute drive of Miamians. The perception of isolation is reinforced by the long-standing policy prohibiting students who live on campus from having automobiles in Oxford. However, because about half of Miami students live off campus, automobiles are in ample supply.

As with students at Grinnell, many of the students who attend Earlham College (Richmond, Indiana, population 40,000) are from communities more than 500 miles from Richmond; about 40 percent are from the East Coast. Thus, facing the transition from large metropolitan areas to a small college in a relatively small town — by their standards — makes it seem as though Earlham is isolated. The mission of Earlham, to create a utopian environment in which Quaker principles can be applied, also contributes to a sense of isolation, a sense of a place apart.

Neither Iowa State University nor the University of California, Davis, is located in a metropolitan area; thus, these campuses may seem isolated to many students. This perception is shaped somewhat by the agricultural roots of these institutions that continue to influence the curriculum, campus climate, and traditions. At the same time, both universities are within a short drive of their state capital, where internships in government agencies and business and industry have been developed for students.

It seems foolish to claim that Stanford University, located thirty minutes from San Francisco, is isolated. But many Stanford students sense that they, too, are in a place apart; 85 percent of Stanford's undergraduates live on the 8,000-acre campus which is adjacent to, not surrounded by, Palo Alto. Many students affectionately call UC Davis and Stanford "the farm," as both institutions were established on farmland. These factors make these universities seem more geographically isolated than they are.

Students at Mount Holyoke in South Hadley, Massachusetts, perceive the college as a supportive, somewhat protective women's community. Yet Mount Holyoke participates in the Five College System, a consortium of the University of Massachusetts at Amherst, Amherst College, Hampshire College, Smith College, and Mount Holyoke College, which makes available a large variety of curricular offerings and social activities. The Evergreen State College is but twenty minutes from the urban sprawl of Olympia, Washington, the state capital. Only about 27 percent of the students live in college-owned housing. But the heavily wooded campus that borders Puget Sound has a very rural, remote feel to it and many students — including adult learners — feel as though they have gone away to college.

Thus, isolation is a construct with physical and perceptual properties that are a product of the institution's distance from a population center, the distance students travel from home to attend the institution, and students' reasons for attending the college, such as a residential experience in a pastoral setting.

Surrounded. The converse of the argument for isolation provides the warrant for an institution located in a metropolitan setting. Most urban areas provide many options for public transportation and numerous off-campus employment opportunities. Cities also offer a multitude of opportunities for student learning through recreational, social, and cultural activities that are not easily replicated in isolated settings. Museums, zoos, theaters, parks, hospitals, and businesses and industries are available to students at urban Involving Colleges. Of course, students must want to take advantage of these opportunities in order to learn. Herein is the distinctive feature of urban Involving Colleges: they use their metropolitan setting to shape and further their educational purposes. The city is their "campus."

There is an important distinction between merely being located in an urban setting and being committed to serving the needs and interests of people in the metropolitan area in which the institution is located. For example, although the University of Chicago is located in an urban setting, its mission emphasizes research and rigorous liberal arts education rather than meeting the needs of the Chicago metropolitan area. The critical factor for using the urban setting to educational advantage is the extent to which the institution and its agents—faculty members, administrators, and staff—have accepted and are enthusiastically pursuing the institution's mission as an urban or metropolitan university.

> [A] university located in a city may simply be a resident of that city with few interactions between the city and the university. An urban university is a participating citizen of the city in which it is located. It has developed many interactions with the city and the overwhelming majority of its students reside in the surrounding metropolitan region [Grobman, 1988, p. 9].

> Certain obligations accrue to an urban public university by the very fact of its being "of the city," not just "in" it. This implies that the urban university becomes an integral part of the city's economic, political, social, and cultural milieu, and is not

merely geographically located in the city [Jones and
Damron, n.d., pp. 6-7].

All four of the urban institutions in this study have formed
partnerships with their cities to foster economic development.
Consider the University of Louisville (U of L).

As described in Chapter Four, seven years after the U
of L joined the state system, the Kentucky Higher Education
coordinating board designated the University of Louisville "the
urban university" in the state system. This designation affirmed
the University of Louisville's municipal heritage (for a long time
the university received funds from the city). Under the leadership of President Donald Swain, the University of Louisville
aspired to be "one of the best urban institutions in the United
States." To realize this vision, the university began to develop
and nurture relationships with government, business, industry,
and civic groups and acknowledge the long-standing educational
and cultural traditions of Louisville and Jefferson County. The
university is committed to making the institution and the metropolitan area in which it is located almost interchangeable. Swain
modeled this philosophy when he served as the president of the
Louisville Chamber of Commerce. Another example of cooperation is the public-private partnership established between the
university and Humana Hospitals. Humana took over the administration of the downtown teaching hospital, which treats
many indigent patients. As a result of the revenue-sharing partnership, an annual loss of about $4 million for the university
has blossomed into a surplus of $1.5 million.

Involving Colleges in metropolitan settings acknowledge
the increasingly permeable boundaries between the campus and
the larger world by developing programs and activities that take
advantage of the opportunities that only metropolitan areas can
provide. It would be erroneous to imply that because institutions are located in metropolitan areas, educationally appropriate
experiences off the campus require little attention by institutional agents. While such opportunities are close at hand, institutional effort and resources are required to link students with
internships, public service agencies, and cultural activities. The

urban institutions that meet this test have unusually strong relationships with the surrounding community. Wichita State, as some told us, "grew up with the community"; because WSU was once a municipal university, many Wichita residents continue to believe it belongs to the city. There is an easy, almost natural, ebb and flow of people on and off the campus. Students—even traditional-age students—report that the city offers as much to do as the university. The important point is not that, compared with small residential institutions, urban universities offer fewer interesting things to do on campus, but rather that students are free—and are encouraged by city officials and residents—to take advantage of the city's resources.

When we began this project, some advised us not to study commuter universities since they have few students in residence, enroll many adult learners (older than the traditional age of eighteen to twenty-three), and do not have many of the features of traditional college life. We were told that life on commuter campuses simply was not rich enough to provide insights into student involvement. Indeed, students at urban institutions are often more diverse in terms of age and educational objectives than their counterparts at predominantly residential colleges and universities (Rhatigan, 1986). At Wichita State University (WSU), more students own their own homes than live with their parents or on campus. Also, more than 80 percent of WSU students work, most off the campus. For many WSU students, their priorities are family, work, church, and college, in that order. Because of their family and work commitments, most of these students do not have the option of attending college elsewhere. These factors have profound and often misunderstood implications for an institution's mission and educational programs, issues described in more detail in Chapter Ten. It would be difficult to argue that the experiences of many students at urban institutions are the quantitative and qualitative equal of students at residential colleges. However, because of their location, urban institutions can offer different types of learning opportunities for their students that are not easily reproduced by isolated colleges and universities. Whether conventional expectations for where and how student learning best occurs limit

creative efforts on the part of institutions to encourage students
to take advantage of these opportunities warrants serious consideration, a point to which we will return in Chapter Ten and
Part Three. Suffice it to say for the moment that it is important
for institutional agents to be knowledgeable about how student
characteristics, the institution's mission, and the institution's location influence student learning.

Connected, Yet a Place Apart

To take advantage of the setting, some institutions must
appear to be two contradictory things at once: connected to the
outside world, and a place apart.

Because of an increasingly pluralistic world and shifting
economic conditions, institutions of higher education are no
longer ivory towers, detached and sheltered from pressing social, economic, and human rights issues. As a consequence, geographically isolated colleges have purposefully entered into consortium arrangements and developed curricular opportunities
for students to get first-hand experience in applying classroom
and laboratory learning to the problems and issues they will confront after college.

The impetus for both structured and spontaneous out-
of-class experiences that connect students to the outside world
is sometimes the institution's mission. As mentioned in the
preceding chapter, from their inception, Berea, Grinnell, Earlham, and Mount Holyoke have been committed to public service. At Berea, for example, the college's ethos of Christian service promotes student voluntarism. Students, until recently,
fought fires in nearby townships and still work with community-
based organizations, such as boy's and girl's clubs. It is said that
all one needs to do to get twelve to fifteen volunteers is to call
a Berea residence hall and ask for help.

Examples of structured activities linking students with societal issues include programs sponsored annually by the Miami University Honors Program wherein students typically work
in an urban area, Stanford's Washington, D.C., campus, and
the internship programs at the University of Louisville, Iowa
State University, and the University of California, Davis.

One of the distinctive qualities of American higher education has been the creation through architecture and green space of a physical setting that clearly separates an institution of higher learning from its environs and symbolizes the life of the mind (Thelin and Yankovich, 1987). Several Involving Colleges in urban settings are linked programmatically, economically, and politically with the surrounding community while presenting a physical appearance that conveys the message that the institution is a center of higher learning.

One of the things that makes urban institutions stand out from their surroundings is the well-kept grounds and physical facilities. Because most students at urban institutions commute from their homes to attend classes, the physical appearance of the campus is important to creating the feeling that the campus is different from, and thus demands different behaviors than, home, work, and church. Consider Xavier, not an urban institution by mission but located nonetheless in the heart of a major metropolitan area. Set apart by freeways and a canal, Xavier is an island in the midst of urban blight.

Shortly after President Swain arrived at the University of Louisville in 1980, he envisioned the university as a place apart from the metropolitan area. He asked the buildings and grounds personnel to make a concerted effort to remove debris and to plant flower beds, trees, and shrubs to make the Belknap campus, where the majority of arts and sciences and professional students attend, more attractive. In addition to well-cared-for green spaces, Wichita State University has become a place apart by limiting vehicular traffic to the perimeter of the campus. Other efforts to create a "campus" setting at WSU were described in Chapter Four.

In summary, Involving Colleges use the qualities of their location to educational advantage and develop curricular programs and out-of-class experiences to compensate for disadvantages inherent in the setting. In many ways, these institutions are places apart; at the same time, their missions, policies, and practices, which are described in Chapter Six, ensure that students are not isolated — intellectually, morally, or socially — from the outside world. Although Involving Colleges have been successful to varying degrees in striking this balance, all recognize the importance of making certain that students contend with real world issues while pursuing their learning and personal development goals.

Physical Properties

The physical environment of Involving Colleges, both the natural and constructed aspects, contributes to student learning and development in two important ways. First, the properties of the physical environment shape behavior, either encouraging or discouraging students from taking advantage of learning opportunities. Second, student involvement in the process of designing and redesigning the physical environment can promote student learning and development. In general, the physical plants of Involving Colleges are attractive, well maintained, and complement the institution's educational mission and purposes. Intentionally or not, Involving Colleges have made good use of the properties of their natural environment by developing a human-scale physical plant.

The concept of human scale is multifaceted. Taken together, human-scale properties permit students to become familiar with and feel competent in their environment. In this sense, human-scale environments engender a sense of efficacy and confidence (Hall, 1966). Human-scale physical structures permit a sense of environmental mastery and control and encourage interactions that contribute to social cohesion and feelings of security and safety. Human-scale environments are not overcrowded, blend in with the natural surroundings, and accommodate small numbers of people in structures usually no more than three stories above the ground (Hall, 1966).

The benefits of human-scale properties are well known. For example, smaller, low-rise dormitories seem to be more cheerful, friendly, relaxing, and spacious than larger, high-rise dormitories. A greater sense of community and increased incidents of helping behavior are exhibited by residents of low-rise units when compared with counterparts in high-rise units. In addition, cohesion and social interaction characteristic of small living units seem to mediate tensions and stress common to academic communities (Bickman and others, 1973; Moos, 1979).

Small Spaces, Human Places. The principle of human scale is clearly in evidence at all the residential campuses (except Iowa State) as few buildings are more than two or three stories high. Stanford University houses 85 percent of its undergraduate students in more than 70 campus houses and dorms. None of these facilities accommodates more than 280 students; most have fewer than 60 residents and some have as few as 30 residents.

Although many of the Iowa State residence halls are multiple-story structures, each floor — called a house — of the residence halls is considered a living unit unto itself. Over time, many traditions have been established that effectively reduce the size of these residence halls and nurture a sense of community for students in each of the houses. The ISU house concept and Stanford residences, which will be described in more detail in Chapter Eight, are intentional efforts to compensate for the physical expansiveness of the campuses and to create human-scale residences.

Complementarity Between Mission and Physical Plant. At some Involving Colleges, complementarity between the mission and philosophy of the institution and the physical plant is striking. Messages about what is important and expected are not merely slogans printed in a catalogue but are also reflected in campus physical structures. For example, the Xavier University campus, with its limestone main building replete with arches, spires, and religious statues, is a lasting monument to its Catholic heritage.

The Quaker values at the core of the Earlham College ethos are also reflected in the architectural style and arrangement of the physical plant. There is a functional simplicity about the place; just enough is provided in terms of facilities to advance the teaching and learning process. Here, as with most of the other Involving Colleges, no building is more than three stories tall. Earlham also maintains a college farm nearby, another manifestation of the utopian life-style consistent with the Earlham mission and philosophy described in Chapter Three.

Mount Holyoke students enjoy an extraordinary collegiate landscape: turreted ivy-covered brick buildings and sleek contemporary structures surrounded by towering trees and campus greens. A sense of purposeful unity pervades the grounds and the buildings. The campus has been shaped by an "assiduous attention to appearance which seems very English" (Werth, 1988, p. 36). The founder, Mary Lyon, considered the campus "plain, though very neat" (Horowitz, 1984, p. 17). Carefully located to preserve the natural space and to frame other spaces and buildings, physical structures are distributed across the 800 acres of land. Buildings blend into the contours of the land and do not compete with or dominate one another. The meticulous care given to the physical grounds is consistent with the care extended to students, faculty members, and visitors.

Idyllic yet homelike, Mount Holyoke is a place where students can think and study undisturbed. Waterfalls, ponds, and bridges create a peaceful setting. Nooks, crannies, and details of the architecture correspond, if not by intention then by coincidence, to the ideals of the women who founded and built the college. There is a harmony among the buildings, the natural physical setting, and the institution's mission which creates an impression of spiritual power. One can always find consolation in the beauty of the campus no matter how difficult things may be. The beauty and serenity of the lakes and woods offer places for contemplation and thought. The campus environment creates a tone of thoughtfulness, scholarship, and high achievement. The physical setting draws one in, compels one to explore one's own ideas as well as the ideas of others (Manning, 1989).

At Grinnell College, the union is called the Forum, a facility that hosts meeting rooms, a snack bar, student life offices, student government offices, and so forth. Located near the center of campus, the Forum attracts a large number of students. A cup of coffee is only 16 cents, a price that encourages students and faculty members to use the facility between classes. The name of the building indicates what is expected to take place there. "Open Forums" are presented frequently, an opportunity for students to state and debate their position on matters of importance to the Grinnell community and beyond, such as women's safety and cultural and ethnic issues. Thus, the Forum is a physical manifestation of one of the guiding tenets of the institution's mission: involvement in current social and political issues.

The Miami campus is "what a college should look like"; "it is a Hollywood view of a college campus." Considerable effort is put forth by the building and grounds staff to maintain Miami's pleasant, well-kept image. Georgian architecture is used consistently throughout the campus, with the exception of Western College and the art museum. The campus is laid out in a geometrically proportioned grid. The "Miami way to do things" is to be conventional, deferent to authority, mindful of bureaucracy, authority, and tradition, and well prepared. For example, dining tables in residence halls and in the campus union are covered with tablecloths. The food, in generous supply and attractively presented, is of high quality. The walls in some of the dining rooms are covered with wallpaper and attractive furniture is common in residence halls, the union, and elsewhere on the campus.

Some consider the consistent Georgian architectural style to be a bit stifling; most, however, view the uniform style as an asset. The consistency and coherence of architecture makes Miami University exceptional in a national system of higher education characterized by a hodgepodge of building styles and materials. Miami's reverence for history and tradition is demonstrated by the establishment of a committee on campus historic preservation charged with setting priorities for the possible preservation of thirty-nine university buildings, including all those constructed before 1930.

The entrance to the Stanford University campus is a mile-long approach lined by palm trees culminating in a memorial arch. The academic core of the physical plant of the university includes classroom buildings, athletic facilities, a medical center, and student residences. Lands contiguous to the campus include faculty-owned homes on land leased from the university; the Stanford shopping center, containing such stores as Macy's, Saks Fifth Avenue, Neiman-Marcus, Nordstrom, and many others; a very large industrial research park that is the heart of Silicon Valley; and many inviting vistas of open spaces in nearby foothills. Almost every dorm or house at Stanford has green space in view from most windows, an intentional effort on the part of planners to allow the open feel of the campus to drift into the relatively small dorm rooms, making the rooms seem larger than they actually are.

The Stanford campus attempts to make every place work for people without a stifling or overly formal sense about the architecture. There is a blending of images of a cloistered Romanesque monastery, California's missions, and English collegiate quadrangles. In this sense, both the traditional and the contemporary are honored. The Romanesque quadrangle is homogeneous in design and sense of purpose; it suggests institutional stability and is an architectural match to the climate and natural surroundings. The Quadrangle is constructed with "homey and friendly little columns, not mammoth or huge but rather of human scale;" one can actually put an arm around each of the columns. The structure is dotted with "user-friendly" components — hearts on columns, small pieces of stone in earth tones. But at the same time, there is a sense of formality in the symmetry and the arcades. Arcades connect all the academic buildings and denote connections among different elements of the physical environment and among the academic disciplines. In this sense, the arcades reflect the unity in a diverse set of activities — the academic buildings, student residences, and playing fields — that one expects to find in a high-quality educational environment.

The University of California, Davis, campus is flat and heavily wooded. Buildings are, for the most part, no more than two or three stories high and are arranged so that at no point can one see the entire physical plant. The effect is much like walking from one room to another in a large house, visually reinforcing the impression of intimacy and smallness at each point. On the occasion of his inauguration, Chancellor Theodore Hullar described the Davis campus: "We are human-scale in our human relationships and in our environments. We create and sustain living environments conducive to learning, particularly for the freshmen. . . . [M]ost importantly, we provide a supportive environment for students." The Davis campus and community are relatively isolated geographically; thus, students are forced to live the lives of students. There are few of the distractions of a large urban center; as one alumnus noted, "it is the only show in town."

Opportunities for Spontaneous Interaction. Involving Colleges encourage spontaneous interactions through the use of space in campus facilities and the natural landscape of the campus. For example, as a result of renovations, most of the academic buildings at Stanford offer places where small groups can congregate. Wider hallways and stairwells and the addition of benches allow students to stop and visit without obstructing the movement of others. Bulletin boards and small chalkboards are placed in the entry foyers of houses and dorms so that students can communicate with one another with little effort.

Community groupings at Stanford are not dense; small gathering places have been established around the campus that engender a sense of closeness, of community. Informality marks the little courtyards or "eddies," small physical spaces out of the main flow of traffic. Each is different so that people may gravitate to those in which they feel most comfortable. These outdoor spaces are places where community building can occur.

Tresidder Union and White Plaza form the center of the Stanford campus. Tresidder faces the Plaza; outside entries to various union rooms take advantage of the pleasant climate. Other architectural features of Tresidder create "crossroads" and "magnets" which draw people into the facility. Thus, the Plaza itself creates an interdependency of buildings and functions.

The Evergreen State College maintains a thirteen-acre organic farm for a small-scale program in organic agriculture; the farm also is a place to get away from the hustle and bustle of the main campus. Red Square is a plaza paved with red bricks that is the campus crossroads, a place that everyone must pass when going from on-campus residences to most classroom buildings and from the parking lots (which are screened by woods) to the Campus Activities Building (CAB) or to the library. Red Square is a place to meet friends or to catch up on things that are happening on campus or just to hang out. In the words of one TESC administrator, "Red Square is a place where students can go for human contact." Red Square is surrounded by green grass and trees with benches and other places for sitting. In front of Red Square is the bus stop for transportation to and from Olympia and environs. To enter the CAB, one must pass the ubiquitous craft tables where sellers are in their uniforms, clothing reminiscent of the 1960s, and posters abound on numerous bulletin boards, none of which is neat. The CAB also includes a health food co-op, the bookstore, and a cafeteria run by an outside caterer — a concept not popular with all students.

A physical plant can encourage interaction if it is arranged in such a way that one or more physical features bring students together or serve as a central meeting point of the campus. At Berea, Earlham, Stanford, and Grinnell, the centrally located campus post office is the area, in addition to the union, where information is exchanged via posters and notes on bulletin boards, and where students interact when they make their daily trek to mailboxes. To encourage informal interaction among students and between students and faculty members, Wichita State University has created small eating spaces in the union and in lounges in academic departments. At some institutions, community meeting places are decentralized to residences, such as the small dining rooms at Mount Holyoke and Stanford. Similarly, the University of Louisville has created small dining areas in several academic buildings so that faculty and students can spend time together before and after class.

The physical plant can also be used to reinforce educational purposes. Wichita State is justifiably proud of its outdoor sculptures which are distributed throughout the campus. No matter where students go — to class, to the recreation center, to the library, or to one of the numerous parking lots close to academic buildings — they cannot get to their destination without passing at least one sculpture. This is a deliberate attempt on the part of the university to expose students to fine art.

Psychological Properties

It is not the number of buildings or acres, but rather the accessibility of the campus that determines whether the physical plant encourages or discourages student initiative and learning.

Thus, the principle of human scale also applies to the psychological size of Involving Colleges. Even at relatively large institutions, such as Miami or Wichita State, there is a sense that the campus is compact and easy to navigate. In part, the psychological size of a place has to do with the degree to which people are friendly and helpful as well as the size and arrangement of the buildings.

The "feel" of an Involving College campus seems appropriate for its size: comfortable, personal, and manageable in larger institutions, diverse in living options but homey in the smaller residential colleges. For example, students and faculty members at Miami University talk about the "great dissonance between the size we really are and the way we behave." A staff member described the ambience to be more like a liberal arts college "because of the attention and support for freshmen, the small-town setting, the small residence halls, and the architecture." Miami *feels* like a small college despite the fact that it is a state university with almost 16,000 students.

The smaller institutions have features, some intentionally developed, to create small subcommunities that promote a sense of manageability and satisfaction. For example, at TESC, the Coordinated Study Program is the core of the curriculum and also serves as the basic affinity group for students, a practice that ensures that students are known by their peers and faculty members. Program participants include a team of two to five faculty members and 40 to 100 students. Thus, students taking the same program make up the primary group of peers with whom a student interacts, lives, and develops significant relationships. The program, which may last an entire academic year, usually requires a full-time commitment from a student. Illustrative titles from the 1989–90 list of programs include: Great Books; Pursuit of Virtue; Reconstructing the Past; and Earth, Wealth, and Democracies Promised. As one faculty member said in response to a question about how well faculty know students: "You really end up knowing more [about them] than you want to. After all, we are with them, and only them, for at least eighteen hours a week!" The Coordinated Study Program is described in more detail in Chapter Nine.

Because Earlham College has five residence halls and

twenty-three small college-owned houses for its 820 residential students, the number of students in any housing facility is relatively small, never exceeding 140. However, the basic unit of organization in student residences is the "hall," a group of 12 to 15 students including students from different classes (first-year students through seniors), supported by undergraduate "conveners" or resident counselors. Students are expected to create their own subcommunities using consensus and other Quaker principles. The balance between individual rights and community values is continually tested. Students are encouraged to arrive at their own resolutions rather than be instructed by administrative intervention. For example, one of the dorms, which is a collection of halls, recently voted to secede from the college as a result of a difference over policy. Thus, Earlham has intentionally created an environment where every student feels ownership for, and contributes to, the quality of life, and uses Quaker values and principles to learn and make decisions.

Informed Sources at Wichita State is a place to obtain information about campus programs, services, and parking, and hosts the ride board, textbook exchange, and so forth. Operated by students, Informed Sources provides another opportunity for students to become involved in the university and, by sharing information and facilitating student access to needed programs and services, reduces the psychological size of the university.

Faculty members create a positive psychological climate in routine interactions after class and through symbolic gestures. For example, on his course syllabus, Mel Kahn, a professor at Wichita State University, extends to any student who completes his class an invitation to dinner at his home. At Miami University and the University of California, Davis, the Dean Witter fund provides financial support for faculty members to take students to lunch. At TESC, potlucks are the initial cement of the programs, a time when students and faculty get to know each other, where friendships blossom, and where the bonding that is so much a part of the Evergreen program begins.

Small colleges can be oppressive if they screen out diversity, stifle divergent views, shelter students from challenges to comfortable patterns of thinking and behaving, and are cut off, even psychologically, from critical issues in the outside world. As mentioned earlier, most small Involving Colleges have programs — such as Berea College's Students for Appalachia and Mount Holyoke's volunteer program where students work with pregnant teenagers in local communities — that encourage students to leave the campus, so that students are forced to deal with some of these challenges.

Absence of Anonymity. At Involving Colleges, particularly the small residential institutions, it is difficult, perhaps impossible, for a student to be anonymous. The importance of enhancing peer groups whose values are compatible with the institution's educational purposes has long been recognized (Clark and Trow, 1966; Newcomb, 1962). Involving Colleges have attempted to instill and promote the importance of students supporting each other, becoming independent and interdependent, and developing group norms that are consistent with the institutions' educational purposes. The prolonged absence or change in disposition of a roommate or floor or house member is usually noted. This is not to say that tragedies do not occur or that debilitating personal behaviors are checked immediately by peer pressure, or that no one ever feels anonymous. However, students who live on an Involving College campus tend not to get lost.

First-year students meet with advisers at Stanford, Iowa State, and Miami. At Stanford, about 150 of the 240 frosh advisers are faculty. Academic advisors live in the residence halls with Miami freshmen. Miami students who are in academic difficulty are contacted by their adviser with offers of assistance; upper-class students in the College of Arts and Sciences are contacted by a college staff member if their grades drop below the standard established by their major field.

Involving Colleges have successfully encouraged the formation of multiple student subcultures. As Clark and Trow (1966) pointed out decades ago, institutions should encourage the emergence of more than one dominant student subculture so that students whose values differ from the mainstream can find others with whom to identify and affiliate. When two or more dominant subcultures exist, students can choose from among alternative affinity groups. Multiple role models are also available.

Appropriation of Personal Space. Most Involving Colleges provide places to which students can escape and find solitude if desired. Students cannot be, in the language of Xavier University, "on tap" all the time in public. Escape places are more than a library carrel or a single room in the residence hall. The availability of personal space — such as the foothills at Stanford, the Miller farm and back campus at Earlham, the pond at Western College at Miami University, the river at Mount Holyoke, and the organic farm and Puget Sound at TESC — allows students to relax and to think.

To the degree possible, students are also able to take ownership, albeit temporary, of their surroundings. The relationship between the ability of students to influence their physical environment through psychological ownership and their satisfaction and feelings of belonging are well documented (Moos, 1976; Schroeder, 1980, 1981). Examples include settling into one of the dining nooks in the union at Wichita State University and the cubbyholes created in the lavatories in Stanford dorms and houses where students can leave their toiletries in a space that is theirs alone. Thus, students are able to exercise temporary ownership over some aspects of the collegiate environment. Also, many Involving Colleges have policies that permit students to adapt their residence hall rooms to personal tastes through painting and construction of unusual furniture configurations (that meet safety standards, of course).

Organizational Properties

How the collegiate experience is organized seems to influence learning and personal development. In Involving Colleges, transactions among students and between students and the institution take place at the level of the institution where students can exert responsibility and influence. Involving Colleges have, for the most part, reduced the distance between a student's experience and his or her individual sense of responsibility. In other words, authority and responsibility have been dispersed to individual students. For example, at Stanford, Earlham, Grinnell, Mount Holyoke, and Iowa State, many decisions are made at the dorm or house level rather than at the campus level. Other examples include the numerous clubs related to academic major or department and the college- and university-level orientation programs at Iowa State (described in Chapter Eight), the role of the residence hall president at Mount Holyoke in adjudicating honor code violations (described in Chapter Nine), and residence-hall-based academic advising for first-year students at UC Davis.

Involving Colleges offer abundant opportunities to participate actively in campus activities. Any student who wishes to become involved can do so. These opportunities include leadership positions and other roles in departmental and social clubs and organizations; recreational sports, campus and off-campus work opportunities or internships; cooperative education arrangements; paraprofessional roles in student affairs and other areas on the campus; and representation of their peers in various levels of student government, such as their residences, Greek organizations, community assemblies, and the board of trustees.

At some institutions, opportunities for involvement are fostered by the size and nature of the place. For example, Earlham, Berea, Grinnell, and Mount Holyoke (along with most other small residential colleges) must involve students in meaningful ways to get the business of the institution accomplished. When governance structures require representation from fairly small units (residence hall floor, residences, clubs, and organizations), more opportunities are created for students to participate in meaningful ways. More than 10 percent of the Earlham College students are active in choir and other choral groups, 30 percent (340 students) participate in varsity athletics, and fully 10 percent are involved in the radio station. More than 125 students signed up for the April 1989 bus trip to Washington, D.C., to lend support to women's right to choose abortion.

According to the dean of freshmen at Mount Holyoke:

> Students here are strongly encouraged to be in-
> volved in out-of-class experiences. . . . We recog-
> nize the implicit connections between out-of-class
> experiences and in-class experiences. . . . The in-
> volved student is happy and successful. There is
> an enormous array of opportunities — don't let [them]
> pass you by. But the message also has to do with
> balance — involvement means there are going to be
> tugs.

Indeed, the report from the Mount Holyoke Task Force on the
Quality of Student Life stated:

> Large numbers of students complain of having very
> little free time, of being fixated on calendars and
> schedules, of not being able to take advantage of
> the wealth of cultural and cocurricular events at
> their disposal but beyond the range of their ener-
> gies. The elements are here for a challenging edu-
> cation and for a life outside the classroom that is
> purposeful and enjoyable.

Therefore, having a multitude of opportunities and institutional support for involvement, while essential, are not
sufficient to ensure that students will be able to avail themselves
of the opportunities.

At large institutions, participation has been successfully
stimulated through campuswide encouragement of involvement
and the intentional development of leadership roles. For example, there are approximately 5,000 leadership positions for students at Iowa State. Because the undergraduate enrollment exceeds 20,000, approximately one-quarter of all undergraduates
may hold leadership positions at any given time. Also, the tradition of involvement at ISU seems to be handed down from
one generation of students to the next. Students get this message before matriculation through participation in 4-H events

throughout the state, orientation programs, and resident assistants' descriptions of what is expected of students. Also, faculty and staff encourage students to become involved in one of the 133 departmental clubs that link the students' majors with a variety of in-class and out-of-class activities and leadership opportunities.

A large number of the more than 400 ISU student organizations extend invitations for membership, and a range of supportive programs encourage leadership development and participation. Remember the Iowa State student quoted in the introduction to Part One: "They said . . . that students who got involved in campus activities usually perform better academically." For those students who were not actively involved in high school, Iowa State established TULIP (The Undergraduate Leadership Intern Program) to help students acquire and sharpen leadership, time management, and organizational skills so that they can fully participate as leaders in out-of-class experiences.

Miami University students are expected to get involved in campus life. One undergraduate peer adviser said: "Student life here is hectic, nonstop, and challenging—if you want it that way. There's pressure to do things and it's expected that you'll get involved. That way you feel like you're making a contribution. You feel guilty if you're just getting good grades." On any given night, there is something going on that was programmed or orchestrated by students. Students coordinate many important events and organizations, such as the Wellness and Physical Fitness Programs, Laws, Hall & Associates, and Homecoming. More than 11,000 students participate in at least one intramural activity.

The institution encourages involvement by providing extensive opportunities for participation; Miami has more than 300 student organizations. In the School of Business (SOB) alone, there are eighteen student organizations (half the students at Miami major, or are planning to major, in business). One of the SOB organizations has over 600 members. The Astronomy Club attracts students and faculty from other disciplines, thereby reinforcing the institution's commitment to liberal education. Musical performance groups are open to nonmajors, another interesting example of an "undermanned environment." For example, Miami's Symphony Orchestra consists of 50 percent nonmajors and they regularly perform off campus; music majors make up less than half the membership of most choirs. It is not unusual for the first chair in several sections of the orchestra to be held by a nonmajor. In this sense, Miami was said to have a "tolerance for talent." The point is, at Involving Colleges there are more than enough opportunities for those who wish to be involved.

Moreover, Involving Colleges have ways, formal and informal, to encourage students to become involved. Prior to arriving, new students — through admissions office literature and summer mailings — are sent the message that becoming an active member of the community is important. This aspect of the anticipatory socialization process will be described in more detail in Chapter Six. Also, orientation programs emphasize that students are expected to become involved; students are encouraged to join, in some cases are even "rushed" (in the best sense of the term) to take part in activities. The message Involving Colleges send to students is clear: "We want you to be a part of this!"

Because numerous formal organizations are active at Involving Colleges, the size of the groups is relatively small and students can obtain positions of responsibility and feel as though they are integral members of the organization. This involvement breeds a sense of connectedness to other groups and organizations and belongingness in the institution. Even when the number of members is adequate to do the work of the organization, many Involving Colleges practice the ethic of membership described in Chapter Three. Intercollegiate sports are open to anyone at Grinnell College. Students sometimes play on the football team for the first time as a junior. One student asked the swim coach whether he could join the team. The team did not need another swimmer, particularly one *who could not swim,* but the coach agreed and the student eventually learned how to swim. For the record, in recent years the Grinnell swim team has been very strong, usually winning its conference meets.

Students at Involving Colleges are not always actively engaged in formal or institutionally sanctioned programs, organizations, and events. Involving Colleges have struck a balance between formal and informal opportunities for students to organize; not all out-of-class learning and personal development experiences are sanctioned by the institution. As Moffatt (1988) discovered in a study at Rutgers, students in the 1980s seem to spend less time in the formally sanctioned groups and activities typically associated with the formal extracurriculum than did students in past decades. Many institutions tend to underemphasize or overlook the importance of students creating their own learning and personal development opportunities. One example of an institution that encourages such experiences must suffice.

At The Evergreen State College, it is common for students to describe how they spend their time as "hanging." While some "hang" time is purely social and relaxing, some "hanging" events take the form of powerful learning experiences. For example, one student reported spending a weekend evening with friends sharing various ways that Passover can be celebrated. "Then we talked about what Passover meant to us." As with some other Involving Colleges (Earlham, Mount Holyoke, Stanford), mealtime is not only or primarily an opportunity to discuss social events or personal problems but also a time to examine personal assumptions and beliefs in the context of information acquired in class, from peers, and from the national media.

Summary

Involving Colleges take advantage of the qualities of their location. They intentionally or unintentionally allow their mission and philosophy to influence the arrangement, dimensions, and appointments of the physical plant. Most Involving Colleges adhere to the principle of a human-scale environment; they use both the natural surroundings and the physical structures to create social and personal spaces that reduce even further the size of what are relatively small living environments so that students do not feel anonymous. Students can appropriate personal space when desired and create new avenues for involvement. The interaction of the influence of mission, philosophy, and educational purposes, campus culture, and established policies and practices cannot be overlooked.

In the next chapter, we consider the role of policies and practices in encouraging meaningful involvement on the part of students in the life of the institution.

6

Policies and Practices

Policies and practices at Involving Colleges are influenced by mission and philosophy, culture (including the institution's history), and student characteristics. As at other colleges and universities, context-specific organizational structures have evolved over time. For example, the offices and institutional agents that monitor student admission and financial aids, advising, and internships have different titles and responsibilities across Involving Colleges. These areas are assigned to student affairs at some institutions, at others to academic affairs, and at still others, to auxiliary services. In spite of the variety in organizational arrangements, however, Involving Colleges share, to varying degrees, some policies and practices that encourage students to take advantage of opportunities for learning and personal development.

Involving Colleges know their students (and other constituents — students' parents and graduates) well. Faculty and student affairs staff know students so well that they have been able to establish workable, developmentally appropriate boundaries and expectations for students' academic and social behavior. Expectations are set fairly high, at a level that demands the very best of students. And students rise to meet these expectations. These institutions take students *seriously;* this goes beyond appointments to campus committees.

Moreover, Involving Colleges *trust* their students, but they emphasize in various ways that trust and responsibility are mutually dependent; students are expected to take responsibility for their actions. How the institution communicates and implements this expectation differs across institutions, although in each instance the means selected are responsive to the institution's mission(s) and, equally important, the capacity of students to be autonomous, self-directed, and responsible.

Six clusters of policies and practices more or less characterize these fourteen colleges and universities: (1) recruitment and socialization practices that clearly and consistently articulate the institution's educational purpose, values, and expectations; (2) formal and informal induction activities that welcome students and teach them how to act; (3) policies that give students responsibility for learning and maintaining community standards; (4) blurred boundaries between in-class and out-of-class learning and personal development opportunities; (5) resource allocation processes driven by educational purposes and priorities; and (6) policies that enable and support multiple subcommunities. These six clusters of policies and practices take slightly different forms at different Involving Colleges because implementation is influenced by each institution's mission, philosophy, size, and culture.

Anticipatory Socialization

A salient institutional mission coupled with consistently expressed educational purposes permits an institution to present itself clearly to outsiders (Heath, 1981; Keeton, 1971). Involving Colleges are unusually effective in articulating the institution's mission-driven expectations and values to prospective students, their families, and others.

Anticipatory socialization is the process by which newcomers become familiar with the values, attitudes, norms, knowledge, and skills needed to function acceptably in a new role or environment prior to actually entering the setting (Bragg, 1976). Involving Colleges use effective anticipatory socialization processes during the period between a prospective student's first expression of interest in attending the college or university and matriculation.

As mentioned in Chapter Three, through individual contacts and various publications directed to external audiences, an Involving College describes, in plain language, what the institution values and is trying to accomplish. Prospective students are told what they need to know to become responsible citizens of the campus community. For some of these institutions, parents who are graduates and older siblings who have attended the institution help create expectations for, and thus shape, the behavior of students.

What could be a routine campus tour of buildings and grounds is an introduction to an Involving College's culture. Tour guides — almost all of whom are undergraduate students — have stories to tell about student life, faculty members, historical events, and traditions that make the campus quickly become a place of people, not merely bricks, mortar, and green space. Tour guides and institutional agents use institution-specific language, the "terms of endearment" described in Chapter Four, to communicate aspects of the institution's history and culture and share insights into why and how the institution is the way it is. Thus, through reading literature from the institution, visiting the campus, and talking with current and former students, prospective students get a clear picture of whether they can expect to find "people there like me."

For example, because of its land-grant heritage, traditions, and mission, some prospective students first hear about Iowa State from staff in the local county extension office. University-sponsored county extension programs throughout the state reach more than 500,000 Iowans annually. This system also communicates to rural communities the involvement and service values of the institution and shapes and influences the attitudes and expectations of potential students in very positive ways. A large number of current ISU students first visited the campus to take part in summer programs related to agriculture or leadership development prior to their senior year of high school. The relationship between word-of-mouth recommendations and college choice is well known (Hossler, 1984), and ISU admissions staff encourage students to talk with others from their town who have attended Iowa State. By the time a typical undergraduate enrolls at Iowa State, he or she is likely to be familiar with the institution and its expectations for student behavior and performance.

Students new to Stanford University receive fifteen mailings during the summer prior to their matriculation. Letters come from a Resident Fellow (a faculty member living in the dorm or house), a resident assistant, the president, the provost, the dean for undergraduate studies, the dean of student affairs, and others. The messages contained in those letters are coordinated by members of the Frosh Information Project (the term "freshman" is not used formally at Stanford although students continue to use the term) who are drawn from various campus offices and whose work is considered important for a successful transition to university life. One of the mailings contains a publication that is a pithy, light-hearted description written by sophomores of the cycles, extremes, and challenges of collegiate life. In the margins for more than two-thirds of the book are quotations from students, many of which poke fun in some subtle and not-so-subtle ways at the Stanford experience. Most important, repeated throughout the document are themes such as responsibility, trust, making one's own decisions, and acting as a responsible adult. These themes make up the core of Stanford's attitude toward the undergraduate experience.

Stanford does not send tuition bills or grades to parents. Stanford staff and faculty emphasize to students (and their parents) long before they matriculate that they are expected to be responsible for their own behavior. Decisions about where to live, whether and how to use alcohol, what classes to take, and with whom to share grades are made by students, not the university. Of course, Stanford students are bright, motivated, and — in most cases — self-starters; thus, they are well on their way to becoming autonomous, self-directed, responsible adults before they arrive on the campus. Earlham, Grinnell, and Mount Holyoke students are similar to those at Stanford in this regard.

Earlham college admissions materials offer insightful, accurate descriptions of various aspects of campus life. The Office of Admissions sends, along with the acknowledgment of the student's acceptance of admission, an academic and residential planner. This is an opportunity for a student to communicate his or her preferred learning styles, academic interests, and the type of person with whom she or he would prefer to live. The registrar receives the advising information and the housing office receives the information about roommates. The Student Development Office does two additional mailings during the summer; Resident Counselors (RCs) also write to new students. The letter from the RC describes what the student can expect with regard to life in a residence hall and reinforces some of the Quaker principles and values described in the Earlham publications. International and transfer students get an additional letter.

The use of alumnae in national recruitment seems to be important for giving an impressive picture of Mount Holyoke and its values, opportunities, and outcomes. In the words of one senior, "I met alumnae who were in charge of their lives, and that was something I knew I wanted"—they seemed "special," so "I thought there must be something special" about Mount Holyoke. In addition, prospective and new students receive a large amount of written materials about Mount Holyoke. The recruitment and orientation publications were viewed by students as accurate and welcoming. Mentioned as particularly useful was the "Big Sis-Little Sis" handbook prepared by juniors for incoming first-year students: it "helped me to visualize where I was going."

Students come to Mount Holyoke expecting a small-college atmosphere, a rigorous academic experience, and extensive and varied out-of-class opportunities. If anything, their expectations for involvement in and out of class seem to have been exceeded, in terms of what they are able to achieve—self-confidence, social and political awareness, and a sense of themselves as women; we heard from many students that "I've accomplished things I never expected to"—and in terms of the value they come to place on being part of a women's college. Almost every senior we talked with told us, "I didn't come to Mount Holyoke because it's a women's college, but I *stayed* because it's a women's college."

Thus, the period during recruitment and following admission is viewed by Involving Colleges as an opportunity for anticipatory socialization, and is used not only to describe the institution in an attractive manner but, more importantly, to articulate clearly and consistently the values of the institution. Students learn the expectations by which they will be measured as successful and responsible members of the campus community.

Welcoming Newcomers

As several students reported in the introduction to Part One, going to college can be a frightening experience. Both seventeen-year-old and thirty-seven-year-old students must prove to themselves and others that they are competent, can perform satisfactorily in the academic program, and can be accepted by their peers. Consistent with the ethic of membership described in Chapter Three, Involving Colleges expect newcomers, once matriculated, to act as full members of the community. A combination of formal and informal induction activities prepares students for being successful and meeting their own learning and personal development goals. Through these activities, which are different at each college or university, the bonding process of student to institution and student to student begins and an Involving College says to its newcomers: "We were expecting you!"

Formal Induction Activities. Involving Colleges direct resources to assist students in acclimating to college life and attaining academic and social success. The importance of orientation to a smooth transition is well documented (Dannells and Kuh, 1977; Upcraft, Gardner, and Associates, 1989). Orientation programs — either summer or fall or both — are used to communicate standards and expectations for academic and social behavior. The national colleges, such as Earlham, Grinnell, Stanford, and Mount Holyoke, do not offer summer orientation programs because most of their students live too far away to make summer programs feasible. Thus, a fall orientation period — often a full week — is used. Most of the students who attend Iowa State, Miami, Wichita State, and the University of Louisville live close enough that they can participate in summer programs.

Stanford orientation activities are scheduled over a week's time and are a blend of academic and social activities that most students remember vividly. Students are warmly welcomed by RAs and orientation volunteers wearing bright cardinal-red T-shirts. The picture book identifying frosh by dorm or house prepares RAs and orientation staff to greet students by name when they arrive. It is not unusual for a new student to be greeted by his or her first name when arriving at the dorm, and have several people swarm around, pick up his or her belongings, and move everything to the new student's room. Imagine the surprise on the part of a new student who arrives in front of his or her place of residence and is addressed by name! Some students are a bit taken aback (after all, this is a cosmopolitan group who rarely are called by their first name when encountering strangers); however, most students recognize that this is a sign that the institution is glad they are there and wants them to be members of the community.

> I remember distinctly during freshman orientation when all the freshmen went into Memorial Auditorium with Dean Fetter and President Kennedy and I remember sitting there and thinking, "Wow, I can't believe that all these people are here and I am part of the whole thing" [Stanford University senior].

Stanford frosh have an academic adviser with whom they meet during orientation. The advising relationship continues until the student chooses a major. About 150 of the 240 frosh advisers are faculty.

Frosh Field Day is one of the major social events of the Stanford orientation week. The Stanford Band, which has a reputation for zaniness, marches around the campus in the early afternoon to pick up the frosh from the various houses and dorms and leads them into an open field where Field Day takes place. Later that afternoon, the band jumps into the pool (followed by many frosh) and continues to play in the water!

At Berea College, orientation provides another opportunity for the institution to affirm its purposes and clarify the institutional mission:

> During orientation, President Stephenson talks about the Seven Great Commitments. Also, other administrators and the head residents mention them. Really, that whole week, you hear them over and over and over again. Then, when something real controversial comes up, the situation is analyzed in terms of the Seven Great Commitments. You sometimes also hear the Commitments mentioned by students and the director of student activities sometimes brings them up when we talk about certain kinds of programs [Berea College student].

Some Involving Colleges extend the formal effort to introduce students to college life beyond the few days just prior to the beginning of classes. For example, Xavier provides special programs such as SOAR, a summer program that prepares students for analytical and scientific reasoning expected in college, and University 1010, a semester-long orientation course that addresses study skills and provides information on university and community resources and services. In one of the U1010 sessions, new students view a film describing the circumstances leading up to the founding of Xavier University, including the meeting between the founder, Mother Katharine Drexel, and the pope, who encouraged her to establish the institution.

Because 90 percent or more of all first-year students at the University of California, Davis, Stanford, and Miami University live on campus, the residential life experience is used to communicate standards and expectations and to inform students about facilities, programs, resources, and opportunities to become involved. The freshman-year residential experience at Miami University and the University of California, Davis, are described in more detail in Chapter Eight.

A comprehensive orientation program at the University

of Louisville has been developed under the auspices of the Tender Loving Care initiative, described in more detail in Chapter Ten.

Informal Induction Activities. Students at Involving Colleges are expected to exercise appropriate judgment and responsibility and that expectation is communicated clearly in informal induction activities. On the first night new students arrive at Earlham College, each "hall" (groupings of twelve to fifteen students) is expected to set social and community standards by means of consensus. For most students, this is the first opportunity to learn about and to use consensus, the cornerstone of decision making in this Quaker community. The norms for halls are established by students themselves, albeit with some encouragement and guidance from residence life staff. Similarly, at Grinnell and Stanford, few rules govern life in the residence halls; students are expected to determine and monitor community standards.

At Earlham, the Humanities Program is a continuing academic and social orientation program as well as a rigorous academic experience. The Humanities Program is a core requirement for all first-year students in which they are introduced to the tenets of humanistic education, are given a crash course on the mechanics of writing, argument, and inquiry (a paper is due every Monday morning), and learn about Earlham's dual emphasis on mastery of material and cooperation in group discussions and projects. The focus at Earlham is on collaborative, interdisciplinary learning. Sunday evenings are typically hectic with everyone trying to meet the Monday morning Humanities paper deadline. According to students, this experience seems to weld each class together quickly ("misery loves company") and bind first-year students to the college community as a whole ("a rite of passage"). As the focal point of the first year, the Humanities Program is the perfect vehicle to infuse the Quaker ethos into the lives of new students.

As with Earlham's Humanities program, Grinnell College's Freshman Tutorial, the college's only required course, serves as both an academic and a social induction experience.

There are no more than twelve students in a tutorial; the faculty tutor also serves as the student's academic adviser until the student declares a major. Faculty tutors determine the content of the tutorial and students choose the tutorial in which they are interested from a list of those available. While the content of the tutorial is important, learning how to learn is also emphasized. Tutorials are designed to improve writing skills and oral presentation skills, and help students become familiar with the library and campus computing networks. Approximately $100 is available to each tutor to meet the cost of events, such as dinner or picnics, that bring students and faculty together. Thus, the tutorial encourages establishing close relationships between students and faculty as well as among students, and often serves as a bridge to interaction beyond the classroom.

Because the dorms and houses at Stanford are relatively small, bonding among residents is encouraged through traditions specific to houses or dorms. These include: Club Ujamaa; Yost Wedding; "DIK" T-shirts at Potter House; Rincadelt — a campus-wide party sponsored by Rinconada, an all-frosh dorm; the initiation week of Alpha Sig (a coeducational house) during which residents are introduced to the traditions of the house; the self-op and co-op "work weeks" prior to the opening of school where the house is cleaned and prepared for the year; and spontaneous trips to the beach taken by residents.

At Involving Colleges, student subcultures often communicate and model appropriate behavior. At a time when American higher education is experiencing a "crisis of community" (Boyer, 1990; Bresler, 1989), a topic to which we will return in Part Three, many Involving Colleges are advantaged in that institutional values and traditions are reinforced by student subcultures. Because most of these groups have been in existence for years, we cannot describe exactly how these subcultures formed. We can speculate, however, on why student subcultures are enhancing rather than countercultural (having values that conflict with the institution's purposes and values) (Martin and Siehl, 1983). Involving Colleges state clearly to prospective students what the institution expects before the students arrive on campus. One of these expectations is that students will be responsible for their own learning, a theme we take up next.

Student Responsibility

In general, Involving Colleges encourage student responsibility and freedom of choice. Students are trusted and expected to be responsible for their own learning and development, as well as for handling violations of community norms. For the most part, students are given the freedom to learn from their own decisions, experiences, and, in some cases, mistakes.

The amount of structure imposed on students at Involving Colleges varies widely according to institutional mission, philosophy, and student characteristics. For example, few external constraints are placed on students at Earlham, Grinnell, Mount Holyoke, and Stanford, whereas students at Xavier, Miami, and Iowa State are given considerably more structure. The key here is the extent to which the institution knows and understands its students and their needs and capabilities. This issue will be discussed in more detail in the section on ladders to success.

The purpose of both structure and lack of structure is to encourage development of student autonomy and appropriate student behavior. At Grinnell College, for example, students are held responsible for the success of their educational experiences. Thus, students must make intelligent choices about what to do with their time out of class.

Stanford students are expected to be responsible for their own behavior. Few rules exist and those that do are enforced by students. At the same time, university administrators, faculty members, and staff members state, in various policies and in public forums, that they trust students. Although few policies are sacrosanct, and almost anything is open to challenge, one institutional practice that cannot be challenged is the honor code.

Honor Systems. An honor code constitutes a statement of trust, student responsibility, and dedication to academic integrity. The Stanford honor code, which applies to both students and faculty, was initiated by students in the 1920s, at which time it was received with serious misgivings on the part of faculty. Yet the honor code has persisted uninterrupted and means, among other things, that at Stanford there are few proctored exams.

The honor code makes everything more laid back.
You don't have to worry that people are looking
over you and making sure you don't cheat. It is in-
sulting when people put that much faith in you and
then make sure you don't cheat. It is nice to know
that they do place confidence in you [Stanford
University student].

Stanford students exercise considerable influence over the
governance of their dorms and houses, the acculturation of new
students, the selection of courses, and the governance of student organizations. For example, the members of each house
can determine for themselves appropriate behavior standards
and how house members will respond when those standards are
violated. Students also assist the Resident Fellow (each of the
faculty members who live in thirty-seven of the houses and
dorms) or the Resident Assistant in planning and implementing educational and social programming. In some housing units,
students also do their own cooking, including purchasing the
food and planning menus.

The honor code at Mount Holyoke College encompasses
both academic and social life and is viewed by students as a positive factor in the community. In the words of one senior: "The
honor code treats all members of the community as adults and
with respect — the implicit assumption is that students are intellectually capable and responsible." Students are permitted to
take final exams anytime during final exam week; they merely
show up at the exam site and ask for the correct exam. During
the 1987–88 academic year, only five challenges to the honor
code were brought before the campus committee that deals with
such violations. Many more infractions occurred, the majority
of which were handled by residence hall presidents, students
who are selected on the basis of leadership and interpersonal
skills. Although some violations can be expected, the honor code
has worked so well for so long that it is now an unquestioned
part of the Mount Holyoke experience.

Ladders to Success. Colleges and universities attract students with varied capacities to handle ambiguity successfully

and to exercise responsible judgment in selecting courses and regulating social life. Problems occur when a great difference exists between students' ability levels and conceptual complexity, on the one hand, and institutional expectations for autonomous, responsible, and self-directed behavior, on the other. Many psychologists recommend that an individual's cognitive style and cognitive complexity be taken into account in designing educational practices (Hunt and Sullivan, 1974; Messick and Associates, 1976). Hence, many institutions must provide a range of options for students who need more or less structure to succeed than the majority of students. When the student body tends to be homogeneous in ability and cognitive complexity, the range of structured options tends to be narrow.

At some Involving Colleges, structure is provided to help students become autonomous and self-directed. Berea and Xavier, for example, have programs and procedures in place to help students succeed, particularly in their first year of college. Xavier has established a "ladder" or set of programs and activities with steps, or rungs, to help students get involved, feel supported, and become academically successful. The institution says to students that "these are the steps you must take if you are to be successful here."

Steps in the Xavier ladder, such as summer programs (see Chapter Nine), the orientation course (U1010), and tutoring, are visible and are emphasized without apology to students or anyone else. As one student said, "when you enter Xavier University, you need a crutch of study skills." Half of Xavier's students are involved in peer tutoring, either as recipients of tutoring or as tutors. Tutoring announcements are found on almost all bulletin boards. Other steps, such as strict rules and regulations and instructions for how to use student services, are described in the student handbook. The university's vice-president for academic affairs reported that, at Xavier, standards are applied "with sympathy" and "strictness and understanding." Expectations for students are consistent with the institution's mission and philosophy and the students' characteristics, and tailor-made policies and practices provide ladders to help students succeed.

One student described Berea as "a rehabilitation institution." Most Berea students are from poor backgrounds; in fact, a student whose family can contribute more than $2,100 annually to college costs is not eligible for admission to Berea. As many as two-thirds of Berea students are from families facing difficult circumstances, such as alcoholism, incest, and black lung disease. It is not surprising, therefore, that some Berea students require considerable assistance in developing study skills and the confidence necessary to succeed.

Safety Nets. Students at Involving Colleges are not immune to the manifold hazards and difficulties endemic to everyday life (Prins, 1983; National Association . . . , 1987). They get sick, have parents, spouses, children, and friends who get into trouble, and sometimes have difficulty managing the stress that often accompanies the life of a student. Involving Colleges are cognizant of these obstacles to success and have, each in its own way, developed "safety nets" to help students in trouble. These structures are more or less visible, depending on the institution's mission, philosophy, and student characteristics.

At institutions where autonomy and personal responsibility are expected from the first day, an ethic of care is represented by all-but-invisible safety nets; help is available to students who want it, but support systems are not obvious. In this way, student responsibility and autonomy are protected; assistance is not intrusive. At Stanford, the Residence Deans, a group of people who are, in effect, "trouble shooters," constitute one of the institution's "invisible safety nets." A major responsibility of the residence deans is to coordinate institutional resources (faculty, medical and counseling resources, parents, and others) in response to students who are in trouble academically, socially, emotionally, or physically. Resident Assistants, however, are not responsible for discipline or "police" functions.

Informal networks of faculty, staff, and students have developed over time and work together in times of crisis to assist students in need. A number of Involving Colleges have not created policies and procedures to control or mold student behavior but rather have attempted to remove obstacles to students' pursuit of their academic and personal goals. The director of the Counseling Center at TESC trains peer counselors to listen for problems during program group discussions as well as in other groups and residences. Because the curriculum is all-consuming, and students are affectively involved in their learning, student problems tend to surface in such discussions. When help is needed, peers are prepared to assist by offering help or referring students to the appropriate institutional agency. Miami and UC Davis have similar peer-assistance programs.

Wichita State University, like many urban institutions, attracts a substantial proportion of at-risk students, many of whom are first-generation college students whose parents know little about the collegiate experience. For several years, the institution has offered a credit-bearing course for parents which, among other things, introduces them to the support services available to their children and the kinds of advice and counsel parents can provide to their son or daughter. Financial aid is available to cover up to half the tuition of the parents' course.

Special advising and orientation programs and administrative structures such as University College have also been established at WSU to guide students and, in some instances, to "hold" them in place until they are capable of navigating the collegiate experience on their own. To assist new students — many of whom have been away from studies for several years or more — in meeting the university's academic standards, WSU developed the transition semester. After students receive grade reports at the end of their first semester, if their grade point average is below 2.0, they may request that all grades be changed to credit/no credit. All grades of A, B, and C are translated to credit, and lower grades are entered as no credit. In the following semester, the student may not enroll for more than twelve hours and must earn a grade point average of at least 2.0.

Many senior Wichita State faculty members consider themselves part of a network of helpers, an invisible safety net, and refer students with problems to student affairs staff. They seem to be aware of students in trouble and know what to do when problems arise. Counseling Center staff, another important thread in the safety net, conduct programs "all over campus," are very responsive to faculty referrals, and are perceived by faculty as a place to refer students who need help.

> At one time I got behind in my housing payments
> and didn't know what to do. I was close to being
> kicked out. . . . I went to talk to the Dean and ex-
> plained my situation and told him that my mother
> was sending me money but she was having a little
> problem. He just said, "Don't worry about it. We
> will take care of it. We know that you are an honest
> person." He told the landlord to hold off for a while
> until my mother could get me the money. I don't
> think you can go to too many other predominantly
> white campuses and find that sense of support
> [Wichita State University student].

At the University of California, Davis, the House is a
student-run drop-in center where students can get help in dealing with problems. The First Resort, also student-run, provides
referrals for students who need more assistance than can be typically provided by a paraprofessional. The former is affiliated
with the Counseling Center and the latter with the academic
advising program.

No matter what degree of structure is present, a clear,
consistent, and unwavering message is sent to students: we trust
you; we expect you to perform up to the (high) standards of
the campus community; if you get into trouble, someone is available to help you help yourself. The absence of rules at many
Involving Colleges does not indicate lack of care or concern but
rather is evidence that the institution is willing to encourage students to take risks to become responsible for their own learning. Institutions with strict rules and behavioral regulations, such
as Berea and Xavier, recognize that the types of students that
they attract may not be able to succeed without such guidance.
When rules do exist, they are periodically evaluated to make
certain they are responsive and appropriate to changing times
and student characteristics.

Blurring Between In-Class and Out-of-Class Learning

Intentionally or not, Involving Colleges blur distinctions
between in-class and out-of-class learning experiences. They

have taken seriously John Dewey's (1916) admonition that the whole student comes to school. Any event or activity in which a student engages can provide insight into the institution's driving values and assumptions, how the institution conducts business, and where and how students learn.

The pervasive ethic at Berea College is clear: one must work for everything. Berea is one of five colleges that have labor programs; the others are Blackburn, College of the Ozarks, Alice Lloyd College, and Warren Wilson College. The Labor Program provides a sense of self-worth and accomplishment — very important for students who come to college with low self-esteem. Students also gain an appreciation for how different aspects of their life work together and can be complementary; they learn how to balance activities and to cooperate.

> I had nothing when I came here and was able to work my way up to being a head resident, which is a prominent position on this campus. I supervise and evaluate each resident assistant, no easy job. Also I learned how to plan, coordinate, and evaluate social functions. Just seeing my achievements has been a real high point for me [Berea College student].

Because Berea College could not exist without student workers, students derive a sense of contributing to the college. The Labor Program is described in more detail in Chapter Nine.

Berea also offers a series of convocations which bring in outside speakers and allow faculty, staff, and students to focus on broad social, cultural, and artistic themes and issues. Students must attend a minimum of ten convocations each semester, a requirement that encourages students to use out-of-class time to meet the institution's educational purposes and further students' learning and personal development. The convocation series is an intentional effort to blur the lines between in-class and out-of-class learning and underscores the relationship between how students spend their time out of class and desirable outcomes of college.

Through the Earlham College Office of Co-curricular Studies students are encouraged to integrate in-class and out-of-class learning experiences. A Service Learning Program challenges them to get involved as volunteers for various civic projects in the local community. Other illustrations of the blurred boundaries between in-class and out-of-class learning include the Earlham College Humanities Program and the Freshman Tutorial at Grinnell, which were described earlier.

At Miami University, the honors program is an intentional effort on the part of the institution to increase the "intellectual vibrancy" of the campus:

> The honors program was created to provide a vehicle for students to do things to enrich the intellectual life of the community. The students put out a newsletter, plan off-campus service projects in urban areas in the midwest, and have created a black-white relations committee. The symposium committee plans special seminars and programs. . . . If students feel a sense of intellectual efficacy outside of class, this sense of community will enhance their performance in class [Miami University honors program director, Richard Nault].

Perhaps the best example of the integration of in-class and out-of-class learning is The Program at The Evergreen State College. During our first visit to TESC, we inquired about the relationship between in-class and out-of-class learning. Both faculty members and students were puzzled at this distinction. As noted in Chapter Three, TESC was founded as and remains an alternative school where standardization and academic routines were rejected in favor of collaboration and student responsibility for their own education. The following statement from the TESC Viewbook challenges the usual rhetoric and provides an evocative illustration of how an academic community can be a holistic, interconnected experience for students: "Social life at Evergreen begins in the academic community." More will be said about the seamlessness between academic routines and out-of-class learning at TESC in Chapter Nine.

Serendipitous blurring occurs when an institution's educational purposes are met through an out-of-class experience without an expressed intention on the part of an institutional agent to structure a student's out-of-class time for that purpose. Examples include the student who visits the library to complete a class assignment and discovers a book of poetry or a piece of literature, or the student who becomes involved in research with a faculty member that is not related to a class assignment.

> Today over a noon brown bag lunch I'm presenting my paper on the effect of vitamin A on regenerating sound mimeograms to my lab group — two other undergrads and two grad students. I'm working on a manuscript for publication. I talked with some experts in the field at a meeting at Urbana-Champaign. They think I've got a good chance at getting it published [Miami University student].

> My sophomore year I coordinated Black Liberation Month . . . I was just scared to death . . . I didn't know how to use resources on campus, I didn't know how to sit in front of a group of people and say, 'Okay, we are going to do this' and delegate authority. But I learned a lot quickly — you have to. How to do budgets, write proposals, get funding, put out publicity, where to go on campus for resources and information, how to use a computer, everything. I got to know a lot of people on campus. And Black Liberation Month came off pretty well. I was glad about that [Stanford University student].

In some institutions, what was serendipitous blurring has become intentional. At Miami University, Laws, Hall & Associates is a student-run advertising firm that contracts with a major company each term to produce an advertising campaign. Open to students from any academic field, this program is described in more detail in Chapter Eight.

Involving colleges also use internships, cooperative education programs, and leadership opportunities to bridge in-class

and out-of-class experiences. No matter how the blurring occurs, however, what is important is that students, faculty, and
staff recognize that student learning and development are seamless processes.

Resource Allocation

All colleges and universities have infinite appetites. The
amount of resources available to Involving Colleges varies. Size
of endowment can be misleading in this regard. For example,
Berea has a very large endowment for a college of its size. However, because students do not pay tuition, endowment income
must cover a considerable amount of annual expenditures.

Discussions about the amounts and availability of resources are beside the point when considering use of resources
at Involving Colleges. More important is how resources are used
and the process by which these difficult choices are made. Because there is never enough money to honor all requests, students, administrators, and faculty members must make conscious, deliberate, often difficult decisions about what is valued
and necessary. At Involving Colleges, groups charged with the
authority for allocating resources rarely use the rationale or excuse, "we simply don't have the money." A more typical response
is, "we cannot honor your request because of the following reasons."

Involving Colleges allocate resources according to expressed priorities consistent with the institution's educational
purposes. These institutions "put their money where their *mind*
is." Equally important, students participate in resource allocation decisions, particularly for funds generated through student
fees and revenues. Involving Colleges adhere to five principles
in allocating resources: (1) substantial resources are focused on
incoming students; (2) students control and are responsible for
the allocation of a substantial amount of resources; (3) students
have relatively easy access to funds; (4) specific groups are targeted for resources; and (5) resources are committed to support
out-of-class learning.

New Students a Priority. In general, Involving Colleges are committed to directing resources to new students. The assumption underlying this commitment is that, by devoting resources to new students, the college will enable them to be productive, academically successful, and socially confident, and help them remove obstacles to attaining their learning and personal development goals. Examples of directing resources to new students at Involving Colleges are numerous and include: Xavier University's SOAR program and University 1010 mentioned earlier; the freshman residence hall and advising program at Miami University, described in Chapter Eight; the Tender Loving Care initiatives at the University of Louisville and the University College at Wichita State University, described in more detail in Chapter Ten.

Student Control of Resources. By permitting students to control a substantial amount of resources, the institutions act on the assumption that students are responsible. At Wichita State University, for example, the Student Fee Board holds hearings in the spring and fall and makes recommendations to the Student Senate about funding levels for a variety of activities. The list of such activities is extensive and includes programming in the Campus Activity Center (the union), intercollegiate athletics, the health service, the Heskett Center (the campus recreation facility), club sports, the campus pre-school, and the Women's Resource Center. In 1989 proposals totaling $3.5 million were reviewed and approved by this board. The student senate has the option to modify proposals before they are considered for action. Presumably, the university president can amend what is approved, but that is unlikely. At Wichita State, students control how their fees are spent.

The Coffee House at the University of California, Davis, is operated by students and has a high volume of sales; the profits are controlled by students. At Iowa State University, the residence hall student government prepares and allocates its annual budget without the involvement of administrators. The Iowa State Director of Residence Life could not remember any instance during his twenty-year tenure in which he overruled a student government decision. Thus, students at Involving Colleges are able to plan, set priorities, and be held accountable by their peers in the development and expenditure of resources.

Because resources are finite, not all existing programs can be continued if new initiatives are added. Thus, hard decisions must be made not only about which new programs warrant support but also as to whether currently funded programs should be continued. Many of these decisions involve discussions and debates and can be teachable moments as students are forced to choose among attractive, worthwhile options, an exercise that approximates life after college. The resource allocation process itself furthers students' attainment of educational goals.

Ease of Access to Funds. At Involving Colleges, students who wish to create a new organization or outlet for their interests are encouraged and supported. Thus, two or more students with common interests and concerns can form an organization to pursue their mutual interests as long as these interests are compatible with the institution's educational purposes. Unallocated or discretionary funds are intentionally held back so that pockets of money are relatively easy to obtain from a student affairs or other campus office to support new organizations and activities created in response to emerging opportunities.

For the most part, Involving Colleges have been able successfully to blunt the rising tide of bureaucracy and the hardening of organizational arteries common to many campuses. The process by which students and student groups obtain these funds is not bound by overly bureaucratic procedures. At Wichita State, the Student Senate can approve requests from student groups for funds on a weekly basis. Thus, if special needs arise outside the typical semester review process, worthy projects can be supported. At Grinnell College, where $115,000 is available for student activities, organizations can form quickly and within a few weeks receive funding from student government. This process was designed deliberately to facilitate student access to funds and to respond to emerging needs on the campus. Earlham has a similar process to establish and fund new organizations.

Sensitivity to Special Needs. In any institution, certain groups of students have special needs and Involving Colleges make special provisions to meet these needs. At the University of North Carolina, Charlotte, for example, commuting students must drive considerable distances to campus. While they compose the majority of UNCC students, commuters are not as well represented in out-of-class activities as the university would like. UNCC encourages commuting students to participate in out-of-class experiences through a newsletter sent to students on a periodic basis. The newsletter publicizes campus-based activities and resources with the obvious intent to encourage students to take advantage of these resources.

Many students at the University of Louisville are first-generation college students and come from disadvantaged educational backgrounds. The university has implemented a faculty mentor program in which students meet with a faculty member to obtain assistance in academic planning, study skills, course selection, and preparation for examinations. A total of 776 students were matched with faculty members in 1987–88. Fourteen faculty members are active in the program and they receive $1,000 a semester for their contributions. Also, fourteen peer advising leaders (PALS) work with the faculty mentor program. PALS are selected from among students who have been academically successful and have had a faculty mentor. They receive an hourly stipend of $3.45 and work about six hours per week.

Resources Directed to Out-of-Class Experiences. Involving Colleges make funds available to support student participation in out-of-class learning and personal development experiences. For example, the Miami community has embraced and supported public service. Student Recognition Day is in its fourth year; students are nominated for recognition in one of three categories: student employee on campus, service to the Oxford community, or service to the Miami University community. Ten students in each of the three categories get presidential citations; the others receive a Parent's Council Certificate. Thus, virtually everyone nominated receives a certificate. The university has allocated about $7,000 for dessert and certificates to recognize 800 participants. The nominators are invited to join their student winners at the ceremony.

The Government of the Student Body at Iowa State University disburses about $750,000 annually. The amounts that student governments have to support student activities vary, of course. The point is that while there are never enough resources to fund all activities, the amounts provided to students by Involving Colleges are adequate to support a wide range of activities that complement the educational purposes of the institution.

The five principles described above interact with one another during the resource allocation process. Critical issues are how the money is spent, the rationale for allocating funds, who participates in the allocation process, and an active bias that enables students to organize interesting, educationally purposeful out-of-class experiences. In this way, Involving Colleges direct resources toward activities that complement the institution's educational purposes.

Enabling Multiple Subcommunities

Involving Colleges purposefully promote the establishment of multiple subcommunities. As discussed in Chapter Three, multiple subcommunities are groups of persons with like interests and, very often, similar racial, ethnic, and cultural backgrounds. However, multiple subcommunities need not be based on racial or ethnic heritage. Academic interests, life-style preferences, and political interests are examples of other reasons for the establishment of distinctive living-learning groups.

At Miami University, Western College hosts an alternative community that occupies a corner of the larger Miami University campus. Western College is actually the School for Interdisciplinary Studies. Originally founded as a liberal arts college for women, Western was absorbed by Miami University in 1974. The Western architecture is different from the Georgian architecture used throughout the rest of the Miami campus, and many Western students are different in aspirations and attitudes from the "mainstream" Miami student. Although only

300 students are part of the Western College program, Western College has often been the locus of political and social ferment at Miami. Western College students are very tolerant of differences and are liberal and independent in their thinking; in a sense, they conform to nonconformity and relish challenging the status quo. To some degree, Western College students' behavior and attitudes are shaped by classroom and out-of-class activities, such as serious discussions over meals or residence hall colloquia where they are strongly encouraged to exhibit high levels of critical thinking. Few Western College students are affiliated with Greek-letter organizations; many are involved in political and social justice movements. For example, the Democratic Socialists of America group at Miami is located at Western College.

Another subcommunity nurtured at Miami is the aforementioned Honors Program, which is also seen as an incubator for social change on the campus. The honors program has approximately 900 participants, most of whom have ACT composite scores of 29 to 30 and graduated in the top 5 percent of their high school class. The honors program was a deliberate attempt to link academic and cocurricular activities and to enhance the degree of intellectual excitement on the campus. Participating faculty members are released from teaching a course and are encouraged to take intellectual risks (in what is a conventional academic environment) in designing learning experiences for their students. The honors program also has a strong service orientation to both the external community and the Miami community. Service projects number ten to twelve annually. One example is the Habitat for Humanity Project where, during the 1988–89 academic year, students spent several weeks in Columbus, Ohio, building a house.

In one sense, Stanford is a community unto itself. About 88 percent of the undergraduates live on campus. One might argue, then, that Stanford could develop a cohesive, coherent sense of community among its undergraduates. However, Stanford has also made a commitment to multiculturalism, individuality, and egalitarianism. As noted earlier, the Stanford mission states that the university will provide instruction and opportunities for students to enhance "human and self understanding . . . in their own and other cultures; [and] in the fundamental skills and methods needed in a rapidly changing world." Because Stanford is a national college, students come from all over the country with prior significant leadership, athletic, artistic, and other accomplishments. They are from different socioeconomic classes and from different racial and ethnic backgrounds. Slightly more than a third of Stanford students are students of color (black/African American, Asian American, American Indian, Native Alaskan, and Mexican American/Chicano or Chicana). The institution's commitment to becoming a multicultural learning community keeps cultural, ethnic, and racial differences at the forefront.

As mentioned earlier, most of the Stanford living units are relatively small. Within this array of houses are many different living arrangements: co-ops, student-managed residences, apartments, academic and ethnic theme dorms, and many different traditions of life-styles and dining arrangements such as eating clubs. Except for one all-female house and ten all-male fraternities, housing is coeducational. Four of Stanford's dorms are cross-cultural residences: Casa Zapata (Chicano theme house), Muwekma Tah Ruk (American Indian theme house), Okada (Asian American theme house); and Ujamaa (African American theme house). These houses are intended not only to provide supportive communities for their specific groups but also to enable students who are not members of those groups to expand their cultural experience and be open to learning about people who are different from themselves. Daily contact with cultural differences in a living-learning setting promotes personal development as well as greater understanding of issues of race and pluralism on campus and in society.

At The Evergreen State College, 27 to 30 subcommunities of about 100 students each are created every term when new Programs begin. The Program, the basic organizational unit for learning and socializing at TESC, will be described in more detail in Chapter Nine. Other examples of subcommunities include the academic theme houses at Earlham and the Iowa State "house" system, and various residential living environments at the University of California, Davis, all of which are described in Chapter Eight.

The rationale for enabling multiple subcommunities in the context of an Involving College is sound. For students to be successful and feel valued, they must have their interests and backgrounds acknowledged, legitimated, understood, and — a longer term goal — appreciated. In addition, with the existence and recognition of multiple subcommunities, college campuses more accurately reflect the larger society. By enabling multiple subcommunities to coexist and flourish, Involving Colleges have made a strong statement about the nature of American higher education in the future and the need to acknowledge cultural pluralism. We shall return to this issue in Part Three.

Other Policies and Practices

Involving Colleges have many other context-specific policies and practices that encourage participation on the part of students in learning and personal development activities. For example, The Evergreen State College has purposefully avoided the creation of structures that might inhibit educational experiences for both students and faculty. Minimizing administration is one of the founding ideals of the college that has survived. An example of TESC's aversion to bureaucracy is Disappearing Task Forces, which are committees formed to address pressing issues (and there are committees for nearly everything) and which operate in a participatory manner. These groups typically meet on Wednesdays, the day of the week set aside for faculty governance and related business, and disband after their issue has been addressed. This demonstrates TESC's aversion to permanent structures that might outlast their usefulness and take time away from the primary business of the enterprise — teaching and learning.

Because the student body at the University of North Carolina, Charlotte, includes a large number of commuter students, the institution has gone to unusual lengths to involve students in the life of the campus:

> Because of multiple commitments, many of our students can spend only a limited amount of time on the campus. We were able to keep 12:30 P.M. to

2:00 P.M. on Tuesdays and Thursdays free. No
classes are held during that time so that student organizations can meet and students can meet with
faculty [Charles Lynch, Vice-President for Student
Affairs, University of North Carolina, Charlotte].

As with UNCC, almost all classes at the University of
Louisville and Wichita State University are taught by faculty
members. While this is due in part to smaller graduate programs
than might be found at Iowa State, Stanford, or the University
of California, Davis — and thus a smaller pool of graduate students to teach courses — the emphasis on undergraduate education has become an integral part of the institutional mission,
and having faculty as teachers is often reported by students to
be a positive characteristic of their experience. The role of faculty
members at Involving Colleges in student involvement in learning will be discussed in the next chapter.

Consistent with the traditions of The Society of Friends
(Quakers), the Earlham College community has been successful in discouraging many status differences. One manifestation,
and an important shaping influence, is the president's preference, as with Donald Kennedy at Stanford, to be addressed by
his first name. An alphabetical picture directory of all Earlham
faculty and staff is provided to each student; at first glance, the
directory does not appear unusual until one realizes that all
names are alphabetized without regard to title, position, or role.
This diminution of status differences is, in addition to being an
egalitarian aspiration, absolutely critical to ensuring the viability
of decision making by consensus. For consensus to work, all
members of the community must be free to speak and to have
their opinions taken seriously and valued by others in the community.

Other important policy issues concern questions of who
is admitted to the institution, how they are supported, and how
faculty are used and their availability to students. For example, Stanford and Grinnell have need-blind admissions policies;
that is, admission decisons are made without regard to students'
financial resources and the institution is committed to meeting

students' financial needs. The Berea admission policy and the Labor Program have a leveling effect as they ensure that all students have two things in common: they are from modest to low income backgrounds, and all have jobs. The symbolic message of these Berea policies is that "we must all tend the commons" and contribute to the welfare of the institution. In these ways, the policies and practices of Involving Colleges attempt to establish a level playing field or game board on which students can play. Although this analogy is not perfect, the point is that Involving Colleges do what they can to ensure that all have an opportunity to succeed and can succeed if they put forth effort.

Summary

For the most part, Involving Colleges are sensitive to the importance of anticipatory socialization of students and the role of formal and informal induction activities in the acculturation of newcomers. They provide students as much responsibility as they can handle — and sometimes more — with the assistance of appropriate ladders and safety nets. Involving Colleges recognize that the number and nature of rules must be consistent with the mission, educational purposes, and student characteristics. Some establish relatively few rules and regulations in order to encourage student responsibility and freedom of choice. These institutions also recognize that learning and personal development are products of both in-class and out-of-class experiences and they avoid policies that rigidly segment these learning opportunities. Resources are allocated according to publicly expressed priorities consistent with the institution's educational purposes and philosophy. Multiple subcommunities are enabled, acknowledged, and valued within the larger campus community.

Policies and practices that are effective in one institutional setting may be inappropriate in another. Differences in history, mission, educational purposes, traditions, and other factors contribute to the idiosyncratic nature of what works. Through many vehicles — brochures or viewbooks produced by the admissions office, videocassettes of the campus, tours of the campus or contacts with graduates, contacts with former students — Involving

Colleges clearly express their educational purposes and values and leave little doubt about the institution's mission and values. In fact, policies and practices at Involving Colleges are effective *because* they are mission-driven and are constantly evaluated to assess their contributions to educational purposes. As we shall see in the next chapter, institutional agents are always searching for better ways to respond to changing times and circumstances in a manner consistent with the institution's philosophy and purposes. Thus, the key to evaluating policies and practices is knowing how the institution works and toward what ends. We will return to this point in Chapter Fourteen.

The role of institutional agents and students in encouraging learning and personal development is the focus of the following chapter.

7

Administrators,
Faculty, and Students

The descriptions of Heartland College and Metro University in the introduction to Part Two illustrate that people constitute the core of an Involving College. Indeed, in the final analysis, people are at the heart of any enterprise. Institutional mission and philosophy, campus environments, culture, policies, and practices represent the aspirations, values, commitments, and visions of a group of people. This chapter describes the role of institutional agents and students in encouraging student learning. Five categories of institutional agents are considered: president, academic administrators, student affairs staff, faculty, and others such as trustees and librarians. Students are not typically considered agents of the institution. However, because Involving Colleges *expect* students to take responsibility for their learning and consider them full members of the community (ethic of membership), their contributions to an Involving College are also examined. In each section, the major themes related to each group are identified. Examples are provided to illustrate these themes in various institutional contexts.

The President

Although they once were teachers, scholars, and academic leaders, presidents of colleges and universities today must also be chief executive officers (Green, 1988; Kerr, 1984; Kerr and

Gade, 1986), focused as much on issues and groups external to the institution as on academic programs and personnel. The changing nature of the presidential role requires that a president devote considerable time to external constituencies such as alumni and alumnae, state legislators, governing boards, accreditation officials, and local businesses and industries. The institutions participating in this study were included because they were perceived by experts to be doing extraordinary things with regard to out-of-class experiences of students. What role, if any, do presidents play in facilitating such experiences? Does the president articulate how out-of-class experiences contribute to attainment of the institutional mission and educational purposes and, if so, in what forms and through what forums?

In Involving Colleges

1. The president provides symbolic leadership by communicating the institutional mission and priorities and a vision for the institution to different constituents, including students. The role of the out-of-class life of students is often emphasized through speeches, during orientation events, and in literature distributed to students, graduates, alumni, and others. In some instances, such as Berea, Earlham, Grinnell, and Stanford, the president models interest in and concern for students and the importance of involvement in out-of-class activities for students.
2. The president is able to articulate how institutional history and traditions underscore the importance of students' participation in out-of-class activities to learning and personal development.
3. The relationship between the president and the chief student affairs officer is characterized by trust, loyalty, support for decisions, and mutual respect and trust. This mutual respect is obvious to faculty and students.
4. Presidents may or may not encourage faculty involvement with students out of class. This has no apparent impact — positive or negative — on student participation in out-of-class activities. The president's impact occurs primarily at the institutional level in speaking about the mission and the

importance of involvement to various members of the community as well as to other constituents.

The role of the president in setting the tone for out-of-class life is mediated by institutional features such as size. For example, small-college presidents tend to be more knowledgeable about the out-of-class life of students than presidents at large universities. Also, individual features, such as the president's previous experience, length of tenure at the institution, and interests and personality, influence the values and insights a president brings to the role. For example, Donald Kennedy, the Stanford University president, was once a resident assistant in a Harvard residence. This experience may have contributed, in part, to his keen insights and sensitivity about the power of the residential experience in attaining the institution's educational purposes.

Analysis of speeches and other public statements reveal much about the importance a president attaches to student involvement in out-of-class experiences. In his 1988 State of the University Address, Paul Pearson, president of Miami University, challenged faculty and students to strive toward "vibrancy" in campus life. What does vibrancy mean at Miami?

> Quality teaching that gives shape and direction to the undergraduate experience . . . a strong sense of community between faculty and students . . . opportunities for students to pursue research and other projects with faculty. Students are truly caught up in the excitement of learning.

Pearson emphasized that vibrancy should not be confined to the classroom or laboratory:

> Faculty and students . . . realize that student learning extends beyond the classroom and into the larger community. . . . We must also look beyond the walls of the traditional classroom and explore ways to get students to work in a variety of different

environments. . . . We need to stimulate . . . link-
ages between students and external publics (e.g.,
businesses, schools, and governmental agencies)
through community service projects, internships,
and collaborative research projects; student participation in off-campus professional and career-related activities; employment programs that allow
students to serve the university and assist their peers
in academic support, career guidance, job searches,
and educational activities.

Pearson asserted the importance of out-of-class experiences
for the quality of student life. Students not only learn leadership
in those settings but also have fun, which is very important for
a balanced collegiate experience, satisfaction, and persistence.
In addition, out-of-class experiences encourage bonding to the
institution which forms the basis for alumni loyalty and support.

A highlight of Frosh Orientation Week at Stanford is
President Donald Kennedy's annual speech to the new students.
His comments during the 1988 fall orientation were powerful;
unfortunately, space limitations preclude reproducing all of
them. A few paragraphs must suffice:

In this community, we care for one another's welfare. The orientation volunteers you have seen, the
RAs, the faculty members who commit themselves
to residential life, we advisers, and our student advising associates — all represent one form of that
commitment. . . . In a different but no less important way, the emphasis on voluntary and public service evident in the work of the Public Service Center . . . is another signal of the value we attach to
helping one another.

In residential education and elsewhere, racial understanding has properly become a powerful theme. It is important for you to acknowledge
that theme, and to recognize it as an integral part
of the education you will receive here rather than
as some extracurricular sideshow. I hope you will

start this process by taking advantage of the programming provided by the ethnic orientation committees.

We have assembled an extraordinary fac-
ulty. . . . We will try to challenge you in the classroom, not just to learn but to think for yourselves
and to apply your knowledge to new situations. . . .
We will give you every incentive we can think of
to extend your intellectual commitment beyond the
classroom.

You have come to a community that has
worked hard to open itself to you, and that will try
to make you feel at home. It will grant you opportunities for friendships, for service to others, and
for joy. But most of all it will supply you with a
chance at new ideas, new possibilities, and new
challenges. Whether you take them up is a decision that the creators of circumstances cannot make
for you. But we will be watching, hoping, cheer-
ing—and waiting for the call to come.

One of the Stanford traditions is that the president is the
students' president, as well as the president of the faculty and
other staff. Kennedy is also the president of the two Stanfords
described in Chapter Three: the research university which encompasses and, in some ways, dominates the second Stanford,
the undergraduate college. Kennedy spoke passionately and ar-
ticulately about the important role of the residential experience
to the "other Stanford":

I'm a college president and a university president.
In spite of our best efforts there is still a gap between what faculty think ought to happen in the
residential education component and what does
happen. Another problem is that some members
of the Dean of Student Affairs staff don't understand
the academic enterprise well enough and faculty
don't understand the high degree of professionalism

and the quality of support given [by student affairs staff] to the out-of-class experience of students. Unlike experiments in a laboratory, we don't understand clearly what happens in residential education or how it happens. We know good things happen, but it is not under our control; that is, we can't create positive outcomes every time we take risks or present challenges. . . .

This place has a tradition of students helping students. Peer relationships and pride in taking care of our own community are cornerstones of the Stanford way. . . . How do you bring together teachers and students? Who are the best role models? Faculty are not always comfortable or competent for that matter in sitting down with an eighteen- or twenty-year-old. . . .

And students have a responsibility here too. The number of undergraduates who lay claim to the resources of faculty is relatively small. . . . [My job, and that of student affairs] is to be more active in arousing students' interests; arousal produces opportunism. That is, how can we get students' attention and have them think, ponder, and agonize about what constitutes punishable racism and protected speech? We will do a lot of teaching around that issue here in the near future.

Kennedy is not a detached (or perhaps typical) president as far as the collegiate experience is concerned. He makes twenty to twenty-five appearances in student residences each year! While recognizing the many challenges associated with integrating the research university with the collegiate experience, and while attempting to attract the best and brightest faculty (not always people who have a keen interest in lives of undergraduate students), Kennedy always keeps one eye on the quality of student life. His words symbolize the high expectations Stanford has for students and for creating the idea of a multicultural learning community, as described in Chapter Three. This can be a two-edged sword because, when misunderstandings and racial incidents occur, students feel let down and frustrated by the institution's failure to live up to these expectations. More will be said about this complicated issue in Part Three.

As mentioned in Chapter Four, the contributions of some presidents, or chancellors on campuses that are part of a multicampus system such as the University of California, take on almost heroic proportions in the shaping of appropriate ways for students to spend time out of class. As noted earlier, chancellors Mrak and Meyer had great influence in establishing a participatory tone for the UC Davis campus. The legacy of Mrak's philosophy—"students helping each other succeed"—was described by one Davis faculty member:

> Students maintain the continuity of events which are not structured by staff or faculty. Mrak's influence and his guiding theme—students helping each other—has kept the psychological size of Davis small, even though it is close to 20,000 students today. Faculty and staff still think of the place as more of a small college than a large research university.

The Evergreen State College (TESC) has had a noteworthy sequence of presidents. Each has played both a special role and a role special to his time. The first president, Charles J. McCann, continues to serve on the faculty. McCann was brought to TESC as president after the institutional philosophy had been established through dialogue between a consultant, Joseph Tussman, and many of the key figures writing about higher education at the time. This was during a very frisky time in American higher education—the 1960s. McCann was a powerful advocate of individualized education and shaped many of the college's qualities and structures that continue intact. In 1977, while reflecting on his presidency, McCann wrote:

> My ideas for Evergreen were composed of a list of negatives (no departments, no ranks, no requirements, no grades) accompanied by a vaguer list of

positives: we should have cooperative education (internship) options for students, we should be interdisciplinary, there should be as little red tape as possible among the faculty members and students and what's there to be learned, freshmen — everyone — should have the opportunities and obligations presented by seminars, evaluation should be in narrative form, library and computing services should have disproportionately large shares of the budget, students should be able to study on their own when they're capable of it.

The second president, Daniel J. Evans, came to Evergreen from his position as governor of Washington and was very instrumental in providing TESC with the political protection it needed. The college was, after all, young and without the usual loyal constituencies that older and more established schools take for granted. Evans is now a United States Senator.

The most recent president, Joseph Olander, had — by necessity — a different role. His agenda included creating and implementing a strategic plan, stabilizing and routinizing the relationships between the college and the state, implementing administrative procedures (something quite foreign, even now, to the Evergreen way of doing things), and continuing to clarify TESC's mission to state legislators and others.

Minimizing administration and the visibility of administrators were two of McCann's founding ideals that have persisted. By articulating only a few value-based organizing principles, not an a priori organizational design characterized by a complex system of policies and rules, faculty, administrators, and students were able to create institutional policies and practices needed to meet current and future exigencies. The TESC administration is more the keeper — rather than the leader of — the community. The TESC community, including students, more or less leads itself. The academic vice-president and the deans do not make their administrative roles a career; rather they are "taking time away from their faculty duties" to take their turn at administration and do their share to organize and keep the academic system running. All expect to return to the faculty after a three- to five-year administrative appointment.

According to faculty and student life staff, President Elizabeth Kennan of Mount Holyoke College has demonstrated the importance of out-of-class life and the contributions of student affairs professionals to the institutional mission by investing additional resources in student affairs. Because of Kennan's commitment to recruiting high-quality faculty with scholarly interests, many of whom may not devote a lot of time to students after class, student life staff promise to become even more important at Mount Holyoke in the future.

The Grinnell mission — focused on human rights and human dignity — is clearly articulated and actively modeled by the president, George Drake, a Grinnell alumnus and former member of the Grinnell governing board. President Drake often takes meals in the campus residence halls and asks students about their involvement outside the classroom. According to students, he is very accessible: "Any student can see him. All you have to do is try." Drake believes that his job is to know and understand students.

> I spend more time on campus than many of my counterparts at peer institutions. I'm gone a fair amount, of course — perhaps an average of one week a month. . . . I could be out there raising more money. But the college is in good shape financially, so I have a choice. . . . Most presidents don't have the opportunities I do to get to know students [Grinnell College president, George Drake].

But Drake warned that an administrator or faculty member must be authentic when interacting with students; one should not spend time with students just because others value the activity. One must genuinely enjoy spending time with students. And Drake does!

At some institutions, such as the University of California, Davis, Miami, Mount Holyoke, and Iowa State, symbolic gestures and statements on the part of the president encourage involvement; the student culture does the rest. But at other institutions that attract students less autonomous, self-assured, and self-directed, more structure is needed. For example, President Norman Francis of Xavier University believes that "students need to be brought around as they are less sure how to get involved." He feels responsible for helping faculty show students how they can make a contribution to society—through tutoring elementary and high school children, helping in special schools, working with the elderly, voter registration and leadership development, and working with black professionals in the university neighborhood and beyond. As with Kennedy at Stanford, Kennan at Mount Holyoke, and Drake at Grinnell, Francis models what Xavier is about, an institution that shows students how to be successful through commitment, hard work, and self-respect.

In some instances, presidents are appointed because the institution desires a change in mission or direction. At Berea College, however, presidents are selected to "do Berea"; that is, to keep the institution on the same course that has made it successful in the past. Out-of-class activities are described by Berea College president John Stephenson and others, such as the vice-president for labor and student life and the director of student activities, as "service," consistent with the clearly articulated, long-standing mission of the institution. In Stephenson's words, "there are enough centrifugal forces that drive people apart even at a place the size of Berea that we must do everything we can to hold them together." Out-of-class activities, particularly the Labor Program in which all students participate, are a source of self-esteem, self-sufficiency, and responsibility, and feelings of mutual dependence are fostered through these activities.

It is no surprise that learning through out-of-class experiences is considered important by presidents at predominantly residential institutions. But even at urban institutions with a high proportion of commuter students, the out-of-class experience is perceived not only as a desirable adjunct or diversion but also as an integral part of the undergraduate collegiate experience.

Chancellor E. K. Fretwell, of the University of North

Carolina, Charlotte, who retired in 1989, was a dynamic, visionary leader and is responsible for much of the development of UNCC. His desire was that campus life be so interesting and rich for adult learners and part-time and commuter students that they would never want to leave the campus.

Donald Swain is the self-described "action-oriented chief executive officer" of the University of Louisville. Swain insists that the university take seriously its designated mission as the urban institution in Kentucky. His vision for the University of Louisville is that it be the boldest, most innovative school in the state. Swain is an articulate spokesperson for the importance of out-of-class life in realizing the urban university's mission. He recognized that the more students are involved in campus life and out-of-class activities, the happier and more satisfied they will be and the greater the likelihood that students will persist to graduation. Swain also emphasized that the institution must become responsive to the needs and interests of nontraditional students. One manifestation of this is the hundreds of people who now participate in commencement events on campus. Because involvement is a major challenge at the University of Louisville, as at other urban institutions, Swain and the Board of Trustees (who are also very interested in the quality of student life) have presided over the development of several innovative programs, described in Chapter Ten.

When presidents meet with counterparts from other institutions, out-of-class experiences of students are rarely on the agenda. Yet many of the institutional leaders with whom we talked acknowledged the role that out-of-class experiences play in enabling students to become responsible members of a community and learn to deal with the conflict inherent in building and maintaining community (Palmer, 1987). Student involvement in activities that integrate students into the culture of the institution is perceived to be critical.

Chief Academic Officer

Because presidents spend much of their time involved with external constituencies, the portfolio of the provost or chief academic officer (CAO) has expanded beyond academic program development and faculty matters. The role of the chief academic officer is complicated by multiple expectations. Faculty expect the chief academic officer to champion their rights and, above all, look out for their welfare. The president and trustees expect the CAO to encourage research, curriculum development, and academic excellence. These demands, and others too numerous to mention, do not necessarily preclude the CAO's interest in the out-of-class learning of students. Where do the out-of-class experiences of undergraduate students fall on the CAO's agenda?

1. In general, the chief academic officer is detached from student life, although many are able to talk about the importance of a mutually enhancing relationship between out-of-class life and the curricular goals of the institution;
2. The degree to which out-of-class experiences are considered important by the CAO is influenced by the ability of the chief student affairs officer (CSAO) to articulate the contributions of student life to the academic mission of the institution and by the personal relationship between the CAO and the CSAO.

Some CAOs were more articulate about out-of-class experiences than others. Some were actively involved in and sensitive to the symbolic power of their role in this regard, particularly those at residential institutions. The provost at Stanford, James Rosse, acknowledged the importance of investing money in residential education and providing good "safety nets" for students:

> It is the case that many faculty simply do not acknowledge or recognize that there is a second half of a student's life which is, in some ways, more important. Many faculty have a romanticized recollection of the quality of the intellectual experience they had as undergraduates. Not all students will have the same level of intensity as far as their intellectual experience is concerned. However, it is Stan-

ford's responsibility to give all students an opportunity; the out-of-class experience — particularly
through residential education — can enhance the
possibilities that students will be challenged intellectually at various places and times throughout the
undergraduate collegiate experience.

High on the agenda of Carol Cartwright, the vice-chancellor for academic affairs at the University of California, Davis,
is increased student contact with faculty out of class. Such contact is believed to be necessary so that students can learn more
about the faculty role and life-style. According to Cartwright,
because of the shortfall of faculty expected around the turn of
the next century, "we simply must do more to introduce undergraduates to the academic life-style. Only through developing
personal relationships between faculty and students are students
likely to view a faculty role as more attractive." This goal will
be increasingly difficult to attain as the professional energies of
faculty seem to be inexorably drawn away from activities that
could result in close, personal relationships with students.

Some chief academic officers know a lot, and speak author-
itatively and passionately, about student and faculty life and
the institution's mission. According to Sister Rosemarie Kleinhaus, vice-president of academic affairs at Xavier University:

I meet with the department chairs a day before the
fall faculty institute and I try to inspire them to be
leaders, not act as administrators, hand in course
schedules, and so forth. Then I meet with the new
faculty once a month during their first year to tell
stories about this place, about why Mother Katharine founded the institution, about our policy with
respect to cheating, about advising students, about
the athletic program and how it ties into the academic program. I also talk about the history of the
university to the new students in all sixteen sections
of U1010, the required orientation course. As we
grow, I don't want to lose the spirit that makes
Xavier unique.

The attitudes of the chief academic officer were either neutral toward or supportive of the learning potential of out-of-class experiences. Because presidents were enthusiastic supporters of the importance of out-of-class experiences to the undergraduate collegiate experience, it was no surprise that the CAO would reflect at least a passing interest in and familiarity with how student life contributed to the educational goals of the institution. In no instance was a breach perceived between the role and functions of student life programs and services and the academic enterprise.

Student Affairs Staff

As institutions of higher education have become more complex organizations, and as students with more diverse backgrounds, abilities, and interests have matriculated, responding to student needs has become more challenging than ever (National Association . . . , 1987). Typically, student affairs professionals are the institutional agents expected to deal with students' out-of-class lives. What can be said about student affairs staff at Involving Colleges?

1. Student affairs staff work unusually long and odd hours, are energetic and enthusiastic, and are sensitive and committed to the institutional mission and how that mission is best accomplished in student life.
2. As faculty members spend less time with students outside of class and less time in nonacademic areas of concern, student affairs staff increasingly are expected by trustees, the president, and the students to bridge the academic program and out-of-class life.
3. Student affairs staff are the heart of the early warning system and the safety nets that assist students in academic, social, emotional, and physical difficulty — the support system that encourages students to take responsibility, take risks, and learn about themselves in relationship to those different from themselves. They also serve as the authoritative voice to the institution and other constituents about the attitudes and behavior of students.

4. Student affairs staff, in concert with a shrinking group of student-centered faculty, enable and empower students through one-to-one interactions, develop opportunities for student involvement through educational and social programs, serve as role models, and challenge students to get the most out of their college experience by examining their assumptions about people who are different and taking responsibility for their learning and behavior.

At Involving Colleges, the student affairs division, particularly the CSAO, enjoys respect across cabinet-level administrators. This mutual respect seeps down, across, and through organizational lines and units. Faculty, student life staff, and other administrators recognize and value the contributions each makes to the enterprise.

Provosts and presidents readily admit that student life staff are the campus experts on students. To many faculty members, student affairs is a black box, a set of functions about which little is understood and even less is noticed. At all these institutions, however, faculty members are proud of their student life colleagues and are quick to compliment the quality of their work. Faculty at UC Davis suggested that because of student life staff and programs, the university has been able to maintain the image and feel of an institution smaller than it actually is (21,000 students). In the words of a UC Davis faculty member, "there is a wealth of student services and the people are great, simply outstanding." We share this comment to demonstrate that, on some campuses, the relationship between the academic and student life functions is complementary, even synergistic.

In general, student affairs staff at these institutions have a deep commitment to the institution's mission and purposes. They are dedicated to maintaining distinctive, precious community values and have high expectations of students, colleagues, and themselves. At the same time, they are pragmatists; they recognize that they "must play the cards they have been dealt," in that student characteristics and the institutional culture shape their work.

In many Involving Colleges, the chief student affairs officer (CSAO) has held that position for a decade or more. In several instances in which a new CSAO was recently appointed, the philosophy of the predecessor is being carried forward with renewed enthusiasm. In a few cases, however, a change in student affairs leadership coincided with a shift in direction in student life that was supported by faculty and administrators, including the president.

Whether characterized by continuity of leadership or new directions, the student affairs units at Involving Colleges are vibrant and forward-looking. The CSAO and his or her principal assistants are sensitive to changes in institutional policies and practices necessitated by changes in the external environment and in student characteristics. Through continuous monitoring of external and internal environments, they anticipate, and prepare their staff and students for, potential problems and challenges that may demand changes in institutional policies and practices.

Student affairs staff at these institutions are generally willing to support or encourage students to question institutional policies. Because more than a quarter of the undergraduate students are new to the institution each year, each generation of students must learn for itself how to live in an increasingly multicultural community, to identify institutional values and commitments, and to understand how the community functions. Administrators rarely say in response to a student's question, "we've always done it this way." In this way, routine decision-making opportunities can be transformed into "teachable moments."

As with staff at most of the other institutions in this study, residence life staff at Earlham teach students how to take care of themselves and one another, rather than intervening when students encounter problems. By trusting students and taking them seriously, student life staff, other administrators, and faculty encourage students to cope with the consequences of community and conflict. The goal is to use creative dissonance for educational benefit. Thus, student affairs staff serve as catalysts for raising relevant questions and protecting freedom to doubt and question in the out-of-class domain.

At some of these institutions, such as Mount Holyoke, Grinnell, Stanford, and UC Davis, institutional agents have given up the pretense of being in control of student behavior and instead require students to become responsible for their own behavior. This is not to say that student life staff do not attempt to intentionally influence students' behavior. They focus their energies on teaching and explaining the rationale behind policies, practices, appropriate behavior, and so forth. At other institutions, such as Berea and Xavier, student life staff play a very active role in requiring that students make choices consistent with the institution's mission and the expectations of parents.

The human development philosophy adopted by the University of California, Davis, is reflected in a commitment to the professional development of faculty and staff. The entire spectrum of institutional support services, including student services and human relations, is assigned to student affairs—a staff of 720, including police, residence life and housing administrators, intercollegiate athletics, and institutional research. Members of this division study UC Davis students, informing themselves, faculty members, and others about shifting student characteristics and attitudes.

At some Involving Colleges, some student affairs staff reported that presentations at professional meetings focusing on professionalism and the breach between academic and student affairs were, for them, irrelevant. Unlike many of their colleagues elsewhere, they are seen as full members of the educational team of the college. Indeed, they do many of the same things as their professional counterparts elsewhere. But at TESC, for example, student affairs staff do not sense that their contributions are distant from or irrelevant to the academic mission of the institution, or are in any way devalued. They administer the usual variety of student services (admissions, counseling, medical, organizational advising, orientation, and so forth) but these are seen as integral to attaining the educational purposes of the college. The key factor may be that TESC faculty members, as described elsewhere, tend to see, and work with, the whole student, not just the student learning some specific discipline during some set class hours each day—a living, breathing, learning human being all of the time.

Faculty

The importance of meaningful interaction between undergraduate students and faculty members to positive student
outcomes was summarized in Chapter One. Student expectations for amount and kind of interaction with faculty vary. For
example, many students — particularly first-year traditional-age
students who lack confidence — feel uncomfortable around faculty
out of class. Other students, usually upper-class students, yearn
for more personal relationships with faculty members. The folk-
lore of higher education and higher education research (Astin,
1977; Gaff and Gaff, 1981; Wilson and others, 1975) suggest
that student-faculty contact outside of class is desirable. What
does this contact look like on campuses known to provide high-
quality out-of-class experiences for students?

1. Student-faculty interaction out of class, when it occurs,
   usually is directly or indirectly related to academic activities and concerns:
   - Contact is "after class," through extending points made
     during class discussions; these contacts sometimes evolve
     into conversations about personal or career concerns
     and issues. These interactions are encouraged by the
     availability of benches or clusters of chairs in the hall-
     ways of classroom buildings or accessible departmen-
     tal lounges.
   - During these contacts class material is often related to
     "real world" matters such as learning through coopera-
     tive education and internships.
   - Other contacts usually focus on major-related activities
     or clubs, undergraduate research, or undergraduate
     teaching assistantships.
   - A few contacts are initiated by faculty and sometimes
     evolve into a mentoring/sponsoring relationship with
     undergraduate scholars who have potential to become
     faculty members.
2. Two faculty cultures exist as far as out-of-class life is concerned: student-centered faculty members — those who are

committed to involvement with undergraduates (they tend
to be older, tenured faculty), and those who are not involved
with undergraduates out of class (often younger faculty or
cosmopolitan scholars).

3. Changes in the faculty reward system and institutional ex-
    pectations are altering faculty roles and priorities. How-
    ever, institutions with salient missions as teaching colleges,
    such as Berea, Earlham, Grinnell, Evergreen, and Xavier,
    attract faculty who are willing to invest themselves in those
    students and missions.

4. Students perceive faculty to be available and involved with
    them, particularly in the academic arena. Those students
    who develop relationships with faculty out of class usually
    have taken the initiative to do so.

5. Faculty members at Involving Colleges are generally sat-
    isfied with their work and their institution. They like the
    students with whom they work and some give their time
    and talents to undergraduates in extraordinary ways.

According to Larry Vanderhoef, the executive vice-chancellor at the University of California, Davis, it may be a myth
that faculty care more about students at UC Davis than at some
other institutions. Nevertheless, faculty at UC Davis believe it,
and their students believe it also, underscoring the power of the
myth in American society (Campbell, 1988). These strong beliefs may also prompt "involving" behaviors on the part of both
students and faculty. Powerful mutual shaping occurs as institutional history and traditions influence how students, faculty, and
administrators perceive and relate to one another.

We expected to find a high level of out-of-class interaction between students and faculty at Involving Colleges, particularly the smaller, residential colleges. Although more faculty-
student interaction may occur on these campuses than many
others, contacts between faculty and students are likely to be
initiated by the students and to be related to a class assignment
or a faculty member's teaching and research interests. Thus,
faculty contributions to student life may best be seen as occur-
ring *after class,* emphasizing the temporal connection between

discussions emanating from class or laboratory. This kind of interaction, connecting with students through academic experiences such as class assignments and seminars, is based on more realistic assumptions about what can be expected of faculty and is different from the Mr. Chips analogue in which faculty members actively participate in various aspects of student life that are removed from the academic arena.

The number of student-centered faculty members whose primary commitment is to the institution and to the welfare of undergraduate students is shrinking. These are the faculty who advise student organizations, who dine on occasion with students in their residences or the union, who agree to serve on student life (and other campus) committees, who attend intercollegiate (and sometimes participate in intramural) athletic events, and who take part in social events, such as the homecoming dance, that are intended for students. These faculty members are articulate spokespersons for the importance of the role of student life staff and maintaining a campus climate conducive to teaching and learning, both in and out of class.

In many instances, when student-centered faculty members retire, or leave, they are replaced by younger faculty who have been socialized to a model of faculty behavior that emphasizes research and scholarship first, followed by good teaching. Faculty at most institutions in this study are being pushed to increase their research and grant-writing activities. Also, urban universities are employing increasing numbers of part-time faculty. This trend has been noted by administrators although the impact on the quality of student-faculty relations has not been specifically addressed.

In the words of one Miami University department chairperson: "The ante has been upped considerably in the College of Arts and Sciences for promotion and tenure." When young faculty "hang out" with students, they often get negative feedback from colleagues and department chairs. Another department chairperson said: "In my department, we tell nontenured faculty, 'You should be spending more time writing and publishing.' Others have heard the message and are cranking out publications." This tension between different types of expectations for faculty has existed for some time but has intensified in the past decade.

Junior faculty at many institutions receive fairly clear messages about how much time, if any, to spend with students. Moreover, young faculty members assume a professional risk when they spend time on teaching-related activities and with students after class. These faculty get off to a slower start on a program of scholarship and research. In the event that a faculty member is not awarded tenure or must seek an appointment at another institution for whatever reason, his or her curriculum vitae may not be competitive with that of peers who have worked at institutions where research has been encouraged and, perhaps, even supported with grants and reduced teaching loads. As a consequence, avenues to maintaining a sense of campus community and connecting faculty with students out of the classroom are increasingly limited.

There are other factors affecting faculty involvement with the out-of-class lives of students. Many junior faculty are in dual-career relationships. This situation sometimes compels faculty, particularly those at colleges in small towns, to live some distance from the campus to increase job prospects for the other person and reduce commuting time for both. A junior faculty member's discretionary time may be further reduced by child rearing. One example will suffice; with some variations, the following description fits most of the colleges and universities in this study.

Until a few years ago, new faculty members at Mount Holyoke College were encouraged to live in one of the many white frame houses bordering the campus. For some faculty, athletic and intramural playing fields and classroom buildings were literally in their backyards. In the 1960s and 1970s, new faculty frequently encountered students walking from their home to class; they dined in student residences with little disruption to their daily routine; they found it convenient to take part in campus and community social and cultural events. Today, few junior faculty live in those white houses. They live in nearby towns in closer proximity to where their spouses are employed or where child care is available or where the public schools seem to be of higher quality. The scholarly productivity and national visibility of the faculty, as with other institutions in this study, is increasing; yet they are good, even excellent teachers. The younger faculty are not unwilling to spend time with students outside of class. During our visit, we saw numerous groups of students and faculty having coffee after class, and students reported their time with faculty to be of high quality and importance. At the same time, these contacts seem to be declining in frequency and variety. For example, faculty are less likely to dine in the residence halls during the week as "dinner is family time."

Nevertheless, many faculty members at Involving Colleges take time to help a student who faces debilitating personal experiences, such as parental (or their own) divorce, illness of a child or parent, a roommate with a serious illness, or financial difficulties. In the words of a Xavier student: "Faculty care about us"; "Professors take time for us"; another student put it this way: "[Faculty] believe in you." In some cases, the institutional mission provides a touchstone for determining how faculty are expected to behave. At Berea College, for example, where Christian service is the institutional mission, faculty members are acutely aware of problems, such as relatives who have black lung disease, that threaten the success of their students.

And some faculty members do take initiative in getting to know students out of class:

> On my course syllabus, I offer to have lunch with
> every student. After students graduate, they have
> a standing invitation to dinner once a year with my
> wife and me in our home [Wichita State Univer-
> sity faculty member].

Some Involving Colleges have developed programs and policies to encourage faculty to spend time with students beyond the classroom. At Iowa State, departmental clubs are very active; they "rush" new members with the same enthusiasm as fraternities and sororities. Every departmental club has one or more faculty advisers. One person observed: "We don't have to beg for faculty advisers" at Iowa State.

At Stanford, thirty-one of the thirty-seven Resident Fellows (RFs) are faculty members. Resident Fellows reported that the RF experience has made them better teachers; they involve students in research projects and teaching assignments, and solicit student opinions about classroom teaching strategies. As RFs invite their colleagues to their home (dorm) for dinner, more faculty meet and become involved with students out of class. Students become more interested in independent study options as a result of meeting with faculty in the dorms. It is worth noting that the tenure rate for RFs is comparable to their counterparts who have not been RFs. The Resident Fellow program is described in more detail in the next chapter.

A powerful socialization experience for new faculty members at Earlham is their involvement in the Humanities Program. Each year a committee of Earlham faculty develops a new reading list and exams for the Humanities Program. Some new faculty members are appointed to this committee. As one might expect, there is a good deal of discussion and some debate within the committee and within the faculty group teaching in Humanities Program. Because of the emphasis on interdisciplinary work, new faculty learn that the department designation is of less importance than an interdisciplinary approach to discovery as well as the importance of core Earlham values, such as collaboration and applying knowledge to social problems. Equally important, the expectations for faculty with regard to research have not, according to Len Clark, the provost, changed over the past twenty-five years. As is the case at Grinnell and TESC, Earlham remains a teaching college with no pretense or interest in becoming known for research.

At Stanford, the debate about Western core readings and racism extends to houses and dorms where, through formal programs and spontaneous discussion following dinner, students are encouraged by Resident Fellows and resident assistants to debate such matters. Students and faculty members at Mount Holyoke take advantage of post-dinner conversation to discuss issues related to cultural pluralism, racism, and heterosexism. Involving Colleges are hotbeds of intellectual and social-emotional introspection!

Most students at these institutions were very grateful for

the time faculty members spend with them outside the classroom. In the words of a faculty member at Miami: "When students run into a faculty member in sweats or shopping at Kro-
ger's, it changes the student's experience at the university."
Another faculty member who exercises two large, playful dogs
on the campus said that "the animals are a vehicle to discussions about something else — politics, whatever." She added that
when she encountered students from her class at the art museum
in a nearby city, "the students came bounding up like two
labrador retrievers happy to see a familiar face." We also heard
from faculty members at urban institutions that they are just
as likely to encounter students in the shopping mall or downtown as between classes or elsewhere on campus.

What goes on out of the classroom sometimes competes
for students' time and energy with the purposes of the academic
program. Understandably, faculty members have difficulty taking students seriously when they miss exams because of a "commitment to complete the homecoming float on time." However,
student interaction with faculty out of class usually has a salutary effect on student satisfaction and feelings of belonging. For
example, when students encounter faculty after class, as when
attending a faculty member's presentation in one of the residence halls or interacting with them in their role as advisers
to a club or organization, they often come to know faculty members for the first time as real human beings, not detached scholars
on a pedestal. Students sometimes become interested in faculty
members' areas of expertise and may be motivated to take one
or more classes from them. After exposure in the class, students
may wish to find out more about how faculty live, how they
spend their free time, and what they enjoy the most about their
work — all the things Carol Cartwright, the UC Davis vice-
chancellor for academic affairs, believes are keys to attracting
able undergraduates to the professoriate. As with other important lessons in life, there is no substitute for human contact in
acquiring these insights.

Is it possible that we have overstated the point that some
years ago more faculty spent more time with more students outside the classroom or laboratory? We do not think so. The role

of faculty in students' out-of-class lives is changing. In some instances, the slack is being taken up by student life staff and by students themselves.

Other Institutional Agents

People who play other roles in colleges and universities also make important contributions to creating an environment conducive to student learning and personal development. The work of librarians, trustees, secretaries, custodial staff, and buildings and grounds workers is important to making students feel welcome and comfortable and challenging students to do their best.

The influence of Earlham College librarian Evan Farber is noteworthy. Farber views librarians as "custodians of the tradition" and the library as a key vehicle to discovery of intellectual treasures. He supplies important information to the dozen or so Earlham faculty members researching the history of Quakerism. Farber is also viewed as a persuasive, tireless advocate for the liberal arts. He takes an active interest in virtually every major field and regularly scans a wide variety of journals. Occasionally, he photocopies pages from tables of contents for faculty who may have an interest in the topics addressed in that particular journal. He pins photocopied portions of articles to a bulletin board in the library, calling students' attention to various issues in which they should be interested. Farber knits the community together by his support of faculty and students' intellectual interests.

The library was also described as important to out-of-class life at Miami. A number of powerful out-of-class learning activities at Miami University, such as Laws, Hall, and Associates and the Honors Program described in the next chapter could not exist without financial and personnel support from the library. Evidence of the importance of the library to out-of-class learning of Miami students includes: high traffic through turnstiles, rising reference, circulation, and other statistical information on use, a relatively healthy budget for books and materials designated primarily for undergraduate students, student use of information technologies, a service-oriented staff responsive to student needs in designing search strategies, encouragement and responsiveness to student requests for new materials, and employment of a large number of student workers, which provides opportunities for out-of-class learning.

The degree to which trustees are actively involved in the daily life of an institution varies widely, influenced by history, the previous role of the trustees at an institution, and the knowledge and interest of individual trustees. Trustees at Involving Colleges have a good sense of the institutional expectations for their role. They are familiar with and committed to the mission and philosophy of the institution and appreciate the history and traditions that communicate core values. They have a sense of discovery that is compatible with the institution's educational purposes and they willingly share responsibility for what happens, or does not happen, on campus.

To underscore the importance of campus life to learning, University of Louisville trustees established an annual award for the faculty member who makes a noteworthy contribution to the quality of campus life. As University of Louisville trustee George Fischer said: "It's obviously more difficult here [at an urban university] to create a sense of college community. But we are committed to doing whatever it takes to increase the quality of campus life. . . . We want students to succeed." The quality of campus life award carries a one-time cash stipend of $5,000. Funds to underwrite the award come from an annual assessment of $300 per trustee; thus, the trustees' award does not compete with academic programs for support.

Other staff members perform important roles in communicating institutional ethics of care and membership. Early one morning during our spring visit to Grinnell College, we stopped at the Forum snack bar for a cup of coffee. At 7:15 A.M. the place was empty except for the snack bar attendant. A few minutes later, a student came in. Before she could get to the counter, the snack bar attendant greeted the student with a soft, caring tone in her voice. "Mary, hon, how are you doing this morning? Dear, you look tired. Been up all night studying again?" Their conversation continued for a few minutes. This kind of interaction was repeated several times in the next ten minutes as other students arrived; the counter attendant would greet students by name and inquire about how things were going for them. At lunch, grill orders are placed by first name. When the order is ready, the name is called. We retrieved our sandwiches. Later, when one of our team members returned to the counter for a cookie, the attendant turned and said, "Oh, George, what can I get you?" Nothing in this description represents a powerful learning or personal development experience. But it does suggest something about the power of the small gesture to engender feelings of belonging and to create a campus climate conducive to learning and personal development.

Students

College students are diverse in many ways, including educational aspirations, socioeconomic background, age, ability, and cultural and ethnic background. Characteristics of student bodies at Involving Colleges range from relatively homogeneous to diverse. At Miami, Stanford, Berea, Grinnell, Earlham, UC Davis, Iowa State, Mount Holyoke, and Xavier, the vast majority of students are traditional age (eighteen to twenty-three years old). At some colleges (Grinnell, Earlham, Stanford, Miami, Mount Holyoke, UC Davis), the majority of students are from the top 10 percent of their high school graduating class. Berea, TESC, and Xavier enroll many students who probably would not be in college were it not for the mission and philosophy of those institutions. One TESC student told us, "I want to be the first non-high school graduate to give the student commencement address." At the urban institutions, students are diverse in age, ability, cultural and ethnic heritage, and educational aspirations. At the two California institutions, Stanford University and UC Davis, where more than a third of the undergraduate students are people of color, the cultural and ethnic backgrounds of students reflect the demographics of the West Coast.

Six themes characterize students at Involving Colleges:

1. Student learning in and out of class is seamless; that is, students do not partition what they learn into experiences from the classroom, laboratory, library, residence, and other ac-

tivities. Rather these events and activities blend together in students' minds.

2. Students know how the institution works (or think they do); that is, they know how to use the college's resources to achieve their purposes.

3. In general, most students take seriously the institution's expectations that students will be responsible for their own lives and their own learning.

4. Students may or may not have close, personal relationships with faculty or staff members. Those who have such relationships usually initiated the contact.

5. Students learn as much from peers and others outside of class as they do from classes.

6. Most student subcultures promote student involvement in activities that complement the institution's educational purposes.

Seamless Learning. Most students perceive in-class and out-of-class experiences to be seamless. That is, what is learned during college is not easily partitioned into courses, friendships, organizations, library work, laboratory assignments, recreational activities, and so on.

> Some people view working with student groups as extraneous to achieving academic goals. I've found that they complement each other. What I learned outside of class is just as important as what I learned in the classroom. And what I learned in class I've applied out of the classroom. The leadership experience I've gained out of class I've used in group projects in class. . . . In the introduction to philosophy and ethics course I discovered that social values are not necessarily cut in stone — that they are a product of the times. Well, I can apply that when working with a group who rejects capitalist ideas or with a group trying to motivate themselves to bring social change to Latin America [Earlham student].

Stanford is a learning institution. What you learn is up to you. There is academic information around. That's kind of a minimum. After that, Stanford has so much to offer in research . . . and leadership positions and special interest voluntary organizations, and fund-raising opportunities and just different types of people [Stanford student].

What we learn in class is interwoven back at the dorm, at dinner, at [milk and crackers]. You learn more at dinner sometimes than in class. And being really stretched doesn't necessarily occur only in the classroom [Mount Holyoke student].

For two years I worked as a runner for a law firm and last year I was an assistant campaign manager in a state representative race. . . . A lot of the stuff I did [at the law office] was connected with the city and county government so I got to know how that system worked better. Also, as the Kentucky Supreme Court rulings came down I was able to read them. A lot of my work related to political science theory [University of Louisville student].

I've learned balance here — personal, social, professional, intellectual. It has been a painful process at times, but I am ready to strike out on my own now to mix biology, what I learned in my internship in industrial hygiene, and medicine [UC Davis student].

Classrooms, laboratories, student living environments, and work settings all can provide powerful learning opportunities. For example, at Stanford, the Structured Liberal Education Program is offered in student houses and dorms as are components of the Honors Program at Miami University. Senior faculty members teach in both programs. The Honors Program at the University of Alabama, Birmingham, is housed in an old church on campus and provides a campus "home" for its largely commuter student population. It is common at Involving Colleges for student living groups to organize discussions about current issues or to arrange trips to plays, to the beach, to cultural or other public events. Students are responsible for planning and coordinating many of these events. The dorm or living group is their "family unit," a place where they will be supported and with which they will establish a strong identification and attachment.

Knowing How the Institution Works. Students at Involving Colleges take initiative — in learning, in getting to know faculty, and in taking advantage of the institution's resources. At Stanford, for example, an entrepreneurial ethos pervades which, among other things, encourages students to initiate new ventures. To obtain funds to support these ventures, students often must contact several of the many sources of funding around the campus. Stanford students design and sell computer software and clothes and operate food services such as a cookie delivery service. While many of these businesses come and go from year to year, others remain. In 1982 three students proposed a frozen yogurt and pizza operation for the Tresidder Union. In the first year, the business grossed one-quarter of a million dollars and now generates over half a million dollars a year.

Miami is a meritocratic institution where acknowledging status and following lines of authority are very important for success. Miami's rich sense of history and tradition reinforces the importance of the hierarchical or "corporate" (Miami) way of doing things. A high value is placed on doing things "the right way," on using appropriate channels, on maintaining schedules and routines, and on behaving and "looking right." For example, when students meet with the board of trustees, they are well versed in appropriate behavior for such a group, prefacing their comments with "Mr. Chairman, members of the board . . ." and the like. Civility, or politeness, on the part of students is the norm. We were told that "student organizations at Miami are run with professionalism"; meetings begin and end on time, an agenda is developed in advance of the meeting, and officers have prepared reports. One faculty member, who for several years had dined in a residence hall about three times a week, received a memo from students asking to "schedule" lunch, an indication of the planning and structure students perceive is necessary and important to be successful. When electronic bulletin boards were introduced on campus, a group of students established by-laws for the use of electronic bulletin boards. This is the Miami way: anticipate problems, coordinate responses, carefully design the implementation of the response.

In general, students figure out, or readily adapt to, how Involving Colleges work. However, at many, but not all institutions, some students are "outsiders," such as, in some cases, students of color or students with alternative life-style orientations. Some members of historically underrepresented groups become frustrated when the means by which business is conducted is not consistent with or is foreign to their cultural upbringing. Black students at Stanford, for example, interpreted the need to forage for financial support for activities from a variety of sources as begging, and felt uncomfortable doing it. We will return to this point in Part Three.

Student Responsibility. Students take responsibility for themselves, for each other, and for their living and learning environments. In some instances, the institution's history and traditions carry strong messages urging students to take care of each other. As noted in Chapter Three, the founding president at Miami University, Robert Hamilton Bishop, underscored the need for students to teach each other after the enrollment increased more than tenfold in one year even though the number of faculty stayed the same. Thus, from the earliest days, students were expected to make important contributions to the life of the Miami community and to learn from one another.

The second chancellor of UC Davis, Emil Mrak, established the participatory tone that characterizes the campus with his philosophy of "helping students to help themselves." Former chancellor James Meyer encouraged broad consultation and involvement on the part of students in campus committees, thereby continuing this legacy of cooperation which is communicated from one generation of students and faculty to the next. A current manifestation of the legacy of cooperation can be found in a brochure, "Students Helping Students," distributed by the office of the vice-chancellor for student affairs, which identifies fifteen different advising units that use peer advisers. An informal variant of students helping students exists at Wichita State:

> I feel I have to push the younger students. They
> need a person with more experience to take charge —
> to push them about their schoolwork. They call me
> up for a pep talk [Wichita State adult learner].

Through the various patterns of anticipatory socialization and formal and informal induction experiences described in Chapter Six, students at Involving Colleges receive fairly clear and consistent messages about behaviors that will be successful and tolerated by the student cultures and by institutional agents. As discussed in the preceding chapter, Involving Colleges have varied expectations for student responsibility. Some institutions, such as Miami University and Xavier University, provide specific guidelines to which students must adhere, particularly in the freshman year. Other institutions, such as Grinnell College and Stanford University, allow students to determine what behaviors are acceptable and appropriate. At Mount Holyoke, much of the administration of life in the residences is left up to students.

> At first it bothered me [that the institution did not
> monitor alcohol or marijuana use]. But I realized
> that this is really important — that you are allowed
> to be responsible for your own behavior, unless it
> gets to be a serious problem. Then if a friend goes
> to an RA, an RA might start talking to that person,
> or suggest that they go to a mental health center.
> But it is always up to the individual to choose what
> is best for themselves [Grinnell student].

> Stanford says take care of yourself as far as your
> dorm life goes. You set your own responsibilities,

> your own priorities. We aren't going to tell you
> when to study and how to study. We aren't going
> to tell you how to run your social life. We will offer
> you the opportunities for help if you need them.
> But we will not force anything on you [Stanford
> student].

In other instances, the academic program forces students to take charge of their own learning. For example, the Program at TESC is structured to require a large measure of student responsibility. The Program encourages students to learn how to work together as a group by emphasizing expectations for equal participation by students and faculty. Because the seminars are small, students typically take responsibility for certain aspects of the reading and discussion; the small number of people in each seminar promotes interaction which affords students opportunities to articulate ideas with precision, to discuss difficult concepts, and to work independently as well as interdependently with others. The Program is also the context for many student-initiated activities. Students regularly organize and conduct book seminars where they read and discuss a book related to their Program (Chapter Nine).

Student Relationships with Faculty and Staff. In general, students perceive that faculty members and others are approachable and responsive. For many students, developing a meaningful relationship with a faculty member was a significant aspect of their collegiate experience. Although not all students at Involving Colleges develop a close, personal relationship with a faculty member, for those who take the initiative and connect with a faculty member, the results are deeply satisfying.

> Working with a very well-known philosopher has
> definitely been an intellectual highlight. I got to
> work six months, spending one-on-one time with
> this man who has devoted his life to the philosophi-
> cal issues I had been thinking about. To have him
> listen to my ideas and to take them seriously or criti-
> cize them, it just helped my confidence . . . here this

great philosopher was respecting what I had to say
[Stanford student].

I found professors and staff that were truly interested in me and challenged me both in and out of
the classroom. The French department has a small
number of majors so the faculty are very involved
with the students. Almost all of my professors have
been that way, although I have often had to take
the initiative [Wichita State student].

My contact with professors here has been really
wonderful. Faculty are interested in helping students learn and think. Professors have had confidence and interest in me. One gave me a "C" and
said, "Rewrite it—you can do better." I initiated
contact—from my desire to learn—stopped by their
offices, stopped to talk after class [Mount Holyoke
student].

On a few occasions, a faculty member will select a student to
sponsor.

I got involved with research in the pharmacy department. . . . I did it as an elective because the
professor kept asking me, so I said, "What the heck,
I will do it." We applied for a big grant . . . and
we got it. The research was pharmaceutical chemistry. . . . It was pretty intense but very interesting.
At times I was frustrated. . . . He would say, "What
will you do now?" I would say, "I don't know, you
are the one with the Ph.D." And he would say, "I
know, but tell me what you think." So that made
me think, and stretch [Xavier student].

For others, connecting with an adult—whether an upper-
class student or a coach, or a student life staff member—created
an important, personally meaningful relationship.

Some student leaders were role models [for me]. One of the most important was [someone in student affairs] — professional, articulate, intelligent, and also a woman [Wichita State student].

I and my friends had the "Gang of Five" to turn to, five black staff members who befriended me and my friends and helped me in my leadership role with the African American Student Union. In fact, one of these people was instrumental in making events like Black Family Day successful [UC Davis student].

I have a very good friend, an older friend who is almost like a father. I appreciate him and I love him and I'm not afraid to tell someone that I love them and I do regularly with this guy. He has had such an impact on me. He is not a professor. He was one of my labor supervisors. . . . We attend church together, we play on the same softball team. Bob was the first one I told about my hardships about being here at school. And he listened and I guess from then on, I've always gone to him with problems [Berea student].

As their undergraduate experiences draw to a close, some students express disappointment that they did not become closer to a faculty member.

At the present time I'm helping a graduate student with her research, a special lab project. I would love to do something with a professor, but my time is running out. I was just looking at the bulletin boards to find something and this research jumped out at me because of the content of the research, so I was looking more for that than to work with the professor. I wish I had done something with a professor, though [Stanford student].

Learning from Peers. Students often mentioned relationships with other students as the high points of their undergraduate experience. They recognized that their peers influence them
in ways that faculty members or classes never could. Students
used words such as intelligent, enthusiastic, diverse, and supportive to describe their peers.

> I'm a lot more conscious of so many things be-
> cause *everything* was really challenged. I had to de-
> fend the way I thought to other students so that
> made me think. Like three-hour debates about
> abortion [Mount Holyoke student].

> There is something that happens when you are
> around really bright people for four years — things
> change. You start looking at things in a new way.
> You start always looking at something, always
> thinking. It's hard to describe but I just know when
> I leave Stanford I can tell I am not at Stanford
> [Stanford Student].

> The opportunities to be with other students who en-
> joy talking about intellectual issues, who enjoy in-
> tellectual challenges, have meant so much. I'm not
> certain I have taken full advantage of all the interest-
> ing people I've been around but I can look back and
> appreciate what I do when I do it [Earlham student].

> I feel that I have accomplished something, if not
> the 4.0, it has been a sense of I have developed as
> a person. I can communicate well with all types of
> people. I have learned a lot. Not only in class, but
> out of class. I have learned about people, how they
> think, how they perceive the world, how they per-
> ceive you. I think if you can do that, then that is
> a great achievement [Miami University student].

Involving Student Subcultures. Many of the colleges and
universities in this study were advantaged by having two or more

student subcultures that promoted activities that were, for the most part, congruent with the institution's philosophy and educational purposes. Western College and the Student Foundation at Miami, the Greek organizations and residence hall "houses" at Iowa State, and the traditional-age student and adult student organizations at Wichita State and the University of Louisville all have heroes and heroines with which different types of students on those campuses can identify. Equally important, these groups and others perpetuate rituals and traditions that provide a sense of continuity and belonging for members of the community. For example, VEISHEA — the spring festival at Iowa State (described in the next chapter) — is essentially a weeklong, student-run celebration of the academic roots of the institution. Picnic Day at UC Davis, a campus celebration with beginnings similar to VEISHEA, is also described in the next chapter.

> Right now I am finalizing plans for the Afro-American graduation ceremony. It is so important to show excellence in my culture and share that with the other graduates. We need to show our endurance and what can happen when we work and build together [UC Davis student].

These examples provide a sharp contrast to the student cultures that have recently been described as anti-intellectual and in competition with the educational missions of the institution.

None of the small residential institutions selected for participation in this study had social fraternities and sororities. In recent years, such groups have been criticized because they allegedly perpetuate certain anti-intellectual behaviors and traditions that are incongruent with the institution's educational purposes. While some respondents at the larger Involving Colleges expressed reservations about the presence of Greek organizations on their campus, at most of these institutions the values of fraternities and sororities were not altogether different from the values of the dominant student subcultures. That is, the Greek system was but one student subculture, the values of which were generally consonant with the institution's educational purposes. At some institutions, such as Miami, Greeks were the dominant subculture. At other institutions with Greek systems, such as Stanford, institutional agents have been actively discouraging the growth of these organizations.

Summary

In some respects, the people who work at and attend an Involving College are similar to those in other types of successful organizations. Those in leadership roles, whether administrators, faculty members, staff, students, or others, reflect characteristics of leaders of high-performing systems (Vaill, 1984). That is, they spend a great deal of time attending to important matters; they also have a reverence for the past and take a long-term view of the future. They have a deep commitment to the institution and their work and are focused on the important elements of the teaching and learning process in and out of the classroom and on the institution's purposes.

The whole of the contributions of institutional agents is greater than the sum of their individual parts. The mix of agents and their complementarity, commitment, and communication are critical for creating an Involving College. The match between priorities of faculty and student affairs staff, the blending of academic and student life objectives, and the compatibility of both with the institutional mission help to create a climate conducive to high-quality out-of-class experiences for students. At Earlham, this complementarity takes the form of, but is more than, decision making through consensus, educative hassles, and student responsibility. At Wichita State, the focus on the individual student, the pastoral approach of the CSAO that permeates the philosophy of the student affairs staff, and the networks of support contribute to, but cannot fully explain, why the institution exceeds expectations for getting students involved. "The whole" of the Mount Holyoke experience is more than the sum of traditions, rituals, and governance structures that challenge, support, and empower women.

The commitment on the part of institutional leaders influences how faculty, staff, and students view the degree to which out-of-class experiences are important to attaining the institutional mission. Institutional leaders articulate the appropriate role of faculty and others in the out-of-class life of students. Moreover, students receive signals from faculty about the importance of taking advantage of opportunities in the environment and using institutional resources appropriately. Thus, institutional agents work in combination with the other factors and conditions to contribute to student learning and personal development.

8

Large Institutions

Since 1950 the number of colleges and universities has increased by 60 percent while enrollment has increased by 400 percent (The Study Group . . . , 1984). As institutions become larger, they can also become more impersonal and bureaucratic. The size of classes becomes larger, high-rise residence halls are built, and campuses sprawl. But the quality of student life does not have to suffer because institutions grow to meet enrollment demands.

At the beginning of Part Two, we described a hypothetical institution, Heartland College, where students have rich out-of-class learning and personal development opportunities. It would be difficult for any institution to duplicate Heartland College, but the residential institutions in this study have many of the properties that characterized Heartland. In this chapter, programs and practices are described that exemplify student learning experiences compatible with the missions and philosophies of the four large residential Involving Colleges, those with more than 5,000 students: Iowa State University, Stanford University, Miami University, and the University of California, Davis.

Residential programs and practices at these four institutions are emphasized because substantial numbers of first-year students live in campus residences. These universities commit resources to their residential systems so that students can make the transition from home and family to the college community with relative ease and begin the bonding process between entering students and their university. In other words, these universities have developed ways to make students feel at home and not be overwhelmed by the institution's size.

Iowa State University

In this section, we describe three programs at Iowa State to illustrate several distinctive characteristics of Involving Colleges: the residence hall house system, a successful attempt to create human-scale living environments for students in large housing facilities; VEISHEA, a spring festival that is a celebrative event consistent with the educational purposes of the institution; and new student orientation, which illustrates how a large university can welcome and prepare students for college life.

The House System. Among the first things that one sees when approaching a residence hall at Iowa State are the banners with names of the houses in bold, colorful letters on the side of the building. The banners indicate that the large residence hall is, in fact, made up of smaller units. The following description of the ISU residence hall house system illustrates one way in which a large university has achieved a human scale, making the institution feel manageable by creating a sense of floor community and militating against feelings of anonymity. In addition, the houses offer ISU students, especially freshmen and sophomores, opportunities to develop leadership and educational programming skills through involvement in house government.

The house system at Iowa State was started in 1948 by then-director of housing, Dr. J. C. Schilletter. Previous attempts to make ISU's only residence hall, Friley Hall (which housed 637 men), feel smaller had been unsuccessful. Residence hall staff thought that if students identified more closely with where they lived, they would be more active participants in activities and events in the living unit. The attention of housing officials turned to fraternities, which became the model for the residence hall house system. Iowa State's house system now consists of residence hall floors or similar size units, usually housing fifty to sixty students. Houses at ISU look like typical residence hall floors. The lounge on the floor where our staff member stayed was called "the Den," a name that makes it feel different — more homey, more private — than a lounge. Inside the Den were a television set, newspapers and magazines, and tables for study purposes, board games, or card games. In this particular complex, chalkboards are located in the bathrooms so that students and staff can write notes to each other, thus making the common bathroom a great source of communication for residents of a house.

As previously mentioned, each house has a name that is displayed on the outside of the building as well as in the house. Indeed, what makes the continued presence of names on the outside of the residences especially powerful is that the university has regulations that restrict the use of banners. Pressure has been brought from time to time to remove the names from the exterior of the buildings, but to this day they remain.

All but one of the houses are named for deceased Iowa State University faculty, staff, or regents. The exception is a house named for a former residence hall officer who was killed in a car accident the year after he served in office. Most houses have a crest; some crests are those of the families after whom the houses are named whereas others were designed by student residents. The crest often appears on house T-shirts, sweatshirts, and stationery.

How strongly do students identify with their houses? We were told stories about how roommates who did not get along well, when given the option of splitting up and moving to different houses or staying together in their house, chose to stay. We also learned that it was common for graduates to visit their houses when they returned for Homecoming.

The study atmosphere in the houses warrants comment. Classes for the spring term began the day our team member moved in. He was warned that it might be hard to sleep or concentrate late at night, but this was not the case. The floor or house was quiet, and while there was plenty of interaction among the residents (going in and out of rooms to visit or study together), the atmosphere appeared to be ideal for serious study. Later on, he learned that the house had been designated for strong academic students, but a quick check of other houses in the building indicated that the study atmosphere elsewhere in the residence hall was every bit as good.

VEISHEA. VEISHEA is a four-day spring festival described as the largest student-organized celebration in the country. Thus, VEISHEA provides a vivid example of the emphasis placed on student involvement at Iowa State. Also evident in VEISHEA events and activities is the land-grant mission of the university, and the many ways in which academic and nonacademic aspects of ISU student life are blended into a seamless experience.

VEISHEA was begun in 1922 when an Iowa State College student, Wallace McKee, suggested that the agriculture, engineering, and home economics colleges combine their spring "open houses" for high school students into one celebration that would also provide athletic events, honor ceremonies, and musical entertainment for the campus community; in 1925 a parade was added to the festivities. "VEISHEA" was coined using the first letter of the name of each college in existence at the time: V for veterinary medicine, E for engineering, IS for industrial science, HE for home economics, and A for agriculture. Today, the VEISHEA festival attracts participants (estimated at over 250,000 people) from the entire Iowa State University community and Ames, as well as throughout Iowa and the Midwest.

VEISHEA still includes academic open houses for prospective students. The colleges, including their clubs and divisions, have displays and demonstrations; high school students also attend presentations on career and academic planning and have campus tours. The displays are judged by a panel of students and faculty on the basis of creativity and quality of information, and prizes are awarded to the winners. An example of a recent open house display is that of the Hotel, Restaurant, and Institution Management Club of the College of Family and Consumer Sciences (formerly Home Economics). This group's exhibit illustrated the modernization of food preparation equipment and the history of the cherry pie, an item the club has sold at every VEISHEA since 1922.

The tradition of the VEISHEA parade has continued, although parades in the late 1980s have had nearly 100 entries, including floats built by residence hall and Greek houses, marching bands from area high schools and colleges, and "novelty units" such as the Barker Brigade, residents of Barker House (a floor in Lyon Hall) who perform tricks and drills with lawn chairs. Expenses incurred in replacing lawn chairs that break during practice are covered in part by funding obtained from the residence hall government.

Athletic competition remains an important part of VEISHEA. Sporting events include: Design College Boat Races; 5k and 10k runs; bicycle and canoe races; tennis, golf, and softball tournaments; water balloon launch; mud and sand volleyball tournaments; "slam-n-jam" dunk contest (including a 9-foot hoop for players under 6'3"); 5-on-5 basketball; and a 1400-mat Twister game coordinated by the Inter-Residence Hall Association. The Iowa State University football team also plays an exhibition game during VEISHEA weekend.

VEISHEA entertainment has expanded from the "Scandals of 1922" to include a carnival, rib cook-off, Battle of the Bands contest, beach party, "art in the park" fair, and an outdoor party. One of the highlights of the weekend is "Stars Over VEISHEA," a student musical production; the stage version of "Grease" was featured in 1989.

VEISHEA is coordinated by a central committee of students, including a business manager, computer coordinator, and chairs for publicity, open houses, parade, events, entertainment, and Stars Over VEISHEA. Two former committee chairs serve as "student advisers" to the central committee, along with two faculty advisers. Students also form the committees that implement the various VEISHEA events and activities. A 1989 press release stated that "VEISHEA started as a seed in the mind of a single student and has blossomed" into an event run by over 200 students, and enjoyed by thousands more.

VEISHEA reflects the university's land-grant mission and its emphasis on service to the state through college exhibits, programs for high school students, and involvement of state and local organizations and people in all of its activities. In addition, just as involvement is part of the life-style in the small towns that make up much of the state of Iowa, it is also an important aspect of student life at Iowa State. VEISHEA is part of the tradition of involvement that has been handed down from one student generation to another. It is now, as in the beginning, the responsibility of students to make VEISHEA happen. Students who have been involved in VEISHEA planning and leadership serve as advisers for those who are new to their tasks.

There is a continuity in that many of the activities that constituted the early VEISHEA still take place, although change is constant; something new is added every year as student interests and the social context change. For example, the 1970 VEISHEA took place two days after the Kent State killings, and so the parade consisted of a protest march.

The strength of Iowa State's residence hall and Greek organization is also evident in the high level of involvement of these groups in planning, funding, and implementing VEISHEA events. This practice, too, is evidence of the tradition of student participation in decision making and student autonomy in developing and allocating funds to support their activities. Although some students describe VEISHEA as an "all-Greek" festival, residence hall governments and houses have become an increasingly visible and influential presence, to the point where VEISHEA seems to be a celebration of, and for, the entire student body.

Orientation Programs. Orientation programs for new Iowa State students demonstrate and reinforce the complementarity and integration of in-class and out-of-class experiences. These programs also provide important socialization for students and parents in the Iowa State way of doing things and begin the process of making a large university feel comfortable and manageable.

Seventy percent of all students who are admitted to ISU attend orientation. Of that group, 95 percent enroll at ISU, and of those who enroll, 99 percent stay for two semesters. Students who have not decided on a major are placed in the orientation program of Science and Humanities, Iowa State's liberal arts college.

Orientation for new Iowa State students is two-tiered: activities and events related to the entire university, and features specific to individual colleges. The orientation committee at ISU is chaired by a faculty member and has thirty members, including faculty, administrators, and student representatives from the Government of the Student Body (GSB) and former Cyclone Aides (summer orientation paraprofessionals). Chaired by a faculty member, the group functions as a coordinating committee since much of the actual work in orientation takes place at the college and department level.

Each college provides its own orientation in conjunction with the university orientation program. College-level orientation is planned and implemented by administrators, faculty, and staff from the individual colleges and academic departments. College orientation programs begin with a welcome from the dean of the college, including a bit of history about the college, identification of famous alumni and alumnae, demographics of the student body, and information about student life, such as recreational sports and Greeks, opportunities in the residence halls, and departmental clubs. Students are told about college and departmental activities and organizations and are encouraged to participate. Orientation is used to encourage students to become involved in out-of-class activities for two reasons: student involvement is a tradition at ISU that is passed on to each generation of students, and the university is attempting to help students develop themselves in ways that potential employers find attractive.

Course placement tests are also a part of college-level orientation. After placement testing, each college hosts a meeting to provide information about the curriculum and expectations for how students can best work with their academic advisors. Expectations for involvement in departmental clubs are described. After the advising meeting, students check into the residence hall for their night's stay. A dinner buffet is provided for students and their parents, selected faculty, administrators, and the Cyclone Aides. After dinner, students talk with the Cyclone Aides in small groups. Making the academic and social transition to college, involvement in clubs and other activities, and class work are topics of discussion.

On the second day of orientation, students have a meeting at 8:15 A.M. at which the registration process is described and questions are answered about classes. Later in the morning, the students have individual meetings with advisers. Because literally thousands of students participate in summer orientation at ISU, the personal meeting each student has with an adviser underscores Iowa State's commitment to make a very large university feel small. While students meet with advisers, their parents participate in "ISU in Action," a program that describes faculty activities at Iowa State, including application of research to everyday life for Iowans. The orientation program for students and parents ends at noon on the second day.

Iowa State maintains contact with students throughout the summer. After orientation, students receive additional mailings from clubs, churches, and special-interest groups. Students also receive a confirmed schedule and a bill before they return to Ames in the fall. Most of Iowa State's colleges offer an orientation course for freshmen in the fall, mostly for the purposes of providing survival skills for college. In some colleges the course is required, while in others it is not.

Special orientation programs are designed for minority students and transfer students. Topics that address the unique needs of these students are included in the orientation programs they attend. Transfers register in the spring with the students who will be their classmates in the fall. There are also special orientation activities for adult learners and one for international students. Students who miss the summer orientation may attend orientation in the fall.

Stanford University

In this section, some distinctive elements of Stanford student residences are described. Residence life is a crucial aspect of the "other Stanford" — the undergraduate collegiate experience. Resident Fellows and Resident Assistants welcome newcomers by name — easing the transition to their new home — and continue the process of "socialization" to Stanford's expectations for student responsibility and autonomy. As has already been mentioned, Stanford dorms house from 15 to 280 students and so encourage the development of small living communities within the larger university. The dorms are also one of the places in which the institution's commitment to multiculturalism and multiple subcommunities is implemented as well as reinforced.

Two goals provide the foundation for Stanford houses and dorms: to develop inclusive communities, and to stimulate intellectual life. The 5,500 undergraduate students who live on campus have a wide variety of housing options from which to choose. Consider the food service options: self-operated food service; university-operated food service; cooperative food service; individual dining rooms; and dining commons. Among the housing program alternatives are standard dormitories, cross-cultural theme houses, cooperative houses, suites, mobile homes, apartments, and fraternities. Just over half (55 percent) of the Stanford freshmen live in all-frosh houses, while the balance live with upper-class Stanford students.

Stanford Resident Fellows include approximately thirty-seven faculty and staff who live in the houses and dorms and serve as in-house advisers, counselors, and academic program planners. These people are committed to the welfare of students and the Stanford collegiate experience. One RF pointed out: "My wife (who is also a Stanford graduate) and I decided to become Resident Fellows and live in a dorm to give back something to the university which has meant so much to us."

The Resident Fellows live rent free with their families, spouses, or significant others and take meals in the dorm. While RFs do not receive a stipend, they can save a significant amount of money on housing and food costs. This program has been so successful that the number of applications far exceeds the number of vacancies. The Resident Fellows are uniformly enthusiastic about the RF concept and recognize that their work is one of the building blocks of the Stanford collegiate experience.

What do RFs do? According to the RF position description, the RF is, above all, an educational leader. In addition, RFs play a role in community development, supervise RAs (undergraduate assistants who work in the houses and dorms), perform academic and personal counseling, promote multiculturalism, and serve as liaisons with the Office of Residential Education. Resident Fellows also teach classes in the residences, arrange for faculty visits, speakers, discussions, debates, and cultural outings. Film series are planned, guests are invited for dinner and workshops, and discussions and programs are designed to help students clarify their views on challenging issues. Fine arts programs, such as theatrical productions or musicals, also occur, as do community service projects.

In spite of the impressive array of programs offered by RFs, the job description offers one further element that is the heart of the program:

> Resident Fellows can also provide invaluable mentoring to undergraduates. Knowing the students as individuals, RFs can influence students' learning by such simple gestures as loaning a book, clipping a newspaper article of interest, bringing together students interested in the same subject, or suggesting avenues of research and faculty contact.

Stanford Resident Assistants (RAs) serve on resource teams, monitor student behavior out of the classroom, and invite students to take part in planning activities that are meaningful and challenging to previous ways of thinking and knowing. Stanford RAs do not perform a disciplinary role. RA training emphasizes the importance of embracing and appreciating differences of race, class, gender, sexual orientation, religion, and other background differences so that RAs can help students learn from living in a pluralistic community.

Miami University

In this section, two "involving" practices at Miami are described: special opportunities and programs for first-year students, which illustrate how a university targets resources to help newcomers succeed; and Laws, Hall & Associates, a student-run advertising agency, which illustrates how boundaries can be blurred across disciplines, academic routines, and out-of-class life.

Freshman-Year Experiences. One of the strengths of Miami is its commitment to providing powerful bonding and socialization experiences in the residence halls; newcomers are made to feel very welcome. According to one administrator, values are "caught more than taught" at Miami, and the residence halls, including RAs and advisers, are an important part of the process of inculcating new students in the "Miami way" of doing things. Also, the almost protective attention paid to freshmen is very much a part of the "Miami way."

All freshmen, except those who live with their parents, must live on campus. Twenty of the thirty-seven residence halls are designated as freshman halls. The ratio of professional staff to students is impressive: one full time freshman adviser (a title used synonymously with resident director) for every 200 students. In freshman halls, the Resident Assistant (RA) to student ratio is 1:20 and in upper-class halls it is 1:35. The importance of the RA to a smooth transition to life at Miami cannot be overestimated. These upper-class students teach newcomers how to negotiate the system, what is valued and what is considered to be appropriate. Resident Assistants also send letters to their corridor members during the summer.

The purpose of the freshman advising program, which is centered in the residence halls, is to facilitate the transition from home and high school to college life. Each freshman must meet with his or her adviser at least once during the first semester. This level of attention to first-year students makes them feel important and valued. Of course, not all students take full advantage of the advising program, although most students learn that they can go to their freshman adviser for virtually anything. The adviser will often make telephone calls to assist students in resolving their problems. About eighteen inches of manuals describe the role and responsibilities of the freshman adviser. Responsibilities of the freshman adviser include hall administration, RA supervision, committee work, counseling, discipline, and organization of freshman mixers, which are an important part of the first few weeks of the fall semester. The freshman advisers also have academic advising responsibilities; they receive training (two and one-half weeks) in course planning, academic programs, the registration process, procedures for dropping and adding classes, and so on.

Freshman advisers do a degree audit report and check mid-term grades and contact students who are having difficulty. Periodic meetings are held between freshman advisers and academic departments throughout the year, another factor that helps to integrate residence life and students' academic programs.

All RAs are encouraged to select a Faculty Associate for their corridor. It is not always easy to find a faculty member willing to serve in this role (eat an occasional meal in the residence hall, attend concerts or lectures with groups of students from the hall). Humanities, particularly language department, professors are usually the most willing to participate. However, serving as a Faculty Associate (or "Dorm Dad" or "Corridor Pop") does not always provide the most satisfying type of interaction between faculty and students as far as some faculty are concerned.

At the beginning of the fall semester, each hall has a banner welcoming its new student members. In many residence halls, almost every night for the first week, corridor members participate as a group in exchange activities with other corridors of men and/or women. No wonder that most freshman students feel supported and welcomed when they arrive at Miami!

There are some potential disadvantages associated with Miami's approach to the first-year experience. First-year students live in single-sex freshman halls that tend to isolate many freshmen from role models and members of the opposite sex. As a result, the halls are seen by some faculty, students, and staff as a breeding ground for immature relationships between men and women.

Laws, Hall & Associates. Laws, Hall & Associates is both a four-credit semester-long course offered by Miami University's marketing, mass communication, and art departments and a student-run advertising organization that provides students the opportunity to deal with real-world companies and their advertising problems. Laws, Hall & Associates is a program consistent in all aspects with the "Miami way" of doing things. Miami's mission is to provide a high-quality undergraduate liberal arts education that includes faculty-student involvement and professional preparation for students, as well as an emphasis on faculty scholarship. Laws, Hall is also an excellent example of the ways in which academic and nonacademic experiences can be integrated to create a valuable learning experience for students.

Established in 1971, Laws, Hall involves approximately 160 students and 6 faculty from marketing, mass communication, and art each year; student involvement is competitive and the faculty members serve as the Laws, Hall board of directors and advisers. Student participants are divided into three competing interdisciplinary "agencies," or teams, led by student account executives and charged with producing advertising campaigns to meet the promotional needs of a paying client. The campaigns include market analysis, strategies and tactics, budget and media plans, electronic media productions, and art work and layouts for print media and direct mail; the teams have access to state-of-the-art market research and computer technologies, and art and broadcasting production equipment and facilities. At the end of each semester, completed campaigns are presented to, and judged by, the client.

Previous clients of Laws, Hall & Associates include Proctor & Gamble, NCR Corporation, Marshall Field, BF Goodrich, Avon, Miami University, J. M. Smucker Company, the Stroh Brewery Company, and Ford Motor Company. Clients' fees ($15,000 in 1989–90) are used to cover campaign development and production costs, student agency expenses, and the cost of recruiting potential clients. Top-level representatives of the client meet with students to describe their needs and provide assistance throughout the semester. In many cases, the client uses ideas generated by the student teams in actual promotional campaigns.

The interdisciplinary nature of Laws, Hall & Associates makes it unique among experiential advertising programs. Students bring preparation and training in their majors to their team: marketing students develop campaign objectives and strategies and perform marketing research tasks; mass communication majors develop audio and video productions, from script to completed presentation; and art students design print and visual materials. Each of the three academic departments provides one-third of a faculty load per semester, as well as facilities and equipment, to the program, and faculty members in graphic design, mass communication, and marketing consult with the teams. The three faculty members directly involved with Laws, Hall & Associates provide guidance and advice, and evaluate the teams' progress throughout the campaign.

The interdisciplinary nature of Laws, Hall provides students and faculty with the experience of working cooperatively with colleagues whose ideas, viewpoints, and problem-solving methods are very different from their own, a process that encourages a broader perspective about each individual discipline and advertising as a field of endeavor. Faculty members use Laws, Hall & Associates to gain support for, and involve students in, their research agendas, and expand off-campus contacts with practitioners in their fields. Thus, Laws, Hall & Associates "demonstrates the potential for achieving professional excellence in a liberal education environment."

The student initiative and competition that are integral to Laws, Hall & Associates are also characteristic of student life at Miami. As with many other out-of-class activities, students cannot simply volunteer or sign up to participate in Laws, Hall, but must submit to a rigorous and competitive screening process. Once accepted for the program, students are assigned to competing teams, only one of which is selected "the winner" by the client. Team competition mimics real-world experience and builds real-world skills, and the demand for efficiency, accuracy, dependability, and interpersonal effectiveness that one finds throughout the Miami student culture is affirmed and perpetuated.

Students are encouraged from their first contact with the university to take the initiative to "get involved" — "there are so many things to do here, so do them" — in out-of-class activities as a means to "give back" to the community, keep busy and have fun, and build career-related skills. In addition, we heard over and over again about the importance placed at Miami on integrating in-class and out-of-class experiences. Laws, Hall & Associates epitomizes the out-of-class experience at Miami: blending interdisciplinary coursework with real-world practice, involving students with faculty outside the classroom, providing service to a client (while promoting Miami), and giving students the opportunity to work — and compete — with other students to create something of value.

University of California, Davis

Three involving characteristics of UC Davis are highlighted in this section: the campus housing program, which is another view of how a large campus can provide a human-scale environment for resident students; the administrative advisory committee system, which illustrates how history and tradition encourage students to become involved in campus governance; and several campus community celebrations that underscore the institution's commitment to multiculturalism.

Student Housing. Residence life at UC Davis is an important vehicle for formal and informal induction experiences for new students. Campus residences are also a means to make the university feel small in that a number of housing alternatives are available so that students with common interests can form residential communities. In addition, as was mentioned in Chapter Five, the size of Davis residence halls is kept to no more than two or three stories, a practice that also fosters a sense of human scale.

Almost 90 percent of the first-year students at UC Davis live in residence halls and the first year is seen as a time for students to learn about what is available at the university. Residence hall staff assume responsibility for informing freshmen about the campus, its programs, and its resources. Emphasis is placed in the halls on community development, appreciation for diversity, leadership opportunities and training, and educational programming. Students reported that the community of friends developed in the residence hall was the group with which they continued to live even after moving off campus.

Before students arrive on campus they receive a Resident's Workbook describing special programs and offering information about adjusting to life in the residence halls. During the

academic year, hall staff offer sessions on roommate relationships, communication skills, and expectations for student learning and development. Because UC Davis has so many ways for
students to be involved, hall staff work with new students to
help them identify their preferred avenues of involvement.

Residence hall staff return to campus for training a month
before classes begin. Preparation of hall staff receives considerable time and effort, in part because staff preparation is believed
to be essential to helping students get the most benefit from their
residential experience. Another reason for an emphasis on knowledgeable and skilled hall staff is that few Davis students live on
campus for more than one year, so the most must be made of
that year in providing skills for autonomous and responsible off-
campus living.

In addition to residence halls, UC Davis has a number
of "alternative" residences. Baggin's End Domes are fourteen
fiberglass domes built in 1971. The Domes house twenty-eight
students and feature gardens, fruit trees, and chickens. Pierce
Co-op is a frame house that provides space for eleven students
who share concerns about the environment. The residents of
the Agrarian Effort, another co-op, share interests in home economics and agriculture and maintain a large garden.

Administrative Advisory Committees. The administrative
structure of UC Davis includes extensive use of a system of advisory committees, an important means by which students' full
membership in the university community is acknowledged and
supported. As mentioned in previous chapters, these committees were established by former chancellor Mrak and perpetuate the culture of participation and collaboration he initiated.

Thirty administrative advisory committees ranging from
"Animal Use and Care" to "Regents Professor and Lecturer" are
actively involved in channeling student input into the affairs of
the campus. A general application form for participation in these
committees with an accompanying letter of invitation by the
chancellor is circulated throughout the campus to solicit the involvement of faculty, staff, and students. The chancellor also
sponsors occasional Open Forums and a Chancellor's Retreat,

and has several student assistants working in his office. This level of participation apparently has nurtured a culture of leadership among students. As of 1989, three of the five student regents for the University of California system had come from UC Davis.

Campus Celebrations. During the spring quarter, numerous activities are scheduled that focus attention on and celebrate the multiple communities of UC Davis. These events are usually student-initiated and student-run (with, in some cases, some staff assistance), and so are useful examples of the importance of student initiative at Davis. Some of the events also integrate the academic and the nonacademic in ways that celebrate the total educational experience of students.

"Picnic Day" is a campus-wide celebration that takes place in the spring of the year, attracting many Davis graduates and residents of California's Central Valley. Attendance at the 1988 event was estimated at 60,000. Originally designed to attract off-campus guests, this largest of campus activities began about fifty years ago as a day for students and residents to view animals and new farm equipment. Beginning with a parade followed by a rodeo, Picnic Day is now an open house for departments and groups to perform demonstrations, provide information booths, conduct performances, and sponsor activities such as sports events and dachshund races. Students, faculty, and staff work at food booths and other activities on this festive occasion, which takes place on the second or third Saturday in April and is funded by student fees and university departments.

"Whole Earth Festival" grew out of the ecology movement and continues as an important expression of the Davis ethos. Hosted early in May by the Experimental College, this activity emphasizes education for a more holistic life-style. People come from all over the Western states to partake of the natural and ethnic foods, dancers, performers, speakers, and crafts offered by student and community volunteers called the Karma Patrol.

"Cultural Days" are four distinct celebrations corresponding to each of the largest racial and ethnic groups represented on campus: African American, Native American, Mexican

American, and Asian American. Support of these events is consistent with Davis's expressed value of appreciating cultural diversity.

African American Family Week originated around 1970 after some black students who had attended Picnic Day decided that they wanted to plan an event for their families and themselves. One of the black fraternities was a key organizing group for a time, but in recent years the African American Students United has assumed responsibility for the event. African American Family Week has become so large — 30,000 in attendance from all over the West — that it is co-chaired by a student and a staff member who coordinate seventeen different committees. The event demonstrates a significant commitment to creating a supportive community for black students and their families. In addition, the event reinforces the plethora of leadership opportunities available to students.

Asian/Pacific Heritage Week highlights the cultural, political, and social activities and issues of Asian Americans. During Asian/Pacific Heritage Week, there is an opportunity to hear guest speakers, view martial arts displays, sample Asian foods, and watch cultural dances.

La Raza Cultural Days are programs and events designed to increase the cultural awareness of the UC Davis campus and community by promoting Chicano/Mexican American culture and history. The organizing committee of La Raza Cultural Days is composed of faculty, staff, and students. Events include distinguished speakers, music and film presentations, dance performances, and picnics.

Native American Culture Days is a celebration of American Indian cultures. It is also a time of fun, learning, and sharing. Programs include poetry, reading, traditional dancers, a pow-wow, and more. American Indian food, arts, and crafts are displayed and sold.

Summary

The examples of programs presented here illustrate ways in which four large universities are meeting the challenge of maintaining a high quality of student life in what might other-

wise be a fragmented and anonymous environment. Each institution's practices reflect its unique setting, people, and mission and philosophy—its culture, so to speak—but in every case,
students are given rich opportunities for learning and personal
development.

Not all institutions of higher education are faced with the
problems and concerns that accompany large enrollments and
residence hall systems the size of small cities. Yet small residential
colleges have problems of their own with which to contend. In
the next chapter, we present some examples of programs and
practices from small colleges.

9

Small Institutions

Six small colleges (5,000 or fewer students) were included in the study: Berea College, Earlham College, Grinnell College, Mount Holyoke College, Xavier University, and The Evergreen State College. In this chapter, selected policies and practices of those colleges are described. While some of the practices are not particularly unique or innovative, they are included because of their importance in the institutional contexts in which they occur. Each is consistent with, and contributes to, the mission of the college; the ways in which the practices are developed and implemented are usually distinctive; and the meaning that the practices have for participants is part of the specialness of the institution.

Berea College

Critical to the implementation of Berea's mission is the Labor Program. In Chapter Three we described the clarity and coherence of the mission of Berea College as stated in the Seven Great Commitments. The Labor Program is described in the fourth commitment: to demonstrate through the student labor program that labor, mental and manual, has dignity as well as utility. Thus, the Labor Program is one of the ways in which Berea's mission is integrated into, and has meaning for, the daily lives of its students. In addition, the Labor Program is both a bridge and a ladder: a bridge between the academic and nonacademic aspects of student life and a ladder for developing personal, academic, and career skills.

215

A word commonly used at Berea in talking about the Labor Program is democratization; because all students have jobs, few, if any, status distinctions among students are made. A similar effort is reflected in the policy that campus activities and organizations be accessible to all students regardless of financial resources; all activities are provided at no, or minimal, extra cost to students. A transfer student stated that she did not have to feel that she was missing out on student life just because she had to work and had little spending money.

Because Berea serves students who would need jobs at any college or university, and who are likely to have limited self-confidence and underdeveloped social skills, the egalitarianism promoted by the Labor Program encourages student involvement in the life of the college. More specifically, the Labor Program ensures student membership on various campus committees and tangible progress and success in mastering tasks and obtaining rewards (such as promotions) for hard work.

Another advantage of the Labor Program to students and the college is that it provides opportunities for students to interact with the faculty and staff who serve as labor supervisors. The importance of such relationships for student satisfaction, retention, integration, and involvement is well established (Hossler, 1984). Berea students, because of their backgrounds, may benefit even more than other students from the attention of caring faculty and staff. Labor supervisors come from diverse educational backgrounds, in some cases similar to those of Berea students, so students usually are comfortable interacting with them.

The Labor Program also helps students prepare for careers. After the first year, students can express a preference for a certain labor position. Many work in areas directly related to their majors; for example, sociology majors may work for Students for Appalachia, a community service agency. As a consequence, labor involvement and membership in departmental clubs are mutually enhancing, blurring the lines between classroom experience and out-of-class life as each portion of the student's experience has a positive effect on the other.

Students change over time in their views of the Labor Program. At first, the job provides the money necessary to go to school. Later, students recognize that they are acquiring important skills and experiences that have implications for their future success. One student told us that labor "grows on" students as they come to realize the many benefits they obtain from it. Berea graduates attest that the Labor Program helped them learn to be responsible, be a contributing member of society, manage time, and behave properly in personal and social situations. Nearly every student with whom we spoke mentioned her or his labor position or Labor Day (celebrating the worth and dignity of labor and laborers) as one of the "most significant" experiences she or he had at Berea.

Earlham College

Described in this section are Earlham's Service Learning Program and residence hall program, both of which support and reinforce the egalitarian values and Quaker ethos expressed in the college's mission.

Service Learning Program. In Chapter Three we described the Quaker values and assumptions that form the basis of Earlham's mission. Those values include the responsibility of each individual in a global community and the application of knowledge to life and service — a value expressed in the phrase, "Let your lives speak." The Service Learning Program (SLP) is a vehicle for enabling students to put these values — and, therefore, the institution's mission — into practice.

Earlham College, as a member of Campus Compact and Campus Outreach Opportunity League (C.O.O.L.), sustains a growing, active interest in encouraging voluntarism among students. The Service Learning Program was established in 1987 to revitalize student interest in providing service to the Richmond community. Approximately 650 students joined SLP in 1988–89, although interest and participation wane occasionally under the press of time demands.

Prior to the development of SLP, the Earlham Volunteer Exchange placed student volunteers in the Richmond community for ten years. In 1986 Earlham's president, Richard

Wood, committed his support to student community service along with presidents from about 120 colleges and universities. Earlham applied for and received a federal government ACTION Grant to provide funding for a director who expanded the Earlham Volunteer Exchange by emphasizing service learning. This restructuring of the volunteer program at the college has resulted in Earlham volunteers encouraging others to enter into community service. The results have been impressive. In the first year, the number of students participating in the program nearly doubled, from 337 to 650, and students contributed 10,652 hours of service to 73 Richmond agencies and community projects.

Volunteers serve the community of Richmond in a variety of roles, including: working in the city's fall and spring cleanup campaigns; assisting with scouting organizations and Big Brother and Big Sister and other youth organizations; working with Special Olympics and with youngsters who have physical and mental disabilities; visiting patients at the local state hospital; and participating in a local pet therapy program. Earlham volunteers also are active in providing support for the elderly, the hungry, and the needy. They serve meals, cook food, tutor students, and work with adults through a literacy program.

There are benefits also for the students who are members of SLP. In addition to the satisfaction of helping, students have an opportunity to explore careers and visit with professionals, apply course work to real-life situations, gain practical experience, develop friendships with diverse groups of people, accept civic responsibilities after college, develop self-confidence, and make a difference in the world around them.

It is easy for students to get involved in the Service Learning Program. All they need to do is inform the program director or a student staff member of their interest. After completing an interest assessment and participating in an orientation, the volunteers are ready to go. They contribute about ten hours a week to the program and may work with the agency of their choice or design their own project.

Residence Halls. The residential environment at Earlham is intentionally arranged to accentuate and implement Quaker values as well as liberal education, another integral aspect of the college's mission. The size of Earlham dorms also helps to make a small college feel even more manageable, but not stifling. Many challenges — to grow, to think differently, to behave responsibly — are provided in the residences at Earlham.

Earlham maintains five dormitories and twenty-two college-owned houses (including four language houses, a Black Cultural Center, and a farm collective) for approximately 800 residential students; all campus residences are coeducational. Key staff people in the halls are Head Residents, resident counselors, and hall conveners. The Head Resident is a full-time, professionally trained staff member whose responsibilities include counseling, encouraging community involvement in programs, and supervising resident counselors and hall conveners. Resident counselors are paraprofessional upper-class students who have training in personal and academic counseling and advising. Hall conveners are volunteers who assist with student orientation and convene hall meetings for such purposes as establishing quiet hours, planning small group activities, and disseminating information.

Dorm Councils are the primary means by which students plan and implement activities within the dorms. Funds are allocated by the councils for special events such as study breaks, dances, and other activities that make positive contributions to the quality of campus life. Head Residents also have small amounts of discretionary funds to support social activities.

Student participation in activities and governance is encouraged by the college, as is social responsibility. Learning is facilitated in the residential environment by role modeling by staff and upper-class students, planning of and participation in activities and events, and determination of community living expectations.

Grinnell College

The autonomy and egalitarianism emphasized in Grinnell's mission and philosophy are demonstrated in many ways, including the campus housing program and varsity athletics. Those practices are highlighted in this section.

Residence Halls. At Grinnell, students are expected to take responsibility for the quality of their lives both in and out of class, an expectation that is communicated clearly—and lived effectively—in the residence halls. The dorms offer numerous opportunities for students to take leadership for programs, activities, and other educational experiences.

Grinnell's residence halls are small and therefore manageable. Each professional residence hall staff member is responsible for from 110 to 180 students, an excellent staff to student ratio. Between 8 and 20 students form the residential living unit (floor, corridor, or wing). One Grinnell administrator observed that students "learn as much outside the classroom at Grinnell as in the classroom."

Students tend to live in the halls for at least two years, although they usually do not stay in the same building for more than a year. Students are intermingled by class standing, which makes for powerful modeling behavior in that under-class students can learn from upper-class students in the living environment. Each year, 150 students, usually seniors, are allowed to live off campus because the campus residence halls are full.

The Grinnell housing system is similar to Stanford's in some respects. Some houses on the perimeter of the campus are organized by themes, including vegetarian dining, Russian language and culture, and Chinese language and culture. The Grinnell alcohol policy is also similar to Stanford's in that Student Advisers are not expected to be police officers and turn in students if they use alcohol. Rather, if a student gets into trouble (such as drinking heavily), the SA may ask the Resident Adviser—the full-time professional staff person—to design an intervention.

According to President George Drake, life in the halls is a key to a high-quality undergraduate experience because it is in the residence halls that students learn about human nature and about themselves. Dorm life is not without problems, as living quarters are tight, but it can also be the most stimulating noncurricular aspect of college, providing opportunities for interaction with other students, more than half of whom are from places 500 miles away from Grinnell.

Athletics. As was mentioned earlier, Grinnell is an institution with strong egalitarian aspirations; the importance of past performance and family or educational background are minimized. In addition, collaborative learning is emphasized. These community values of egalitarianism and collaboration are exhibited and reinforced in Grinnell's athletic program.

Forty percent of Grinnell's students are members of varsity athletic teams. The student body president, a member of the cross-country team, explained that there were forty-three students on the cross-country team, but only seven are allowed to compete in intercollegiate events. The others participated because they wanted to exercise, learn the rules of the sport, and interact with one another. This is a refreshing approach to intercollegiate athletic competition, although not unique among small residential colleges that do not offer athletic grants.

Students move freely from one activity to another across grade levels. This is unusual. Students at other colleges typically become involved in an activity as first- or second-year students and continue to participate in that activity to arrive at a position of leadership as junior or senior. At Grinnell, students think nothing of playing football one year and running cross-country the next. One student, for example, never played competitive football until he went out for the team in his junior year. Another student reported that she and some friends wanted to start a women's rugby team, a club sport. It took about a semester to organize the team, arrange for funding and develop a schedule. Within a very short time, Grinnell was competing against the University of Iowa. Clearly, athletics at Grinnell are for any student who has an interest in participating in a particular sport.

One more anecdote is worth mentioning. During George Drake's first year as president, Grinnell closed the football season by winning its final game. Ten months later, the Grinnell eleven opened the next season with a victory. At that point, some students sought assurances from President Drake that the two-game winning streak did not mark the beginning of overemphasis on athletics at Grinnell!

Mount Holyoke College

As with the other small colleges in this study, residence life at Mount Holyoke is a means by which the institution's mission and educational purposes are conveyed and maintained. In this section, Mount Holyoke residence programs and the Frances Perkins Program for adult learners are described.

Residential Life. We have described elsewhere the importance of a shared vision of what an institution stands for, as well as high expectations for student responsibility, in creating an environment conducive to student learning and personal development. Residential life at Mount Holyoke reflects and reinforces the college's commitments to community and individual responsibility and support. The expectations for excellence, tolerance, integrity, and service that characterize the academic experience at Mount Holyoke are also an integral part of community life.

Residential life at Mount Holyoke is founded on the principles of community responsibility articulated in the Student Handbook (1989–90, p. 31):

> To enter Mount Holyoke is to become a member of a community. Choosing to become a member of this community implies a commitment to the notions of free inquiry and free expression which are central to a liberal arts education. Becoming a member of the Mount Holyoke community also implies a commitment to maintaining an environment in which these goals may be attained. Being a member of this community is a privilege; sharing in this community is a responsibility.

Responsibilities of Mount Holyoke community members include respect for the freedom, rights, beliefs, and feelings of others, and a commitment to an environment in which diversity is celebrated. The responsibilities, as well as the privileges, of community membership are clearly demonstrated in the operation of the college's residences.

Mount Holyoke dorms are small, housing from 60 to 140 students, and range in style from "cottages" to modern multi-level residence halls. Members of all four classes live in each of the sixteen halls, a policy that was described by students as creating important learning opportunities; seniors recalled with satisfaction their early experiences of "being challenged in the dorm"—that is, having lively and challenging discussions with older students about academic, social, personal, and political issues.

Each residence has a living room, lounges, study rooms, a kitchenette, a baby grand piano, a grandfather clock, and a dining room. Meals are served in each dorm by dorm residents. According to students, much of Mount Holyoke's social life is "centered in the dorms," and a great deal of dorm community building, as well as out-of-class learning, seems to take place at mealtimes. The practice of gathering for "m & c's" (milk and crackers) in the dorms at 10:00 P.M. every night was described in Chapter Four.

Mount Holyoke residence halls are "run by students," including a hall president, assistant hall president, and student advisers. In addition, each dorm has a head resident (HR), a part-time staff member of the Office of Residential Life who lives in the dorm and serves as the professional administrative liaison between the dorm and other college offices.

The hall president (HP) is "the chief student administrator" of the residence hall, according to the Student Handbook. She is a junior or senior selected for her leadership, communication, and helping skills. Hall presidents are responsible for coordinating the Hall Committee (described below), facilitating communication among residents, coordinating hall meetings, encouraging and assisting hall programming, advising the director of residential life on matters of policy and community concerns, serving as liaison between the dorm and the Office of Residential Life, communicating college policies to residents, and working to "ease the problems of community living." Each Hall President selects an Assistant Hall President (AHP) who helps the HP and typically coordinates dorm orientation activities. Both HPs and AHPs volunteer their time to these positions, a practice that can be traced to Mary Lyon's emphasis on service — on sharing one's gifts and skills with others.

Student advisers (SAs) are also full-time students, usually sophomores or juniors, who serve as peer advisers and counselors to floor residents. The SAs are responsible for the general welfare of their floors, including community development, effective communication, programs and activities, limit setting, mediation, and problem referrals. According to the Office of Residential Life, important goals of the SA program are to "aid in increasing student responsibility for self" and to be approachable and available to floor residents. The emphasis is on SAs as helpers, rather than policy enforcers. Like HPs and AHPs, SAs are volunteers.

All student residential life staff have extensive pre-service and in-service training in order to prepare them to handle their considerable responsibilities. Training topics include leadership and counseling skills, mental health referrals, programming, issues related to alcohol use and eating disorders, minority and international student concerns, and orientation for new students.

Some students hold paid positions in the dorms. The work chair is a student hired by the head resident to be responsible for making sure that hallways are free of student belongings, monitoring use of the vacuum, and supervising the kitchenettes. A student supervisor is appointed by Food Service to serve as the liaison between the dorm and the kitchen staff. She is responsible for organizing the student kitchen workers and keeps residents informed about special meals and so on.

The residential life staff in the halls (HRs, HPs, AHPs, and SAs) constitute the Closed Hall Committee, a group that meets weekly to discuss dorm life in confidence. An extended Hall Committee is coordinated by the HP and is usually composed of the dorm program coordinator, responsible for all-dorm social activities, dorm treasurer, responsible for developing a dorm budget and managing hall funds, dorm senator, representing the dorm to the Student Government Association, class representatives, fire captain, intramural representative, security representative, and energy representative (works with director of physical facilities on energy issues).

One of the tasks of the Hall Committee is to develop, with the involvement of the dorm residents, a dorm mission statement. Some examples of recent mission statements include the following:

> To be a supportive atmosphere where all students are treated with respect and provided with the opportunity to explore their community and learn about themselves [North Rockefeller].

> The residence hall creates a supportive home which fosters fellowship and celebrates diversity [North Mandelle].

> Part of our mission is to make sure no one is ever chronically lonely within the dorm [South Mandelle].

These mission statements reflect commitments to community responsibility described in Mount Holyoke publications and expressed by faculty, administrators, and students throughout the college.

Undergirding residence hall living is the Mount Holyoke honor system. According to the Student Handbook (p. 34):

> With integrity as the foundation, the honor system promotes community living and maximum individual freedom within the community. The student demonstrates her respect for individual freedom by conducting herself with maturity and honor, and by showing due concern for the welfare of other members of the community.

Therefore, each student is honor bound to abide by and uphold the academic, social, and library regulations of the college. If a student breaks a rule, she is on her honor to report herself to a faculty member (in the case of an academic regulation) or to a member of the Closed Hall Committee in the case of a social regulation.

The Council on Student Affairs (composed of the president of the college, the dean of students, three faculty members, and six students, including the SGA president and the chair of the HPs) may hear cases of serious violation of social regulations (that is, where suspension or expulsion may be considered). As indicated earlier, in the year prior to our visit, only five cases of honor code violations were heard by the Council on Student Affairs. Most violations were dealt with by HPs.

Frances Perkins Program. The challenge, support, and press for involvement both in and out of class that characterize the experience of traditional-age Mount Holyoke students are also important to the adult learners who are Frances Perkins Scholars. The Frances Perkins Program was begun in 1980 in order to make the opportunities and advantages of Mount Holyoke available to women who are older than the typical college student. Named for the Mount Holyoke alumna (Class of 1902) who was Secretary of Labor in President Franklin D. Roosevelt's cabinet, the Frances Perkins Program "is for women with a goal": to obtain a college degree. Since 1982, 103 Frances Perkins students have done just that.

During the 1988–89 school year, eighty-eight women participated in the Frances Perkins Program. Of the twenty-one Frances Perkins Scholars (FPs) who graduated in 1989, sixteen received their degrees with honors and eight were elected to Phi Beta Kappa. Many graduates of the program have gone on to graduate and professional schools, including law and medicine, while others have pursued careers in teaching, business, college administration, art, and social service.

Frances Perkins students are a diverse group. While the vast majority of FPs come from Massachusetts, ten other states were represented in 1988–89. The median age of the 1988–89 participants was thirty-four, although the age range was twenty-two to sixty-six; about a third of the students were married and about half had children. Frances Perkins students have interrupted their educations for three to forty-eight years. Many have attended community colleges, although some have not participated in formal education since high school. According to a program publication, FPs have been nurses, mechanics, waitresses, hairdressers, realtors, legislative assistants, flight attendants, artists, performers, bank officers, and substance abuse counselors prior to entering the program. Many continue to hold jobs after they become students, and some make significant contributions through service to their local communities. Despite their diversity, however, FPs were all described as highly motivated and hard-working students.

Frances Perkins Scholars may attend college part-time or full-time, but they are, in all respects, full members of the Mount Holyoke community. As many as a third of the program students live in the residence halls, and all attend classes and engage in extracurricular activities with "traditional" students. The messages that all Mount Holyoke students receive — "there is so much to do here, so get involved"; "you can be anything you want to be" — are not lost on FPs; program students with whom we spoke included a hall president, a student adviser, and a student government representative.

The special needs of adult learners, for information, financial aid, housing, employment, academic assistance, and personal support, have been addressed in a variety of ways by the college and the Frances Perkins staff. For example, admission to the program is based on a personal interview, as well as on traditional indicators of potential, and life experience is an important consideration and a valued contribution. A special orientation for FPs is held prior to the beginning of each term. The students are introduced to the campus and its offices, meet one another as well as faculty and staff, and attend academic workshops. Some grant aid is designated for program students, and campus employment is available to them as well.

Frances Perkins Scholars also have their own organization that plans social activities, workshops, and programs. A residence hall annex has been designated as the Frances Perkins House, a place where FPs can gather for events, study, and share meals. Some FPs live in the House, although a number live in other residences.

The challenge and support described by traditional Mount Holyoke students were also experienced by Frances Perkins

Scholars. They felt stretched and, in some cases, stressed by the rigors of academic life and the many opportunities for involvement outside the classroom. At the same time, they felt "embraced" by the support systems they found at the college. Program students were especially enthusiastic about the attention and encouragement they received from faculty members, although Frances Perkins staff and other FPs were also mentioned as "lifesavers."

Frances Perkins students, like other Mount Holyoke women, felt strengthened in the environment of a women's college. The emphasis placed by faculty, administrators, and other students on their potential for excellence and for doing "uncommon" things was particularly important to FPs and seemed to motivate them to even greater effort.

In 1983 a second phase was added to the program: Frances Perkins Fellows. The Fellow Program is intended for women who already have a bachelor's degree but who want to pursue further undergraduate study, usually in a field different from their original majors. Fellows receive a Certificate of Achievement upon completion of their courses of study.

The Frances Perkins Program is an example of how a college with a special mission can adapt and expand its programs and services to achieve that mission more fully. Mount Holyoke's mission of empowering women through a rigorous liberal arts education in a supportive environment has easily encompassed nontraditional learners by treating them as full and valued members of the community while meeting their unique needs. In this way, adult learners are given the opportunity to pursue their dreams, including higher education, and traditional students obtain the benefits of interacting with highly motivated older women who have interesting and varied life experiences.

Xavier University

Xavier's founder, Mother Katharine Drexel, believed that people who face overwhelming obstacles can succeed and, in fact, excel, if given opportunities to do so. Xavier's mission — offering opportunities for achievement and excellence in the context of service to the black community — forms the basis for a number of programs intended to help students meet their educational goals. These programs are designed to be "ladders to success" — making very clear the steps to be taken to meet those goals — undergirded by extensive support systems that help students climb the ladders.

The ladders to achievement that are the Xavier way are illustrated here by six programs that prepare students with potential "to get up to speed" for collegiate level work: MathStar, BioStar, ChemStar, SOAR, SuperScholar Excel, and Triple S. All but SuperScholar Excel are designed for potential science majors. All but Triple S are offered during the summer for high school students and have associated costs ranging from $125 (Math-Star) to $500 (SOAR); cost differentials are explained by the length of the programs. A limited number of scholarships are available. Instructors for the programs are drawn from Xavier faculty and advanced students majoring in the areas emphasized in the programs.

MathStar. Implemented in 1987, this program was developed to give a head start to ninth-grade algebra students who have an interest in the sciences. To be eligible, a student must be a member of a group underrepresented in the sciences, have a grade point average not less than 2.75 and C or better grades in math and science courses, and plan to enroll in high school algebra the following year. MathStar consists of ten days of classroom instruction (five hours per day) including lectures, daily quizzes, and discussions of previous lectures and quizzes. As with the other programs described below, about ninety minutes of homework is assigned each day. Laboratory experiments are designed so that small groups of students (16 to 20), led by an upper-class Xavier math or science major with good grades, set up and solve physical models of algebraic equations. As with other programs in the series, group work provides a source of peer support for members and a locus for competition not among individuals but among groups. Groups often develop banners, cheers, and songs to exhibit pride in their group identity. Although the program was originally conceived for about 120 students, about 140 to 150 students enroll; 95 percent are African American, about three-quarters are women. About 80 percent of the MathStar students apply for admission to the next program in the sequence, BioStar.

BioStar. The criteria for admission to BioStar are similar to that of MathStar, except that students are expected to enroll in high school biology, which is usually offered in the tenth grade. This program is four weeks in duration with four hours a day devoted to academic activities, including: traditional classroom activities such as lectures, quizzes, and discussion; experiments that capture the interest of the students; skill-building sessions in vocabulary and reading to help students learn words derived from Latin and Greek and to improve comprehensions of scientific material; and research on biological topics. As with MathStar, students usually make significant gains in their knowledge of the subject as well as in reading comprehension and vocabulary. More than 80 percent apply for ChemStar, the next program in the ladder.

ChemStar. The current form of ChemStar emerged in 1982, although Xavier has been working with New Orleans high school chemistry students since 1974. As with the other programs in this sequence, it is hoped that students will eventually select a career in the sciences. This program, too, is annually oversubscribed; intended for 50 students, it generally accommodates about 150. Because the purpose of the program is to prepare students for high school chemistry, most participants are tenth-graders, usually female African Americans from the New Orleans area. Instructional techniques similar to the first two programs are employed (lectures, daily quizzes, homework). As expected, laboratory experiments are featured. Drill work is used to hone problem-solving abilities. Testimonials similar to those heard in reference to MathStar and BioStar attest to the value of ChemStar: students report that they could not have done as well in chemistry without this course; high school teachers are almost uniformly impressed with the quality of work produced by ChemStar graduates. In addition, more than 80 percent move on to either the SOAR or SuperScholar Excel Programs.

SOAR. SOAR, an acronym for Stress on Analytical Reasoning, is designed to prepare students for entry-level science and mathematics courses in college. Eligibility requirements are the same as for previous programs in the sequence; participants are either about to start their last year of high school or the first year of college. Although it was originally conceived in 1977 for about 100 students, close to twice that number participate each summer. The five components of SOAR tend to emphasize process over content: general problem-solving ability; standardized test-taking abilities; general (not scientific) vocabulary; group competition; and tours of professional and graduate schools and lectures by professionals in health science fields. On average, SOAR participants improve their SAT scores by 120 points; students with low reading scores show an average gain of 2.5 years in both reading comprehension and vocabulary.

SuperScholar Excel Program. Instituted in 1983, SuperScholar Excel is a four-week summer program designed to improve the analytical and critical reasoning skills of high school sophomores and juniors considering careers in the humanities, law, and social sciences. A maximum of 70 students was set in 1987, but the demand was so great that 101 students participated in the summer of 1989. The program is so popular that as many as 180 students have applied to participate in a given year, indicating the high demand for such opportunities. Word of mouth passed from one generation of SuperScholar Excel graduates to their high school colleagues, resulting in the high number of students applying for admission.

The program consists of four weeks of academic and nonacademic activities. Students are divided into groups of no more than fifteen. Each group is organized and coordinated by a recent Xavier graduate who serves as a group leader. This person provides assistance with the various academic components of the program, in addition to the faculty, and also organizes social activities. The group leader also works to motivate and maximize student academic achievement. The subjects introduced include mathematics, vocabulary, history, humanities, philosophy, speech, and analytical reasoning. Besides classroom activities, the students participate in debates, literary tournaments, and a quiz bowl.

Social activities are also part of the program. Events such as a Fourth of July picnic, trips to the French Quarter, and pizza parties are common. But in the tradition of Xavier, all social activities cease at 8:00 P.M. Monday through Thursday evening. At 8:00 P.M. a two-hour study session begins. Distractions from preparing for the next day's classes are not tolerated. The group leader also provides individual attention to motivate students.

Many participants make a two-year gain in reading skills upon completion of the program. Others add as many as 100 points to their SAT scores. Those who participate in the program are twice as likely to complete their college degrees as those who do not participate. Scholarships are available to cover the cost of tuition and fees for a number of participants. For those who are from beyond commuting distance, a limited number of room-and-board scholarships make living on campus possible. Students who complete the SuperScholar Excel program with a 3.0 grade point average are eligible for admission to Xavier. Students with grade point averages between 2.6 and 3.0 may be admitted if they have done well in certain courses and demonstrate potential for success at the college level. A student who had been active in high school and had appropriate letters of reference might be admitted if he or she earned less than a 3.0 in the SuperScholar Excel program.

Triple S. Triple S (Standards with Sympathy in the Sciences) is the final initiative in the sequence of science preparation courses that began with MathStar. As part of the regular freshman and sophomore course offerings, faculty in mathematics and sciences structure their introductory courses, such as general biology, general chemistry, organic chemistry, precalculus/calculus, and general physics, to maintain high standards for achievement and, at the same time, provide support for students who are underprepared academically and psychologically. These courses are standardized with regard to content and pace of coverage. Workbooks are provided so that students know what they are expected to learn and when. Systematic vocabulary building and practice in different approaches to problem solving, such as inductive and deductive reasoning, are other cornerstones of Triple S courses. In addition, the mathematics and science departments jointly sponsor a tutorial center that provides free assistance to any student in a Triple S course.

The six "ladder" programs briefly described here have been successful by any standard. Designed to increase the number of persons from underrepresented groups in the health professions, the programs are consistent with the Xavier way — high expectations for academic performance within a highly structured and supportive academic and social environment. Discipline and expectations for hard work on the part of students are not compromised. Parents are encouraged to participate in parts of the program; if a student is falling behind or misses a class during the summer program, the parents are notified. Small classes and group work allow faculty and other members of the Xavier community, such as upper-class students, to give personal attention to students.

Xavier students are role models for another aspect of the Xavier way — giving something back to the community and to those who are less fortunate. Moreover, the ladders take students where they want to go. Xavier graduates are more than twice as likely to gain admission into graduate programs in the health professions than their national counterparts. Xavier places more African Americans in pharmacy school than any other institution and is second in the number of African Americans placed in medical school.

The Evergreen State College

From the beginning, Evergreen's mission has been alternative liberal education — "alternative" in the sense that it is based on a feeling of collegiality and collaboration between students and faculty and among faculty, a commitment to student responsibility and freedom, and an appreciation for the interconnectedness of academic and nonacademic aspects of education. Certainly the most distinctive characteristic of TESC is the form and mode of the academic program. The academic program consumes the interest and energy of faculty and students alike. In this section, the basic building blocks of the Evergreen experience are described: Coordinated Study Program, Core Programs, and Individual Learning Contracts, including internships.

Coordinated Study Program. The Program is succinctly described in a chapter in an as yet unpublished history of the college (The Evergreen State College, 1989):

> From a faculty point of view, the main structural features of coordinated study include: the Program theme or problem and the faculty seminar. The organizing principle of a coordinated study has two dimensions — the Program Concept and what Evergreen has called the "Program Covenant." The Program Concept refers to the central matter, or questions, or problem to which the year's reading, lecturing, seminaring, and writing will address itself. The Program Covenant refers to a contract among the faculty team for how the central matter of the study will be collaboratively presented. This Covenant functions as insurance against the very understandable tendency to drift toward one's disciplinary strength as against the will required to exercise one's interdisciplinary responsibility in such a program.
>
> A second faculty-centered aspect of the coordinated study is the Faculty Seminar. This arrangement is designed to make it possible for faculty members to teach with each other across their disciplinary specialties by providing them with a time each week for their discussion of the material as it bears on the Program theme for that week. This seminar occurs prior to their meeting with students on the same material and is the glue for collaboration.
>
> From the students' perspective the important structural features of coordinated study include the Program idea and the Faculty Seminar, but also

book seminars, lectures, workshops, the assigned reading and writing, individual conferences, and evaluation. Coordinated study may also include internships, group projects, special-interest seminars, examinations, program retreats, business meetings, and what Evergreen locals call "down days," usually one day a week when faculty prepare to teach and/ or attend college meetings, giving students the opportunity to do likewise.

The Coordinated Study Program is the main feature of the Evergreen curriculum. A Program usually requires the full-time participation of the student, often lasts for the entire academic year, and is made up of a team of faculty numbering from two to five, and with 40 to 100 students.

Most programs are offered for a full year; some are offered for only one or two quarters. Environmental Studies is one of the more popular areas of study, undoubtedly because of the geography of Washington and the Puget Sound. Programs in this area have such titles as: Habitats: Marine, Terrestrial and Human; Principles of Biology; Cells and Organisms; Ecological Agriculture; Tribal Resource Development. Additional areas of study include: Expressive Arts (music, theater, and studio arts), Humanities, Language and Culture Center, Management and the Public Interest, Native American Studies, Science-Technology-and-Health, Center for the Study of Science and Human Values, and Political Economy and Social Change.

The curriculum is always being invented. Although a Program may be offered annually, it is never exactly the same. The teaching team changes; an interdisciplinary team will never teach the same program twice. As a new team finds and prepares to teach a Core or Coordinated Program, the content and the basic approach invariably change.

The manner in which faculty find each other in order to form an interdisciplinary team to offer a program warrants description. Published each year is "The Geoduck Cookbook or Program Planning Among the Evergreens." It is essentially a recipe for curriculum planning that provides an explanation of the roles and responsibilities of members of the college community, guidelines for submitting proposals, criteria to be used in selecting programs, a flow chart of the planning process and a planning timetable, an overview of the curriculum, and tips on planning. It also includes a lengthy chapter about faculty interests and academic backgrounds that helps faculty members find each other to make common intellectual cause. Consider a typical example:

> In 1990–91, I am semi-committed to teaching in the entry-level media arts program but actually would prefer to teach in a coordinated studies program for two quarters and work with advanced media students on a cable-access program for one. Current interests include: (a) global mass communications, taught both on campus with visiting practitioners and a social scientist, (b) a performance-based program that combines anthropology and theater, (c) something that explores the relationship between the moving image, information, and perception (actually I would love to teach a program . . . on women and technology), (d) anything that could combine my interests and experiences in SE Asia, (e) a field-based program that involved documentary production in India, Pakistan, or China. My teaching style has been described as "exacting, intense, project-oriented, witty, organized, active, inventive, and involved." In other words, I have been known to tap dance while at the podium. (Subjects: film history and theory, nonfictional/experimental film, theater arts and production, video production, visual anthropology, visual communication. Biography: B.S., Communications/Fine Arts, Syracuse University, 1969; M.A., Theater, Ohio State University, 1971; Ph.D., Communications/Film, Ohio State University, 1974.

The listing, like all others, included the faculty member's picture, current assignment, and discipline (in this case, Film/Television).

One of the factors that contribute to the students' sense of involvement in, indeed almost ownership of, the educational program is their role in curriculum development. Curriculum ideas are posted on bulletin boards throughout the campus. Students put their ideas on 3 × 5 cards and respond to the ideas placed on the boards by faculty. Students also advise deans and faculty about the shape, scope, and content of the curriculum. More importantly, students often work directly through specialty areas or individual faculty members to develop proposals for Programs.

Besides being the basic academic component of TESC, the Program is also the basis of the social community of the college. At the beginning of a Program, time is set aside to allow students to get to know one another and the faculty. One of the Evergreen traditions that is often mentioned and much appreciated is the Pot Luck dinner, frequently held in faculty homes, where everyone pitches in. Faculty also have organized retreats for Program participants.

The Program becomes the context for many other activities that would be considered "out of class" at other institutions. For example, students regularly organize and conduct Book Seminars where they will read and discuss a book related to their Program. Although the main purpose of the seminars is to examine readings in the context of Program themes, other purposes are also served. Book Seminars help students learn how to work together as a group by paying attention to issues of equivalent participation and relating to implied faculty authority. Moreover, Book Seminars engender an intense intellectual investment by students. The seminars are small, and students customarily take responsibility for certain parts of the reading and discussion. They are designed to be truly interactive and to give students practice in articulating ideas with increasing precision, in being responsible for coming to the seminar prepared, and in becoming both independent and interdependent with the group.

Core Programs. Core Programs are coordinated study programs especially planned for first-year students. While each Core Program has a unique theme, they all expose students to interdisciplinary learning, to certain learning skills, and to the Evergreen approach, which places so much responsibility on the individual student to both learn and teach, to work collaboratively, and to shed any need for competitiveness when it comes to academic performance.

Individual Learning Contracts. Individual Learning Contracts are examples of a student and faculty member working collaboratively. The contract may include reading, writing, painting, photography, research, field studies — any activity that involves the student in what he or she will need to study. These are more common for more advanced students with well-defined goals. Internships are similar to Individual Learning Contracts. There is a one-to-one relationship with a faculty member but also with a field supervisor, usually the student's sponsor at the work site.

Evergreen is a college that puts first things first — learning in an interdisciplinary mode to ensure an integrated experience. Evergreen deliberately avoids the usual tendency to carve students into intellectual (or cognitive) beings on one part, and feeling (or affective) beings on the other, and then dividing their labors along those lines. To the contrary, this college gives meaning to the idea that students are whole persons who think and feel. Consequently, students are recognized and responded to as individuals, take responsibility for their own education, and become autonomous learning partners with their faculty.

Having noted the above, one can find few examples of things at TESC that compete with the academic program. Since many of the students are of traditional age, it is not surprising that they and counselors and faculty report that developing interpersonal relationships is high on students' agendas. All of the learning and trauma that ordinarily accompany this age group are here in full measure as they learn about making, sustaining, and ending relationships. As one faculty member put it, "Around here one does not casually greet a student with the query, 'How are you doing?' unless you are prepared to invest at least forty-five minutes to hearing and discussing the answer."

Summary

The small Involving Colleges in this study are distinctive. Berea is one of only a handful of colleges with a labor program. Quaker traditions permeate campus life at Earlham in countless ways. Grinnell College incorporates individual decision making in academic and out-of-class life. The special missions of Mount Holyoke, a college for women, and Xavier, the only historically black Catholic college in the Western hemisphere, provide powerful learning environments for their students. Evergreen remains an alternative college, true to its founding principles.

Not all colleges have such distinctive missions, nor are all dominated by traditional-age (eighteen to twenty-three) students in residence. For the most part, the colleges and universities described in this chapter, and in Chapter Eight, enroll traditional-age undergraduate students who have moved away from their parents' home to attend college and who probably will move away from the college after graduation. In the next chapter, we will examine how student learning and personal development can be encouraged at urban, commuter colleges.

10

Urban Institutions

One of the most powerful factors shared by the four urban institutions in this study (University of Louisville, Wichita State University, University of North Carolina, Charlotte, and University of Alabama, Birmingham) is the degree to which they take advantage of their setting (Chapter Five). By establishing partnerships with local business, industry, schools, and other community agencies, urban institutions make learning opportunities throughout the metropolitan area accessible to students. Further, when an urban institution shares its resources with the city, the quality of life for all residents, including students, is enhanced. For example, it is common for students and faculty to participate in community-sponsored musical organizations and take advantage of fine arts performances and exhibitions. Students at urban universities often participate in public service projects and other forms of voluntarism coordinated by off-campus agencies. Commuter students attending urban institutions often remain active in the religious organizations of which they were members prior to college and continue to participate in other community organizations.

The converse is true at residential campuses, particularly those geographically removed from metropolitan areas. Rather than suggesting, for example, that students seeking an outlet for their musical talents join the city or town orchestra, such colleges encourage students to become involved in musical groups sponsored by the institution. While some learning experiences are available through off-campus activities, such ac-

240

tivities tend to be fewer in number and variety at a college in a geographically isolated area than what one can find in a city.

To succeed in encouraging students at urban institutions to take advantage of learning opportunities available off campus as well as on campus, the institution's mission, which emphasizes service to the metropolitan area in which the university is located, must be understood and appreciated. Examples are given of how these institutions couple their own resources with those available in the city to promote student learning, and how the institution takes into account the characteristics of students when setting expectations for performance and creating early warning systems and safety nets to help students succeed.

University of Louisville

Out-of-class learning at the University of Louisville is an institutional priority. This is exemplified by the commitment of the University Board of Trustees to enhance the quality of undergraduate life. The board is composed of twenty members, seventeen of whom are appointed by the governor and three of whom are elected: a student (student government association president), a faculty member (head of the faculty senate), and a staff representative. It is not unusual for trustees to take calls from students and city leaders and residents about matters related to the university. In fact, the first program described (Tender Loving Care) was initiated by the trustees. The second is the Center for Academic Achievement.

Tender Loving Care. The University of Louisville has made a conscious effort to direct resources to new students, a characteristic of other successful Involving Colleges. For example, the Tender Loving Care (TLC) effort was initiated in 1987 to increase retention of new and at-risk students. Tender Loving Care was suggested by the then-chair of the board of trustees, George Fischer:

The trustees were concerned about attrition so we set up an ad hoc committee to brainstorm with several groups to address this issue. Out of that came several recommendations that culminated in the TLC program. We wanted to send the message that student success was very important and that all of us — faculty, staff, trustees — were here for only one reason — to help students succeed, and that the university should do everything it can to address that goal, before students get here and after they get here. And we targeted funds for those programs. In short, we're trying to effect a total change in attitude, a cultural change, with regard to the attrition issue, particularly for freshmen.

Although no one aspect of the college environment can be manipulated to reduce attrition, a responsive attitude on the part of faculty and staff which says "we care" and "students matter" is important. Thus, TLC is intended to create a welcoming, friendly atmosphere, enhance student-faculty interaction outside the classroom, and increase communication with new students throughout the first year.

Various interventions (Welcome Stations, Welcome Houses, special events for first-year students such as a Freshman Night, and a pizza party at the Red Barn) were instituted as part of TLC. Other aspects of the TLC initiative included painted sidewalks directing students to important destinations, apples and cookies at snack stations, and exam posts during the year where coffee and cookies are available to students as they move from one exam location to another.

Faculty can also obtain funds ($200) under the auspices of TLC to support interaction with students outside the classroom. One faculty member had students to her home for piano juries; this provided an opportunity for students to practice in front of peers. One serendipitous outcome was that music students, who tend to have few group classes because much of the instruction is individualized, came to know one another. Another faculty member had a "Bring Your Own Rock Party" during which students from the physical sciences were asked to discuss various properties of the rocks they brought to the event. The biology department has used TLC funds to take classes to the city zoo.

Designed to personalize a large university for newcomers, many of whom are older and first-generation college students, the TLC program illustrates how an institution uses resources to meet the special needs of entering students. Approximately $146,000 was spent in the first year. A telephone poll evaluation of the program produced some information about the impact of the program and also resulted in some modifications for subsequent years. In general, TLC seems to have had a positive impact on the campus climate; student retention has improved.

Center for Academic Achievement. Established in 1984, the Center for Academic Achievement assists students in the development of basic skills and problem-solving techniques. It was originally called the Retention Center, but students suggested that the name be changed to reflect more accurately the aspirations and abilities of students. For example, the center offers programs that encourage students to explore different academic fields and participate in career awareness activities. While the center was funded initially with desegregation funds, center programs and services are now available to nonminority students. The center offers three tracks of programs: financial, tutorial, and faculty mentoring.

Tuition remission scholarships are available to qualified students who earn a 3.0 grade point average, as are supplemental aid and work-incentive funds. Work incentives allow students to apply for additional aid in the form of campus-assisted work in areas consistent with their interests, skills, and schedule requirements.

The tutorial track has two programs: Supplemental Instruction and Directed Academic Study Hours (a series of review sessions for a specific class). Supplemental Instruction meets the needs of students enrolled in high-risk courses (those in which 30 percent of regularly admitted students earn a "D" or "F" or withdraw) by providing instructional assistance before students encounter academic difficulty. Supplemental Instruction is now available for about thirty courses. The Directed Academic Study Hours (DASH) program is supervised academic study individually designed for students. One or two hours of small group tutorials are available on a daily basis, and students can receive individual tutoring as needed.

The University of Louisville has great expectations for its students and expects them to succeed academically. The various programs provided under the auspices of the Center for Academic Achievement serve as both a transitional bridge for students by providing them with the academic skills necessary for college-level work and an early warning system to identify students who are encountering difficulty with academic demands.

The Wichita State University

The two programs described in this section, Cooperative Education and University College, illustrate how this urban university uses its location and knowledge of its students to enrich the learning environment.

Cooperative Education. The cooperative education programs at Wichita State are, to some degree, a function of the proximity of the university to the center of commerce and industry in the state of Kansas. The partnerships that WSU has developed with the community allow students to use off-campus resources and expertise through placements in business, government, industry, and health and social agencies. Programs are individually designed, enabling students to work directly with professionals in their field while applying knowledge gained in the classroom. Opportunities occasionally are available for students to refine research methods, apply theories in actual field settings, work with advanced technology, and design original projects and research.

During the 1988–89 academic year, 911 students participated in the 300 co-op sites; over 1,000 were expected to participate in 1989–90. Placements are available in areas such as the personnel office of the corporate headquarters of Pizza Hut, management training at Ford Motor Credit, accounting at National Cash Register, the budget office of a local retirement home, the publications section of the Mid American Trade Center, and a variety of management and sales positions. The students earned an aggregate of $2.1 million in 1988–89; it was estimated that if more sites were available, an additional 700 students could be placed.

Cooperative Education offers both full-time and part-time placements. Students who select the full-time option must participate in a semester of full-time course work before entering a full-time position. Alternating full- and part-time placements allows students to remain enrolled on a full-time basis, which makes them eligible for perquisites such as access to university recreation facilities and student health benefits.

Students placed in cooperative programs must enroll in designated co-op courses and work with a faculty adviser from within the appropriate department. Each placement is assessed by the faculty adviser for its potential to provide learning relevant to the student's professional and educational goals. Academic credit, which generally counts toward university degree requirements, may be earned through co-op placements as determined by the student's faculty adviser. During the work period, students are expected to meet project requirements assigned by their adviser.

Through cooperative experiences, students learn about themselves and the world of work and where their talents and interests can be best directed. A student in real estate, for example, found that property management was a much better fit for him than sales. Students learn about marketing themselves — their strengths and weaknesses — and how to use their remaining courses to educational advantage. Corporations, aware of the impending labor shortage, use the co-op process to introduce promising students to their firm in the hope of recruiting these students to full-time positions after they graduate.

University College. The University College at Wichita State is an administrative and academic unit that provides a variety of services and resources to first-year students, academically underprepared students, students who have not selected a major, students with economic disadvantages, and first-generation college students. The number of programs offered prohibits providing lengthy descriptions of each, so a brief description of selected programs follows.

Academic advising is offered to all students who have not selected a major. A full-time staff member supervises paraprofessional advisers who are on call fifty hours per week; more than 10,000 advising contacts are made annually by paraprofessional advisers.

Specially designed orientation programs are offered to student groups often ignored by many institutions of higher education. For example, programs are offered for transfer, evening, and new nondegree adult learners. A minority mentoring program has been developed to assist in adjustment to campus life. Students of color new to the university are matched with upperclass students who maintain close contact with them.

University College offers a variety of courses, including a seminar for returning adult students, a course for intercollegiate athletes designed to facilitate their adjustment to the university environment, and courses in career exploration and reading and study skills. The Parents' Course is offered for parents of entering students. Using readings and audio tapes, the course provides parents with information about what to expect during their child's first semester of college. Parents are eligible to participate in activities on campus and they may earn credit for the course. Scholarships are available to defray up to 50 percent of the tuition cost.

The Skills Enhancement Institute for College Students (SEICS) course is a safety net of sorts for students who have been dismissed by the university for academic reasons but wish to continue their education. Students must complete the course before they are eligible to resume their studies.

These programs and courses speak to some of the specific, unique needs of Wichita State students that are met by University College. Having one unit deliver all these programs and services is administratively efficient. Moreover, by placing support services and learning opportunities in an office focused on the needs of entering students, University College functions in part as an early warning system for students who are experiencing problems in meeting the institution's high expectations for academic performance.

University of North Carolina, Charlotte

The roots of the University of North Carolina, Charlotte (UNCC), reach back to 1946 with the establishment of the Charlotte Center of the University of North Carolina. The number of World War II veterans seeking educational opportunities was the impetus for the creation of the Charlotte Center and a number of other centers around the state. The Charlotte Center later became Charlotte Community College and was supported by local property taxes during the 1950s. In the early 1960s, Charlotte Community College added junior and senior classes and, in 1965, the University of North Carolina, Charlotte, was created. D. W. Colvard was the first chancellor. E. K. Fretwell was appointed as the second chancellor in 1978 and served until 1989. He was succeeded by James Woodward, the former senior vice-president of the University of Alabama, Birmingham. Located in the largest urban area of North Carolina, UNCC is not the prototype urban institution in that many of its students come from outside the Charlotte area and a number of them live in residence halls or in apartments close to the campus. At the same time, UNCC shares a number of characteristics with other urban Involving Colleges.

For example, the university is involved in the community through its relationship with the adjacent University Research Park (which includes IBM, Allstate, AT&T, the *Wall Street Journal,* Union Oil, and a number of computer firms) and it is one of five component campuses in the Microelectronics Center of North Carolina. Affiliated with both the research park and UNCC is University Place, a developing city with office space, residential areas, a conference facility, a shopping center, recreation areas, and green space. Two programs that take advantage of the relationship between the city and the university are described here: Service-Learning internships and leadership development programs.

Service-Learning Internships. Service-Learning internships are designed to provide learning opportunities for students while meeting the needs of the community. The program was started in 1969 after a visit to the campus by representatives from the Southern Regional Education Board (SREB). The SREB suggested that UNCC develop a program that would involve students in service to the community. University faculty and administrators recognized the learning opportunities inherent in this idea and began the program.

Some of the organizations in the community that serve as sites for UNCC interns include community centers, environmental action groups, the city of Charlotte, Mecklenburg County offices, social service organizations, United Way, the court system, and the district attorney's office. In 1988–89, requests for UNCC interns were received from thirty-five more community organizations than could be accommodated.

Interns typically receive three to six credits for their service. For three credits they must work 120 hours; for six credits the amount of service is 240 hours. In a given year, 20 to 25 percent of the internships carry cash stipends. Upon completion of the service project, the students must submit a report to the faculty member supervising the experience. This program illustrates a UNCC–City of Charlotte partnership that results in an excellent learning experience for students and valuable service for the community.

The success of the Service-Learning Program is contingent on the relationships established between UNCC and the city of Charlotte. The partnership between the institution and the city is another illustration of how an Involving College can take advantage of its setting to create off-campus learning opportunities consistent with the mission of the institution.

Leadership Development Programs. A comprehensive approach to leadership development has been developed for UNCC students. Instructors for these programs include student affairs administrators, faculty, and community leaders.

Designed for freshmen, the Emerging Leaders Program is offered twice a semester. The program consists of a two-day retreat and weekly sessions for ten weeks for 80 to 100 students. The program introduces students to UNCC resources and leadership concepts. Topics covered in the course include the history of UNCC, self-assessment of leadership style, and conflict resolution.

The Leaderworks Program is offered for transfer students and other student leaders and provides a more in-depth view of leadership than the Emerging Leaders Program. Serving about forty students, Leaderworks meets one afternoon a week for nine weeks. Students learn how to market their leadership skills both on and off campus, to recruit and retain members, and to delegate authority and responsibility. Students also address other issues related to leadership, such as ethics.

The Leadershop Program is offered for students who are unable to participate in ongoing leadership programs but are still interested in developing their leadership skills. Leadershop consists of a six-hour program that includes twenty interest sessions as well as an address by the chancellor. Among the topics included are how to complete one's education and be a student leader, advising styles, and effective communication skills. Sixty-eight students participated in the program in 1989.

The Leadership Theory and Group Dynamics course is offered in two sections of approximately twenty-four students each. It provides an in-depth look at the dynamics of leadership, including leadership theory, learning styles, power, and ethics. Simulations and role-playing are important pedagogical features of the course. Any student may take the course, but usually one-third to one-half are education majors.

In addition to the programs described, the office of the dean of students consults regularly with student groups and academic departments on leadership development issues. The involvement of community leaders, such as bank executives, in the leadership programs at UNCC provides an important tie between the university and Charlotte.

The various leadership development programs offered by UNCC introduce students to the ways in which offices of the university operate. By encouraging students to take responsibility for themselves and their peers, UNCC's approach to leadership development is an illustration of the benefits of spending less time designing and implementing programs for students and more time encouraging students to take advantage of learning opportunities available in the institution and the city.

University of Alabama, Birmingham

The University of Alabama, Birmingham (UAB), is a relatively young institution that developed out of the state medical school in Birmingham, Alabama. During the first half of this century, the University of Alabama, from the Tuscaloosa campus, offered educational programs in six cities including Birmingham. The Birmingham center opened in 1936. The medical program was started after World War II and has evolved into one of the foremost medical complexes in the world. The Birmingham operations (medical school and educational center) of the University of Alabama were consolidated in 1966 creating UAB, a comprehensive university. In 1969 the University of Alabama campuses in Birmingham and Huntsville became independent institutions within the University of Alabama system with their own administrative structures and presidents. More than one-fifth of the state's population resides within twenty-five miles of the UAB campus, which is located within six blocks of downtown Birmingham. In addition to providing educational opportunities, UAB is the largest employer in Birmingham. Two initiatives are described here: an orientation simulation and the institution's honors program.

Orientation Simulation. As part of the 1988 summer orientation program, UAB introduced an activity that simulates an academic year to acquaint students with the typical diversions that can detract from academic performance. The simulation is run by the Blazer Crew, a group of orientation paraprofessionals trained in the usual matters related to institutional life. They also receive an introduction to basic interpersonal skills, which helps in debriefing student participants after the simulation.

Four sessions of the simulation are offered; each session

can accommodate up to 225 students. An entire academic semester is condensed into forty-five minutes, during which students are given tasks to complete, such as using the library to discover certain facts related to a scientific experiment or listening to a tape-recorded lecture. While students are completing their tasks, various diversions are introduced. Diversions range from opportunities to listen to music or attend a basketball game to coming down with an illness.

After the simulation, the students discuss their experience for about an hour in small groups never exceeding twenty. Topics discussed include the purpose of the experience, what students learned from the simulation, and how to cope with diversions. Evaluations of the simulation are very positive; approximately 75 percent of the participants rated it as the best event of the orientation program. While the long-term influence of the simulation has yet to be determined, this activity serves its purpose of making students aware of the need to emphasize academic performance over competing interests.

The orientation simulation is another example of how an urban institution can make newcomers feel welcome and create appropriate expectations for college life. In addition to establishing high expectations for academic performance, UAB also provides opportunities for students to acquire the skills needed to succeed academically. In this sense, UAB has made a conscious effort to allocate resources to ensure the success of entering students.

Honors Program. The UAB Honors Program was initiated in 1983 to bring students and faculty together in an intensive interdisciplinary curriculum. The program is also a community of students and faculty whose "home away from home" is Honors House, an old church located in the center of the UAB campus. Honors House is the location of Honors Program classes and other instructional activities, as well as the social life of the program. House facilities include a computer room, kitchen, library, pool table, and places for students to study and talk.

Honors Program courses substitute for the Core Curric-

ulum normally required of UAB undergraduates. The core of
the Honors Program is interdisciplinary course work. A nine-
credit honors course, taught each fall by faculty members from
various disciplines, is offered only to Honors Program students.
This course focuses on a single theme or issue from an interdisciplinary perspective. The honors course for 1988 was "Sex,
Race, Class, and Ideology: Conflict and Compromise," an examination of human rights issues within American society taught
by faculty from sociology, English, history, management, curriculum and instruction, and foreign languages. Honors Program students must take three of the interdisciplinary courses
to remain in the program.

The Honors Program participants also take three honors seminars, courses on special topics that are open to non-Honors Program students as well. Recent honors seminars included "Intuition and Proof in Mathematics," "Choosing Battles—What Is
Worth a Fight?," "Language and Law," and "What's So Funny:
American Humor in the Twentieth Century." These courses
are also taught by faculty throughout the university who take
an interdisciplinary approach to the issues they address.

The Honors Program curriculum includes guest lectures
(the First Thursday Lecture Series is open to high school students from the Birmingham community), field trips to scientific and cultural events, discussion groups, community service,
and social activities. Students are responsible for planning and
implementing many of these events and provide assistance to
the program with recruitment and fund-raising, by means of
yard sales and recycling.

The small size of the Honors Program (about ninety students) and the nature of its curriculum facilitate extensive and
intensive interaction between students and faculty and among
students. Students describe the program as "a family" that includes students and faculty. The Honors Program, then, provides a sense of community and belonging for students who are,
for the most part, commuters. In addition, the program promotes out-of-class interactions between students and faculty
across disciplines, something that is difficult to do at an urban
campus.

Any UAB student is eligible to apply for the Honors Program, and selections (approximately thirty students per year) are made on the basis of demonstrated academic ability and creativity, competence in basic skills, intellectual potential, evidence of leadership or other talent, instructor recommendations, and a personal interview. The interview is more important than such traditional indicators of ability as grade point average or test scores because the Honors Program seeks students who are curious and creative, ask questions, take risks, and are committed to a "total education." Honors Program students have included Rhodes Scholarship finalists, Truman Scholars, members of academic and leadership honoraries, and literary and science prize winners.

Honors students are a diverse group by design; scholarships are available to encourage older students and students of color to participate. The diversity of the Honors Program reflects the diversity of the UAB student body — traditional age and older adult learners; students who have been academically successful and those who are "late bloomers"; students of varied racial, ethnic, economic, cultural, and educational backgrounds; and commuting and residential students — and, like UAB, the program brings them together to achieve a common educational purpose. In this way, the Honors Program is consistent with the mission of the university: to meet the educational needs of Birmingham by providing a wide array of programs to serve a wide array of people.

Like UAB, the Honors Program is new — one of many new and emerging traditions at the university. Honors students and faculty are still creating the Honors Program, shaping it to fit the needs of an urban university, its people, and its surroundings, yet also forming an intimate and rigorous learning community. The director, a member of the English faculty, referred to the Honors Program as a "small liberal arts college experience within a large urban university," the best, perhaps, of both worlds. Indeed, it is not possible for an Honors student to remain anonymous given the amount of interaction that is encouraged by the program. In this sense, the Honors Program is an example of how an urban university can create a human-scale environment for some of its students.

Summary

The four urban institutions in this study are located in the largest metropolitan area of their respective states. In addition, they all have relatively short histories as institutions in their present form. While the University of Louisville and Wichita State have histories that date back to the 1800s, they have been institutions with urban missions for twenty-five years or less. All of the institutions experienced significant growth during the 1970s, reflected by increasing amounts of state aid and growing numbers of students and faculty. Managing growth was a constant challenge for their administrators in the 1970s.

The emphasis given to students' out-of-class experiences is a relatively recent phenomenon at several of these institutions. For example, John Jones, the chief student affairs officer at UAB at the time this study was conducted, was brought to the campus in the 1970s to organize a student affairs divison. The same can be said of the University of Louisville. After receiving encouragement from the Southern Regional Education Board, the institution appointed its first vice president for student affairs in the 1970s. Hence, not only are the urban institutions relatively young with respect to their development as universities, but the division of student affairs is even younger.

For a variety of reasons, students at urban institutions are less likely to participate in a substantial number of out-of-class experiences on campus. Because of their commitments off campus, such as full-time jobs and families, students often can participate in only one or two institution-sponsored activities. This is in stark contrast to residential college students, who are often involved in their place of residence (residence hall or Greek house), departmental organizations, recreational sports, and, perhaps, as volunteers. Too often, there is a tendency on the part of those responsible for out-of-class life at urban colleges and universities to neglect students' out-of-class lives because the students are perceived to be "too busy" or "not interested." However, for many students at urban Involving Colleges, learning outside of the classroom has great potential to enrich their lives and their education.

PART THREE

===

Developing Opportunities for Student Involvement

Colleges and universities are complex organizations, often rich with symbolism and tradition. Each is unique. Some attract more academically able students than others; some are more affluent than others and have better-documented or, perhaps, more frequently invoked histories and more clearly defined constituent groups which provide stability in turbulent times. Some benefit from student cultures that value educationally purposeful behavior, while other institutions — for various reasons not always easy to identify — must cope with students and student groups that behave in ways antithetical to the institution's educational purposes.

This study was based on the assumption that some colleges and universities provide unusually rich out-of-class learning and personal development opportunities for undergraduate students. After observing first-hand the environments at Involving Colleges, and talking with hundreds of students, faculty members, and administrators, we are confident that many other colleges and universities can enhance student learning by examining and, if appropriate, adapting to their setting and students the policies, practices, and other elements that have been effective at Involving Colleges. The factors and conditions that characterize Involving Colleges are summarized below.

255

Factors and Conditions Common to Involving Colleges

Involving Colleges expend considerable effort to encourage students to take advantage of institutional resources. Efforts are directed to: communicating expectations that students fully participate in the life of the institution; creating opportunities for and removing obstacles to student involvement in their own education; and encouraging students to be responsible for the quality of their living and out-of-class learning environments. Student learning is promoted by creating numerous contexts, such as residences, governing bodies, and work, in which students can take significant responsibility for their lives and education.

The factors and conditions shared to varying degrees by the fourteen institutions participating in this study can be divided into five categories: mission and philosophy, campus environment, campus culture, policies and practices, and institutional agents.

Mission and Philosophy

Involving Colleges are "one thing to all people." That is, members of various constituent groups (current and former students, faculty members, administrators) understand and can describe — in their own words — what the institution is trying to accomplish. The *means* (policies, practices, standard operating procedures) through which an institution enacts its mission are consistently expressed. A clear, coherent, and sometimes distinctive institutional mission communicates "great expectations" for students — clear, high but reasonable, challenges — buttressed by an ethic of care. Status differences and interpersonal distinctions are deliberately accentuated or minimized to attain the institution's mission and educational purposes. Programs and services serve as "levelers" and "ladders" to increase students' chances for academic success and satisfaction. The institution's unwavering commitment to celebrating, encouraging, and enabling multiple subcommunities is symbolized through strong statements about the value of individual and group differences.

Noncurricular programs and services complement the institution's educational purposes, suggesting that "we're all headed in the same direction."

Campus Culture

There is "something special" about an Involving College. The institutional culture and dominant subcultures promote involvement and a sense of ownership among institutional participants. An ethic of membership communicates to students that "this is your home." Once matriculated, students are treated as full members of the community and are expected to attain their educational objectives while participating fully in the life of the institution. Student- and institution-sponsored rituals, ceremonies, and traditions reinforce the importance of involvement and communicate important institutional values and expectations. "Terms of endearment" (institution-specific language) are used by students and others to encourage feelings of belonging and being a full member of the institution. Stories about heroes and heroines are told with affection and reverence to illustrate institutional values and expectations for student, faculty, and administrator behavior. All the elements described—in addition to the shaping influences of regional and local cultures—create a shared understanding of how the institution works, what is valued, and how to get things done.

Campus Environment

The institution uses the properties of its location to educational advantage. Whether located in a rural area or in the midst of a major metropolitan area, an Involving College proclaims, "this is a good place for a college." Involving Colleges are human-scale organizations that create "small spaces and human places" by making certain that: (1) the physical plant is well maintained and not overpowering; (2) the psychological size—the "feel" of the place—is appropriate, comfortable, and manageable so that small colleges seem larger than they are and large universities seem smaller; (3) students are not anonymous; (4) indoor and outdoor nooks and crannies encourage informal, spontaneous interaction among all community members; (5) students can appropriate personal space and be alone if desired; and (6) opportunities for meaningful involvement are in ample supply, such as leadership positions and other roles of responsibility in major-related and social clubs and organizations, recreation, campus jobs, and off-campus work or internships.

Policies and Practices

In general, institutional policies and practices are consistent with the institution's mission and values. An Involving College makes a concerted effort to help newcomers feel welcome while at the same time articulating what the institution stands for. It is as if an Involving College says to each student, "Welcome, we've been expecting you. You are one of us." Institutional anticipatory socialization processes help prospective students and other constituents know and understand what it is like to be a student there. Prospective students receive enough information from the institution to know "if I will fit in here" and "if there are people here like me" and learn what will be expected of them when they arrive. Induction activities, both formal — such as major-related and institution-sponsored new student orientation programs — and informal events and activities carried out by student subcultures or living groups model appropriate behavior and communicate standards for both social and academic performance.

Students are trusted and expected to be responsible. Boundaries between in-class and out-of-class experiences are blurred. Small subcommunities of students are intentionally established to create "a home away from home" for all students.

By allocating resources in ways consistent with educational purposes, Involving Colleges "put their money where their *mind* is." Students participate in allocating resources and must grapple with the tough choices forced by finite resources. Trade-offs, such as discontinuing funding for certain activities in order to support new initiatives, are acknowledged and debated.

Institutional Agents

Involving Colleges are like other types of successful organizations in some respects. Institutional agents reflect characteristics of leaders of high-performing systems (Vaill, 1984) in that they are willing to take a long-term view and devote more than eight-hour days and five-day weeks to their job, have a deep affective commitment to the institution and their work, and are focused on the important elements of their work and the institution's purposes.

Administrators. The president provides symbolic leadership by communicating the institutional mission and priorities as well as a vision for the institution to constituents, including students. The role of the out-of-class life of students is often emphasized by the president through speeches, during orientation, and in written material distributed to students, parents, graduates, and others.

The chief academic officer (CAO) may be detached from student life, although most CAOs acknowledge the importance of a mutually enhancing relationship between out-of-class life and the curricular goals of the institution. The degree to which out-of-class experiences are considered important by the CAO is influenced by the ability of the chief student affairs officer (CSAO) to articulate the contributions of student life to the academic mission of the institution and by the personal relationship between the CAO and the CSAO.

Student affairs staff have a broad view of higher education and understand how in-class and out-of-class experiences are complementary. They are energetic and enthusiastic, are sensitive and committed to the institutional mission, and understand how the mission can be accomplished in student life. Student affairs staff are the heart of the early warning system and safety nets that signal the need to assist students who are in academic, social, emotional, or physical difficulty. These same supports encourage students to take responsibility, take risks, and learn about themselves as well as those different from themselves. At some institutions, particularly large universities, student affairs staff have become the caretakers of the collegiate culture as faculty members immerse themselves in research and publication activity.

Faculty Members. Student-faculty interaction out of class, when it occurs, is often directly or indirectly related to academic activities and concerns. Contact is "after class," pursuing points made during class discussions. Students perceive faculty to be available and involved with them, particularly in the academic area; those students who develop relationships with faculty out of class usually have taken the initiative to do so. Two faculty cultures exist as far as out-of-class life is concerned: those who are committed to involvement with undergraduates and those who are not. On balance, faculty members at Involving Colleges are satisfied with their work and their institution; they are committed to the students with whom they work and some give their time and talents to undergraduates in extraordinary ways.

Other Institutional Agents. Trustees, alumni and alumnae, and support staff also make important contributions to establishing and maintaining an environment that promotes student learning and personal development. By offering support and encouragement to students, faculty, and others, they derive a sense of satisfaction and accomplishment in helping the institution attain its purposes and contribute to student learning.

Students

"Involving" student subcultures promote student behavior compatible with the institution's educational purposes. Student groups perpetuate important campus traditions of involvement. At some institutions, such as Miami, Grinnell, Earlham, and Mount Holyoke, the vast majority of students are of traditional age (eighteen to twenty-three years old). At the urban institutions, students tend to be more heterogeneous in age, ability, and educational aspirations. Students at Involving Colleges: know how the institution works; perceive their in-class and out-of-class lives to be seamless; take seriously the institution's expectations that students are responsible for their own lives and their own learning; may or may not have close, personal relationships with faculty members; learn as much from peers as they do from classes; and experience "resonance" with the institution in that the match between a student's expectations and intellectual ability and the demands and environmental press of the institution are congruent. Institutional agents and peers typically present enough challenges that students must expand their behavioral repertoire in order to be satisfied and successful academically and socially.

Caveats and Overview

Partitioning a college or university into what appear to be separate factors and conditions does not acknowledge the holistic nature of an institution of higher education as a learning enterprise. The elements of an Involving College are woven together and mutually shaping; missions, campus environments, institutional cultures, policies and practices, and people work together to promote student involvement. To isolate one for emphasis is to overlook the symbiotic relationship among the parts of the whole.

The factors and conditions common to individual Involving Colleges are context bound and are, therefore, not generalizable. Because something — a program or policy — works (or seems to work) in one setting does not mean it will be effective in another. However, the principles on which the factors and conditions are based are *transportable* because institutional agents in other settings can reflect on how these ideas can be adapted to, and make the best use of, the learning opportunities present in their institution's context.

At the least, these factors and conditions should stimulate discussion about what they would or could look like on another campus. This study will be only partially successful if a lot of "creative swiping" (Peters, 1987, p. 78) does not occur. We hope that many institutions will see utility in many of these ideas and adapt them for use on their own campuses.

Before institutions can take action with regard to any of these factors and conditions, their current state of affairs must be understood. Chapter Eleven presents some principles for conducting institutional audits designed to discover the out-of-class learning and personal development opportunities an institution provides. Chapters Twelve through Fourteen discuss the implications of institutional mission, campus environment, and policies and practices that institutional auditors — as well as other faculty, administrators, staff, students, and others — should consider when conducting an involvement audit. In Chapter Fifteen, conclusions from the study are presented and recommendations are made for institutional agents committed to improving the conditions for student involvement. Some unresolved issues related to student involvement and community on campus are discussed.

Because institutional culture influences all aspects of a college or university, the cultural implications of our findings are incorporated in each chapter rather than presented separately. When going through the implications and recommendations, the reader should think about how the questions, issues, and challenges posed in this section can be used in his or her institution.

11

Discovering
Institutional Strengths:
The Campus Audit

Automobile clubs provide maps, sometimes called "triptiks," that clearly mark the most direct or most scenic route from the traveler's point of departure to the desired destination, as well as all roads, turns, detours, refueling points, intermediate stops, and recommended lodging. Because institutions of higher education are constantly evolving and complex organizations, it is impossible to provide a triptik, or a step-by-step process, for transforming a college or university into an Involving College. Although we have a pretty good idea about what the destination — an Involving College — looks like, we cannot prescribe exactly how an institution can get there. Nor can we say precisely what form learning and personal development opportunities, or the environment that supports them, will (or should) take at a particular college or university. Moreover, we do not propose that one best Involving College model exists for providing high-quality out-of-class learning opportunities.

In the previous chapters, we have described a constellation of factors and conditions (mission and philosophy, campus environment, campus culture, policies and practices, institutional agents) that seem to encourage a high level of student participation in the life of the institution and in their own education. In this chapter, we begin with some general comments about campus audits. Then we provide a guide—in the form of eleven principles—that institutional agents can use in order to figure out what their own institution is and does. As with many developmental journeys, the first step to becoming an Involving College is self-discovery.

The Audit Process

The process of institutional discovery is described here as a "campus audit," and persons who undertake it are called "campus auditors," even though the audit may focus on only one or several aspects or subunits of the institution. This terminology implies that the discovery process requires systematic (yet open-ended) effort, and reflects the depth and breadth of scrutiny required to understand a college or university.

Although institutional assessment is becoming increasingly important (Ewell, 1985; Marchese, 1987), frameworks have not been developed to guide institutional agents in assessing the quality of the out-of-class experience. The eleven principles described in this chapter were distilled from our experience as well as that of others (see Chaffee and Tierney, 1988; Clark, 1970; Kuh and Whitt, 1988; Morgan, 1986; Schein, 1985; Van Maanen, 1979a, 1979b, 1988) who have studied and written about colleges and universities as organizational cultures. The principles are intended to serve as general guidelines for institutional discovery and understanding when used in concert with the more specific questions for guiding audits contained in the Involving College Audit Protocol (ICAP, Resource E).

Principles for Institutional Discovery

Principle 1: Culture is both the lens through which institutional participants interpret and make meaning of their world and "the glue that binds an institution" (Kuh and Whitt, 1988, p. 96); *therefore, to understand an institution, first understand its culture.*

Cultural aspects of an institution play an important role in shaping its character. According to Chaffee and Tierney (1988, p. 7):

> The most fundamental construct of an organiza-
> tion, as of a society, is its culture. An organization's
> culture is reflected in what is done, why it is done,
> how it is done, and who is involved in doing it. It
> concerns decisions, actions, and communication
> both on an instrumental and a symbolic level.

Aspects of the culture of Involving Colleges were described
in Chapter Four as well as in other chapters. We concluded that
high-quality experiences that promote student learning are guiding cultural values at Involving Colleges, values that are expressed and maintained in institutional mission, philosophy, history, traditions, and other cultural artifacts.

We also described the complexity inherent in using cultural perspectives to study organizations, as can be seen in the
following descriptions of culture: culture is context-bound; culture is constantly evolving; culture is not always visible to its
participants; and an institution's culture is a composite of several
subcultures. Although the process of understanding an institution's culture is complicated, it is not impossible, as the following principles illustrate.

*Principle 2: A campus audit of opportunities for student learning
can begin almost anywhere in the institution, focusing, for example, on
the mission, or the environment, or policies and practices, or institutional
agents.*
Conducting a campus audit is somewhat like word pro-
cessing. One can begin entering information at almost any point
in the document. As one reflects on the implications of the information being gathered and entered, information can be aug-
mented, deleted, modified, or moved to enhance the quality,
precision, and coherence of the presentation.

For example, auditors might conclude that the institution's mission and philosophy are communicated clearly to relevant constituencies and so elect to focus first on identifying
aspects of institutional culture or certain groups of institutional
agents that promote student behavior consistent with the institution's educational purposes. As the audit unfolds, the institu-

tional mission might be reexamined in light of discoveries about the culture or roles of institutional agents. Symbolic actions on the part of the president or faculty members may or may not be consistent with the mission. Similarly, campus rituals and traditions may inhibit attainment of the institution's educational purposes. Thus, auditors studying student involvement in learning could begin their work at any point in the institution, or with any of the factors and conditions common to Involving Colleges. A pertinent caveat is, however, presented in the next principle.

Principle 3: The factors and conditions that contribute to high-quality opportunities for student learning are inextricably linked; none of the factors is separable from the others, nor will focusing attention on one, or even a few, produce an Involving College.

Mission and philosophy, policies and practices, campus environments, institutional cultures, and institutional agents work together in different ways in different places to create educational experiences that are distinctive to each institution. For example, while the institution's mission serves as a rudder, helping the institution stay on course, the mission is effective in that role only to the extent that the institution behaves in ways consistent with the mission. Therefore, encouraging a higher degree of student involvement is a task for all functional areas of, and all people in, the institution.

Principle 4: An institution and its cultures must be examined from the perspectives of its members to create a complex, comprehensive description of the institution.

Discovery and understanding demand that auditors develop a picture that is "thick in description and rich in nuance" (Chaffee and Tierney, 1988, p. 14). Therefore, auditors must resist the impulse to reduce complexity by focusing only on certain types of people, experiences, or opinions, or moving quickly to draw conclusions from the first stories they hear. Auditors should listen to what is said but also probe for the meaning of what is offered. They must be sensitive to what is not heard. Silence often communicates a message—disengagement, fear, hurt, bitterness, fatigue, or uncertainty. Silence may also communicate a lack of awareness. To interpret silence as, for example, evidence of satisfaction or dissatisfaction without exploring the reasons underlying silence may lead to erroneous conclusions. Further, a silent student (or faculty or staff member) has thoughts and feelings that are necessary to understand if an accurate portrayal of the institution is to be developed. The challenge for institutional auditors is to try to understand what people are not saying as much as what they are saying. For example, students often respond to issues of diversity and pluralism with silence. Auditors must gather as many and as diverse — even contradictory — perspectives of the institution as is possible.

The audit team should attempt to create settings in which participants can express their feelings and viewpoints to promote better understanding throughout the institution. One way to do this is with the use of focus groups. The purpose of focus group discussions is to share one's point of view and to listen to the views of others, not to negotiate demands or pursue one's personal agenda (although this does happen at times). When appropriately facilitated, a focus group can generate information that will be useful in discovering beliefs and perceptions held by various groups. When focus groups are created, they must include representatives of historically underrepresented groups, such as adult learners, women, and people of color. To promote free and open sharing of ideas, participants should be encouraged to make their first response one of seeking to understand and to suspend judgment, for a moment, in the spirit of increasing understanding and communication. One of the Quaker principles from Earlham College is worth considering as a ground rule: Do not come to a meeting (or a focus group) with your mind made up.

A variety of information-gathering techniques, such as interviews, observations, and analysis of documents, should be used as each provides different kinds of data — data that may conflict with, or confirm, other data. In addition, auditors should seek the perspectives of insiders (students, faculty, administrators, graduates, staff, and others) on the impressions, interpretations, and understandings that develop during the processes of data collection and analysis. Continuous feedback from insiders about the auditors' emerging understandings will help auditors develop a picture of the institution that accurately reflects the experiences of insiders, yet enables people outside the institution to obtain a "native"'s point of view.

Finally, producing an accurate description and understanding of a college or university demands lengthy engagement with that institution, or as lengthy as possible (Lincoln and Guba, 1985; Schein, 1985; Whitt and Kuh, 1989). The amount of time spent in the setting is influenced by: available resources, such as time, number of auditors, and money; the breadth or depth of the audit's focus, for example, an entire institution, an academic affairs division, or a residence hall; and the size and complexity of the organization under examination. Chaffee and Tierney (1988) asserted that, in order to study an institution, auditors ought to observe "a full cycle of time" (p. 14), such as an academic year. In this study, we sampled different parts of the cycle. Observing a full cycle of time enables auditors to see the beginning of the semester as well as final exam week, to observe the development of events and crises, and to talk with seniors in the fall and shortly before graduation.

Principle 5: Campus audits cannot be conducted exclusively by insiders.

Outside auditors are needed to help insiders "transcend their own immersion" (Chaffee and Tierney, 1988, p. 4) and discover what is to insiders so familiar and commonplace that it may be overlooked, or consider from a fresh perspective long-embedded and unquestioned assumptions and practices. Insiders may, for example, take for granted that the institution warmly welcomes all types of students, while outsiders may discover policies and practices that inhibit the assimilation and progress of one or another group. College publications may project an image that is no longer consistent with "reality," an issue that may be uncovered only as outsiders talk with new students who consistently describe a feeling of "not fitting in here." Insiders may point out policies and practices that encourage tolerance of differences but which, from the perspective of an outsider, seem to define what is politically or ideologically acceptable in that setting. At some institutions, students may perceive that a liberal agenda is at work. At others, faculty members may be accused of promoting tolerance to avoid confronting troublesome, unpopular, or simply inappropriate ideas. The help of insiders, however, is essential to modify the questions in the Involving College Audit Protocol (Resource E) so that they are relevant to the institution's context.

Outsiders should acknowledge, however, that they, too, have assumptions, beliefs, values, and expectations regarding what is appropriate, and cannot shed them completely when studying another institution (Masland, 1985). While the influence of these values on what an auditor sees, interprets, and understands cannot be eliminated entirely, the influence can be ameliorated by extensive and intensive focus on insiders' perspectives (Crowson, 1987; Whitt and Kuh, 1989). Again, this means that the auditors must spend considerable time in the setting, listening to the perspectives of many insiders with diverse points of view.

Principle 6: Campus audits cannot be conducted exclusively by outsiders.

This point is also reflected in Principle 4, but it cannot be overemphasized. Although experienced and open-minded outside auditors can, with time, become familiar enough with an institution to discover and understand it (Chaffee and Tierney, 1988), discovery and understanding require the assistance of insiders. If, for example, an institution's culture resides in the hearts and minds of participants, then that institution cannot be understood unless its members reveal what is *in* their hearts and minds—their attitudes, values, beliefs, and assumptions (Kuh and Whitt, 1988) about the institution in which they live and work. Outside auditors, then, need insiders to provide the primary data for the audit, to react to the auditors' emerging impressions and interpretations, and to achieve an accurate portrayal of the institution.

Also, while many insiders know a lot about their particular part of the institution, their focus may be limited to that subunit. While some insiders, such as the president or the chief academic officer, have broad knowledge and understanding of the institution as a whole, they may lack specific information about some subunits. Therefore, discovering what an institution is and how it works demands considerable commitment, effort, and contributions on the part of individuals and groups *throughout* the institution.

Although interviews are the primary sources of data for a campus audit, other sources of valuable information include documents, institutional histories, reports, handbooks, catalogues, newspapers, admissions publications, and observations of events and activities. Outside auditors should request, and study, as many relevant documents as possible prior to visiting the campus in order to become familiar with the institution as well as to generate interview questions and a list of events to observe (Dobbert, 1984; Whitt and Kuh, 1989). After spending time in the setting, auditors will learn of additional useful documents, events, and activities.

Principle 7: To discover, understand, and appreciate what encourages student involvement, auditors must "uncover the mundane as well as the more vivid aspects" (Morgan, 1986, p. 131) *of an institution's culture.*

If the focus of the audit is only on those events that are most obvious or most colorful, such as new student orientation, homecoming, or commencement, the daily routines by which institutional values and assumptions are expressed will be missed. For example, students may be told at orientation that they are expected to be responsible adults and fully participating members of the college community, but an examination of housing regulations, billing practices, and institutional decision-making processes may reveal that the institution says one thing and does another. Homecoming festivities may evoke a sense of community that is experienced only once a year. Thus, policies and practices, mission and philosophy, organizational structures, and campus environment are as much artifacts — and therefore evidence — of institutional culture, as are history, traditions, rituals, and symbols, and should be treated as such by auditors.

Principle 8: Accentuate institutional strengths by focusing on current resources and realistically appraising the institution's capacity for creating learning opportunities for students.

As campus audit teams, presidents, trustees, and other institutional agents consider what is required to maximize the conditions and factors on their campus common to Involving Colleges, their institutions will be best served by forsaking some of the practices of conventional planning, such as conducting needs assessments or emphasizing institutional limitations or obstacles to student learning out of the classroom. As Mathews (1989) observed, a powerful symbolic message often accompanies the notion of needs assessment: "You and your community are sick; you can only get well with the help of professionals who will supply what you are lacking. . . . [B]ut a sense of inadequacy only breeds inadequacy" (p. 83). Instead, institutional agents should concentrate on capacity enhancement, on identifying and taking advantage of the resources and learning opportunities already present, rather than conducting comparisons with other institutions or documenting shortfalls.

We encourage institutional agents and students to emphasize their collective strengths and capacities and not become paralyzed by "needs" that, if only they could be met, would surely promote student involvement in appropriate out-of-class activities. Campus audit teams and other institutional agents should not view their task as searching for solutions but rather as describing the variety of learning opportunities inherent in the college environment and the larger community.

Becoming an "involving" institution will not be easy for some colleges and universities. Some campuses have difficult physical obstacles to overcome, such as high-rise residences and other facilities that are far from human scale. Although identifying these and other obstacles to student involvement provides useful information, a more important task is helping institutional agents and students become aware of the possibilities and opportunities that are present in the college environment for students to become actively involved in educationally purposeful ways. By focusing on what already exists and what the institution aspires to be, a vision can be created of what a college can become.

Principle 9: Auditors must respect the integrity and distinctiveness of the institution being studied.

Auditors should avoid making generalizations to the institution under study from other experiences or organizations. For example, auditors should not assume that because a cooperative student ethos contributes to learning at institutions with which they are familiar, it is the most appropriate ethos for all students. Auditors should also avoid making evaluative judgments about the worth of particular practices, traditions, or symbols, but instead attempt to discover what they mean to different groups in that setting and how they influence attitudes and behavior (Whitt, forthcoming). A striking example is the mascot of Miami University—a Miami Indian. Because many universities have dropped Indian mascots in response to the concerns and requests of American Indian people, an outsider might assume that the Miami mascot is evidence of lack of respect for American Indian culture. However, the Miami mascot was "given" to Miami University by the Miami Indians and remains a symbol of understanding between the university and the tribe.

In addition, there are ethical issues that must be considered by institutional auditors: some institutional agents may not be prepared to accept feedback about their unit; the results of an audit may increase the institution's vulnerability, both internal (demands for rapid change, conflicts, morale problems) and external (alterations in constituent support, image problems); and the auditors' analysis could be inaccurate, and provide an incorrect basis for institutional action or public consumption (Schein, 1985). Therefore, institutional auditors have an obligation to understand the potential consequences of their work, and to protect the welfare of the institution under study (Schein, 1985). Unless otherwise negotiated, any products, such as a campus audit report, are the property of the institution, not the audit team.

Auditors must make sure that insiders understand the potential consequences, both internal and external, of self-discovery and self-revelation. An audit should not be undertaken without the consent of the participants and a commitment to confidentiality. Insiders should not be interviewed or observed without their consent, which should be based on a clear understanding of the ways in which the information obtained from them may be used (Lincoln and Guba, 1985; Whitt, forthcoming).

Auditors must also be committed to providing as accurate a portrayal of the institution as possible. As already stated, accuracy can be enhanced through prolonged engagement with the institution and by obtaining many and diverse perspectives from insiders.

Principle 10: Qualitative research methods — those that produce data in the form of words and analyze data by means of the use of human instruments, that is, the auditors — are necessary to discover and understand colleges and universities and their cultures.

Qualitative methods are particularly effective for identifying, describing, and interpreting concepts that are difficult, if not impossible, to quantify, such as the interplay of attitudes, values, beliefs, and assumptions (Goetz and LeCompte, 1984; Morgan, 1986; Van Maanen, 1979a) of administrators, faculty, and students that influence students' learning and personal development.

Assumptions underlying qualitative research methods include the following: (1) the central goal of research is understanding, rather than identifying causes or laws, proving or disproving hypotheses, or generalizing results from one study to other settings (Crowson, 1987); (2) understanding cannot be achieved without direct, first-hand experience in and knowledge of the setting under study (Van Maanen, 1979b); and (3) understanding cannot be achieved without viewing behavior, events, and actions from the perspectives of persons within the setting (Van Maanen, 1979b; Whitt and Kuh, 1989). These assumptions are compatible with the challenge of institutional self-discovery.

There are a number of detailed and helpful descriptions of methods for qualitative data collection and analysis (see Goetz and LeCompte, 1984; Lincoln and Guba, 1985; Merriam, 1988; Miles and Huberman, 1984; Spradley, 1979, 1980; Whitt and Kuh, 1989) with which institutional auditors should be familiar. Suffice it to say here that we believe the use of interviews, observations, and documents, concurrent data collection and analysis, and continuous feedback from insiders are essential to develop the rich and complex — and accurate — picture of the institution that is necessary for understanding.

On occasion, other forms of data collection, for example pencil-and-paper instruments such as the College Student Experience Questionnaire (Pace, 1984a), may be combined with the descriptions generated using qualitative methods to understand certain aspects of student involvement. Because pencil-and-paper instruments are not able to provide the depth and richness of insights needed to perform a campus audit, information from survey questionnaires should be used only as a supplement to, not a substitute for, interviews, focus groups, and other qualitative methods.

Principle 11: Campus audits can be time-consuming and expensive.

Participants — students, faculty, administrators, staff, graduates, trustees — must give of their time to talk with auditors about their experiences and perspectives. Participants should also be called upon to give feedback about the evolving institutional picture developed by the auditors: Does it fit their view of "reality?" What should be added or deleted? With what other participants should the auditors talk? Students, faculty members, administrators, and others are often very busy. Finding the time for more meetings will not be easy, but important choices must be made. If such gatherings provide useful results, the time spent will be well worth the effort.

Inside members of the audit team can expect that the audit process will consume a considerable amount of time. Outside auditors will usually require travel costs and consulting fees for their time, both on site and in preparing a report of their findings. Additional expenses might include recording equipment, typing and copying costs, meals or refreshments for institutional participants, and the like. The breadth and depth of the focus of the audit will influence the number of auditors and on-site visits by outside auditors and the amount of time required of the auditors and institutional participants.

Auditors' personal characteristics can facilitate or inhibit them in meeting the demands of institutional audits. Auditors who have experience with a variety of colleges and universities are likely to be better prepared for what they ought to look for or what they might see than those with limited experience (Whitt and Kuh, 1989). Further, auditors with broad knowledge of higher education may be more credible to faculty, administrators, students, and others in the setting, and so may elicit more useful information (Crowson, 1987). No matter what the auditors' backgrounds and experience, however, effective communication skills, both in interview and presentation settings, are a must.

A high energy level is also essential; conducting interviews, talking with people and observing events at all hours, gathering multiple and varied perspectives from insiders, and trying to understand an unfamiliar setting are exhausting. Patience and flexibility are required in working with insiders to make sure that their opinions and experiences are accurately reflected in the audit, and that a shared picture of the institution is achieved.

Auditors must also be tolerant of ambiguity. While institutional audits should be systematic, auditors must be open-minded. As one learns more about an institution, more questions and gaps in knowledge become apparent and more information is necessary to fill the gaps (Lincoln and Guba, 1985; Whitt and Kuh, 1989). In addition, nothing ever goes as planned; participants miss interviews, outdoor events are postponed because of rain, flights are delayed, tape recorder batteries expire, and an emerging campus crisis explodes the minute outside auditors arrive (Whitt and Kuh, 1989). One can only smile and be flexible, sensitive, and responsive.

Potential Salutary Effects of Audits

A campus audit that combines these principles with the questions provided in the ICAP (Resource E), and any other questions relevant to the process of learning about a particular institution, can be used by a college or university to identify current strengths and limitations relevant to the factors and conditions that contribute to student involvement in learning. In addition, a campus audit can enhance understanding about a variety of matters that may or may not seem, at first glance, to have implications for students' education, such as the condition of the physical plant or the morale of classified staff or opportunities for students to hold leadership positions.

The process of conducting an audit may, in and of itself, have salutary consequences for the institution and its participants. For example: students may feel as though they are important, that they are being heard and valued; administrators and faculty can receive accurate information that could be used in decision making; areas of conflict can be identified and, perhaps, ameliorated; students, faculty, and administrators will learn more about one another; and the feelings and ideas of people are acknowledged in what may otherwise be perceived as increasingly complex, bureaucratic, and unresponsive organizations.

Although a campus audit is time-consuming and hard work, those faculty and staff who serve on audit teams or participate in interviews will find that trying to discover and understand an area of campus life that too often receives little systematic attention is an interesting, productive use of their time. Faculty participants may be surprised to learn about the many and varied learning activities in which their students are engaged and the number of students who effectively balance multiple commitments. Most important, widespread participation in an involvement audit has the potential to enrich student learning, a goal that is often underemphasized in institutional planning and governance activities, or in the day-to-day operation of the campus.

Summary

The list of principles described here is not, by any means, complete. Each institutional audit reveals its own lessons about how the process can be accomplished more effectively. What an audit should look like varies from place to place and over time. Institutions interested in undertaking an audit should be reminded that, while there are many roads to an Involving College, none is well lighted or free of obstacles. Each does, however, offer the opportunity for a fascinating journey of self-discovery and understanding. That journey can begin right now for those who will consider the implications and recommendations provided in the following chapters in light of what they already know about their own institution and its cultures.

12

Clarifying
Institutional
Mission and Philosophy

An institution's mission provides the rationale for what a college or university is and aspires to be and the yardstick against which students, faculty, and others can determine if their activities and institutional policies are educationally purposeful. In this sense, the mission represents the ends the institution wishes to attain.

An institution's philosophy consists of values and assumptions about teaching and learning, and about how good learning communities ought to function. Values are beliefs "about the importance of certain goals, activities, relationships, and feelings" (Kuh and Whitt, 1988, p. 23). Often stated in general terms, some values are explicitly articulated and serve "a normative or moral function by guiding members' responses to situations. Most institutional values, however, are unconsciously expressed as themes" (Kuh and Whitt, 1988, p. 23). Values can be espoused (what people say they believe but may or may not actually do) and/or enacted (beliefs that people or the institution put into practice) (Argyris and Schön, 1978). Espoused values may be institutional aspirations, such as a "commitment to increasing minority representation in the student body and faculty, assertions about the importance of undergraduate instruction in research universities, and mission statements un-

277

278   Involving Colleges

derscoring [the importance of] students' holistic development"
(Kuh and Whitt, 1988, p. 25). Assumptions form the unquestioned reality of individuals within the institution — how things
get done, what the purpose of the institution is, and what is considered appropriate behavior (Berger and Luckmann, 1966) —
and undergird institutional values. Because assumptions are
widely accepted and generally not debatable, they exert considerable influence over behavior by defining and constructing
the roles to be played in the institution. Thus, an institution's
philosophy guides the process by which the institution attempts
to realize its mission.

In Chapter Three, we illustrated how the mission and
philosophy of Involving Colleges set expectations for and shape
student behavior. This chapter addresses issues that should be
considered by institutions when examining how their mission
and philosophy shape student learning and personal development.

Refocusing the Mission

While relatively stable over time, an institution's mission
may change in response to events and conditions in the external environment (Keller, 1983; Zammuto, 1986). Commitment
to mass higher education in the United States, a decreasing pool
of traditional-age students, special interests of external groups,
uncertain funding sources, and increased organizational complexity of institutions have forced many colleges and universities to attempt to be all things to all people.

The ebb and flow of institutional life can also contribute
to a shift in institutional mission. New presidents are appointed.
Expectations for faculty performance shift. Faculty and staff
come and go, as do student cohorts. At many campuses, each
year more than a third of the students enroll for the first time.
Student characteristics and academic and vocational interests
change.

When institutional missions change, conflicting messages
are often sent to students and faculty about what is expected
and valued. As an example, the agenda of a new president, with
the support of the trustees, may require changes in policies and

practices to emulate perceived "higher status" institutions, such as altering admissions standards to appeal to students of higher ability or modifying promotion and tenure criteria to seek and reward faculty members with outstanding records of research. In another instance, an institution may create merit scholarships to attract traditional-age students from beyond the institution's designated service area. While an attempt to improve the academic quality of the student body may please certain audiences, it may cause concern for others. The message to first-generation and minority students, who perceive the institution as a "bootstrap" university — a place where they can be successful and realize their dreams — may be that they have become less important to the institution.

Another example of a change in mission is the liberal arts college that begins to recruit part-time students to increase head count and tuition revenues. To attract the new student clientele the college begins to offer career-oriented studies and internships in local businesses and industries. Before long, the institution is asked to provide retraining programs for the employees of local firms. Faculty are appointed from applied fields to meet student demand and requests from local industry. Over time, the college's mission has changed.

A change in an institution's mission almost always shifts, and requires more, resources. For example, when urban institutions attract increasing numbers of traditional-age students from beyond commuting distance, more housing and residence space, and health and counseling services are needed — needs that are usually not offset by new revenues. When more part-time students enroll at residential colleges and universities, policies and practices must change, such as keeping offices open during the noon hour and evening hours to accommodate part-time students and modifying financial aid policies so that adult learners and part-time students are eligible for loans, scholarships, and on-campus employment (Shriberg, 1980). These and other issues and trends influence the institution's mission — what it is and what it would like to be.

Reaffirming Institutional Values. Gardner (1990) warned that, without constant attention by leaders and others, the core values of an organization can decay and no longer be shared by enough members to guide behavior. Taking institutional values for granted during periods of change allows for the possibility that other values will take root that are incompatible with the institution's mission and philosophy.

To keep the institutional mission in view, the mission and philosophy must be reviewed and reinterpreted in the context of current and emerging issues and challenges. Equally important, the mission must be publicly reaffirmed by institutional leaders and various constituent groups on a regular basis. Only in this way can a college or university mission remain clear and coherent and provide the desired direction for student, faculty, and staff behavior.

Discovering the Mission. The first step institutions might take in determining how the mission influences student learning is to discover what the institution is and what it aspires to be in the future. We started by asking various groups a simple question: "What is special about this institution?" What, if anything, do the responses of students, faculty members, administrators, alumni and alumnae, community leaders, and friends of the institution say about what the institution is and aspires to be? What are the institutional values and aspirations emphasized by each group? In what written statements, symbols, or traditions can the salient elements of the institutional mission — the "something special" — be found? Are the respondents' descriptions of the institution congruent with what is described in the "official" mission statement?

As a result of talking with a number of people (the number will vary depending on the size and complexity of the institution), the college's distinctive values and assumptions may begin to emerge. Some of these qualities may not be obviously related to mission and philosophy. For example, aspects of the institution's culture, such as language and the influence of heroes and heroines on policies and practices, will be mentioned. If the focus is kept on the reasons for the institutions' existence, and on the values and assumptions that people associate with the college, the mission and philosophy — what people actually do (enacted), not necessarily what the "official" mission statement says (espoused) — will become more clear.

In order to identify one or more aspects of the mission that are, or could be, salient to an institution's constituents, institutions should review their history to note critical periods or points at which the institution made a commitment to certain values that now characterize the college or university, such as admitting women and members of ethnic and racial minority groups or implementing key programmatic ventures, such as work or cooperative education programs. A review of the impact of institutional heroes or heroines on shaping institutional values or current policies and practices may identify one or more core assumptions and beliefs about what the institution stands for and the modes of teaching and learning that can best accomplish the mission.

The influence of student leaders on the behavior of peers is often underemphasized; yet peers are very influential role models for undergraduate students. Thus, heroes and heroines from different student subcultures also may personify some important institutional values that should be considered.

To increase the clarity and coherence of the mission, some combination of institutional values, aspirations, people, and programs must be consistently and persuasively communicated to prospective and current students, faculty, administrators, and others so that, over time, the institution will become known for that aspect of its educational program and be (at least) one thing to all (or most) people. For example, the continuing importance of the agricultural heritage of Iowa State is reinforced through contacts with prospective students and community leaders by county extension agents. Contact with county extension agents by Iowa State faculty and administrators is necessary to reaffirm to people throughout Iowa the institution's fidelity to its heritage.

Aspects of the institution found to be "special" should be underscored repeatedly in institutional advancement materials developed for prospective students, graduates, and others, public addresses by institutional leaders, and statements in publications, such as the student newspaper and faculty newsletters. For example, the video prepared for prospective Wichita State students, "Where Dreams Begin," is an inspiring illustration of how students — for many of whom WSU is the only higher education option — can use the university's resources to forge a better life for themselves, their families, and their community. The Mount Holyoke video, targeted for a very different audience, presents the *raison d'être* of the college: preparing women to become — in the tradition of "uncommon" Mount Holyoke women — anything they want to be.

The search for threads in the institution's "invisible tapestry" (Kuh and Whitt, 1988), or culture, that have meaning for most people is both time-consuming and complex. Clarifying an institution's mission and the values and assumptions on which its philosophy is based requires a long-term commitment. Identifying the institution's values and assumptions, while complicated, will be easier than deciding which value-driven themes should be emphasized. Community members may disagree on what values are most important and should be emphasized. Thus, this process holds the potential for conflict.

Establishing Expectations

When a college articulates what it is about, what it stands for, and what it does, prospective students, faculty, and administrators can peer into the fabric of the place and sense whether they belong there. Students are able to determine whether they can expect to find others there who are like themselves. As a result, students who have a choice about where to attend college can make better choices. Moreover, all students — even those for whom a particular college is their only option — learn what to expect from the institution and what the institution expects from them. This is important because it decreases the possibility that students will be surprised by the academic demands and social challenges they are likely to encounter and gives them time to prepare themselves psychologically for the student role at their college.

To direct student attention and energy to educationally purposeful activities, the institutional philosophy enacted by institutional agents must articulate high, clear expectations for students. Heath (1968, p. 243) eloquently underscored the importance of salient expectations for student and faculty performance:

> A college community that has an ideal or vision has, in effect, expectations of what its members are to become. Such ideals or expectations . . . may be more silent than vocal; they may work their effects out of awareness; they may constitute the invisible college . . . and when such expectations are consistently expressed in all structures and activities of the institution, then different communal experiences may mutually reinforce one another.

As mentioned in Chapter Three, faculty members and others at Involving Colleges have high expectations for student performance. An institution's expectations for students are, in part, a function of its educational purposes, which may follow from religious, ideological, or philosophical beliefs. For example, at Berea College, the Seven Great Commitments have a pervasive influence on the curriculum and on campus life. At Earlham, Quaker principles shape student and faculty behavior. At Iowa State and the University of California, Davis, the agricultural heritage, emphasizing practical applications of knowledge and service to others, is expressed through the curriculum and through major-related organizations. At urban universities, such as Wichita State and Louisville, commitment to meeting the needs of the people of the metropolitan area has a significant influence on their constituents' perceptions of the institutions' missions.

Ideally, salient aspects of the institutional mission can be translated into expectations for student performance. Expectations must also be realistic and appropriate for students. Therefore, institutional agents must have adequate, accurate information about students—their ability, backgrounds, attitudes, and aspirations. Information about students contributes to a better understanding of student behavior by faculty members and administrators and can be used to determine appropriately high standards for student performance. At a minimum, faculty members should know about student aspirations and role commitments (spouse, parent, employee, student leader). Such information, however, is not intended to make excuses, or lower expectations for student performance.

Expectations for Student Performance. Although much of the behavior of members of the two faculty cultures described in Chapter Seven differs, many members of both groups share some assumptions about students and learning that influence expectations for student performance. For example, many faculty members at Involving Colleges assume that all students can learn anything, given the proper circumstances. At Involving Colleges, most faculty members expect students to apply knowledge and make it personally relevant. For many students, these processes require concrete experiences that help them to obtain and incorporate new information and insights. Of course, just as abstract conceptualization is not a preferred learning style for everyone, neither is concrete experience. Learning is also personalized when students are expected to share their thinking and learning with peers. This requires that situations be created in which students cannot rely solely on past repertoires of behavior and must respond intellectually, situations where students must read, and think aloud. This happens best perhaps in small groups of peers.

Language is a powerful tool for establishing expectations for student behavior. The power of language is based on the unconscious nature of its symbolism; language "is a complex mechanism that can be grasped only through reflection; the very ones who use it daily are ignorant of it" (Saussure quoted in Polkinghorne, 1983, pp. 159–160). The strong statements about multiculturalism made by the president of Stanford University, Donald Kennedy, were noted in Chapter Seven. Kennedy's welcoming remarks at new student orientation suggest to students that Stanford is, or should be, marked by sensitivity to differences and inclusive behavior, an environment in which differences are embraced and celebrated. When these expectations are not met, however, institutional agents must deal with the student anxiety, frustration, and uncertainty that result.

Using language to pursue institutional aspirations is fraught with potential pitfalls because words are easily misinterpreted or misused. However well intentioned, statements that portray an institution very differently from what it is may create expectations on the part of students that cannot be met. Language must not be based on espoused values or aspirations too far removed from enacted values or the current situation because the words may be misleading and, therefore, have a negative effect on morale and trust. Ethical issues also arise when campus leaders say things that do not accurately describe current conditions.

At the same time, symbolic leadership is considered an important function of institutional leaders. Herein lies the paradox of language as a lever for symbolic action. On the one hand, visionary leaders are encouraged to use language to inspire people to higher levels of performance. On the other hand, describing an institutional vision as though it were reality can be perceived as misleading at best and deceitful at worst.

Establishing high expectations for student performance is not without some risks. Holding students to high expectations may exacerbate student stress. For example, Mount Holyoke students are encouraged to behave as, and see themselves as, "uncommon women" who can be anything they want to be. These words establish high standards for performance and may promote high achievement. At the same time, these standards can create pressure to overachieve, as well as to view some career and life choices — such as marriage and child rearing — as unworthy.

Ethic of Care. Another important aspect of an Involving College's philosophy is a web of values and assumptions that communicates caring and belonging to students. When faculty members, administrators, students, and others subscribe to an ethic of care, powerful messages are sent to students about the importance of respecting all individuals as persons of worth and dignity.

As one University of California, Davis, staff member said, "We can't care for students if we can't care for ourselves." Effective learning communities attract supportive people who mix freely with others in active pursuit of shared ideals, principles, and values (Heath, 1968). In order for students to take intellectual risks necessary for learning, they must feel they "matter" (Schlossberg, Lynch, and Chickering, 1989). Students also must feel they are full members of the community, not merely transients, temporarily occupying space on campus. To feel as though they are responsible for themselves and where they live, students must feel, and be treated as though, they are full members of the college community (ethic of membership). They must be, to a degree, comfortable in their environment and feel supported, not threatened. At the same time, they must have responsibility and freedom to act as adults. The stakes associated with risk taking must be at a reasonable level; when students perceive the chances for failure are high, they may cheat more easily, may eat too much, abuse alcohol and other controlled substances, and avoid taking risks to become involved.

As previously noted, students at Involving Colleges *perceive* faculty to be available and involved with them, particularly in the academic area; those students who develop relationships with faculty out of class usually have taken the initiative to do so. This is a matter of perception; the amount of student contact with faculty may or may not be more frequent at some institutions. What is crucial is the students' perceptions that faculty care and are interested, responsive, and available.

Institutional agents at Involving Colleges recognize that students get sick, have parents, spouses, children, and friends who have problems, and sometimes have difficulty managing the stress that often accompanies the life of a student. As reported in Chapter Six, an institutional ethic of care is evident in safety nets made up of faculty and staff who reach out to students who are encountering problems that impede learning. If the institutional safety nets are too obvious, they may smother, or discourage initiative on the part of, students who must learn how to cope independently and become autonomous, self-directed learners. When safety nets are invisible, however, certain groups of students, such as students of color, may not perceive that the institution cares about or for them. At times, safety nets that seem to work pretty well for white students fail to "catch" students of color who are encountering difficulties.

The power of the small gesture in encouraging students to take advantage of out-of-class learning opportunities cannot be overemphasized. A query by a staff member to a student about how he or she is feeling today (as in the description in Chapter Seven of the counter attendant at Grinnell College), the marginal notes made by a professor about a student's thinking in an essay, the effort made by a member of the maintenance department to take care of a plumbing problem in a residence, the note written by the dean of students to congratulate a student for an achievement are all seemingly insignificant events that, nevertheless, contribute to a feeling of belonging and self-worth in students.

Ethic of Membership. A guiding assumption of the philosophy of Involving Colleges is that students are appreciated for what they bring to the institution; students are not perceived as a drain on institutional resources or as an unwelcome diversion of faculty attention from research and scholarly activity. When this assumption permeates the institution, it becomes an ethic of membership. But, at the same time, faculty members and others at Involving Colleges send a clear message to students: "You are here because we believe you can succeed."

Campus ceremonies and traditions often communicate the propriety of inclusionary behavior. Examples of traditions that reflect inclusionary values include celebrations of cultural and ethnic heritage, such as Picnic Day at UC Davis, and celebrations of academic diversity, such as VEISHEA at Iowa State (Chapter Eight). Some events are primarily of interest to students, such as informal induction rituals in the dorms and houses at Stanford and Iowa State, and they serve as unifying, affirming experiences for many students.

Not all institutionally sanctioned events and traditions or student traditions and rituals are compatible with an institution's educational purposes. Some of the most debilitating traditions are those that are not formally sponsored by the institution but are tacitly accepted or endorsed by institutional agents, either by pretending the traditions and rituals do not exist, or using ineffectual means to stop them. An example is the classic dilemma faced by most campuses — the tailgating parties at football games where alumni are allowed to use alcoholic beverages but students are not. This practice sends conflicting messages to students at an institution where alcohol use on campus is prohibited.

The difference between institutional sponsorship and tacit acceptance is important. The former are events that are valued by the institution and actively promoted by institutional agents because they reinforce the mission of the institution. The latter include traditions that take place at a campus but are not sponsored by the institution and are antithetical to espoused institutional values and educational purposes. Some traditions, such as hazing (the Rush Week and Hell Week of fraternities, branding of black fraternity pledges), denigrate the worth and dignity of individuals or certain groups and, at worst, threaten lives. Recent campus controversies have arisen over such traditions as: flying the Confederate flag on some southern campuses, an action that black students find offensive; beauty contests; theme parties, such as "Arabian Nights" or "Minstrel Shows," that may trivialize the experiences and cultures of certain peoples; and fund-raising events, such as "slave auctions" and "pin-up" calendars, that emphasize historical and insidious stereotypes. Institutions must discover the messages communicated by their traditions and develop strategies to revise or eliminate those that are inconsistent with the values the institution espouses. This is not an easy task given the bonding function that traditions play, especially within student organizations and, in some cases, for graduates.

Institutions should consider the role of traditions in promoting educationally purposeful behavior. What values do campus and student traditions and rituals support? Do those values affirm the institution's mission and purposes? Institutions should also note which members of the institution participate in which traditions. For example, are people of color well represented at institutionally sponsored events such as the opening convocation, homecoming, and commencement? How many faculty members participate in these events? Who are active participants? Most important, what do these ceremonies communicate and reinforce? What are the symbols of community building? What other messages are given to participants and observers?

Attempts by institutions to determine whether student rituals and traditions are consistent with their mission and philosophy can set up a struggle for control over student life. On occasion, it may be helpful to ask: Whose campus is this? Whose experience is this? Who benefits and who pays? What, according to the institutional mission and philosophy, ought student experiences to encompass and what ought to be avoided? On some campuses, too much energy is devoted to attempts to change or thwart essentially harmless but nevertheless important (to students) rituals. A sense of balance must be maintained. Of course, events with the potential to do physical or psychological harm to participants or others have no place in the academy and cannot be tolerated.

Asserting that an activity is antithetical to the institution's mission and values requires that those making the assertion know and are able to articulate the institution's mission and values. Not all institutional agents are able to do so, particularly residence life staff, who are the first level of contact with many traditional-age students on residential campuses. They are sometimes not perceived by students to be authentic in their reasons for challenging student behavior because their voices lack the moral authority (Gardner, 1990) which is legitimated by the core of values in which institutional policies and practices should be grounded.

Articulating the institutional mission is not merely a matter of parroting the purposes of the academy — pursuit of truth through teaching, research, and service. Rather, moral authority comes from the values reflected in the institution's mission, culture, policies, and practices. To use the institutional mission and philosophy as moral authority demands that institutional agents discover and understand the institutional mission and philosophy and the role that the mission plays in legitimating behavior. Consider how one institution responded to a well-intentioned student tradition, certain aspects of which had outlived their appropriateness.

At Stanford University, a gift exchange (most gifts are

under two dollars) among students living in on-campus housing has been customary every December. The practice came to be known as "secret Santa" and reinforced institutional values of caring and concern for each other during the stress of final exams. However, as more students from varied racial, religious, and ethnic backgrounds matriculated, some were offended by the term "Santa" because it was associated with Christmas, a Christian tradition not shared by all Stanford students. With some encouragement from residence staff, the custom is used now to engage residents in discussion of holiday traditions of different religious and ethnic groups. In some houses, the secret Santa practice has been replaced by a "Bhudda Buddy" or Holiday Helper. Thus, a value-driven custom was modified in an effort not to alienate any member of the community. While the institutional values of care and concern were preserved, a teachable moment was seized as the modified custom encouraged students to learn more about other religious and ethnic heritages. On balance, events that emphasize inclusionary values and behaviors are more likely to engender a sense of community, a point to which we will return in Chapter Fifteen.

Interpersonal Distinctions

Status and other types of distinctions are manifested in various ways and serve different purposes on college and university campuses. For example, distinctions are sometimes made to acknowledge unusual achievements, such as academic achievement reflected by membership in Phi Beta Kappa or Mortarboard. Status distinctions indicated by titles may reflect responsibility, such as student government officers, or authority, such as an administrative role. Special privileges, such as reserved parking or dining facilities for faculty members and athletes, are also forms of distinctions that may or may not have educational merit in the context of a particular institution. Whether distinctions among students and others promote, or become obstacles to, student involvement depends on whether the distinctions are compatible with the institution's mission and educational purposes. For example, color-coding parking lots by age of students is surely irrelevant to educational purposes.

If distinctions are relevant to the institution's mission, they must be clearly articulated. Without discussion of the existence and purpose of institutionally endorsed distinctions, it is not possible to determine if the distinctions are serving desired ends.

The key issue is whether institutionally sanctioned distinctions, or the absence of distinctions, are compatible with the institution's mission and make a positive contribution to student success and attainment. For example, if position titles are placed on doors, desks, and in the telephone directory, what do these titles represent in the context of the institution? Perhaps the message is that "we want to make it easy for students to find the information they need from the right person." Or the message may be that "titles are symbols of achievement that should be acknowledged and respected." Institutions should not assume that the desired message is being received by students, and should take time to check how institutional actions are being interpreted and, if necessary, offer suggestions for how the messages can be made explicit.

Some Involving Colleges attempt to reduce status distinctions such as teacher-pupil or expert-novice. At these institutions, formal titles, such as Doctor, President, or Professor, are perceived to make people seem more different than they really are, and, in the process, denigrate the worth of someone. Diminution of status is believed to encourage collaboration in discovery, and shared responsibility for teaching and learning. As previously noted, at the Evergreen State College, where egalitarianism prevails, faculty members often are referred to as "senior learners" and students are "junior learners," signifying that all participate in and benefit from the learning process equally. The egalitarian traditions of Earlham make it unheard-of for a family name to earn privileges for a student.

Race distinctions are also actively discouraged at some Involving Colleges. As reported in Chapter Three, the sign at the entrance to the Berea campus is a constant reminder of Berea's commitment to members of all races. Similarly, excessive trappings of wealth are antithetical to the Berea College philosophy. In addition, the casual student attire at Earlham and The Evergreen State College reflect students' interest in spending more time being who they are and learning what they can become than appearing to be someone they are not.

However, the characteristics of some students, such as need for support and encouragement to be successful, are a rationale for creating distinctions. At Xavier, for example, developing a strong self-concept is a prerequisite to learning what one can become; distinctions, in this case, enhance self-esteem and help students achieve their goals. Xavier students, faculty, and administrators go to great lengths to appear, and feel, confident, successful, and goal-directed—all those things that people of color have not felt in predominantly white institutions of higher education. Xavier students and faculty call one another by their last names and titles as a sign of respect, important role modeling for students. Xavier students dress up for special events, showing pride in themselves and their institution and respect for the activity. It is also acceptable, even necessary, to be tutored, because tutoring at Xavier is a sign that a student is doing what is necessary to be successful in that academic environment.

Whether status or other distinctions encourage or detract from student involvement in out-of-class learning opportunities depends on the culture or cultures in which the distinctions are made. If status differences are promoted, institutions should try to determine if the distinctions are consistent with the guiding values and assumptions operating in the community. What do these values and assumptions say about who can learn and what can be learned here?

Collaboration, a superior condition for learning (Johnson and Johnson, 1975; Kohn, 1986), is common in collegiate communities where distinctions are intentionally diminished. Institutions characterized by interpersonal distinctions often engender competition among students. Thus, another task is to identify whether competition is healthy and is consistent with the institution's mission or if competition leads to bickering and status distinctions devoid of educational purpose. For example, debates about whether it is better to be a member of the Kappas or Alphas are irrelevant to the educational purposes of most institutions and usually irrelevant to development of an individual student's sense of identity.

Undesirable behaviors can be manifested and reinforced through competitive behavior that exacerbates distinctions among students. Competition for the sake of determining who is better at something (anything) is antithetical to the mission and philosophy of some Involving Colleges. However, competition for and about the right things (activities valued by the mission of the institution) is not always discouraged. For example, contested student elections can be a sign that students are interested in, and take responsibility for, self-governance. In other contexts, such as Mount Holyoke, single-candidate tickets have been common because students have preferred to avoid such competition; this practice is fading, however.

Institutions must determine whether competition encourages or discourages student learning. For example, are members of certain subgroups discouraged from becoming involved in the life of the community? To determine whether interpersonal distinctions encourage or discourage student involvement, institutions should consider whether their mission and philosophy emphasize meritocratic or egalitarian values and behaviors. On a campus that encourages status distinctions, it may be impossible to modify inappropriate behavior associated with such distinctions. Because the institution sends messages that distinctions are accepted, it is extremely difficult to get students (and sometimes faculty and administrators) to see that certain distinctions do not contribute to attaining the institution's purposes. This is particularly confusing if the institution espouses egalitarian values. The critical question is whether competitive behavior — in whatever form — is consistent with the institution's mission and philosophy.

Whether or not distinctions are consistent with the mission and philosophy, Involving Colleges acknowledge and celebrate the question of *individual differences*. On this point, institutional agents must exercise caution when generalizing about students and students' experiences. Athletes, musicians, students of color, women, and many other types of subgroups exist on most campuses. These groups have different needs and concerns that should receive attention. How does the institution recognize the worth and dignity of each individual?

The Multicultural Imperative

The importance of culture and cultural differences is often minimized in the United States. The consequences of having one's senses conditioned by a different culture, such as the Asian culture, while trying to cope with white teachers and white educational materials is receiving more attention (Hsia and Hirano-Nakanishi, 1989). Moreover, African Americans, Mexican Americans, Asian Americans, American Indians, and other people of color are often treated as though they were recalcitrant, undereducated, middle-class Americans of northern European heritage instead of what they really are: members of culturally differentiated enclaves with their own languages, traditions, and values. Because of this "a-cultural bias" (Hall, 1966, p. 173), we seem to want to believe that differences among the peoples of the world are superficial. Demographic realities (Hodgkinson, 1985) require that colleges and universities change to increase the chances for success of people of color, including student involvement in out-of-class learning and personal development experiences.

Institutional Commitment to Multiculturalism. To become a multicultural learning community, an institution's commitment must be fourfold: to advance knowledge and intellectual understanding of differences among groups of people; to encourage interaction among members of different subcommunities (ethnic, cultural, gender-based, academic living groups); to promote the appreciation and valuing of commonalities across all students; and to build on commonalities while acknowledging the important and unique contributions that members of different groups can make to the academic community.

Members of any group value themselves to the degree that their group is valued (Skinner, 1953). It is increasingly important that students be willing to acknowledge, understand, and appreciate the cultural heritage, values, and life-styles of the racial and ethnic groups (including their own) that make up our society. Students must also develop a capacity to understand and appreciate sex differences in ways that do not reflect stereotypes or traditional role expectations. To develop this capacity, students need opportunities to share their understanding and interpretation of differences. Understanding and acceptance of oneself in relationship to others does not usually come about in a lecture hall or laboratory. Rather, for many students, learning about their biases and ignorance toward people who are different requires articulating and sharing their thoughts and feelings, debating and challenging stereotypes, and dealing with their uncertainty about cultural differences in the presence of peers. This kind of personalized learning is risky and often intense. It is, perhaps, best done in the student's subcommunity of choice, such as the residence or an ethnic or academic theme house, where a student usually enjoys a sense of security and psychological safety. Thus, the rationale for enabling multiple subcommunities is to promote self-discovery and the development of self-esteem within a supportive community of choice. Further, the existence of multiple subcommunities allows students to examine different life-styles.

The first level of response by colleges and universities to the matriculation of increasing numbers of students from different cultural, ethnic, and socioeconomic backgrounds was to encourage acknowledgment of the diverse characteristics of students and encourage faculty members, graduates, and traditional-age students — most of whom were white — to demonstrate an increasing *tolerance* for diversity. When the inevitable misunderstandings occurred between members of different cultures and ethnic groups, institutional agents often made rational appeals to members of the majority to exhibit greater tolerance of differences and to the nonmajority to persevere with the promise that conditions would improve. Problems and misunderstandings were often handled through individual and small-group interventions. On occasion, attention to issues of race, ethnicity, and cultural diversity has been brought about through open forums addressing these issues of community concern. Such efforts have produced generally positive, if only modest, results.

Many colleges and universities have not yet created the conditions wherein diversity is tolerated. At too many institutions, the appeals for tolerance became synonymous with benign neglect of authentic differences in life-style, language, and cultural values. That is, as long as relatively few students (and faculty) of color were present, institutional policies and practices remained, for the most part, unchanged. However, at some institutions, which have attracted increasing numbers of students from different racial and ethnic backgrounds, *tolerance* of differences is not a satisfactory aspiration. At these institutions, expectations for higher education and campus life held by students of color often are found to be inconsistent with institutional traditions and practices, although they may be consistent with the institution's *espoused* values and expectations. Dialogue between faculty members, student affairs staff, academic administrators, and students of color revealed what is now apparent on many campuses: differences between the institutional culture and the heritages of students of color are barriers to student achievement and success (Richardson and Bender, 1987). What is needed, then, is movement beyond tolerance of diversity toward development of multicultural learning communities in which the institutional culture supports and appreciates cultural differences. Before institutions can become multicultural learning communities, however, the quality of campus life of women students, the "invisible majority" (Tidball, 1989, p. 167), must receive attention.

Campus Climate for Women. Although women now constitute over half of the undergraduate student population (Pearson, Shavlik, and Touchton, 1989), their status on many campuses is still that of a minority: "outside the norm" (Wilkerson, 1989, p. 29), "outsiders or marginals to the male-dominated world of academe" (Moore, 1987, p. 30), "second-class citizens" (American Council on Education, 1987, p. 5); at best, invisible, and at worst, victims of sexual harassment, violence, and discrimination. The presence of increasing numbers of women students — as well as students of color — demands that we examine assumptions about who our students are, what they bring to our campuses in the way of strengths and needs, and what changes are needed in institutional structures, policies, practices, and programs in order to enhance the quality of campus life for women and take another step toward becoming multicultural learning communities.

Women students are by no means a monolithic group; they are young and old, white and of color, single and married, mothers and childless. Nevertheless, research about women and women college students suggests some commonalities that must be considered in assessing the campus climate for women. For example, although women come to college with higher grades than men, they have lower expectations for their performance in college (Hafner, 1989). First-year female students have lower self-confidence than males with regard to academic ability, math ability, public-speaking ability, and intellectual self-confidence (Hafner, 1989). Worse yet, women's self-esteem declines further during the college years (Pearson, Shavlik, and Touchton, 1989).

The decline in women's self-esteem may, in part, be attributed to the "chilly campus climate" that women students encounter (Hall and Sandler, 1984). For example, Hall and Sandler found a pervasive devaluing of women in a myriad of "micro-inequities" (p. 4) — everyday behaviors that discount or ignore someone on the basis of race, sex, or age and have a pernicious influence on self-esteem. Examples of these behaviors include sexist humor, disparagement of women in general, less time and attention given to women students by faculty and administrators, subtle and overt communication of stereotypical expectations and assumptions about women, sexual harassment, fewer mentoring opportunities for women students, exclusion of women from study groups, and so on.

On many campuses, male students dominate social norms, placing women in stereotypical social roles — such as fraternity "little sisters" or contestants in "wet T-shirt contests" — and depriving them of leadership opportunities and self-respect. The most disturbing evidence of the devaluing of women at colleges and universities is found in increasing numbers of acquaintance and gang rapes committed by male students (Ehrhart and Sandler, 1985). Male dominance of student life is a reflection of male dominance of institutions, demonstrated in hiring and promotion practices, policy and decision making, and the absence of institution-wide commitment to courses, events, and activities focusing on women and women's issues (Hall and Sandler, 1984).

Until recently, male models of development were used to understand women's growth and development during college (Forrest, Hotelling, and Kuk, 1984). However, new theories of women's development based on research about and by women have implications for institutions of higher education. These theories have been described elsewhere (see Belenky, Clinchy, Goldberger, and Tarule, 1986; Gilligan, 1982); suffice it to say here that women experience the world, and function within it, differently than do men; those differences must be understood, appreciated, and reflected in institutional policies and practices if women's developmental and educational needs are to be met.

To identify ways in which colleges and universities can become more hospitable places for women, the authors of the *Report of the ACE Commission on Women in Higher Education* (American Council on Education, 1987, p. v) posed the question: "If an institution were to commit itself fully to meeting the educational needs of women, what would it do?"

An example of an institution fully committed to meeting the educational needs of women can be found in this study: Mount Holyoke. Women's colleges are noted for the career and educational achievements of their graduates. Perhaps equally important are the rich learning opportunities they offer their students: "It is clear that the environment of women's colleges is more enabling of women than is that of coeducational institutions" (Tidball, 1989, p. 160). Mount Holyoke students described their experiences in the following terms:

> I have developed so much more confidence in myself as a woman. I didn't think of myself as smart. That change couldn't have happened at a coed institution; I wouldn't have had the focus on myself. I didn't have access to leadership positions before and that's what made all the difference for me here.

> There's a special kind of bonding that takes place here. People genuinely care about each other and

> they respect differences. If there were men, there'd
> be more of a competitive edge. Women wouldn't
> fill all the leadership roles. We have opportunities
> here we wouldn't get in society in general.

> We have such a strong sense of women's commu-
> nity that can't be duplicated anywhere else. I feel
> a sense of empowerment because I've been chal-
> lenged and been a leader. It's a place you can grow
> in and not feel threatened. An environment where
> women do everything is necessarily strengthening.

Mount Holyoke faculty and administrators take women
very seriously, to an extent that women students have not experienced at other times and other places in their lives. Students,
faculty, and administrators were unanimous in their belief that
what Mount Holyoke provides its students cannot be duplicated
in a coeducational setting: "Whatever you try to do to help
women in a coed environment, you can't create an environment
that is totally affirming, and that kind of affirmation helps you
grow." It is a reality, however, that women will attend coeducational institutions, and that those institutions should, to the extent possible, be affirming environments for women students.

The ACE Commission on Women in Higher Education
developed a set of recommendations, in the form of a "new
agenda" for women in higher education, for institutions interested in becoming places in which women are taken seriously
and can thrive. Included in the fifteen-point agenda are recommendations to: obtain a strong commitment from institutional
leaders to understand and address the concerns of women students, faculty, administrators, and staff; correct inequities in
institutional policies and practices, including hiring, promotion,
tenure, and salaries; create a supportive campus climate for
women; develop an annual status report on women in the campus community; and assess campus values and the ways in which
they influence the status of women and people of color.

Simply adding more women or students of color to a student body, or adding more women and people of color to the
faculty and staff, will not create campus environments in which

members of these groups are valued and taken seriously, and in which their needs are met. For example, a supportive climate for women students cannot be created in the absence of a supportive climate for women faculty, administrators, and staff (Tidball, 1989). Institutional structures and processes must be altered (Moore, 1987), a task that cannot be accomplished easily or quickly. Ways in which institutions can work toward interactive multiculturalism are described in the following section.

Toward Interactive Pluralism. In order to become genuine multicultural learning communities, colleges and universities must reassess and, if necessary, refocus their missions and philosophies so that they promote *understanding, appreciation,* and *respect* for cultural, racial, ethnic, gender, life-style and religious differences to affirm all members of the college community. A shift is needed from the "melting pot" metaphor for community, in which students from varied backgrounds blend together to form a homogeneous whole—thereby ignoring differences—to a "salad" or "stew" metaphor in which the differences among groups are preserved while the contributions and complementarity of subcommunities are highlighted (Smith, 1989).

Understanding, appreciation, and respect cannot develop, however, without interaction among community members. Nor does asserting the importance of and commitment to multiculturalism, in and of itself, create opportunities for forming positive relationships among students of different groups. Colleges, especially residential campuses, can be laboratories for the development of interactive pluralism because students must live and learn together twenty-four hours a day. Nevertheless, on most campuses, practices—such as cafeteria seating arrangements, preferences regarding music and alcohol use, all-white and all-black social organizations—have evolved that permit, even encourage, segregation of students' out-of-class lives by racial or ethnic background.

If colleges and universities are to be models of interactive pluralism, at least three conditions must be met: institutions must change in fundamental ways to accommodate and take advantage of the contributions of students from historically underrepresented groups; opportunities must be available for students to live in and learn about their subcommunity of choice, whether it be based on race, ethnicity, gender, academic interests, or life-style orientation; and boundaries between student subcommunities must be permeable, allowing and encouraging positive interaction and learning.

Creating an environment that is welcoming and hospitable for students from historically underrepresented groups, including women, will require changes in staffing and curricula. More faculty and staff members of color and women faculty and staff members must be recruited. Others have been articulate and persuasive in this matter (Green, 1989; Richardson, Simmons, and de los Santos, 1987; Washington and Harvey, 1989); nonetheless, we would be remiss if we did not make this obvious point. Simply increasing numbers is not enough, however. In most instances, institutions will have to make fundamental changes in their structures and processes in order to create environments in which women and people of color can thrive (Moore, 1987; Rowe, 1989). Furthermore, an institutional mission that espouses interactive multiculturalism should be enacted by a multicultural curriculum, including courses that examine the heritage, traditions, and contributions of a wide range of cultural, racial, and ethnic groups and of women.

In Chapter Fourteen, we describe in more detail the development of multiple subcommunities. Suffice it to say at this point that multicultural learning communities not only enable multiple subcommunities but also encourage permeable boundaries between them so that their members can learn from one another. Students feel free to explore various subcommunities (for example, there are white residents in the ethnic theme houses at Stanford), and subcommunities are open to sharing their experiences with others.

At the same time, membership in a subcommunity should not constrain students' learning about other aspects of themselves. Subcommunity members must be allowed and encouraged to develop along other dimensions and for other purposes than group identity or solidarity. If subcommunities are supported by the community as a whole, and so do not face external threats to survival, they may feel comfortable in acknowledging and encouraging overlapping memberships and shared experiences.

Teachable Moments. When people of different cultures and backgrounds come together in collegiate environments, many teachable moments emerge. A student may unknowingly use language that is offensive to members of some groups. A roommate may be unaware of the cultural roots of behaviors she finds confusing or irritating. Holiday celebrations may create feelings of denigration. The choice of music for an all-campus dance may be viewed by some groups as exclusionary.

Using teachable moments effectively is difficult, however. Moreover, some teachable moments are potentially explosive. The number of misunderstandings between white students, many of whom come from monocultural environments, and students of color will likely increase as students of diverse backgrounds come together in classes, residences, and social situations. Now that women students are in the majority on many campuses, incidents of institutional and individual sexism, however subtle, fuel tensions between women and the institution and between women and men.

Overt racial and sexism incidents demand that immediate, decisive action be taken to resolve the conflicts among the parties involved. In the future, however, such incidents should also be used as catalysts for moving the institution from promoting tolerance for diversity to an appreciation for multiculturalism. This includes refusing to back away from conflict or confrontation.

Involving Colleges do not ignore the tensions that result when members of one or more subcommunities challenge the norms of the larger campus community. This openness to conflict demands a high level of risk taking by students and institutional agents, particularly administrators whose effectiveness is often measured by the extent to which their campus is peaceful and quiet.

The rationale for taking advantage of teachable moments is that, through a series of small but often arduous steps, the nature and quality of relationships among community members can be changed, although not quickly. Groups previously viewed as "different," and therefore deficient, may not quickly become full members of the community. Constant attention to teachable moments can also keep an institution focused on what it should be, what it stands for, and what it can become (Mathews, 1989). Thus, much will be lost if efforts to keep the campus peaceful suppress teachable moments.

Difficult times may be ahead for colleges and universities committed to becoming multicultural learning communities. Institutions that have made the most progress thus far in embracing the goals of interactive multiculturalism are also those that are potentially the most explosive because they have opened themselves to the conflicts that come with differences and high expectations. Two examples are Stanford University and the University of California, Davis, where about 35 percent of the students are students of color. When compared with other institutions in this study, and most other institutions in the United States, Stanford and UC Davis have made considerable progress in moving toward a multicultural learning environment, one in which diversity is a given and now appreciation, understanding, and respect are the goals. And yet both these institutions have faced and will continue to face difficult times as students attempt to learn how to live with and learn from people who are different from themselves. We will return to these issues in Chapters Thirteen and Fourteen.

Unifying the Focus

Continuity and consistency of philosophy across academic affairs and student affairs characterize Involving Colleges. Consistent messages from the president, trustees, faculty, and student affairs staff about the importance of taking advantage of out-of-class learning opportunities seem to promote student involvement. This complementarity of purpose and philosophy is also reflected by student affairs staff who model behavior consistent with the educational mission of the institution. The ability of student affairs staff to influence students' use of out-of-class experiences in ways that complement the institutional mission seems to be related to the extent to which they feel partnership with and respect from faculty and academic administrators.

When student affairs staff have a keen understanding of and appreciation for the institution's mission, they are better able to promote learning because they can explain — to students, faculty, and one another — how these activities complement the institution's educational purposes. Through teaching, advising, and counseling students, and consulting with faculty, student affairs staff translate the institution's values and educational purposes to students. They take advantage of opportunities to instruct and to encourage staff, students, and faculty to reflect on, and occasionally challenge, institutional norms and values.

Summary

While a clear, salient mission and a coherent institutional philosophy are necessary, they are not sufficient conditions to promote student involvement. The mission must be enacted in all aspects of the institution, in the physical settings in which learning takes place, and in the policies that determine, for example, who is admitted, who receives financial aid, and who is permitted to stay. At the same time, the institutional mission and philosophy may need to change in order to accommodate changing times and student populations. Critical questions to be considered include: How can our college or university accommodate the traditions and values of different groups and foster interactive multiculturalism? What structures must be available for different kinds of students to establish a sense of belonging? What strategies can be developed to synthesize intellectual, moral, social, and emotional issues and concerns across racial, ethnic, gender, and other kinds of boundaries? What do the mission and philosophy suggest about affirmative action and how seriously affirmative action is taken?

In the next chapter, we identify some environmental issues that are relevant to student involvement.

13

Humanizing
Campus Environments

The environments of a college or university are not created overnight. They evolve over decades, sometimes centuries, shaped
in part by uncontrollable factors such as climate and natural
disaster. Campus environments are also influenced by the efforts
of planners, architects, administrators, and others who, by
preserving the old while creating the new, become guardians
and curators of their institution's distinctive character (Jackson
and Kleberg, 1989).

In this chapter, we discuss the implications of Involving
College environments that warrant consideration: taking advantage of the setting; creating a human-scale institution; and
providing many and varied opportunities for involvement. Emphasis is given to environmental conditions that can be improved
without a substantial investment of money and other resources,
and to opportunities for student involvement in activities consistent with the institution's educational purposes. We must
stress, however, that it can be expensive to modify important
aspects of the physical environment, such as the size of classrooms and student residences, in order to create settings that
promote student involvement.

Taking Advantage of the Setting

Institutions can begin a study of their campus setting by
asking three questions:

1.   What are the characteristics of the geographical location?
2.   In what ways does the location influence the institution's mission, educational purposes, policies, and practices?
3.   How does the institution use its setting to educational advantage?

Isolated Location. In Chapters Five, Eight, Nine, and Ten, there were examples of colleges located in settings geographically isolated from, close to, or surrounded by a city. Although physical isolation is important for some colleges to attain their missions, learning is not enhanced if students are intellectually isolated from the outside world. Even the most geographically isolated Involving Colleges are not ivory towers, detached from and unconcerned about social, economic, and political issues. Grinnell uses its isolation to immerse students in development of individual responsibility and social consciousness. Earlham uses its perceived isolation to encourage community members to create an environment in which collaboration and egalitarianism are emphasized. Nonetheless, Involving Colleges intentionally provide off-campus learning opportunities that connect students to the issues, problems, and challenges of the outside world. Hence, there is an abundance of internships, work-study opportunities, travel programs, speakers, public service opportunities, and programs about current events.

Isolated institutions should consider whether their educational or intellectual boundaries need to be expanded. If a college is located in a rural area, how is isolation reflected in the mission, philosophy, design, and implementation of programs? Do students use the isolated setting to immerse themselves in the life of the college — "making their own fun" — or do they lament the lack of commercial entertainment available to them? Does the college's location limit students' learning opportunities in ways inconsistent with the mission? In what ways can the outside world be brought effectively to the campus, and how can the students be more actively involved in the outside world?

Surrounded Location. Institutions located in or near a city can use the resources of the metropolitan area to enrich students' out-of-class learning. Merely being located in a city does not, of course, guarantee that students will take advantage of cultural, academic, and employment-related learning opportunities. Considerable effort is required by faculty and administrators to develop cooperative arrangements with the arts community, business, government, and industry to match work and cultural opportunities with students' interests, educational objectives, and career goals. Graduates who live in the metropolitan area and community leaders play an important role in obtaining jobs for students, supervising internships, discussing career plans, helping students reflect on the educational value of their work experiences, and encouraging participation in cultural events and activities.

Many urban institutions are located in impoverished or deteriorating neighborhoods. These colleges have an opportunity—if not an obligation—to enhance the quality of community services in the surrounding area while using it as a learning setting for students, faculty, and staff (Reinert, 1989). Institutional efforts may take the form of volunteer services, political and social action groups, "good neighbor" policies regarding noise and parties, and undergraduate and faculty research opportunities with businesses, community health or social service agencies, or local schools.

Institutions should examine the degree to which off-campus employment and cooperative education opportunities are integrated with the curriculum and are used by students to enrich out-of-class learning. Student access to and use of cultural activities and other resources should also be examined. For example, can costs for the use of local libraries and attendance at cultural events be reduced for students?

No matter where a campus is located—geographically isolated, a short distance from a city, or surrounded by a metropolitan area—that location can be used to educational advantage.

Creating a Human-Scale Institution

Human scale, a key factor in planning towns, neighborhoods, and housing developments (Hall, 1966), is also important in creating rich out-of-class learning opportunities. Human scale at Involving Colleges has both physical and psychological aspects. Evidence of human scale at Involving Colleges includes residence halls with no more than 200 to 300 residents or small subcommunities in larger residences, buildings that are no more than three or four stories above ground, and small classrooms.

Physical Environment

Buildings, signs, traffic patterns, and the landscape communicate messages to community members about the institution's philosophy, such as valuing people over things (Rapoport, 1982), and influence students' feelings of well-being, belonging, and identity. For example, trees, lawns, flowering plants, open spaces, buildings softened with vines, and footpaths and bike trails free of traffic and debris make people feel welcome as well as physically and psychologically comfortable. Seeing green space or a body of water from a residence or faculty office can provide feelings of stillness and openness to the outside. To the extent possible, open spaces and "sacred ground" — such as the "heart" at Earlham, the oval at Stanford, Justice Brandeis's grave at the University of Louisville, the monument commemorating the 1970 plane crash of the Wichita State football team, and Mary Lyon's grave at Mount Holyoke — should be preserved.

Involvement by certain students can be discouraged if facilities are not physically accessible or available at convenient times. For example, for many part-time learners who hold full-time jobs, the noon hour or late evenings are the only times to attend organizational meetings, meet with faculty members, or conduct college business. Students with physical disabilities should have access to every part of the campus if they are to be fully involved in the institution and in student life.

Student residences and academic buildings should be placed so that students experience the campus as an integrated community, not simply as distinct sets of buildings for separate uses (Jackson and Kleberg, 1987). While relatively few buildings may be constructed in the near future, the need for an integrated sense of community that properly placed buildings provide should be a factor in such decisions. In addition, institutions should determine whether vehicular traffic interferes with student movement on campus and contact among peers and faculty members. More space (roadways, parking lots) for automobiles means less space (parks, benches, sidewalks, pedestrian malls) for people to meet and congregate. Walkways and bike paths promote access to people and facilities; when people walk they get to know one another, if only by sight.

Funding for maintenance and renovation of facilities, such as residence halls and open spaces, is likely to receive serious consideration in the coming decade as the large number of buildings constructed in the 1960s require attention. Some simple and relatively inexpensive modifications can be made. For example, on large campuses — particularly urban institutions — it is important that facilities be clearly marked, particularly for commuters and part-time students whose time on campus is limited. Large residence halls can be divided into small, interactive subcommunities.

As noted in Chapter Five, interaction among community members is fostered by the availability of indoor and outdoor spaces where people can come together without much effort. Institutions should consider whether their campuses have adequate places that encourage spontaneous, informal interaction among students. Examples include: accessible departmental lounges; alcoves, benches, and chairs in the hallways of classroom buildings which allow faculty members and students a convenient place to continue class discussions; residence hall and union areas that encourage impromptu interaction, such as lounges with comfortable furniture, wide hallways, and wide stairwells; and meeting facilities with space dividers that permit the creation of small, quiet gathering places.

Psychological Environments

Psychological comfort is a necessary condition for positive out-of-class learning experiences. For example, in the first few weeks of college, students need to feel accepted by their peers (Upcraft, Gardner, and Associates, 1989). Aspects of the psychological environment include sources of support and challenge, availability of personal space, absence of anonymity, and presence of multiple student subcommunities.

Sanford (1962) suggested that readiness to learn is a unique individual characteristic that cannot be manipulated or rushed. Thus, collegiate environments have to provide varying amounts of support and challenge in order to meet individual learning needs. A task for institutions is to discover and describe aspects of the psychological climate that contribute to, or inhibit, learning. For example, is it safe and socially acceptable to discuss issues and questions regarding differences in race, gender, or life-style orientations? How do students react when their views are challenged? Is freedom of inquiry valued and protected? Encouraging faculty members to learn and use the names of students in their classes is an example of a small gesture that can make students feel supported and set the stage for learning. Other indications of psychological comfort are whether students easily become members of groups, whether students exhibit care and concern for one another, and whether safety nets are in place to "catch" students in trouble.

Personal Space. Effective learning environments allow people to be alone. In order to get the most from their college experience, students must reflect on their learning and internalize new information about themselves and others, activities that may be best done alone. Students gravitate to tranquil places — nooks, courtyards, woods, lakes — away from the campus hustle and bustle. However, as campuses become more crowded and as land becomes too valuable to maintain as open space, opportunities for contemplative learning — or just solitude — are reduced. In addition, on many campuses there is safety in numbers and efforts to design safe environments often preclude isolated areas so essential to contemplation. Institutions must balance the conflicting needs of safety and solitude by providing safe places for individuals to get away from the crowds, to have a serene place to think, to absorb and to integrate the lessons of the classroom, library, laboratory, and residence.

Institutions should assess the availability of personal space, keeping in mind the security needs of the campus and characteristics of their students. For example, a largely residential student body will have different personal space needs than one that is made up of commuting students. Are there sufficient places for commuter students to study? Can students in residences find places in their buildings in which to be alone to think, to laugh, to cry, to rest? At the same time, are there places where groups can meet to collaborate on projects?

In addition, as increasing numbers of students bring personal computers to college, students are more likely to study where they live than in the library. From their residence, students with computers can interact with peers and faculty and obtain learning materials from the library. Thus, as living space becomes academic space, additional pressure is placed on students and housing staff to find ways to create environments conducive to study as well as to relax. The level of noise in residence halls and expectations (on the part of students themselves as well as staff and faculty) for student behavior at all hours of the day and night are increasingly of concern. Can students study in their rooms without unreasonable interruptions from their neighbors? Do students responsibly regulate the study atmosphere in residences?

Absence of Anonymity. Another indicator of psychological comfort is freedom from feelings of anonymity. Although we have noted that personal space is essential, too much isolation can inhibit student learning. According to Astin (1977), it is difficult to defend on educational grounds the policy decision to permit—even encourage—colleges and universities to become so large that students become anonymous. In a review of research relating institutional size and student outcomes, Bowen (1977, p. 248) concluded that "smallness is associated with educational advantage." The implication of this observation is that students at large institutions can be educationally disadvantaged, in part because they can easily get lost in the crowd. Redundancy in personal development opportunities usually associated with large campuses can and must be reduced (Chickering, 1969; Kuh, 1981) if student learning is to be enhanced.

Educational advantages of small colleges include stronger commitment to the institution on the part of students, higher levels of participation in out-of-class activities, and recognition for student accomplishments (Hawley and Kuh, 1986). Further, it is usually difficult to be anonymous at a small college. Many desirable outcomes of college, such as critical thinking, responsible citizenship, community involvement after college, and an enhanced capacity for independent judgment, seem to be accentuated by attendance at small colleges (Pace, 1974). Because they cannot escape being noticed, or avoid coming into contact with others who are different, students at small colleges are forced to confront and, it is hoped, respect differences in opinions, beliefs, and values.

Attending a small college does not, however, guarantee freedom from feelings of anonymity. In fact a student's sense of personal isolation at a small college may be particularly painful and destructive because students and others assume that, at such places, students cannot get lost. Small size also may increase a press toward sameness and exacerbate feelings of anonymity by students who are "different," either as a result of race, ethnicity, life-style preferences, or political and social beliefs. As noted in Chapter Four, Earlham students need to be "politically correct" to be accepted. The few Earlham students who do not share the liberal attitudes that dominate the student culture can, indeed, feel that they do not belong.

Although students are less likely to feel anonymous in a small college setting, it is also the case that a small college atmosphere can be oppressive. Small colleges are often "fishbowls" and, in many ways, an individual's private behavior is very public. A homogeneous small college community can hinder the questioning and challenges necessary to student learning and development. For example, small colleges may have particular difficulty dealing with the consequences of diversity. Also, some students prefer anonymity, at least occasionally, over intensive or extensive personal attention (Young, 1986). For these reasons, some students choose large universities; others transfer from small institutions to large, seeking what they perceive to be more autonomy. Small colleges must consider whether the psychological environment suppresses student autonomy and responsibility, or excessively intrudes on student privacy. Is a balance maintained between absence of anonymity and suffocating attention in ways that are consistent with the institution's mission? Do institutional agents' efforts to make students feel welcome and cared for tend to release students from taking academic or personal initiative, or from behaving as responsible adults? Do students feel free to express themselves in appropriate ways in word and action?

Large Involving Colleges have found ways to make sure that students have opportunities to feel that they belong somewhere and that they are known and appreciated — through small residential subcommunities, ongoing new student orientation activities, safety nets, and involved and caring student affairs staff and faculty. Large institutions should assess the extent to which their students feel anonymous. Are feelings of anonymity typical in all segments of the study body, or are there certain groups that are particularly susceptible? What aspects of the psychological environment contribute to students' sense of belonging or isolation?

Institutions small and large should attempt to identify the extent to which students feel a part of the community. Do institutional agents take for granted that students do not feel anonymous, or are there mechanisms in place to make sure that students feel known, welcome, and appreciated by peers as well as staff and faculty? Does the dominant student culture exclude students whose ideas, beliefs, backgrounds, or life-styles differ from what is perceived to be the norm? Are there opportunities for students with different interests and needs to find a niche in the campus community? We will return to the issue of richness of opportunities later in this chapter.

Multiple Subcommunities. Racial, ethnic, and life-style subcommunities on a campus can encourage their student members to take risks and be more actively involved in the life of the campus community. Smith (1989) estimated that the number of members of a subcommunity must approach 20 percent of the total population to constitute a critical mass — an appropriate number to support the learning and development of its members. When the size of a subcommunity reaches critical mass, members have the support and resources they need to explore multiple facets of their identity. Thus, students learn who they are through exploring multiple dimensions of identity from membership in different groups.

Further, the presence of significant numbers of students in a subcommunity allows the diversity within the subcommunity to become apparent and the uniqueness of individual members to be recognized. Members of a subcommunity may feel more secure acknowledging their differences when surrounded by others like them.

Multiple subcommunities create opportunities for some students to learn for the first time about their cultural heritage. For example, in 1988, 86 percent of the African American students at Stanford said it was important for them to be accepted by the Stanford African American community. Most African American students at Stanford came from integrated neighborhoods and high schools. We can speculate that many of these students were not satisfied with their understanding of or sense of self-esteem regarding their heritage, a precursor to becoming comfortable in exploring other aspects of their identity, such as biology major, musician, poet, and so forth. For many African American Stanford students, Ujamaa House, the African American cultural center, is an important source of affirming information about their background and identity.

It may also be the case that group identity, solidarity, and membership are particularly important in a setting in which one's primary identity group has been linked with failure or low status. Students who perceive the institutional setting as academically challenging and, perhaps, inhospitable need to be told by peers, mentors, and others in the institution that they can succeed.

Need for affirmation is of a different order at Xavier where the entire community is committed to empowering black students, and at Mount Holyoke, where the institution's mission is the empowerment of women. Students at historically black colleges and women's colleges are free from the overwhelming need to be protected from and to guard against threats to their self-esteem and personhood. These students do not have to spend considerable time and energy defending their race or sex, or their ways of thinking and acting. Instead, they can focus on personal and intellectual development, unencumbered by stereotypical expectations. A supportive, encouraging environment also provides opportunities to probe more deeply into one's cultural, racial, or gender heritage. At the same time, students of color and women students at these institutions are sent and receive a very clear message: you are expected to succeed here and we expect you to give your best effort to do so.

Institutions should explore the presence and character of student subcommunities. Do women and students of different racial and ethnic backgrounds or diverse life-style orientation have access to supportive groups of peers, faculty, and staff to help them feel comfortable being themselves and, in turn, feel comfortable becoming involved in the life of the campus community? Is the importance of subcommunities reflected in the institution's mission and educational purposes? Are subcommunities given a voice in shaping institutional and student life decisions and policies? If there is not a "critical mass" of students of a particular group to constitute a subcommunity, how can institutional agents help those students feel supported and encouraged to become full members of the institution?

Providing Opportunities for Involvement

One of the three subsystems of Blocher's (1978) ecological model of learning and personal development is the opportunity subsystem, an infrastructure that encourages active participation of students in leadership and other responsible community roles. Behavior setting theory (Barker, 1968) suggests that an inverse relationship exists between the number of students on a campus and the frequency and intensity of opportunities for student involvement (Hawley and Kuh, 1986; Walsh, 1978). Although involvement is not determined by institutional size, it is influenced by the number of students vying for available opportunities to participate actively in the life of the campus.

Institutions should consider what their missions say about the role of student governance, social organizations, and athletics in the institution. Are undergraduate residence life staff and student government officers able to explain the institutional mission to their peers? For this to occur, institutional agents who work with student leaders must understand the mission before they can promote student awareness and understanding of it.

Institutions should examine the number and type of leadership positions available in departmental or social organizations and clubs, intramurals, and various student and institutional governance bodies. Are opportunities for out-of-class involvement available for all students who want them? Are there sufficient leadership opportunities to meet the needs of all interested students? Can additional roles be created in major-related or other organizations to allow students to exercise leadership or take responsibility for group activities?

Institutions should also be aware of who is involved, who is not, and why. For example, new students may be encouraged to "get involved" but may not be given the information they need in order to know how to get involved, or they may not have access to opportunities for integration into organizations and activities. Also of interest should be the characteristics of students who are nominated and subsequently hold academic and social leadership positions and those who receive awards, research positions, jobs in the library, and so forth. Are students of color and women in some of these positions?

It would be particularly useful to know whether leadership roles are widely distributed or whether a few students are in charge of everything. Faculty and staff may believe that asking students with successful track records to assume leadership positions enhances the likelihood that events will be successful. At the same time, other students are not given the opportunity to obtain leadership skills and derive satisfaction from effective leadership experiences. Does the institution provide opportunities for students without leadership experience to develop leadership skills? At Iowa State, for example, the TULIP Program offers leadership training to students who have not served in leadership roles but desire to do so.

Institutions should know the ways in which students become involved in activities and positions of responsibility. Are interviews or other competitive processes required to participate in student organizations? To what degree are the means for attaining membership consistent with the institution's mission and philosophy? At some institutions, a competitive system for student involvement is consistent with "how we do things here," while at others, competition for positions — applying and being selected for student organizations — is inconceivable.

By attending to the other conditions that support learning and personal development, a synergy may result when students and institutional agents interact in ways that foster student interest and a feeling of belonging. The goal is to create environments or situations where all students have opportunities to participate in ways that contribute something to, as well as take something from, an experience. Examples we found include:

- Student-run escort services to and from the library or to evening classes.
- Peer counseling and tutoring programs run by upper-class students for new students and special populations such as students of color and adult students.
- Union or student activities coordinating boards where students actually plan and carry out the events rather than having college staff implement them (for example, negotiating with a performing group and checking the contract with the college or university lawyer, or setting up student security for a concert or event).
- Scholarship or language theme residences with student coordinators.
- Student officials for intramural events.
- Student tour guides for prospective students who know and relay to newcomers important information about the institution's history, traditions, and terms of endearment.
- Student speakers for admissions and alumni/alumnae days.
- Student-led prayers or readings at campus ministry-sponsored events.

- Student-created scripts or musical scores for institutional advancement materials such as an admissions video.

Student-Initiated Opportunities. Another hallmark of an Involving College is an ample supply of student-initiated learning opportunities. Indeed, institutions should not attempt to create all involvement opportunities for students. Students are encouraged to become involved not only by the number and kinds of clubs and organizations available but also by the degree to which they are encouraged to create their own opportunities for involvement and are supported in their efforts to develop and implement their own activities that are consistent with the institution's mission and philosophy.

Moffatt (1988) observed that students are spending less time in the formal extracurriculum (student government, student activities committees, speakers' bureaus), perhaps as a consequence of an increasing need to have part-time jobs, or fatigue from involvement in high school activities, or a tendency to see student activities as childish or unsophisticated. The nature of spontaneous out-of-class activities that students create in their residences is ever changing. These are not usually funded or sponsored by the institution and may or may not be coordinated by a staff member. The extent to which students prefer spontaneous activities to the formal extracurriculum varies by institution and student subculture. Well-organized and planned student activities characterize some Involving Colleges, such as Miami, while students at Stanford, TESC, and Grinnell favor more spontaneous student-initiated events.

One issue worth considering at urban institutions is whether a core group or critical mass of undergraduates, the vast majority of whom are full-time, traditional-age students whose primary role is to be a college student, is necessary to perpetuate student-initiated traditions and a sense of campus community. Student newspapers and student governments at urban Involving Colleges rely heavily on members from this group to get work done. Of course, not all actively involved students at urban institutions are traditional-age students. For example, a past president of the Student Activities Programming Board at the University of Louisville was an adult learner.

Although campuses differ in the ways students prefer to spend their free time, a critical issue is whether students who seek outlets for their interests are encouraged and supported in generating new activities or whether rules or policies create obstacles to student initiative. For example, are there numerous, time-bound steps that must be followed to form a new student organization or club? Are there prescribed criteria for being an "approved" student organization that limit the number and kinds of groups in ways that are inconsistent with the institution's educational purposes? Sometimes assumptions about what constitutes a legitimate student group, such as formal organizational structures and an approved constitution, may serve as a barrier to some groups. For example, Forrest, Hotelling, and Kuk (1984) reported on a women's group that wished to rotate leadership and preferred an informal organizational structure. The group was denied funding.

Institutions should also consider how many activities or campus events are scheduled at various times during the week, or even the semester, and assess whether the number and timing of activities create an overload for members of the campus community, including students, faculty, and administrators. For example, some important community events take place in the spring, in close proximity to final examinations. Do they compete for students' attention and energy, which would be better directed to academic matters? Could these events be better timed to complement, rather than compete with, the academic program?

Rewards for Involvement. As stated in Chapter Four, cultural artifacts, such as institutional traditions, rituals, and symbols, communicate expectations for student involvement in out-of-class activities. Institutions should understand the ways in which they use symbols and ceremonies to acknowledge and reward achievements of individuals and groups in out-of-class learning opportunities. Examples include the Dean's Award for Service at Stanford University, the University of Louisville Campus Award to the faculty member who does the most to enhance the quality of campus life, and the Mount Holyoke President's Award for student involvement. Students of both sexes and of all ethnic and racial backgrounds should have opportunities to participate in and receive recognition at such ceremonies.

Student-Faculty Interaction. Institutions should also focus attention on opportunities for student contact with faculty outside the classroom. Is the nature of student-faculty interaction similar to that reported in Chapter Seven, essentially after class and connected to academic activities?

Institutions should remember that student-faculty ratio and institutional expectations of faculty affect the extent to which students can be touched by faculty in meaningful ways. Faculty members can spend only so much of their time with students. At the University of Texas, Austin, a campus with 50,000 students and 3,500 faculty, 80 percent of faculty reported that they were involved with students out of class, but only about 20 percent of the students indicated that they had contact with a faculty member out of class. The difference in reports of faculty and students regarding out-of-class contact with one another is explained by the disproportionately high number of students to faculty (Hanson, 1989).

Also warranting attention is the role of faculty in advising major-related organizations and integrating off-campus work experiences with the curriculum. A requirement that student organizations have faculty advisers may constrain spontaneous formation of student groups, but it can also affirm that the institution values, and so expects faculty to be involved in, students' lives out of class. Faculty adviser positions in student organizations are, however, only windows of opportunity for encouraging student involvement with faculty out of class, not a solution. At a minimum, student affairs staff should develop programs for faculty advisers of organizations to meet occasionally to share ideas and discuss their experiences.

The nature and number of faculty-initiated after-class contacts with students, particularly the proportion of these contacts that evolve into mentoring or sponsoring relationships, are other opportunities for out-of-class learning. Institutions should consider whether collaboration in teaching and research is perceived by students and faculty to be in sufficient supply and how, or whether, the decreasing number of student-centered faculty and changes in institutional reward systems (including promotion and tenure criteria) influence faculty contact with students beyond the classroom and laboratory.

Institutions might also determine the frequency with which faculty members are invited by students or student affairs staff to present colloquia or guest lectures or to discuss current social and political issues in student residences. Such settings provide powerful learning opportunities for students because they put faculty members in situations where they can model intellectual inquiry. Through such interactions, students and faculty are reminded that members of both groups lead interesting lives out of the classroom.

Summary

The most critical issue regarding campus environments and student involvement is not institutional size or numbers of students. More important to encouraging involvement is creating a sense of belonging, a feeling on the part of students that the institution acknowledges the human needs of social and psychological comfort, and that they are full and valued members of the campus community.

Large universities can be divided into small living-learning or special-interest units to ameliorate feelings of anonymity that often characterize large institutions and to increase the number of opportunities for student involvement. The physical and psychological boundaries of small colleges can be expanded, if only figuratively, to bring the outside world to their students. Any campus can provide spaces and places for students to congregate and to be alone, groups within which to explore one's own identity and the beliefs and assumptions of others, and as many opportunities as possible for out-of-class learning. The challenge to institutions is clear: discover ways to shape the campus environment to encourage and support student involvement.

14

Focusing Policies
and Practices
on Student Learning

In this chapter, we discuss the implications of the categories of policies and practices presented in Chapter Six: preparing and welcoming newcomers; promoting responsible student behavior; enabling multiple subcommunities; blurring boundaries between in-class and out-of-class experiences; and allocating resources.

Preparing and Welcoming Newcomers

In order for students to take advantage of out-of-class learning opportunities, they must be aware of what the institution expects of them, including how decisions are made and how resources are allocated. Using anticipatory socialization efforts and induction activities, Involving Colleges clearly communicate both the expectations they have for students and how the institution does its work.

Anticipatory Socialization. Institutions must make the strange familiar for newcomers and help students become acclimated to the expectations and demands of their new environment. Involving Colleges assume that, for newcomers, everything about the institution is unfamiliar. Therefore, they use recruitment and pre-enrollment mailings, contacts with current

322

and former students, and campus visits to prepare prospective students for what will be expected. These anticipatory socialization experiences enable students to picture themselves in the new institutional setting and envision what will likely happen to them. Equally important, the institution clearly describes its values and what it considers to be appropriate student behavior.

Some institutions have changed their admissions criteria but maintain policies and practices that are no longer consistent with the characteristics of matriculating students. For example, there are institutions that are attracting increasing numbers of students of high ability who may be capable of exercising independent judgment and taking responsibility for their own affairs. However, for various reasons (history, tradition), current policies and procedures restrict student autonomy and limit opportunities for student learning.

Language defines an institution to outsiders and newcomers. Newcomers can feel particularly like outsiders when words and terms have special meanings with which they are unfamiliar. The extensive and rich cultural vocabularies of Involving Colleges were discussed in Chapter Four. Sharing the institutional language with new students helps them become familiar with the usage and meanings specific to that place and gives them a sense of being full members of the institution. For example, matriculating students at Mount Holyoke, Stanford, Grinnell, and Wichita State receive publications that include lists of those institutions' terms of endearment so that new students, upon arrival, are able to sound like, and communicate with, experienced members of the community. Institutions should be aware of whether institution-specific language is used to make newcomers quickly feel a part of the community or serves as a barrier between newcomers and insiders.

Induction Activities. Social integration, a sense of fitting in and being accepted by peers, is considered important to student satisfaction and retention (Tinto, 1987). Social integration is, to some extent, a function of the degree to which a student feels confident in her or his social life and the number of formal and informal groups to which she or he belongs (Betz, Klingen-smith and Menne, 1970). Group membership is also positively associated with personal development and academic achievement (Bean and Creswell, 1980; Hartnett, 1965). Induction activi-ties at Involving Colleges focus, in part, on introducing students to the importance of, and opportunities for, group membership.

Institutions should consider efforts to make students feel welcome once they arrive on campus, to articulate the institu-tion's values, and to emphasize the importance of involvement in both out-of-class and in-class learning activities. These efforts include institution-sponsored activities, such as new student orientation events, frosh convocations, and informal student-initiated induction activities. What, if anything, is said about out-of-class life at orientation and other institution-sponsored induction activities? Who sends these messages? At Iowa State University, department chairs and academic deans are highly visible during orientation and articulate the importance of mem-bership in major-related organizations. It is worth recalling here the comments made to new students by President Donald Ken-nedy of Stanford University (Chapter Seven).

Encouraging new students to join organizations is a pow-erful way for the institution to say "welcome — you belong here and we want you to be a part of us right away." An example is the Iowa State practice of "rushing" new students to become members of major-related clubs. Do orientation activities in-clude information about the complete range of out-of-class learn-ing opportunities and specific ways in which students can be-come involved? Are new students encouraged and supported to run for elected office? Are training opportunities available for new students who desire leadership skills and experience? Can new students readily become members of existing clubs and organizations or form new groups that match their interests?

Many student affairs staff members have been taught to emphasize needs for social cohesion and competence of students in their first weeks and months in the campus community. While these needs cannot be overlooked, they must be balanced with the institution's academic priorities and expectations. To what extent do induction activities and events clearly and accurately describe to students, their families, and others the institution's academic mission and purposes, and "what it is like to be a *student* here?"

Induction activities are also important for new faculty members. Little attention is paid on most campuses to delineating the roles and responsibilities of faculty members with regard to student learning out of the classroom. New faculty members are often left to discover for themselves how to get things done and what is appropriate behavior (Whitt, in press). The role of senior faculty and department chairpersons in socializing new faculty members, and the information that new faculty receive with regard to student out-of-class experiences, merit attention. New faculty can also benefit from learning about the institutional language and campus traditions, such as those that value (or ignore) the power of out-of-class learning opportunities.

Promoting Responsible Behavior

Involving Colleges expect and encourage students to be responsible for their own learning and living experiences. For example, at several institutions (Earlham, Grinnell, Stanford), students determine and maintain community living standards. At all of the Involving Colleges, students play an active and substantial role in institutional governance. Evidence of high expectations for student responsibility at Involving Colleges can also be found in honor codes, housing policies, and practices regarding student initiative.

Honor Codes. Honor codes help students to be responsible for their learning and the conditions under which learning can occur. Honor codes also indicate that the institution trusts its students. For example, in Chapter Six we described the Mount Holyoke Honor Code, which allows for unproctored examinations. For honor codes to be effective, students — and their institutions — must be committed to principles of fairness, honesty, integrity, and self-governance. In addition, students need to be willing to hold their peers, as well as themselves, accountable for violations of the code.

An honor code that promotes responsible behavior will not prevent irresponsible student behavior. Honor codes work best when they are supported by institutional values and behaviors that communicate community expectations of integrity and honesty. Therefore, institutions with honor codes should assess whether the honor code is supported by institutional practices. Also important to consider is the extent to which students are instructed in, and understand, the elements and significance of the code. What does the code mean to students? Do they assume responsibility for its implementation? Institutions without honor codes may wish to consider the feasibility of introducing such a code if a code is compatible with institutional values and practices.

Housing Policies. Institutions should examine campus and off-campus housing policies to see if they are compatible with the institutional philosophy and educational purposes. If, for example, the mission emphasizes student autonomy and responsibility, housing policies should allow students considerable choices of housing options and high levels of freedom to regulate community life. If the mission and philosophy stress the importance of a living-learning community for student development, housing policies should emphasize on-campus living for all students. Are housing programs and policies implemented in ways that promote learning, or is the outcome merely the housing and feeding of students? Does ability to pay affect the type of housing available? If the institution aspires to promote egalitarianism, all students should pay the same amount for housing no matter where they live, whether in an old and well-worn building or one that is new and air-conditioned. Issues related to special-interest group housing, such as fraternities and theme houses, will be discussed later in this chapter.

Student Initiative. Institutions should be aware of the extent to which their policies and practices signal to students that they are to be self-directed and take responsibility for their own education and behavior. Are these policies and practices consistent with the institution's mission and philosophy? At Stanford, tuition bills and grades are sent directly to the student, not to parents. A completely different practice may be appropriate in another institutional context; at Xavier, institutional agents act almost as surrogate parents and apply "strict standards with sympathy."

If institutional agents take responsibility for planning and implementing campus events and activities, they effectively remove responsibility from students for making good use of their time. While programs and activities designed by institutional agents to promote student learning and personal development in residence halls and elsewhere can be quite useful, this type of programming can also discourage student initiative. In addition, when programs are provided for students, students have fewer opportunities to create what may be more personally relevant and meaningful learning opportunities. An appropriate balance between student-initiated and staff-initiated activities and programs is a function of student characteristics, the institution's history and traditions, and institutional mission and philosophy.

Other policies and practices may discourage student responsibility. For example, although rules and regulations may be intended to describe unambiguous behavioral guidelines, they can also allow students to abdicate responsibility for their own lives. A code of student conduct may be seen by students as something for which they have no ownership—"the staff's rules"— or as a challenge to students' creativity in evading accountability. A number of Involving Colleges emphasize, with considerable success, general behavioral expectations based on clear and shared institutional values which are expected to be maintained by the students themselves. This does not mean that students who violate community standards are not sanctioned. These institutions do, however, assert that they value individual responsibility and trust their students, and believe that students must have opportunities to exercise the freedom that trust and individual responsibility demand.

To be sure, there are risks inherent in treating students as adults and giving them responsibility for their living and learning experiences. Institutional agents must carefully assess their students' general level of maturity and readiness for freedom from institutional rules and rule enforcement. "Ladders"— such as those in place at Xavier (Chapters Six and Nine)— which provide clearly delineated expectations for responsibility, and which give students the amount of freedom they can handle at each step, may be appropriate for some campuses.

Institutions should also be concerned with the degree to which responsible student risk taking is advocated. Are students forced to exceed their own expectations for responsibility by forming their own community living standards? Can they, and do they, live up to the trust afforded them? Are students willing to try new activities or "create traditions," rather than rely on what has always worked in the past, or what makes them feel most comfortable? Are students encouraged to regard failure as a necessary consequence of innovation and an important and positive part of the learning process?

Some practices consistent with an institution's philosophy of student responsibility and autonomy may not be appropriate for all students at that institution. Although invisible safety nets—available, but not intrusive—are consistent with the theme of student responsibility, for some students, particularly those of color, the safety nets may be so completely imperceptible that they may not be used when needed. In addition, while the practice of not contacting family members when students face problems may promote the development of autonomy in many students, student autonomy is not always viewed as desirable in some cultures, such as Appalachian, Asian American, and Mexican American. In those cultures, family connections are strong and highly valued, and family involvement is considered essential in helping family members solve their problems.

Each institution must determine to what degree students should be responsible for their own education and welfare. We heard a story about a nineteen-year-old student who entered himself into a hospital because of abdominal pain, which was subsequently diagnosed as appendicitis. The student underwent surgery and the inflamed appendix was successfully removed. All this transpired without the knowledge of any institutional agent or the student's parents. Upon learning of the operation, the student's parents were angry with the institution for not contacting them. After learning that no one at the institution had any knowledge of their son's illness or hospitalization, the parents remarked, "Well, that's the problem with him, he thinks he is an adult!"

By trusting students and taking them seriously, student life staff, other administrators, and faculty members at many Involving Colleges increase opportunities for students to learn from out-of-class experiences. In many cases, this means that students are given considerable freedom and responsibility for their own learning and living. In other institutions, the characteristics of the college, its students, and other constituents require clearer behavioral guidelines and more intentional institutional involvement in students' in-class and out-of-class lives.

Enabling Multiple Subcommunities

Student subcommunities have always been present in American colleges and universities. The role of such groups has increased in importance over the past three or four decades as the size of many institutions has increased and the characteristics of students have become more diverse (National Association of Student Personnel Administrators, 1987). Student subcommunities can provide a haven from what at times seems to be an impersonal, bureaucratized university. In Chapter Thirteen, we described ways in which racial and ethnic subcommunities can support student learning and involvement, as well as community development. However, subcommunities whose values and attitudes are antithetical to the institution's values and educational purposes can threaten the sense of campus community. In this section, we discuss practices that enhance pluralism, including types of subcommunities, language, and special theme housing.

Student Subcommunities. Institutions should consider whether groupings by social interests are consistent and compatible with an institution's educational purposes and values. On some campuses, fraternities and sororities are viewed as subcommunities whose beliefs and values are inconsistent with higher learning and student development (Wilder and others, 1986).

None of the small residential colleges included in this study (Berea, Earlham, Grinnell, Mount Holyoke, The Evergreen State College) has fraternities or sororities. These institutions were not selected for this reason; surely there are small residential liberal arts colleges where both high levels of involvement and fraternities and sororities exist. We speculate, however, that the presence of Greek organizations is more likely to be a negative influence on the quality of community life at small colleges than at large universities. Fraternal groups tend to be exclusive, not inclusive, and contribute to a sense of territoriality and competition, a charge that some also level at ethnic and racial theme houses. The divisions that competition and territoriality create are especially apparent at a small college, and can be especially destructive to feelings of community.

Few campus issues are as important as promoting interaction and collaboration among student subcommunities. Institutional and student leaders are challenged to discover ways to encourage respect, appreciation, and cooperation among student groups engendering a true feeling of community on campus while retaining the important contributions of individual subcommunities to the learning and development of their members.

We are all engaged in the process of discovering what pluralism should mean to a college campus in the twenty-first century. To struggle, explore, take risks, and attempt to cope with the ambiguities present in periods of transition and upheaval are characteristics of powerful undergraduate learning experiences. It is, however, difficult to discover ways in which members of campus subcommunities can learn to live together, help each other cope with emotional issues that accompany diversity, and appreciate and celebrate differences when many students, faculty, and staff know and understand little about such differences. A starting point is to experiment with ways to enhance respect for women and for people of all racial and ethnic backgrounds and life-style orientations. But beyond the matter of respect is the matter of power: pluralism must embody shared power.

Toward this end, institutional language and symbols may be debilitating factors. Terms such as "racism," "patriarchy," and "male-dominated bureaucracies" can enhance anger in victims and feelings of guilt in the accused while creating obstacles to developing methods for working toward understanding and a truly multicultural community. At the same time, discussions of multiculturalism may seem merely pro forma in institutions in which white males hold all, or nearly all, administrative and student leadership and senior faculty positions.

As discussed in Chapter Twelve, diversity and multiculturalism are different concepts and describe institutions at different stages of evolution toward multicultural learning communities. Involving Colleges, too, vary in their progress toward and commitment to multiculturalism. Differences in mission and philosophy, location, and characteristics of students, faculty, and administrators affect what is happening on each of these campuses with regard to diversity, multiculturalism, and student subcommunities. In all cases, however, there is awareness among institutional leaders that the world, even the world of higher education, is changing and new ways of responding to those changes, developing community, and helping students learn are necessary.

Institutions should attempt to discover the extent to which recognizing, becoming comfortable with, and learning from differences are emphasized in their institutional missions and philosophies, as well as educational and social programming. Are students encouraged and enabled to explore issues of racial, ethnic, sexual, and gender identity? Are students encouraged and helped to form empowering subcommunities that, at the same time, respect and interact with one another? At many institutions, assumptions and beliefs may be rooted in the undergraduate student cultures which work against embracing differences, such as the "politically correct" attitude prevalent at Earlham College and Grinnell College.

Another issue to be considered is the extent to which members of student subcommunities participate in activities that are compatible with institutional educational purposes and values. Are subcommunity values consistent with the educational values of the institution? How do student subcommunities perpetuate or inhibit positive traditions of participation in campus organizations and activities? What messages do they communicate to their members about involvement in the life of the campus at large? The power of student subcommunities to enhance or detract from student involvement, the quality of the campus community, and the accomplishment of the institution's educational purposes should not be underestimated.

Terms of Respect. The language of our society and of our colleges and universities has long treated women as invisible. The exclusive use of male pronouns has, in some cases, been eroded, although it is still considered acceptable by many administrators, faculty, and students. The fact that female students make up over half of most undergraduate student bodies makes this practice increasingly outmoded and debilitating. Institutions should be aware of the extent to which their language embraces and affirms or excludes, alienates, and blocks participation of members of certain groups in learning opportunities. Are women and students of color invisible in the language of the campus? What language is used to describe them? Are students of color typically referred to as "minority" students, as though they were all the same, or in some ways less significant than "majority" students?

Terms of respect vary by region of the country, and sometimes by institution within a region. For example, the appropriate term of respect in some institutions for students of Mexican, Cuban, or Spanish origin is *Latino*. At other institutions, particularly on the West Coast, students prefer the terms *Chicano* or *Mexican American*. In other places, the terms *Hispanic* or *Hispanic American* are common. No matter what the location or common practice, students have a right to be called by the name they prefer. Do the student handbook and telephone director employ terms of respect to describe groups and offices that may be of interest to students of color? What is the term of respect preferred by persons with physical or learning disabilities?

Advertisements for programs and activities warrant careful examination. What efforts are made to challenge language that is offensive or reinforces a negative stereotype of a racial or ethnic group or women? By ignoring advertisements that perpetuate negative stereotypes, institutional agents tacitly endorse attitudes incongruent with the purposes of higher education.

Appropriate use of language is a complicated matter. Terms of respect may change during the academic year. Keeping track of the terminology preferred by various student groups may seem an unnecessary distraction from important matters. Nonetheless, it is critical that institutions acknowledge the power of language and reflect a sensitivity to students of color, women, and members of other historically underrepresented groups. Efforts must be made to use language so that all students feel that they are valued, respected, and included in the campus community.

Theme Houses. Colleges and universities have long encouraged students with similar interests to live together, provided those interests were deemed compatible with the institution's mission. Facilities that house a relatively small number of residents (15 to 200 or so) ensure that all residents will know one another, which usually leads to a strong feeling of ownership for the subcommunity. When a residential subcommunity is founded on shared academic interests — such as the study of another culture or language — knowledge and understanding of the subject area, as well as residents' out-of-class learning, are enhanced. Residential subcommunities based on racial, ethnic, or cultural backgrounds also add to knowledge and awareness of the history, traditions, and concerns of the group while providing social and psychological support for residents.

Much has been written about the security, support, and understanding that cultural or ethnic theme houses provide their members (Bourassa, 1989). Several examples of such housing options from Involving Colleges were offered in Chapters Six, Eight, and Nine. Many students of color reported that some of their most powerful educational experiences involved learning more about their ethnic and racial background through experiences with other students from the same background. This is often the case for students of color who come from integrated, or predominantly white, neighborhoods and schools.

However, the presence of racial and ethnic theme houses is sometimes interpreted by white students as an inappropriate accommodation to the special needs of students of color, and a practice that fosters separatism rather than community. Some white students on predominantly white campuses voice concern that too many resources are being targeted for a small proportion of the student body. Individual students—of either sex, any race, or any ethnic or cultural background—may wonder why they are excluded from certain groups or why some groups feel a need to separate themselves from the community as a whole. These are not simple issues to address. The typical "majority" student is frequently unaware of, insensitive to, or confused about the importance of racial or ethnic theme houses to their members' sense of security, self-esteem, and cultural heritage. At the same time, there is a point at which subcommunities create barriers between themselves and the rest of the institution that inhibit understanding, sharing, and learning.

Institutions should consider whether such housing is consistent with institutional values or student needs. What do various student subcommunities want in the way of residential options? What is the campus climate with regard to diversity and multiculturalism? The educational trade-offs between providing special houses for ethnic, racial, and life-style groups and housing all students together must be explored and discussed.

Blurring Boundaries

To determine the extent to which boundaries between in-class and out-of-class learning experiences are blurred, institutions should examine the frequency and range of educationally purposeful programs and events available on and off the campus. Another issue to address is who initiates and implements these activities: is student initiative and responsibility required?

Institutions may also find merit in determining the degree to which cultural or out-of-class educational programs, such as theatrical performances or guest lectures, are linked to the curriculum. Do faculty members attempt to integrate these out-of-class learning experiences into their courses? Do living units hold colloquia following cultural events to encourage students to share their reactions? Although such discussions would probably take place in some student groups anyway, structured opportunities to talk about these matters underscore the importance of viewing learning as something that occurs everywhere and all the time.

In an attempt to blur boundaries between in-class and out-of-class learning, some institutions have developed programs and policies to encourage faculty to spend time with students outside the classroom (Kuh, Schuh, and Thomas, 1985). The Stanford Resident Fellow Program described in Chapter Eight is one example. Virtually all the Involving Colleges have some type of program to link faculty members with students' residences.

These efforts are more or less effective. More important in fostering faculty involvement with students is the extent to which the institutional culture—including history, traditions, and role expectations—supports and affirms out-of-class involvement between students and faculty. In Chapter Eight, we described Iowa State's departmental clubs, every one of which has one or more faculty advisers. One person observed: "We don't have to beg for faculty advisers at Iowa State." Thus, institutional history and traditions and other cultural artifacts influence how students and faculty perceive and interact with one another, as well as how faculty members perceive and fulfill their roles.

When students encounter faculty members out of class, as when attending a faculty member's presentation in a student residence or interacting with faculty in their role as organization advisers, students often come to know faculty members for the first time as multidimensional human beings, not as detached scholars living on pedestals or in ivory towers. This experience can be very important for both students and faculty. The "detached scholar" impression maintains distance between students and faculty and can affect student learning in the classroom, inhibit students from seeking faculty to answer questions, and discourage students from seeing faculty as potential role models and mentors. Students sometimes become interested in a faculty member's area of expertise, or may even be motivated to consider an academic career, as a consequence of out-of-class interaction. A Stanford student told us:

> I met a new professor [in a social setting] and he asked me if I was going to take his class in Political Science. I took it . . . it was amazing . . . I thought Poli Sci was something I would never be interested in because I could never stand the idea that I would have to read so much. But I actually became very intellectually motivated.

The Harvard Assessment Seminars have also underscored the importance of comments made by faculty members to students outside of class. Interviews with Wellesley alumnae, for example, indicate that "critical experiences in college . . . the things that changed students' lives . . . they tend to be more outside the classroom than in, informal rather than formal" (Marchese, 1990, p. 6).

Allocating Resources

One way to understand what a community values is to determine how and for what purposes its resources are used. Merely providing funds to enrich out-of-class learning activities will not guarantee positive outcomes, but without funds, positive outcomes cannot be expected. Institutions should be aware of the ways in which their resources are directed to create and sustain high-quality learning experiences. Is funding available to encourage student-faculty interaction out of class? Are funds used to create and maintain a physical environment that supports student learning? Who decides how money is to be used, and by what processes? Are students involved in resource allocation? Do students have responsibility for allocation of their fees?

Another issue for institutions to consider is whether there are "hidden costs" for students, such as pay-as-you-go student athletic or social events, or activities that require expensive equipment, clothing, or off-campus travel. If such costs are present, ability to pay can affect student participation and highlight socioeconomic differences among students. For this reason, some institutions keep the cost of participation in events and activities low, in some cases by providing significant amounts of funding to student organizations. At the small residential Involving Colleges, payment of one activity fee enables students to attend all events on the campus. This policy is consistent with the egalitarian ethos of those institutions. Many urban institutions have purposefully kept costs of campus events low and make a special point of inviting family members to participate so that students and their spouses and children are able to use the campus for recreation and take part in events. This practice allows families to spend time together, encourages family participation in the educational process, and builds community among commuting students.

The majority of the students in our study at urban Involving Colleges worked off campus and, in many cases, were responsible for paying for their education with little help from their families. Many students at urban institutions face greater financial pressures than their peers at the residential universities and colleges we studied. This is not to say that students at other types of institutions do not encounter financial problems. They do, but their financial problems are, overall, not as burdensome as those of students at the urban campuses. As a result, there are times when urban university students have to forgo participating in campus events because they simply must work. Moreover, work may be the single most powerful out-of-class experience for urban students. Therefore, we cannot urge too strongly that urban campuses, in particular, develop additional, meaningful work opportunities for their students, either on campus or in the metropolitan areas they serve.

Institutions should also determine if sufficient resources are available to support the compensatory structures necessary to help at-risk students achieve academic success. Examples of such structures in this study include the Center for Academic Achievement at the University of Louisville, the University College at Wichita State University, and the summer programs at Xavier University.

In Chapter Six, we described the practice at many Involving Colleges of channeling resources to new students for the purpose of providing the special attention needed to help newcomers make a good start, thereby increasing the likelihood they will persist to graduation. The downside of directing a disproportionate amount of resources to newcomers is that second-year students sometimes feel ignored and unimportant. For example, we observed on several campuses a variant of the phenomenon once described as the "sophomore slump." A related issue is the use of financial aid as a recruitment tool, so that financial assistance for upper-class students is decreased. Such practices warrant examination. Is there evidence that emphasis on the quality of new student experiences is detrimental to returning students? Do the benefits of focusing attention on new students outweigh the problems faced by sophomores (or upper-class students)? Are there ways in which sophomores' needs and concerns can be addressed so that they do not feel as though they no longer matter?

Institutions must also consider to what extent students are given and take control of determining how their resources, such as student fees, will be used. Fiscal control, such as managing large sums of money and contracting with outside agencies, helps students learn responsibility. In addition, the process of resource allocation provides many teachable moments if students have access to forums in which the trade-offs, conflicts, politics, and compromises that are part of institutional resource allocation are discussed. Debates about resources are educationally purposeful if they reveal substantive conflicts, such as discrepancies between an institution's espoused and enacted values and individual and institutional values.

We have already indicated that institutions should be concerned about the amount of money that is available to create new student programs and groups, and whether students can create new organizations or activities without considerable effort. This does not mean that institutions should eliminate all obstacles from the process of obtaining funding or implementing new ideas. The world beyond the campus is replete with such obstacles, and students can learn from such educationally purposeful hassles. What institutions should keep in mind is that it is not just the amount of available funding, but also how students obtain and use resources, that is important to encouraging learning. Are students learning how to overcome obstacles successfully? Are they using resources responsibly?

Institutions should also consider whether certain groups or individuals, such as women or students of color, face particular obstacles in obtaining resources. It is possible that some groups are invisible in the resource allocation process and, therefore, are not informed about how to gain access to funding. As mentioned in Chapter Seven, institutions have developed ways of doing business that may alienate, or ignore the needs of, some groups of students. At some institutions, asking or bartering for funds is considered to be part of "playing the entrepreneurial game." However, it may be that people of color do not interpret the rules of the game the same way, or that the rules are applied differently, depending upon the sex or color of the person doing the asking.

We were told, for example, that the "entrepreneurial" ways of Stanford are offensive to some persons of color. Most white students quickly learn that to gather resources to support an activity, they will have to solicit funds from a variety of offices. Some of these students probably receive at least a few rejections of their requests for support; nevertheless, they move on to the next office more or less undaunted. However, some students of color feel that rejections of their requests reflect the influence of forces other than the university's entrepreneurial spirit. Whether there are other forces, such as racism, influencing the rejections is not clear, but that is irrelevant. What is important is that people of color perceive that, in this case, foraging for funds does not work for them. Their feelings are reflected in the words of a black faculty member at another institution: "I simply have grown weary and exhausted from going around and having to beg for everything I need." Institutions should be aware of how they transact business, and how resources are obtained, and whether students are knowledgeable about and comfortable with these procedures.

Summary

Policies and practices of Involving Colleges are effective because they are consistent with the institution's mission and philosophy, are responsive to student characteristics, and shape student behavior in educationally purposeful ways. Institutions should be aware of the degree to which policies and practices reflect and are integrated with their mission and philosophy. Institutions must also change the way they do business if they are to accommodate and enable students from historically underrepresented groups. For these reasons, we join the chorus of voices calling for changes in institutional policies and practices to celebrate and affirm the heritage, and encourage the full active participation in the life of the community, of members of historically underrepresented groups, such as adult learners, students of color, and women.

15

======

Conclusions and Recommendations for Creating Involving Colleges

No one of the institutional factors and conditions described in the preceding chapters can ensure involvement and learning on the part of students. Nor can an institution's culture, or student behavior, be easily changed or readily manipulated. However, a high level of student participation in educationally purposeful activities can be promoted if these activities, and the policies and practices that support them, are compatible with the institution's mission, philosophy, and culture. This chapter presents six conclusions about Involving Colleges. Recommendations are offered for institutions interested in creating conditions that seem to promote student learning. Finally, some unresolved issues related to student involvement and some insights from this study about developing a sense of community on campus are discussed.

Conclusion 1: Institutions that have a clear mission, kept plainly in view, encourage involvement.

A clear, coherent mission gives direction to student learning and minimizes confusion and uncertainty about what the institution is and aspires to be. Constant scrutiny is required, however, to keep the institutional mission appropriate within its social and political contexts and meaningful to community members. Goals for what and how students learn are examined, and reexamined, to remain compatible with the institutional mission. Student behavior is assessed and, if necessary, challenged in light of the mission and philosophy.

Recommendations:

1. All members of the campus community should be familiar with and committed to the institution's mission and philosophy.

At Involving Colleges, the most powerful factor in focusing student behavior is the institution's mission and philosophy. The mission should be communicated clearly and consistently in institutional publications, at gatherings of community members, and in the process of welcoming newcomers. Socialization activities send powerful messages about what the institution stands for and create lasting expectations for new (or prospective) students, faculty, and staff.

The chief academic officer (CAO), academic deans, and department chairs should play a primary role in teaching new students and faculty about institutional values regarding student learning. For example, academic administrators can make new faculty aware of the importance of using out-of-class contacts with students to educational advantage. The CAO can recommend that new student orientation include more intellectual activities, such as discussions of books assigned to be read during the summer, and can personally encourage students to become more involved in departmental organizations.

Understanding of, and commitment to, the institutional mission and personal values compatible with the institution's philosophy are particularly important characteristics for student affairs staff. Technical competence in areas such as legal aspects of student-institution relationships, counseling techniques, or conflict resolution is important. However, it is easier to acquire new information than to change values. Technical competence cannot substitute for "fit" between an individual staff member and the institutional ethos.

2. Resist efforts to create a mission that is all things to all people; take pride in and emphasize what is distinctive about the institution.

A distinctive mission not only sets an institution apart from its peers in the eyes of outsiders but also gives community members a shared sense of purpose that guides daily activities and serves as a touchstone for making decisions and establishing policies. New initiatives are evaluated in terms of their compatibility with the mission and philosophy. Are they consistent with "how we do things here" and what is valued? Any change in the mission should occur only after thoughtful reflection and healthy debate, and with thorough understanding of the consequences of a change, not as a result of some educational fad or trend or to avoid conflict.

3. Allocate resources in ways that help the institution attain its mission.

What a college or university values is evident in how, and for what purposes, its resources are allocated. If an institution's mission asserts the importance of encouraging and supporting student learning through out-of-class experiences, a significant portion of its financial and human resources must be directed to that end.

4. Assess the appropriateness and necessity of programs and services in light of the institution's mission and philosophy.

Administrators and faculty can become so involved in the demands of daily events that they do not take time to review whether, or in what ways, their efforts contribute to the accomplishment of the institution's mission. In addition, student activities may monopolize students' time and energy in ways that may or may not have anything to do with the educational purposes of the institution or the learning goals of students themselves.

Campus leaders should examine whether opportunities for involvement and the ways in which community members spend their time are consistent with and promote the institutional mission. If so, the complementarity between mission and community actions should be widely acclaimed and assiduously reinforced. If not, why not? Is the mission no longer viable, or have daily routines taken on a life of their own independent of larger institutional purposes?

5. Institutional advancement personnel should use their contacts with external constituents to teach them about the institution's mission, purposes, and philosophy.

One can learn a great deal about a college from what it says about itself. Prospective students, faculty, and staff need accurate information about what life is like at the college, information that may or may not be provided in institutional publications. For example, do admissions materials portray a picture of campus life that is consistent with the perceptions of current students? Do prospective students seem to expect something other than what they find when they visit campus?

Graduates and other potential donors should also have an accurate picture of institutional priorities. With the help of faculty, students, and student affairs staff, institutional advancement staff should develop publications that clearly communicate the institution's mission and values, articulate expectations for student performance both in and out of the classroom, and — to the extent possible — enable students to be informed sources for their peers who are considering joining the community.

6. Be prepared to deal with the conflict, debate, and discussion likely to characterize colleges and universities into the twenty-first century.

College campuses have always been buffeted by the social, economic, and political turmoil of the outside world. Racism, sexism, poverty, homelessness, abortion, health, and environmental concerns in the United States, as well as struggles of people elsewhere in the world, influence college life and the experiences of students. Increasing diversity of college students will likely increase campus tensions as well as enrich learning. In the process, institutions can become harbingers of the future rather than mirrors of history.

How can colleges and universities effectively meet the challenges of internal and external change and its attendant uncertainty? Up to this point, changes in institutional policies and practices regarding historically underrepresented groups have usually been championed by members of these groups. How will an institution respond when students request or demand changes in institutional policies and practices that enable them to feel understood, respected, and appreciated, rather than alienated and invisible? What changes in policies or practices, consistent with the mission and philosophy, should the *institution* initiate?

On many campuses, unrest is inevitable as institutional agents and students deal with what Steele (1989, p. 49) called the *"politics of difference,* a troubling, volatile politics in which each group justifies itself, its sense of worth, and its pursuit of power, through difference alone."* Student affairs staff and faculty are often on the front line and expected to ameliorate campus tensions. However, as institutions evolve from their present state of affairs toward pluralistic learning communities, an active role on the part of the president, as the embodiment of institutional mission and values, will be crucial. For example, people of color and women must be active and powerful, not just visible, members of the president's cabinet. Hiring of senior-level administrators alone will not empower women and students of color, but discouraging messages about institutional — and presidential — priorities are sent to members of these groups when the institutional leadership is predominantly white and male.

Conclusion 2: Institutions that value and expect student initiative and responsibility encourage involvement.
A college or university promotes student learning by establishing high expectations for student and faculty performance and tells students, from their first contact with the institution, that they will be responsible for their own affairs. When students are welcomed as full members of the institution (the ethic of membership), they are told, in effect, that they are expected to help the institution attain its mission and participate in running the institution. Involving Colleges expect, and help, students to be responsible for determining policies and rules for residences and holding themselves and one another accountable for maintaining a high quality of campus life. Again, the amount of assistance students should receive from faculty and administration depends on the characteristics of the students and the institution's mission and philosophy.

Recommendations:
1. Create an environment in which students can be responsible.
In order for students to take initiative and be responsible, certain conditions must be present within the institution: trust, care, and support for risk taking as a vehicle for learning.

Institutional agents must also be willing to share control of the institution with students and be open to the possibility that there are many ways to achieve institutional purposes, some of which institutional leaders may not have considered. One must keep in mind, too, that any learning process requires patience on the part of both teacher and student. The road to developing student responsibility and self-governance is not likely to be short or smooth, but it is certainly an exciting and worthwhile trip.

2. Spend less time designing and implementing programs and more time encouraging students to take advantage of learning opportunities.

Student affairs staff and faculty should not feel responsible for planning, programming, and organizing all student activities. Do not overstructure or overorganize the out-of-class experience for students; do just enough to enable students to develop and implement their own educationally purposeful activities. Experiment with services and programs. Work with students to identify programs and activities that are of debatable utility and suspend them for a year to see if anyone misses them. Use any savings of human or financial resources to concentrate on improving conditions for out-of-class learning.

3. Recognize and take advantage of the power of the small gesture in encouraging and reinforcing student effort devoted to learning.

As with other powerful learning experiences, there is no substitute for personal contact for encouraging student involvement in educationally purposeful activities. At Involving Colleges, institutional agents and students themselves make many small gestures to one another to encourage effort, such as comments in the margin of an essay acknowledging a salient point, a faculty member's words of encouragement after class, and notes from a staff member to students who have attained personal milestones. The confluence of these expressions of interest in students' welfare makes them feel known and valued, and encourages them to stretch themselves, both in and out of the classroom. At a time when a sense of community seems to be unraveling on many college campuses, we would do well to remember that, in many ways, a community is made up of the thousands of small gestures that keep people together and communicate appreciation and belonging. We will come back to this point later in this chapter.

Conclusion 3: Institutions that recognize and respond to the total student experience encourage involvement.

Most colleges and universities are organized to present students with discrete experiences. Different people, at different points in time and in different places (and sometimes with completely different philosophies about what college is for), orient new students, offer advice and counsel, teach classes and labs, get students registered, provide medical care, teach job-hunting skills, provide places to live and food to eat, impose degree requirements, and help organize dances and parties.

The fragmentation of universities as organizations is reflected in perceptions of student life: in-class and out-of-class learning are too often treated as separate aspects of the undergraduate experience. For example, changing reward systems encourage faculty members to isolate themselves from students, thus enhancing the attitude that academic and nonacademic aspects of students' lives are, and should be, distinct. Separation of academic and student affairs within the institutional structure can encourage persons within those areas to view their tasks and priorities as distinct and, in some cases, competing.

Students, however, do not think of their lives as bifurcated by the classroom door. For students, college is a stream of learning opportunities: challenges, relationships, discoveries, fun, disappointments, and successes. *Where* these opportunities are encountered is, for the most part, irrelevant; what is important is that students learn. Just as the institution seeks to help students make sense of courses within a major, students yearn to interpret and make sense of all their experiences.

Involving Colleges seem to be aware of the seamlessness of student experience and of the harvest of learning that awaits students from *all* aspects of college life. By envisioning what the total student experience ought to be, and resolving to use the institution's educational resources — curricular and noncurricular, formal and informal — to full advantage to enable that experience,

Involving Colleges ignore the perceived, artificial distinctions between what is academic and what is educational and between what are "in-class" and "out-of-class" learning experiences. A college takes a step toward becoming an involving institution when it softens or makes permeable the boundaries between curricular and other student experiences.

Recommendations:

1. Know your students, how they learn, and the conditions that affect their development.

In many institutions, students' aspirations, backgrounds, abilities, and roles, such as student, spouse, parent, or worker, have changed dramatically from those of past students, even the recent past. The ways in which these institutions work with and respond to their students must also change — but this can be done effectively only if the institutions know and understand the changes. The effectiveness of faculty, administrators, and staff is enhanced when they recognize and understand differences among individual students and student cultures.

The institutional research office or the student affairs division are likely sources for collection and dissemination of data about students and the quality of student life. Institutional researchers and student affairs staff should obtain up-to-date information about students (characteristics, attitudes, needs, and activities) and share this information with faculty, academic administrators, trustees, and the students themselves. A study of student cultures could provide insights into their influence on learning and personal development, and the ways in which student life complements or competes with the educational purposes of the institution. The best source of information about students is the students themselves; any institutional research effort with regard to students and their lives should include interviews with students.

One should be cautious, however, about making generalizations from composite information about student characteristics to individual situations. Every student is unique, with unique needs, interests, and priorities. At the same time, certain subcommunities of students, such as women or African American students or adult learners, have needs specific to their group, needs that are best identified in intensive and extensive interaction with members of their subcommunity.

The student affairs division should be held accountable for articulating and, in collaboration with faculty and others, responding to students' out-of-class needs. Student affairs staff should be able to describe and appreciate the ways in which out-of-class environments and events influence student learning, as well as the institution.

2. Discover the ways in which students spend their time and are influenced by peers, student cultures, and campus life.

In order to recognize and respond to the total experience of students, institutions must first understand the experiences of their students from the point of view of the students themselves. How do students spend their time? With what activities do they fill their lives? How do students decide how to use their time? In what ways do peers and peer cultures affect students' lives and learning? Are students' experiences consistent with the educational purposes of the institution?

On many campuses, the pace of student life is hectic and overwhelming, demanding too much time and energy from students and allowing too few opportunities to think about what they are learning. On other campuses, student life can best be described as boring. In both cases (and all those in between), students may respond by organizing activities that are antithetical to the institution's mission. Social life, including parties and drinking, may become the focus of students' efforts as they seek to escape from the pressures of overinvolvement, or because they cannot think of anything else to do.

Students' experiences can, of course, stray from fulfilling educational purposes in many ways, including overinvestment in a particular activity or many activities, to the extent that a sense of balance is lost. Throughout this book, we have emphasized learning experiences that are educationally purposeful, but there *are* trade-offs associated with high levels of involvement. Some students at Involving Colleges suffer negative effects of overinvolvement, including burnout. Feeling responsibility or pressure to become involved, to take full advantage of the institution's resources, to be actively engaged in one or more activities all the time, can be debilitating. The balancing act becomes even more difficult when a student has a spouse, children, job, or other commitments. It is not surprising that more than a few seniors told us that, after graduation, they would like to take a year off because they were exhausted!

Institutional agents can help ease the stress associated with overinvolvement by being aware of students who appear to be taking on too many responsibilities and helping them examine what constitutes an appropriate balance of effort in different aspects of their lives. Students may need help in weighing the perceived personal and educational benefits of various activities when deciding how to invest their time. When students become aware, and consider the implications of the trade-offs, the collegiate experience more closely approximates life after college, when multiple and often conflictual personal and professional demands are typical. Institutional agents can also assist students by teaching and modeling the importance of, and skills needed for, living a balanced life.

3. Examine what your policies and practices teach students.

Students learn from what an institution *does* just as surely as they learn from what institutional agents *say;* discrepancies between espoused and enacted values may create particularly fruitful teachable moments. What are the social values an institution espouses? How does an institution invest its funds? Is the campus press as free as public statements about the importance of a free press would indicate? Does the common language of the institution, especially the terms used to describe individuals and groups, mirror the espoused values of the institution?

4. Develop a shared vision of the institution and its students.

All institutional agents (faculty, academic administrators, student affairs staff) are partners in achieving the institution's educational purposes. This partnership requires a shared vision of the enterprise — what the institution's mission is, who its students are, what sort of education the students should have, what behaviors ought to be expected of students, and what qualities characterize a healthy and effective academic community. A shared vision is forged when faculty, student affairs staff, and others spend time together talking about institutional purposes, about the ways in which the institution's mission and philosophy influence their work, and about students.

The relationship between the chief academic officer (CAO) and the chief student affairs officer (CSAO) is a key to clarifying and reinforcing connections between the curriculum and out-of-class learning opportunities. The CAO will undoubtedly underscore the primacy of the institution's academic mission but should, nevertheless, work with the CSAO, students, and others to discover how the institution's educational purposes can be accomplished in out-of-class learning environments. The priorities of academic and student affairs can complement each other if both acknowledge their common commitment to the institution's mission.

The increasing size and complexity of universities and changing expectations for faculty suggest that student affairs staff on many campuses will play an increasingly prominent role in promoting learning experiences that support the institution's educational purposes. Indeed, at some large institutions, student affairs staff have become the de facto caretakers of the undergraduate experience. Along with a few other administrators and faculty members, student affairs staff model how students can respond effectively to the opportunities and responsibilities present in an academic community. Student affairs staff are more likely than faculty to be present to help students take advantage of the many "teachable moments" that occur out of the classroom.

Conclusion 4: Institutions that provide small, human-scale environments and multiple subcommunities encourage involvement.

Involving Colleges make creating and maintaining conditions that promote student learning a priority. Learning is promoted when faculty, staff, and students are familiar with one another and have frequent contact. By providing small residences and classes, maintaining effective communication networks, and widely disseminating information, Involving Colleges allow community members to interact easily and comfortably.

At a small college, students probably know several faculty members and administrators who can assist and encourage them to become involved in learning opportunities that fit their abilities and needs. Such relationships between students and faculty or staff are less likely to be found at large institutions. Large institutions can, however, foster interaction among students and between students and faculty and staff, as well as encourage feelings of belonging, through the development and support of subcommunities. A subcommunity provides a niche in which its members can feel comfortable and connected and where they can find others like themselves, whether those "others" be students of color, social activists, biologists, or women. At the same time, a subcommunity can support its members' efforts to participate in the community at large and establish connections with members of other subcommunities.

Recommendations:

1. Reduce physical obstacles to interaction by dividing large facilities into smaller units, increasing the number and span of communication networks and making more effective use of campus space.

In general, small is better. Small residences seem to build a sense of community among residents much more quickly than large residences. Members of a small community can more easily become full participating members of organizations and activities, such as intramurals and student government. This does not mean that large institutions cannot provide "small" environments. We have provided numerous examples of ways in which Involving Colleges — large and small, residential and commuter — have made the most of the advantages of their setting (as well as other aspects of their physical environment) to compensate for any disadvantages and to meet the needs of community members for interaction and solitude.

2. Make sure that safety nets and early warning systems for students in difficulty are in place and operating effectively.

Despite the emphasis placed at many Involving Colleges on student initiative and responsibility, students are not abandoned by these institutions to fend for themselves. Resources to help students are available, although the services and their visibility vary according to students' characteristics and institutional philosophy.

Institutions should find out what academic support systems exist, and assess the extent to which they meet the needs of all students and are compatible with institutional mission and philosophy. One example of an academic safety net is the option to declare academic bankruptcy after a particularly trying semester, similar to the policy in place for first-year students at Wichita State University (Chapter Ten). For students who come from disadvantaged educational backgrounds, or who have been away from academic work for some years, the possibility of academic bankruptcy may reduce some of the pressure associated with fear of failure.

Student affairs staff are the heart of the early warning systems of Involving Colleges, systems which identify students with problems and—in collaboration with faculty members and students—form the safety nets for them. To expand existing safety nets, new faculty members could be contacted by the chief student affairs officer by letter prior to their arrival and in person by a senior member of the student affairs staff soon after they come to campus. During these contacts, held when new faculty are looking for behavioral cues in their environment about what is important, programs and services available on the campus to help students—and to help faculty help students—can be described. At the same time, student affairs staff establish relationships with new faculty, who now have a contact in student affairs to whom questions can be addressed and students referred.

3. The institution should be a catalyst for multiple subcommunities and cultural pluralism.

Students of color, women, and members of other historically underrepresented groups need support in their efforts to teach others about their background and interests. Although this can be a wearisome task for these students, it is important for achieving understanding and respect for differences among people of all groups. Students in historically underrepresented groups need the help of others within the institution to achieve their goals. Some of the most highly sought-after helpers include faculty and staff who are women or people of color, although their minority status can place extensive and intensive demands on their time; the need for more faculty and staff who are people of color and women has already been discussed. The needs of students of historically underrepresented groups are not, however, the exclusive purview of institutional agents who are also members of these groups. All members of the community, and members of all subcommunities, must care for one another.

Some examples of practices that respond to the needs of historically underrepresented groups follow. Many institutions are already doing these things. They are offered in the hope that other institutions will recognize the importance of these activities in promoting out-of-class learning by students from these groups.

For Students of Color:

- Assess, perhaps by means of an institutional audit (see Chapter Eleven), the ways in which the needs of students of color are — and are not — being met. On the basis of that assessment, work with students of color to create policies and practices that promote their learning and development.
- Establish recruitment and retention programs for faculty and administrators of color (including those at senior levels) in order to provide a variety of role models for all students.
- Emphasize in word and action, at every opportunity, the importance of a multicultural learning community to the institution's educational purposes.
- Develop orientation workshops for new students of color hosted by currently enrolled students and faculty.
- Create opportunities for students of color to meet regularly with one another and with university administrators to discuss concerns.
- Recruit and train students of color to serve on all major campus governance committees, student government, cultural and social programming boards, and the student newspaper.
- Establish cultural awareness weeks around themes of unity and diversity and observe special holidays and celebrations, such as Black Heritage Month, Cinco de Mayo, and Martin Luther King, Jr.,'s birthday.

- Recognize students of color for their service and academic achievements. For other suggestions related to making institutions more hospitable for racial and ethnic minority students, see Fleming, 1984; McHugh, Dalton, Henley, and Buckner, 1988; Moses, 1989; Richardson and Bender, 1987; and Richardson, Simmons, and de los Santos, 1987.

For Women:

The opportunities for women's development at Mount Holyoke are so powerful that we wonder whether some of the enabling elements of the women's college experience can be adapted and incorporated in coeducational institutions, as through single-sex residential units, special theme houses, women's centers, or changes in the curriculum. This may be merely wishful thinking given the domination of most colleges and universities by males and male values. We believe that creating affirming environments for women demands institutional commitment and action, not changes and adaptation on the part of women themselves. Following are our recommendations for women students.

- Assess the campus climate for women: Are women valued or devalued, and in what ways? Are institutional and student resources expended for women's programs and concerns? Are there campus activities or events that are demeaning to, or perpetuate stereotypical roles for, women? Do women serve in senior-level faculty and administrative positions? Are male faculty and administrators supportive of women students? And so forth.
- Establish recruitment and retention programs for female faculty and administrators, including those at senior levels, so that sufficient female role models are available for all students.
- Create leadership development programs for women and encourage women students to seek leadership roles.
- If there is no women's center, create one; if a women's center exists, make sure that it is appropriately funded and emphasized.
- Provide positive feedback to administrators, faculty, and students who take steps to create an affirming environment for women.

- Emphasize in word and action, at every opportunity, the institution's commitment to the education of women (See Hall and Sandler, 1984, and Moses, 1989, for other suggestions.)

For adult learners:

- Assess the campus climate for adult learners; do not take for granted that their needs are being met. Are campus services adequately available to them? Are they able to and do they know how to take advantage of opportunities for involvement? Are support services adequate to meet their needs (for example, child care or adult learner support groups)?
- Invite spouses or significant others to orientation programs specifically designed for them.
- Arrange child care for all campus events, such as orientation, especially for those activities at times when children are not in regular child care (nights and weekends).
- Encourage families to attend events by sending special invitations and by offering reduced rates to spouses and children of students.
- Establish a task force to advise decision makers on policies and services, such as advising hours, financial aid policies, office hours, and registration procedures, to increase access for nontraditional students.
- Create programs (one time and ongoing) that meet special needs of older students, such as single-parent support groups, budgeting for college with a family, and balancing academic demands with a job. (See also Schlossberg, Lynch, and Chickering, 1989, for other suggestions related to adult learners.)

For commuters and part-time students:

- Establish a communications center and provide a campus mailbox for commuters.
- Send frequent mailings to commuters about campus activities.
- Provide a campus space (other than the library or a campus

dining facility) arranged to encourage social interaction so that commuter students can relax and talk informally with faculty and peers.

- Provide easy access to campus events. For example, if there is an all-campus picnic and resident students eat free because of their meal ticket, provide commuters with free or low-cost meals and parking permits.
- Include representatives of special populations on all student government, faculty, and staff committees or task forces. Be sensitive to commuters and students with family commitments; try not to schedule too many meetings that take students away from their families at mealtime.
- Provide peer counselors or student advisers for commuter and part-time students. A resource person who is also a student can provide the kind of information and support that a faculty member or student affairs staff member cannot. (See Jacoby, 1989; and Stewart, 1983, for other suggestions related to commuter and part-time students.)

4. Encourage prospective students to choose a college where they feel they belong and can grow.

Those students who have a choice about where to attend college should recognize that many colleges and universities have a curriculum that will provide them with an education and prepare them for life after college. Some institutions, however, will be better than others in meeting students' unique academic and intellectual needs and motivating them to their best effort.

When visiting a college, prospective students should find out about the nature and number of activities the institution offers for students outside the classroom. Is this a place that will allow them to learn, grow, and develop competence and confidence outside the classroom? With what frequency are opportunities available to hear visiting speakers or take field trips or study abroad? They should determine, as best they can, how important *students* are at the colleges they are considering; undergraduates and their quality of life are more important at some institutions than at others. Is teaching really important to the faculty? Do professors and students meet together informally, such as over a cup of coffee in the union? Prospective students could ask the tour guide how accessible faculty members are and how difficult or easy it is to get involved in various organizations and activities.

Prospective students should also consider whether they prefer competitive or collaborative styles of working and learning. Some colleges have a competitive ethos, in which students are expected to compete with one another in a variety of settings, both in and out of class. At others, a collaborative ethos prevails, so that students are expected to cooperate with one another, and competition and status differences are actively discouraged.

Most important, prospective students should find out what the institution expects with regard to academic and social performance. At some institutions, students are expected to be responsible for their learning and living activities; at others, institutional agents take a more active role in the lives of students. However, even at the places where students are expected to be responsible, there are usually services that students can use when academic or personal concerns become overwhelming. Prospective students should find out what types of assistance are available, and how helpful current students feel these services are.

One of the most exciting and important aspects of college is the opportunity to have one's views and values challenged and to learn from and about a wide variety of people. One's ability to communicate and work with people who are different in backgrounds, opinions, and values will only become more important in the future, so prospective students should seek educational settings that foster experience and skills in tolerance, understanding, and respect. They should get a sense of how the institution and other students treat people from varied cultural and ethnic backgrounds, and how women are viewed and treated by students and institutional agents.

5. Make it clear to students that they are expected to attend orientation.

A college can be an interesting and fun place, but it can also be confusing, especially if students are unaware of where to get answers to their questions, or even what questions to ask.

No matter where a student goes to college, he or she will learn a lot about the institution by taking part in the events the institution has planned to introduce new students to college life and what is required to make the most of that particular college.

Institutions might want to consider an extended orientation program, such as a course during the first semester, to use the interests of new students to full advantage and to meet their needs more fully (Upcraft, Gardner, and Associates, 1989). Whether an extended orientation process is appropriate depends, of course, on the needs and goals of the students, as well as the mission, philosophy, and resources of the institution.

6. Encourage students to live on campus for at least one year.

Personal circumstances make living on campus impossible for some students. But for those students who can do so, living among peers for an extended period of time provides innumerable opportunities to learn about themselves and others. Institutions might want to consider ways in which more students can participate in on-campus living, such as residential scholarships, and ways in which commuting students can be included in the residential community, such as residence-based social activities and educational programming.

Conclusion 5: Institutions that value students and take them and their learning seriously encourage involvement.

Learning occurs most effectively when students are challenged to reach high, but reasonable, educational goals in an environment in which students are understood and appreciated and which makes manageable the risks inherent in meeting such challenges. High expectations should be established for students, faculty, and others; achievements should be acknowledged, and students, faculty, administrators, and others who contribute to a high-quality campus life should be rewarded.

Recommendations:

1. Make the learning experiences of students, wherever they occur, a priority on the agenda of institutional leaders.

The amount of attention institutional leaders devote to student learning and the quality of campus life is a function of the importance they place on those issues. Of course, merely asserting that the quality of campus life is important does not make it so; actions must accompany the words. Concern for and commitment to students' learning and the quality of their lives should be evident in the words and deeds of institutional leaders, from everyday encounters to long-range plans.

Presidents are expected, when talking with trustees, campus constituencies, state legislators, and the press, to discuss issues that matter, including extraordinary achievements by faculty and students, the institution's future, efforts to retain faculty and recruit students, and plans to enhance collaboration with business and industry. Student learning should also be part of these discussions: What does the institution want and expect its students to learn? How are those expectations communicated? Why is student learning important? How does the institution help students learn? What student learning is taking place?

2. Underscore the importance of student life through symbolic action.

As keepers of the institution's vision, leaders (presidents, academic deans, student affairs staff, senior faculty) use institutional symbols, and other cultural artifacts, to protect and shape community values and assumptions. Because the president serves as the symbolic leader for all members of the campus community, how, where, and to what ends he or she spends time sends strong messages to everyone about what, and who, is valued. For example, the presence of the president and other institutional leaders at student functions, such as community service events, concerts, or academic honor ceremonies, sends an eloquent message to community members about the importance of students and their activities.

The symbolic ways in which an institution demonstrates that students are valued vary according to the institution's mission and philosophy. Being accessible to students, affirming the importance of students in speeches, meetings, or conversations with community members, knowing students' names, taking time to talk with students about their concerns and interests, and eating with students in their dining halls or interacting with them in their residences and other gathering places are all potentially meaningful symbolic actions on the part of institutional leaders. To *be* meaningful, however, these activities must be viewed by students as genuine — consistent with "the way we do things here" — and not simply for show. Among campus groups, students are the least impressed by symbolic action. Thus, symbolic actions must be reinforced by institutional policies and practices, such as those described in the previous recommendation.

Language is also symbolic action. The words institutional leaders use may convey an assumption of second-class citizenship, or even invisibility, for certain groups of students, faculty, and administrators, or for all students. Language can also encourage or discourage seeing and treating students as responsible and trusted adults. An anecdote to illustrate the point: In explaining the events that led up to the probation of the university's athletic department, a president (not from any of the institutions in this study) described it as "an adult problem, not a youngster's problem." By using such language, the president inadvertently encouraged institutional agents and students themselves to think of students as lacking the capacity to act like responsible adults.

3. Seek and reward learning-centered faculty members.

Student-centered faculty members (described in Chapter Seven as those who attend student events, serve as advisers to student groups, and regularly interact with students out of class) are no longer in the majority on many campuses, and trying to reverse that trend is probably not realistic for those institutions. Nonetheless, an aspiration to put *learning-centered* faculty members in most undergraduate classrooms seems reasonable. Learning-centered faculty are people who make their love of learning and intellectual inquisitiveness contagious. They create a sense of wonder and excitement in students and view undergraduates as active partners in learning rather than empty and passive vessels to be filled. They challenge students to take full advantage of the institution's resources, including the library, cultural events, and work opportunities both on and off the campus. They have high expectations for student performance and challenge students to discover and use their intellectual capabilities. Learning-centered faculty members treasure knowledge for its own sake and invite students to collaborate on research projects. They also recognize that, for most students, knowledge must be applied to be useful and relevant. For this reason, learning-centered faculty members help students integrate their studies and their lives, in part by relating class material to students' lives and the pressing social issues of our times.

Faculty can also serve as inspiring examples of learners. They illustrate for students the joy of discovery, the rewards of education, and the seamlessness and satisfaction of a learning-centered life. Faculty might, for example, talk about their experiences and reactions to convocations and distinguished lectures and ask students to talk about what they have learned from these events. When a class session has been especially stimulating, faculty members should express appreciation to students; on some campuses, students are too docile or polite to engage faculty in debates or lively discussions about class material. One faculty member told the story about a particularly stimulating class session during which one of her students asked some challenging questions about the material. Several other students approached the faculty member after class to apologize for their peer's "inexcusable, rude behavior!" Of course, many students are uncomfortable speaking in public and need to feel trust and support from the instructor and their peers before they will take intellectual or personal risks in class.

Faculty should focus on intellectual matters when talking with students out of class. While some relaxed conversation may be necessary to develop rapport and trust, student learning seems to be enhanced when faculty members engage students intellectually and relate their in-class and out-of-class experiences to the mission and educational purposes of the institution.

4. Challenge the ethos that encourages faculty and students to avoid meaningful contact with each other.

On some campuses, students and faculty have struck an implicit bargain that says, in effect, "you leave me alone and I will leave you alone." For faculty, this "disengagement compact" has been encouraged by reward systems that favor research over teaching, by the increasing size of institutions, and by efforts to increase institutional status by becoming less like teaching institutions and more like research universities. The student side of the bargain is motivated by the fact that, for too many students, intellectual activity and meaningful interaction with faculty are not what college is about. This attitude seems to be exacerbated by students' tendency to view and use college primarily as job training. In addition, students are increasingly likely to hold at least one job while in school in order to purchase items that used to be considered out of the question for college students, such as cars, stereos, computers, compact disc players, television sets, and refrigerators. Most of these possessions somehow get crammed into the dorm room that twenty years ago held two beds and a clock radio. The impact of such amenities, and the jobs that pay for them, on the quality of campus life and student learning ought to be examined.

Conclusion 6: Institutions that are able to generate feelings of loyalty and a sense of specialness encourage involvement.

An Involving College is a special place — just ask someone who lives and works there. You may hear examples of ways in which students matter, or outstanding programs or people, or crises that have been weathered. Or you might hear that "there's just something about the place," something that, although intangible, is clearly felt by, and sustains, the community. "Specialness" is found in institutional purposes, values, and history, and is reflected in and affirmed by institutional symbols. Involving Colleges know and celebrate, openly and often, who they are. Their cultures are rich in traditions, language, and stories that keep community values alive so that community members feel that they are part of something truly special.

Recommendations:

1. Discover what makes your institution special and celebrate it.

Institutional self-discovery is necessary both to determine what is special about a college or university and to create an environment to enhance student learning. As we said in Chapter

Eleven, make the familiar strange! Review Chapter Eleven and
The Involving College Audit Protocol (Resource E) to determine how information from a campus audit might be useful in
your setting. Learn as much as you can about your institution's
past and present — its history, mission, philosophy, and traditions. The history of the institution and current catalogues and
handbooks may provide insights into campus traditions and how
these traditions influence student learning. Figure out what messages these events send to students about how to spend their
time out of the classroom. Equally useful, and probably more
stimulating, will be talking with campus historians, institutional
heroines and heroes, emeritus faculty and administrators, graduates and students about what they perceive the institution's mission to be and what the mission says to and about students. Take
a tour of the campus with the institutional historian and architect.
Find out why facilities and open spaces are placed where they
are and how students use these and other spaces to attain their
learning and personal development goals.

A keen sense and appreciation of the past and the traditions that bind various constituencies are essential to discovering the assumptions that undergird the reasons for the institution's existence and the ways in which it achieves its purposes.
What makes your institution special? What is distinctive about
your institution's mission and philosophy? How are the special
qualities of your institution reflected in the out-of-class experiences of students? Recognize that an institution's specialness
is as much — if not more — a matter of how people feel about it,
and its traditions and history, as it is of its admissions and fund-
raising success.

2. Leaders should understand and teach institutional cultures.

Senior faculty, administrators, staff, and upper-class students are in the best position to teach the cultures of the institution, including its mission, traditions, symbols, values, assumptions, and beliefs. As with any good teacher, these people must
know their material in order to communicate it effectively. This
requires that the president, for example, and his or her cabinet, understand the tacit, as well as the obvious, elements of

institutional cultures and student subcultures. Campus leaders should become students of the institutional culture, a continuing process of self-discovery described above and in Chapter Eleven. Institutional leaders—or other teachers of culture—should communicate these messages or lessons throughout the institution so that all members can share in the sense of specialness.

3. Create something special.

Some institutions, particuarly those that have short histories or have markedly modified their missions within the recent past, may have cultures that lack an abundance of unifying or celebratory rituals, traditions, or symbols. Although the development of cultural richness requires many years, events, and generations of people, a sense of institutional specialness *can* be created out of the present. Programs and events can easily become traditions; we know of one institution in which a volleyball tournament became an instant tradition when it was designated the "Fifth Annual. . . . " What is important is that the event or activity affirm and celebrate the community's values and purposes.

Every campus has heroines and heroes; make sure that people know about them and that their contributions are periodically heralded. Acknowledgment of student heroes and heroines in particular sends a powerful message that students matter.

The academic year is marked with many milestones—beginnings, endings, achievements, anniversaries—and each offers an opportunity to declare what is special about the institution and its people. Use these times to celebrate the entry of newcomers into the community. Take advantage of these occasions to bring graduates back to the community to affirm the historical continuity—however brief—of the institution. Institutions can be more imaginative about what is considered a milestone or causes for celebration; every institution should find its own ways to express its specialness.

4. Maintain a sense of perspective and humor about the institution.

Along with a sense of specialness, Involving Colleges do not take themselves too seriously (recall the Stanford Band and

Evergreen's "Fighting Geoducks"), a characteristic that enables them to cope with large and small problems without losing sight of what makes them special. Although playful is not a word that is ordinarily used to describe a college or university, some Involving Colleges have developed that quality to remind people to be open to new ideas and new people, and to take pleasure in their work and in one another.

Concluding Thoughts

As we conclude our report of Involving Colleges, two additional matters warrant attention. First, we consider some unresolved issues related to involvement, including the relationship between student characteristics, such as participation in activities in high school or elsewhere, and taking advantage of learning opportunities. Second, we offer some insights from Involving Colleges about establishing, or reestablishing, a sense of community on campus.

Student Involvement Revisited. Students are more likely to take advantage of educationally purposeful out-of-class learning opportunities when both the institution and students devote time, effort, and resources toward this end. Institutional contributions were the focus of this study although, ultimately, the mutually shaping influences of institution and student are not separable. There is, of course, more that can be discovered about how colleges direct their efforts and resources to promoting student involvement in out-of-class learning and personal development opportunities. For example, the out-of-class learning opportunities for students in two-year colleges deserves immediate attention. Also, additional case studies describing in detail how institutions use the factors and conditions described in this book to promote student learning, such as forging relationships with representatives of local business and industry to create employment opportunities, would be informative.

Are students with certain characteristics and experiences more likely to participate in some activities and not others? It is not unusual for students who were active in out-of-class activities in high school to seek similar outlets to express their interests when they get to college. However, students who were not involved in activities, such as musical ensembles, athletics, or student government, in high school or elsewhere sometimes make an effort to get involved when they get to college. Institutions and students could benefit from knowing under what circumstances students without previous experience will attempt to take advantage of out-of-class learning opportunities.

What "involvement" means is also worthy of further investigation. We did not precisely define involvement at the outset of this study because we were interested in identifying the characteristics of natural settings — colleges and universities — which were thought to provide unusually rich, educationally purposeful out-of-class activities for undergraduates. Narrow definitions could have inappropriately constrained our discovery process. The behavioral view of involvement (Astin, 1984, 1985; Pace, 1980, 1986) — that involvement can be found in what students do and how much effort they expend in various activities — served our purposes.

Because the concept of involvement is relatively new, it remains somewhat ambiguous, a state of affairs typical in the early stages of the development of a social science construct. When an idea or construct attracts the interest of researchers, there is a period during which its scope and parameters must be examined before precise definitions can be developed (Baird, 1989). Baird suggested that the concept of involvement encompasses dimensions of behavior in addition to that which can be observed. For example, to understand why students actively participate in some activities and not others, aspects of a student's personality, such as motivation and interests, may be relevant.

In addition, involvement probably has a social component. A student may become involved in an activity because of affiliation needs. For example, a student whose friends are actively engaged in a particular activity may begin to participate in that activity in order to spend more time with her or his friends. Some students feel responsible for advancing the status or causes of their group, such as gays and lesbians, students of color, women, or members of a particular political party.

Information about how peers and affinity groups influence student participation in various out-of-class opportunities would be instructive for those interested in encouraging student behavior toward educationally purposeful ends. Clearly, more needs to be learned about individual student variables that influence student involvement and the mutual shaping of student characteristics and institutional factors and conditions that promote student participation in out-of-class learning opportunities.

Insights into Community on Campus. Student out-of-class behavior antithetical to the aims and purposes of higher education is frequently featured in the news media, such as the *New York Times* (Carmody, 1989) and *Newsweek* (Mabry, 1989), as well as the higher education literature (Bresler, 1989). Acquaintance rape and other forms of physical and emotional violence, alcohol abuse, racist incidents, and even a pervasive lack of common courtesy, have become all-too-common lead stories about college student life. In response to these concerns, presidents, trustees, and others have become interested in the quality of campus life (El-Khawas, 1989).

Some observers of higher education (see Carnegie Foundation . . . , 1990) believe that the quality of life for students will improve if a sense of campus community is established. For many institutions of higher education, achieving feelings of community will be difficult. At universities with tens of thousands of students and many student subcommunities (not to mention faculty and staff subcommunities), musing about a campus community may be more the stuff of fond recollections of a bygone era—when colleges were small, homogeneous, and geographically and socially isolated—than a realistic aspiration.

We did not set out to determine the extent to which a sense of community was present at the fourteen institutions in this study. Nonetheless, institutional agents and students often used the word "community" when describing what was special about their institution. Consider the observation of a Stanford senior a few weeks before graduation: "Be ready for the fact that the university *is* a community. I certainly didn't understand the concept."

Students (and faculty members and administrators) must develop an understanding of the meaning of community and what community may look and feel like in an institution of higher education now and in the future. We believe that by reflecting on the factors and conditions common to Involving Colleges in light of ideals that characterize community, institutional agents can identify ways in which a sense of campus community can be achieved or affirmed.

Gardner (1989) described the qualities that characterize an effective community: wholeness incorporating diversity; shared culture; good internal communication; caring, trust, and teamwork; group maintenance and governance; participation and shared leadership tasks; development of young people; and links with the outside world. All of these qualities can be found in Involving Colleges.

- Good communities incorporate and value diversity.

    We expect and want diversity, and there will be dissension in the best of communities. But in better communities, cooperation, compromise, and consensus building will be widely shared pursuits. In the best circumstances, such communities will have instruments and processes for conflict resolution [Gardner, 1989, p. 76].

Involving Colleges are committed to pluralism in all its forms, and they support the establishment and coexistence of subcommunities that permit students to identify with, and receive support from, people like themselves, so that they can feel comfortable in becoming involved in the larger campus community. However, when subcommunities are allowed to insulate their members from people of different backgrounds and values, they become vehicles for fragmentation and separation, not community building. That is why Involving Colleges also work to develop networks among members of various groups and to promote interaction among students across subcommunities.

- Good communities have a shared culture.

> Social cohesion will be advanced if the group's
> norms and values are explicit. Values that are never
> expressed are apt to be taken for granted and not
> adequately conveyed to young people and new-
> comers. The well-functioning community provides
> many opportunities to express values and relevant
> action. . . . A healthy community affirms itself and
> builds morale and motivation through ceremonies
> and celebrations that honor the symbols of shared
> identity and enable members to rededicate them-
> selves [Gardner, 1989, p. 77].

Evidence from Involving Colleges lends support to Gardner's observations about the necessity of a shared culture (norms,
values, symbols of group identity, legends, heroines and heroes)
for community on campus. These are institutions that convey
their culture by explaining their missions and philosophies
through anticipatory socialization and induction activities and
clear statements about what the institution expects of students
and students can expect of the institution. We have also described
the need for presidents, faculty members, staff, trustees, and
others to discover their institution's culture in order to determine whether rituals, traditions, ceremonies and other cultural
artifacts promote student learning.

- Good communities foster internal communication.

> One of the advantages of the small group is that
> frequent face-to-face communication is possible . . .
> [A] community is strengthened if there are occa-
> sions . . . in which extensive, informal interaction
> is possible [Gardner, 1989, p. 77].

The human-scale qualities of Involving Colleges create
opportunities for students to know, work with, and understand
faculty, staff, and peers. Through assiduous attention to providing small living units and small classes, and maintaining effective communication networks, Involving Colleges create con-

ditions under which frequent face-to-face interaction occurs and information is disseminated to those who need or want to know. Whether it is the chalkboard in the residence hall or house foyer or lavatory, the weekly student newspaper, electronic bulletin boards, mimeographed sheets on the dining-room table, or posters in the campus post office, communication is a priority at Involving Colleges.

• Good communities promote caring, trust, and teamwork.

> A good community nurtures its members and fosters an atmosphere of trust. . . . There is a spirit of mutuality and cooperation. Everyone is included [Gardner, 1989, p. 78].

The ethics of care and membership undergirded by invisible safety nets common to Involving Colleges mirror Gardner's qualities of caring, trust, and teamwork. However, in the case of some small colleges or separatist subcommunities, we, like Gardner, observed that "a community can be too tightly knit, suppressing the dissent and constraining the creativity of its members" (p. 78).

• Good communities have group maintenance processes and governance structures that encourage participation and sharing of leadership tasks.

> It is not uncommon . . . that the groups most involved in the affairs of the community all come from one or two segments of the community. All segments must participate . . . everyone need not participate actively . . . we must guard the *right* to participate while recognizing that some will choose not to do so [Gardner, 1989, p. 79].

Opportunities for student involvement in institutional governance characterize Involving Colleges. Students are, for example, often expected to determine rules and regulations for their living units compatible with the mission and values of the institution.

• Good communities foster the development of young people.

Preparing future generations of informed, responsible citizens is, undeniably, one of the fundamental purposes of a college or university. Gardner (1989, p. 80) emphasized the role of out-of-class learning experiences toward this end:

> The opportunities for individual growth will be numerous and varied for all members. . . . [O]n the playing field, and in group activities in and out of school and college, they will learn teamwork. Through volunteer and intern experiences outside of school they will learn how the adult world works and will have the experience of serving their society.

An opportunity-rich environment is but one example of the factors and conditions common to Involving Colleges that reflect this quality. Other aspects include policies and practices that give students responsibility for determining how to allocate their money, and "ladders" that provide students with steps to follow to academic success.

• Good communities have links with the outside world.

> The sound community has seemingly contradictory responsibilities: it must defend itself from the forces in the outside environment that undermine its integrity, yet it must maintain open, constructive, and extensive relations with the world beyond its boundaries [Gardner, 1989, p. 80].

An Involving College is, in some respects, a haven for its students, "a place apart" with permeable boundaries. The realities and challenges of the outside world influence teaching and learning and how students spend their time. While some students should, perhaps, be protected for a time from the more destructive forces, such as racism, sexism, and poverty, at work in the larger world, at some point in their education they must have their attitudes, values, and knowledge tested on and off the campus. Involving Colleges provide opportunities for students to render service to their communities beyond the campus through local, regional, and international programs. As we have illustrated, Involving Colleges intentionally create opportunities for students to learn firsthand how their education can be used after college by providing, for example, employment opportunities to broaden and enrich the undergraduate experience.

We do not assert that attending to the institutional factors and conditions shared to varying degrees by Involving Colleges will guarantee a strong and positive campus community. However, the process (a campus audit or some other means) through which an institution discovers the degree to which these factors and conditions are present should also provide some insights into what an institution must do to establish, or reestablish, and maintain the qualities associated with good communities.

A Final Word

Educational renewal initiatives in the 1980s emphasized the curriculum, including such perennial issues as what constitutes general education and how learning during college can be assessed (Ewell, 1985). Renewal efforts must also address the quality and frequency of student relationships with faculty, staff, and peers, as well as the contributions of student affairs and other administrative staff who help establish expectations and an appropriate intellectual tone for student cultures (Gaff, 1989). Because "everything that happens on a campus has curricular implications" (Gaff, 1989, p. 14), a college or university must have not only integrity in the curriculum (Association of American Colleges, 1985) but also integrity between the curriculum and the college's ecology (Gaff, 1989). At a college with integrity, institutional policies and practices, both curricular and noncurricular, are consistent with the institution's mission and values.

So we have come full circle, back to the mission and philosophy of the institution as the basis for all that a college or university does, or ought to do. Only through a renewed understanding of what the institution is and aspires to be—its mission—can people learn their roles and responsibilities, understand why the institution works the way it does, and develop a shared vision of the institution's future. When all members of a college or university community, including faculty, administrators, trustees, staff, and students, believe that all aspects of the institution's environment contribute to student learning and personal development, the institution can take another step toward realizing its potential and fulfilling its obligation to be a community committed to learning in all forms and forums.

RESOURCE A

Members of
the Panel Chosen
to Identify
Involving Colleges

The experts invited to nominate institutions included: directors of the six regional accreditation associations; representatives of fourteen associations or agencies with special interest in higher education and the undergraduate experience, such as the American Council of Education, American Association of Higher Education, Education Commission of the States, National Association of Student Personnel Administrators, and Campus Compact; twenty higher education scholars with long-standing interest in the college student experience, including Alexander Astin, Zelda Gamson, C. Robert Pace, and David Riesman; seven college and university presidents, including representatives of single-sex, historically black, and urban institutions; and eleven chief student life officers, several of whom were current or former presidents of the American College Personnel Association or the National Association of Student Personnel Administrators.

The following persons participated in one or both rounds of the nominating process (March through July, 1988) used to identify institutions that provided rich out-of-class learning experiences for undergraduate students:

Robert E. Albright, president, Johnson C. Smith University

Kay J. Anderson, director, Western Association of Schools and Colleges

Alexander W. Astin, professor, University of California, Los Angeles

Margaret J. Barr, vice-chancellor, Student Affairs, Texas Christian University

James F. Bemis, director, Northwest Association of Schools

Richard D. Blackburn, executive director, Association of College Unions-International

Howard Bowen, professor emeritus, Claremont Graduate School (now deceased)

Nevin Brown, assistant director, Urban Affairs, National Association of State Universities and Land-Grant Colleges

Judith Chambers, vice-president, Student Life, University of the Pacific

John W. Chandler, executive director, Association of American Colleges

Bob Childers, executive director, Southern Association of Colleges and Schools

Burton R. Clark, professor, University of California, Los Angeles

Richard Correnti, vice-president, Student Affairs, Florida International University

David Crockett, vice-president, American College Testing Program

Mary Maples Dunn, president, Smith College

Larry Ebbers, professor, Iowa State University

Elaine El-Khawas, vice-president, American Council on Education

Robert Fenske, professor, Arizona State University

Zelda F. Gamson, professor, University of Massachusetts, Boston

Dennis C. Golden, vice-president, Student Affairs, University of Louisville

Don Hossler, professor, Indiana University

Marvalene Styles Hughes, vice-president, Student Affairs, University of Toledo

Cynthia Johnson, professor, Teachers College, Columbia University

Joseph Katz, professor, Princeton University (now deceased)

Robert Kirkwood, director, Middle States Association of Colleges and Schools

Susan Komives, professor, University of Maryland

Robert E. Leach, vice-president, Student Affairs, Florida State University (now deceased)

Arthur Levine, president, Bradford College

Phyllis Mable, vice-president, Student Affairs, Longwood College

Theodore Marchese, vice-president, American Association of Higher Education

Warren Bryan Martin, senior fellow, Carnegie Foundation for the Advancement of Teaching

Marcia Mentkowski, institutional researcher, Alverno College

Michael Nettles, vice-president for assessment, University of Tennessee

Elizabeth M. Nuss, executive director, National Association of Student Personnel Administrators

C. Robert Pace, professor emeritus, University of California, Los Angeles

James Rhatigan, vice-president, Student Affairs, Wichita State University

Eugene Rice, senior fellow, Carnegie Foundation for the Advancement of Teaching

Richard C. Richardson, Jr., professor, Arizona State University

David Riesman, professor emeritus, Harvard University

Patricia Rueckel, executive director, National Association of Women Deans, Administrators, and Counselors

Arthur Sandeen, vice-president, Student Affairs, University of Florida

Charles C. Schroeder, vice-president, Student Development, St. Louis University

Gloria D. Scott, president, Bennett College

Daryl Smith, professor, Claremont Graduate School

Allen Splete, executive director, Council of Independent Colleges

Susan Stroud, director, Campus Compact

Patricia Thrash, executive director, North Central Association of Colleges and Universities

Nancy Walborn, executive director, National Association of Campus Activities Foundation

RESOURCE B

Results of
the College Student
Experiences Questionnaires

In the spring of 1989, the College Student Experiences Questionnaire (CSEQ) was administered to random samples of students at twelve of the fourteen colleges and universities that participated in the College Experiences Study. While all fourteen institutions originally agreed to administer the CSEQ, students at The Evergreen State College refused to participate, a typical response by TESC students to questionnaire surveys, and at Xavier University the completed questionnaires were misplaced. The CSEQ was subsequently administered at Xavier to a convenience sample of about 120 students.

The sampling strategy was based on the number of full-time undergraduate students at each institution. For purposes of their own institutional research program, some institutions, such as UC Davis, requested permission to augment the number of instruments provided by the study. For some institutions, particularly the urban universities, obtaining current mailing addresses was a problem; hence, the number of CSEQs distributed varies somewhat from campus to campus. In the parentheses following each institution, the numbers of instruments returned and distribued are presented: Iowa State (270/994), Miami (538/1000), Wichita State (209/934), Louisville (317/965), UC Davis (725/1486), Stanford (192/690), UAB (316/748),

UNCC (201/750), Berea (236/398), Earlham (85/400), Grinnell (264/605), Mount Holyoke (180/396), and Xavier (68/120). A total of 9,486 students across the thirteen institutions were actually asked to complete the CSEQ. The response rate was 38 percent based on 3,601 usable instruments.

Because these colleges and universities reputedly provided unusually rich out-of-class learning and personal development opportunities for students, it was no surprise that in most instances the quality of effort expended by students at Involving Colleges often exceeded the mean scores for similar institutions (doctoral universities, selective liberal arts colleges, and so forth) reported in the *CSEQ: Test Manual and Norms* (Pace, 1987) (see Table 1). The exceptions (lower mean scores) tended to be urban institutions. It is not uncommon for students at urban, commuter campuses to spend less time (Rhatigan, 1986) and therefore expend less effort on many of the activities listed on the CSEQ. However, the topics of conversation and gains in learning for students attending urban institutions tend to be more focused on academic matters. This is an issue that deserves more attention but is beyond the scope of this presentation.

Moreover, students at Involving Colleges tend to invest time in a greater range of activities — what Pace calls "breadth of involvement" (personal communication, October 1989) — than students at similar institutions. The breadth index was defined by Pace as the number of scales on which an *individual* scores above the middle (closest to the 50th percentile) of a norm or comparative group of similar institutions. The breadth score was determined by noting whether the midpoint (closest to 50th percentile) at the institution was higher (+), the same (0), or lower (−) than the midpoint of the norm group. In Table 2, a distribution of breadth scores for individuals (the national sample) provided by Pace (personal communication) is compared with students at Involving Colleges. Apparently, students at Involving Colleges spend more time in a greater variety of activities (using the library, interacting with faculty, talking about information presented in their courses, and so on) than students at other institutions. Thus, the CSEQ results corroborate the opinions of experts who helped identify the institutions for the study.

Table 1. A Comparison of CSEQ Quality of Effort Scale Mean Scores with CSEQ Norms.

School	LIB	FAC	CRSE	AMT	UNIN	ATHL	CLUB	WRIT	PERS	STAC	SCI	DORM	TPS	INFO
ISU (DGU)	19.1+	19.1+	28.4	18.7+	17.2+	18.2+	20.2+	24.0	20.4	23.0	15.9	27.2+	28.4	14.0
Louisville (DGU)	19.5+	19.0+	30.7+	17.1	15.7	13.5	14.6	25.5+	20.1	21.7	14.6	14.9	26.2	14.1
Miami (DGU)	19.5+	21.1+	30.0+	21.6+	19.5	20.5+	23.8+	25.2+	24.4+	25.8+	14.0	28.1+	31.4+	15.2+
Stanford (DGU)	19.2+	18.6	29.1	22.4+	18.4	21.5+	23.1+	26.9+	22.7+	29.4+	15.8	27.3+	31.0+	14.5+
UAB (DGU)	19.0+	20.0+	30.9+	16.7+	18.5+	15.6+	16.7+	26.1+	20.4+	23.8	15.9	19.2	27.6	14.6+
UC Davis (DGU)	18.9+	18.7	29.2+	18.8	21.0+	18.9+	19.6+	25.9+	22.4+	26.4+	16.3+	25.5	30.2+	15.0+
UNCC (CCU)	19.2	19.4	29.7+	16.8	19.2	16.0+	18.2	25.8+	20.9	23.3	15.6+	22.9	27.0	14.2
WSU (CCU)	18.4	19.9	29.6+	18.0+	19.9	15.8	17.6	24.9	21.6	24.5	14.3	24.3	27.9	14.4
Xavier (CCU)	19.5	20.6	28.7	18.8	24.4+	15.6	22.3+	26.6+	22.9+	25.8+	18.0	22.6+	31.7+	14.8+
Earlham (SLA)	23.3+	24.5+	30.4+	25.8+	24.5+	20.3+	27.7+	25.5	24.6+	27.7	15.0	25.7+	31.4+	16.1+
Grinnell (SLA)	21.4	23.1+	30.5+	24.4+	25.4+	20.9+	25.5+	26.3+	24.2+	29.6+	15.4+	26.0+	32.1+	15.5+
Holyoke (SLA)	21.1	22.3	30.5+	22.7+	23.5	20.9+	26.4+	26.1+	24.3+	29.7+	14.6	25.1	31.6+	15.2+
Berea (GLA)	23.4+	22.4+	29.8+	23.8+	25.9+	20.6+	22.1+	26.3+	23.5	28.9+	15.8+	27.2+	30.6+	14.8+

Table 1. A Comparison of CSEQ Quality of Effort Scale Mean Scores with CSEQ Norms, Cont'd.

Legend for Table 1

Scale position notation: A "+" following the scale number means the score is above the norm. Scores not so marked are at or below the norm.

College and university abbreviations

Berea	Berea College
Earlham	Earlham College
Grinnell	Grinnell College
Holyoke	Mount Holyoke College
ISU	Iowa State University
Louisville	University of Louisville
Miami	Miami University
Stanford	Stanford University
UAB	University of Alabama, Birmingham
UC Davis	University of California, Davis
UNCC	University of North Carolina, Charlotte
WSU	Wichita State University
Xavier	Xavier University

Institutional classifications (Pace, 1984a)

CCU	=	Comprehensive Colleges/Universities
DGU	=	Doctoral Granting University
GLA	=	General Liberal Arts College
SLA	=	Selective Liberal Arts College

Column abbreviations

LIB   = Library experiences scale
FAC   = Experiences with faculty scale
CRSE   = Course learning scale
AMT   = Art, music, theater scale
UNIN   = Student union scale
ATHL   = Athletic/recreation facilities scale
CLUB   = Clubs and organizations scale
WRIT   = Experiences in writing scale
PERS   = Personal experiences scale
STAC   = Student acquaintances scale
SCI   = Science scale
DORM   = Dormitory/fraternity/sorority scale
TPS   = Topics of conversation scale
INFO   = Information in conversations scale

Table 2. Comparison of Breadth Scores of Students at
Involving Colleges with Counterparts at Similar Types of Institutions.

National Sample		
Score 0–3	low breadth	27%
Score 4–8	medium breadth	49%
Score 9–13	high breadth	24%
Involving Colleges		
Score 0–3	low breadth	25% (3 schools)
Score 4–8	medium breadth	33% (5 schools)
Score 9–13	high breadth	42% (5 schools)

RESOURCE C

Notes on Methods Used in the Study

In this section, we elaborate on the data collection and analysis methods used in the study. This information, coupled with the material in Chapter Two, provides a detailed description of the inquiry methods used in the College Experiences Study.

The Research Team

The ambitious scope of the project required multiple investigators. One or two individuals could not conduct the number of interviews required to provide a rich, cumulative description of fourteen Involving Colleges. Field research using qualitative methods requires that the research team be familiar not only with appropriate inquiry techniques but also with the phenomena under study. With these criteria in mind, the research team was composed of nine members: four faculty, including a former college president and university provost, a former academic dean and department chair, the head of a preparation program in college student affairs administration, and a former dean of students; three student life administrators, including one chief student affairs officer with twenty-five years experience at private institutions of higher education, one associate vice-president at an urban institution who also has extensive residence life experience, and one dean of students who has served at both commuter and residential universities; and two graduate students, one of whom had experience in student affairs administration at a women's college and at large public universities.

The nine members brought a variety of experiences relevant to identifying and understanding institutional factors and conditions that seemed to be significant in promoting involvement. The research team members also brought different styles and ways of thinking about higher education. Most important, all were willing to challenge assumptions about student learning and personal development when analyzing and interpreting the data.

Selection of Institutions

There were 252 institutions mentioned in the first round of nominations: 78 small residential institutions, 67 large residential institutions, 49 urban institutions, 33 single-sex colleges (some of which were subsequently deleted from that category because they were no longer single sex, such as Haverford), and 25 historically black colleges.

A list of those institutions receiving two or more nominations (27 small residential, 29 large residential, 21 urban, 16 single-sex, 14 black) was sent to the panel of experts. They were again asked to identify those that they believed provided high-quality out-of-class experiences for undergraduates. In the second round, 85 institutions were nominated by four or more experts: 20 small residential, 23 large residential, 16 urban, 15 single-sex, and 11 black. After the second round of the nominating process was completed, twelve experts were interviewed by telephone to learn more about the criteria they had used in making nominations. Focusing primarily on the results of the second round of nominations and telephone interviews with a dozen members of the expert panel, the research team engaged in a series of discussions to identify institutions to visit.

Negotiating Entry

In late August and early September 1988, the chief student affairs officer at each institution was contacted to invite her or his institution's participation in the study. The oral agreement was subsequently confirmed with a letter describing the study's purposes and the process by which the fourteen institutions were selected and requesting information about the institution (Resource D).

Data Collection and Analysis

Data collection and analysis were conducted concurrently. In this way, we were able to use existing data to inform collection and interpretation of additional data (Lincoln and Guba, 1985; Miles and Huberman, 1984).

Respondents. The institutional contact person was asked to schedule the initial round of interviews. The selection of interview respondents was based on the technique of status sampling (Dobbert, 1984). In this instance, status sampling required that interviews be conducted with the president, the chief academic and student affairs officers and their principal assistants, faculty members, professional staff who work directly with students, and student leaders and other students.

The principle of inclusion was emphasized to the contact person — that is, we needed to gather information from as many perspectives as possible (Miles and Huberman, 1984). For example, we wanted to be certain that we talked with students who held informal leadership roles as well as some who were not well integrated into the social system. We also wanted to talk with faculty who might not have had a lot of contact with students outside of class.

We employed a variant of "snowball sampling" (Dobbert, 1984). At the conclusion of interviews, respondents were asked to identify others whose opinions and out-of-class activities and experiences differed from their own, such as students who seemed to be less involved in campus life. In addition, we did some impromptu interviews in cafeterias, library foyers, student centers, residence halls, and other living units, such as fraternity and sorority houses.

All respondents were asked to sign a consent form giving

their permission to use information obtained from them in the study. Respondents were told that their participation was voluntary, and that they could withdraw from the study at any time (Dobbert, 1984).

Interviews. Individual interviews and focus groups (Merton, Fisk, and Kendall, 1956) were the primary methods of data collection. Focus groups are discussion groups that meet only once and concentrate on a specific topic, such as factors related to students' out-of-class experiences. Interviews were conducted to obtain respondents' constructions, as well as to confirm and expand information already obtained (Lincoln and Guba, 1985). Although the degree of structure imposed on the interviews varied from more to less as the investigation proceeded, a set of questions was developed for each category of respondent, such as the president, students, and so forth. Initial questions were developed from the research questions presented in Chapter Two. The interview protocols were used by all investigators at all of the sites. Questions were added as interviewing progressed and additional questions were necessary for clarification or to obtain additional information. Thus, the respondents generated additional questions for the study.

Interviews were recorded by means of a tape recorder so that all information obtained could be retrieved. Transcripts were made of interviews that were deemed to be especially useful, such as those of student leaders and faculty members. Interview data were compiled by the investigators on interview summary forms (Miles and Huberman, 1984) in order to identify themes, questions, and reactions generated by each interview. This information was used to develop additional questions and during data analysis.

Observations. A secondary source of data was observations of programs, events, and activities that took place during the campus visits. Observations were considered to be secondary because they were typically used to generate topics for interviews. Observations fell roughly into three categories: regularly scheduled events, such as convocations and lectures; spontaneous events, such as frisbee matches on the green; and events conducted for the purpose of the visit, such as a tour of the campus.

We did not actively participate in the events observed; rather, we recorded notes and impressions (Dobbert, 1984). Points for clarification and questions were addressed later to appropriate individuals. Data from observations were recorded on observation summary sheets (Miles and Huberman, 1984) in order to facilitate the process of identifying further questions and emergent themes.

Documents. Documents were another secondary source of information and, like observations, provided topics and questions for interviews. Documents were also used to describe and understand the institutional context (Dobbert, 1984). We obtained numerous documents in advance of the visits (Resource D). The following documents were found to be particularly useful: handbooks for policy, procedure, student, faculty, and staff, promotional pamphlets such as admissions viewbooks, student and organization recruitment brochures, institutional mission and goal statements, institutional histories, and other documents that referred to the integration of students' out-of-class experiences with the academic mission of the institution. In addition to printed documents, we reviewed other media designed to communicate with constituents, including videotapes used for institutional advancement or recruitment purposes.

Data obtained from document analysis were recorded on document summary forms (Miles and Huberman, 1984). Information from the forms was used to generate questions for respondents at the institution, as well as to develop constructions of the institutional context.

Data Analysis

Data analysis was conducted throughout data collection and focused simultaneously on analysis of data within the individual sites and across sites. A description of each of these processes follows.

Within-Site Analysis. A coding scheme was developed to identify categories for the purpose of organizing and retrieving data (Miles and Huberman, 1984). Categories encompass a single theme, containing those units of data that relate to the same content (Lincoln and Guba, 1985). A preliminary list of category codes was formulated by the research team from the conceptual framework, purposes, and guiding questions. These categories were: (1) the role of institutional agents regarding out-of-class experiences; (2) description and role of student subcultures; (3) description and role of institutional history and traditions; (4) description and role of institutional policies and practices; (5) description and role of institutional mission; (6) characteristics of student involvement in out-of-class life; (7) tentative explanations, speculations, and hypotheses; and (8) other (creating additional categories as necessary). Each of the categories was discussed by the team in order that all could understand and agree upon the category definitions (Miles and Huberman, 1984).

After each site visit, each investigator recorded his or her interview and field notes on interview summary forms (Miles and Huberman, 1984). In addition, each investigator completed a case analysis form, in which data from interviews, observations, and documents were placed in the categories developed by the group.

These forms, as well as tapes and interview notes, were forwarded to the investigator designated as the site coordinator. The first task of the site coordinator was to compile all of the site data, including notes from team meetings on-site. The coordinator then clustered the data into categories; case analysis forms from the other investigators were used as a means to assess the completeness of these categories. If necessary, additional categories were developed in order to include all of the site data (Miles and Huberman, 1984). Categorization at this point in the analysis process served two purposes. First, having the site data in categories enabled the development of a case report, summarizing findings and conclusions for the first visit. Second, categorization of site data provided a basis for analysis of data across sites, a process that is described below.

The case report of the first visit served as an "interim site summary" (Miles and Huberman, 1984, p. 75), synthesizing what was known about the institution and identifying remaining questions to be explored. The case report was then circulated among all members of the research team in order to inform data gathering at other sites. The report was also sent to respondents at the institution in order to allow them to confirm or deny the investigators' constructions of their words and feelings through the debriefing process. Debriefing will be discussed later in the section on trustworthiness.

Cross-Site Analysis. Data from all the first-round campus visits were compiled and analyzed at a meeting of all project staff in December 1988. For the purposes of cross-site data analysis, data from the individual sites were "standardized" (Miles and Huberman, 1984, p. 152) by means of common categories and common reporting formats using forms. Analysis of the standardized data took place in four stages: development of a meta-matrix, clustering of data, identification of patterns, and development of propositions (Miles and Huberman, 1984).

In developing meta-matrices, "the basic principle is the inclusion of all relevant data" (Miles and Huberman, 1984, p. 152). For the purposes of this study, a meta-matrix was developed from summaries of within-site analyses. Data from each institution were described by categories: (1) the role of institutional agents regarding out-of-class experiences; (2) description and role of student subcultures; (3) descriptions and role of institutional history and traditions; (4) description and role of institutional policies and practices; (5) description and role of institutional mission; (6) characteristics of student involvement in out-of-class life; and (7) tentative explanations, speculations, and hypotheses. Institution-specific categories were, in most cases, subsumable into the original set of categories.

Once the meta-matrix was prepared, research team members proceeded to cluster data in order to identify commonalities and differences in categories across sites (Miles and Huberman, 1984). In addition, commonalities and differences were described according to the five types of institutions (small residential, large residential, urban/commuter, single-sex, and historically black). Thus, we were able to discover that, except in the case of urban/commuter institutions, the various institutional types had many more commonalities than differences.

The cluster of "things in common" was then examined in order to identify patterns or themes emerging in each category. From those themes, a set of propositions was developed to describe and explain (however tentatively) factors and conditions associated with high-quality out-of-class experiences for undergraduates. Those propositions, then, were discussed in debriefing sessions with respondents and evaluated by the research team throughout the second round of site visits.

Establishing Trustworthiness

Lincoln and Guba (1985, p. 290) proposed the standard of trustworthiness to answer the question, "How can an inquirer persuade his or her audiences (including self) that the findings of an inquiry are worth paying attention to, worth taking account of?" Criteria for trustworthiness include credibility (the constructions arrived at are credible to the respondents), transferability (the study may be useful in another context), dependability (the reporting of results considers possible changes over time), and confirmability (the data can be confirmed by someone other than the inquirer). Mechanisms for meeting the criteria for trustworthiness are described below.

Credibility. Three of the mechanisms cited by Lincoln and Guba for establishing credibility (triangulation, peer debriefing, and member checks) were used in this study. Triangulation is a technique for judging the accuracy of data and requires the use of multiple data sources and/or multiple methods of data collection. Multiple sources of data may include multiple "copies" of one kind of source, such as respondents and different sources of the same information (Lincoln and Guba, 1985). In this study, data were obtained from five different types of institutions of higher education. In addition, at every institution, respondents in nine general categories (students, presidents, chief academic affairs officers, chief student affairs officers, faculty, student affairs staff, institutional historians, graduates, and trustees) were interviewed. All nine types of respondents at all five types of institutions were asked to provide information about the out-of-class experiences of undergraduates, the role of institutional agents in those experiences, and the connections, if any, between out-of-class experiences and the academic mission of the institution.

Debriefing of the inquirer by a peer is used: to ensure that the inquirer is aware of her or his personal perspectives and perceptions and the impact they have on the study; to develop and test next steps to be taken; and to test hypotheses that are emerging from the data. Debriefing sessions were particularly critical for the credibility of this study as nine "human instruments" were involved. First, visits to Grinnell and Wichita State were conducted by two teams of investigators in late September. All nine members of the research team then met by conference call in order to debrief the first visits, make adjustments to interview protocols and other data-gathering techniques, and identify other sources of information that were found to be beneficial.

Throughout the study, team members at each site met at the end of each day of data gathering to discuss findings, determine additional questions that needed to be answered and identify additional respondents, and discuss tentative (and temporary) conclusions. Follow-up phone conferences were conducted in order to discuss data and impressions further.

Debriefings were also conducted at project staff meetings, held four times during the course of the study. These debriefings were used to test ideas, obtain feedback on methods, such as interview techniques and identification of themes, and discuss the next steps.

Member checks are, in effect, debriefing sessions with respondents for the purposes of testing the data, analytical categories, interpretations, and conclusions — in short, for judging the overall credibility of the findings of the study (Lincoln and Guba, 1985). Member checks occurred throughout the study and were informal as well as formal. At the end of most interviews, the investigators reviewed what they had heard the respondents say, seeking immediate feedback and clarification of the interview. Also, after the first round of site visits, we began to "recycle" data among the respondents at each institution. Respondents from each category received both a case report about their institution developed by the site team and a list of tentative constructions about factors relevant to high-quality out-of-class experiences. Conversations were held with respondents, either by phone or in person, in order to obtain reactions to the questions, comments, concerns, and experiences described by other respondents. This process served to focus later interviews and reinforce the constructions that were emerging during data analysis.

Finally, copies of our preliminary propositions regarding factors and conditions associated with high-quality out-of-class experiences of undergraduates were sent to respondents at all fourteen sites. Their reactions to the propositions were used in the process of developing conclusions to the study as well as to inform the second round of site visits.

Transferability. To address the issue of transferability, the inquirer must demonstrate the degree of similarity between the sending (the setting of the study) and receiving (a setting to which the study may be applied) contexts (Lincoln and Guba, 1985). Therefore, he or she must provide a thick description of the sending context so that someone in a potential receiving context may assess the similarity between them and, hence, the transferability of the study. Thick description entails the broadest and most thorough information possible. In reporting the findings and conclusions of the study, we provided as accurate a description of the setting and respondents as concern for confidentiality would allow, as well as an extensive discussion of themes, including statements from which they were derived.

Dependability and Confirmability. In order to meet criteria for dependability, the inquirer must provide evidence of the appropriateness of the inquiry decisions made throughout the study (Lincoln and Guba , 1985). Confirmability of the data is demonstrated by showing that the findings are based on the data and that the inferences drawn from the data are logical (Lincoln and Guba, 1985). Dependability and confirmability can be established by means of an audit, in which an external auditor examines both the processes and the products of the study. During the course of the study, we developed an audit trail (Lincoln and Guba, 1985) composed of: (1) raw data, including tapes, interview notes, and documents; (2) products of data reduction and analysis, including field notes, interview and document summary forms, and case analysis forms; (3) products of data reconstruction and synthesis, including category descriptions, case reports, and ongoing reports of findings and conclusions; (4) process notes, including notes on methodological decisions and trustworthiness criteria; and (5) materials relating to the intention and disposition of the research team, including notes of debriefings, staff meeting minutes, and staff correspondence.

RESOURCE D

═══

Materials
and Individuals
Consulted in
Campus Visits

College Experiences Study Institutional Profile Materials

To make the best use of our time on your campus, it would be very helpful if we could receive the information listed below in Part I two weeks prior to our visit. Single copies are sufficient unless noted. We would like to review the materials in Part II when we are on campus.

Part I (to be received prior to the visit)

A.   Undergraduate catalogue (3 to 4 copies if possible).
B.   Organizational charts (including position titles and names) for the institution and student affairs division.
C.   Mission statements for the institution and student affairs division.
D.   Sample admissions material (viewbooks, brochures, and the like). If a video cassette is available, we would like to view it during our visit.
E.   Student demographic information, such as biographical data, ability, aspirations, attitudes (for example, CIRP data), and any student participation/involvement data (for example, Pace's CSEQ data).
F.   List of student organizations (formal and informal).

G. Student handbook (or alternatives).
H. Public statements or policies that address the out-of-class experience (for example, recent presidential addresses, news releases).

Part II (to be reviewed during the visit)

I. Annual reports prepared for various groups (for example, trustees, graduates, parents) that describe student life or special programs.
J. Sections of reports prepared for accreditation associations that describe the quality of student and campus life.
K. Reviews of student affairs units or other departments that have responsibility for students' out-of-class experiences.
L. Student government annual reports.
M. Samples of student newspapers, including copies of pertinent articles.
N. Institutional histories or anthologies.
O. Lists or descriptions of opportunities for student involvement.
P. Samples of alumni/alumnae publications and participation rates (for example, annual giving campaigns).

Persons and Groups to Be Interviewed During the First Campus Visit

Individual Interviews

President
Chief Academic Officer
Chief Student Affairs Officer
Student Affairs Principal Assistant (1 or 2 persons)
Historians (formal and/or informal)
Student Body President (and/or members of student governance organizations)
Student Newspaper Editor
Others to be determined

Focus Groups

Faculty (2 groups)
Student Affairs Professionals

Residence Life Staff (paraprofessionals/RAs included)
Student leaders
Students of color
Adult learners
Other students
Trustees (could be individual interviews)
Recent alumni(nae)

Each session is expected to last between forty-five minutes and one hour. Please try to schedule the meetings every ninety minutes. This will give us a few minutes to summarize our notes at the end of each meeting and prepare for the next session. If possible, please try to divide the interviews evenly across the two full days we will be on your campus. Because two or more project staff will participate in the visit, two persons/groups can be scheduled concurrently. One or two evening meetings can be accommodated. If necessary, we can conduct one or two interviews the night before the first full day or the morning following the second full day.

RESOURCE E

Involving College
Audit Protocol:
A Guide for Assessing
Campus Environments

Overview and Use

The Involving College Audit Protocol (ICAP) is a guide
to help colleges and universities learn whether the out-of-class
experiences of their undergraduate students are compatible with
the educational purposes of the institution. The questions provided in the ICAP are *not* interview questions. Rather, they
and the categories of institutional functioning they represent are
intended to direct attention to the multiple factors that may influence student involvement. For example, faculty, administrators, and students can use the ICAP to determine if institutional
policies and practices encourage students to take advantage of
learning opportunities. In this sense, the ICAP is a formative
assessment tool that can help institutions identity areas of campus
life that promote student learning as well as aspects of out-of-
class life that warrant attention. Student learning is broadly
defined and includes the acquisition by students of any lasting
knowledge or skill consistent with the educational purposes of
the institution.

Patterns of involvement or active participation in learning activities are as diverse as American colleges and universities. The elements that make up an Involving College (IC) cannot be easily separated or isolated, although we have done so for the purposes of analysis and understanding. The distinctive factors and conditions described in this book work together in different combinations and toward different purposes, depending on the institutional context, mission, and expectations for students, faculty, and staff. To be useful, the ICAP must be adapted to reflect the institution's missions, culture, and student body. In that sense, the ICAP is a tool for institutional self-discovery, not a set of prescriptive questions. Hence, sections and questions should be modified so that they fit the institution. Some questions may be inappropriate for institutions with many commuter and part-time students.

The ICAP is designed for use in conjunction with the ideas described in this book and in accordance with the principles for conducting campus audits explained in Chapter Eleven. We recommend that those conducting a campus audit begin with a question like: "What is special about this institution?" or some other question designed to elicit diverse impressions and perceptions. Follow-up questions should focus more specifically on areas suggested by the ICAP.

I.   Mission and Philosophy
     A.   Is the institutional mission clearly communicated and understood? Mission refers to the broad, overall, long-term purpose of the institution which guides institutional priorities and practices in ways that are consistent with the expectations of its constituents both on and off the campus. An institution's mission may be, but is not necessarily, described by written mission statements.
          1.   What is the institutional mission?
               a.   Where and in what forms is evidence of the mission to be found?
               b.   What is *not* included in the institution's mission?

       c.   When, where, how, and to whom is the mission communicated?

       d.   How does the mission influence student learning and the student experience?

2.   How do members of the institution describe the mission?

       a.   What similarities and differences exist among these descriptions? Do they agree or disagree with "formal" mission statements, such as in the catalogue?

       b.   Do those similarities and differences affect the experiences of students?

3.   To what extent are institutional values and aspirations consistent (or inconsistent) with the mission?

4.   To what extent do students, faculty, and administrators have shared understandings of the institution's philosophy, and of how the institution works, what is valued, and how things get done?

       a.   To what extent do students perceive that they are actively involved in institutional decision making?

       b.   In what ways is the philosophy consistent or inconsistent with the mission?

       c.   In what ways does the institutional philosophy influence students' learning?

5.   To what degree is the institution committed to the appreciation, encouragement, and enhancement of multiculturalism in race and ethnicity, in life-styles, in gender, in physical abilities, and in opinions and world views, both on the campus and within society? How are these commitments manifested in the mission, philosophy, and practices?

B.   Do expectations for students present challenges that are appropriate for the students, consistent with the institutional mission, and buttressed by an ethic of care? The ethic of care is an institutionalized support system that communicates to students that they are important; resources are devoted to helping students succeed.

1. Is pertinent information about student characteristics, such as ability, attitudes, and educational aspirations, made available to faculty, administrators, students, trustees, and graduates?

2. To what extent is knowledge about student characteristics used to influence institutional policies and practices, including expectations for student behavior? To what degree are faculty and staff members' assumptions about and expectations for student behavior congruent with the characteristics of students?

3. In what ways do academic and social expectations for students enhance or diminish stereotypes?

4. Does an "ethic of care" permeate the institution?
   a. How are students in difficulty noticed and helped?
   b. What forms of assistance are available? Are they known by students?
   c. To what extent is seeking or accepting assistance encouraged or discouraged by faculty, by administrators, and by students?

5. Does the institution manifest an "ethic of membership"? An ethic of membership means that upon matriculation, a student becomes a full member of the community. The institution sends the message: "We are happy to have you here. You belong here and you are, by the very act of choosing us, a full member of the community with all the rights *and* responsibilities that come with community membership."

      a. To what extent are students acknowledged and encouraged to act as full members of the community?

      b. Are there groups or individuals who feel that they are not acknowledged as full members of the community? If so, why?

C. In what ways are individual differences acknowledged?

    1. By whom and how are the worth and dignity of individuals and groups emphasized?

    2. What means, if any, are used to acknowledge differences in achievement, year in college, or students' capacity to act responsibly? Are these means consistent with the institution's educational purposes? How do they influence student learning?

    3. Is the institution characterized by meritocratic or egalitarian values, or some combination?

      a. Are these values consistent with the institutional mission and philosophy?

      b. How do these values, and the ways in which they are enacted, affect student learning?

    4. Is competition or collaboration a dominant theme?

      a. Are these themes consistent with the institutional mission and philosophy?

      b. How do these themes, and the ways in which they are enacted, affect student learning?

II. Campus Culture

A. How do the institutional culture and dominant student subcultures promote student learning?

B. What traditions and events introduce and socialize students to core values of the institution? Which are antithetical to the values of the institution?

    1. How do students learn about expectations for their behavior?

> 2. What opportunities exist to celebrate the campus community? What role do students play in these celebrations? Are there segments of the campus community who feel that they are excluded from participating in such celebrations?

C. What language is used by students, faculty, and others to communicate the importance of students and their learning?

> 1. Is the language of the culture inclusive and embracing or alienating?
>
> 2. Does the language of the culture communicate respect or disrespect for individuals and individual differences?
>
> 3. What "terms of endearment" are used to communicate the special qualities of the institution to insiders and outsiders? Terms of endearment are words and expressions that have context-bound meanings and encourage feelings of belonging in members and express institutional values and beliefs.
>
> 4. How do newcomers learn the language of the institution?

D. What symbols and symbolic actions communicate the importance of out-of-class experiences to student learning?

> 1. What is communicated about student life to prospective students, and in what ways?
>
> 2. What is communicated about expectations for student behavior at orientation activities, and by whom?

E. What messages and institutional values are communicated by other cultural artifacts, such as mascots, mottoes, traditions, stories, institutional heroines and heroes, history, and myths?

III. Campus Environment

A. In what ways does the institution's setting influence its mission and practices?

B.   What are the special circumstances or resources that the setting provides? Are these circumstances and resources used to promote student learning?

1.   What cultural, political, social, or service opportunities are available to students? Do students take advantage of these opportunities? Why or why not? Which opportunities are most attractive to students and why?

2.   Do students take advantage of the educational opportunities the setting provides? How?

3.   Do students have access to work that can be matched with their educational and career objectives?

4.   Is transportation available for students to take advantage of off-campus opportunities?

5.   Are local graduates, community leaders, and other friends of the institution used as resources by students?

C.   In what ways is the campus "human scale?" A human-scale setting is one which people have a sense of mastery over, and feel comfortable and confident with, where they live and work.

1.   Physical plant

a.   Is the campus attractive and well maintained?

b.   Are facilities clearly identified for newcomers and visitors?

c.   Are facilities accessible to students and at times convenient to students' schedules?

d.   Are residence halls, libraries, and recreational facilities placed to encourage use by, and interaction among, faculty, staff, and students?

e.   Does vehicular traffic interfere with access to facilities and contact among community members?

2.   Psychological aspects of the environment

a. How are common campus issues communicated? Do students have access to information?

b. In what ways does the psychological climate influence feelings of comfort for students?

c. Are large facilities, such as classroom buildings and residence halls, constructed — or can they be modified — to promote a sense of mastery, comfort, and interaction? If so, in what ways?

d. To what extent are students free from unwanted feelings of anonymity?

   1) Do faculty know students' names?
   2) To what extent, and in what ways, do students exhibit care and concern for one another?
   3) Are "safety nets" in place to help students in trouble, and do students take advantage of them? A safety net is a network of faculty and staff who reach out to students in difficulty.
   4) Can students easily affiliate with one or more groups?

e. Are there places on the campus that encourage spontaneous, informal interaction among students? Between students and faculty? Among students, faculty, and staff?

   1) What central meeting places are available? To what extent are they used, and by whom?
   2) To what extent are gathering places accessible (both physically and psychologically) to all students?

f. Are there spaces in residence halls and other campus buildings that encourage impromptu interaction?

g. Can students find personal space when needed? Where, when, and how can students be alone if they desire?

h. In what ways are students encouraged to participate actively in the life of the community?

   1) What opportunities exist for student involvement in institutional groups, and other activities?

   2) Are there enough opportunities to meet all students' needs for involvement?

   3) To what extent do students take advantage of these opportunities? Who does and who does not, and why?

   4) Are these opportunities compatible with the institution's educational purposes?

   5) Are too many opportunities available for student involvement?

i. How do students get involved?

   1) To what extent are students welcomed and encouraged—even "rushed" (in the best sense of the term)—to become actively involved in the life of the community?

   2) To what extent are interested students excluded from participation, such as by membership limits, special qualifications, dues or fees, or narrow interests?

   3) To what extent are interviews or other competitive processes required to become involved? Are these processes compatible with the institution's espoused educational philosophy and purposes?

j. To what extent are students who seek outlets for their interests encouraged and supported in creating new clubs or organizations?

    k.   What leadership positions are available?

        1)   Are there enough leadership positions to meet the needs of students for leadership experiences? Are leadership roles widely distributed or are a few students "in charge of everything"? What, if any, students are most likely to fill these roles and why?

        2)   Are opportunities to develop leadership skills and followership skills widely available? To what extent do students take advantage of these opportunities?

IV.   Policies and Practices

    A.   Do institutional policies and practices promote student learning in ways that are consistent with the mission and student characteristics?

    B.   How are newcomers made to feel welcome? How are the institution's values articulated and by whom?

        1.   What means are used for anticipatory socialization of students, faculty, and administrators? Anticipatory socialization includes all the things students learn about the college before they matriculate. How effective are anticipatory socialization efforts at communicating the institutional mission and values?

            a.   Do preadmission contacts clearly and accurately describe "what it's like to be a student here"?

            b.   What is done between admission and matriculation to teach new students what it means to be responsible, self-directed members of the institutional community? To communicate institutional values and expectations? To make new students feel welcome?

    c. What role do current students play in these anticipatory socialization efforts?

  2. How are newcomers formally and informally "inducted" or made to feel like full members of the institution? Induction activities include those events (planned and spontaneous, sponsored by the administration and by student subcultures) that provide clues to students about what is appropriate behavior.

    a. What are these induction activities, such as orientation or convocations? Do all or most new students attend? If not, why not?

    b. What messages are sent to new students about the importance of taking advantage of learning opportunities?

    c. What roles do academic administrators (for example, president, provost, academic deans), student affairs staff, and students play in orientation? Do they invite and encourage students' active participation in the campus community?

C. To what extent does the institution communicate that students are expected to be responsible and self-directed?

  1. How does the institution communicate what is considered to be responsible behavior in the collegiate community?

    a. Do anticipatory socialization and orientation processes clearly communicate expectations and standards for academic and social performance?

    b. What messages about appropriate behavior are communicated by students and student subcultures?

    c. Do students, faculty, administrators, and others have the same view of what is appropriate student behavior?

  2. What opportunities exist for students to exercise initiative and responsibility?

       a.   Are students given responsibility for their residential and organizational experiences?

       b.   What educationally purposeful "hassles" (educational or bureaucratic obstacles to getting what is needed or wanted) do students encounter? How do students cope with these hassles? Do they see them as positive learning opportunities?

       c.   Do students take initiative?

       d.   Are students responsible for their own learning? What impedes students from taking responsibility (for example, parietal rules or student immaturity)?

  3.   Are students encouraged to take risks?

       a.   What is the price of failure?

       b.   Are safety nets available?

  4.   Do students take or share responsibility for planning academic and social learning experiences? In what areas?

D.   Are boundaries between academic and other student routines blurred?

  1.   Do students, faculty, and administrators acknowledge that the student experience is an integrated whole? Do institutional policies and practices reflect that seamlessness?

       a.   To what extent are residential groups, such as Greeks or residential living units, encouraged and expected to engage in activities consistent with the educational purposes of the institution?

       b.   To what extent do athletics promote or inhibit student learning?

  2.   Are educational—that is, both academic and nonacademic—learning opportunities available in student living areas?

       a.   What are the frequency and range of these opportunities?

       b.   Who initiates, plans, and implements these opportunities?

        c. How do these opportunities influence student learning?

    3. To what extent are students involved in academic or major-related out-of-class activities (for example, research with a faculty member or active participation in departmental clubs)?

        a. Do faculty members as well as students participate in these activities?

        b. Is participation encouraged by the institution?

    4. What intentional connections exist between educational experiences for students and the concerns of the institutional setting or "outside world," such as volunteer services, political and social action groups, "good neighbor" policies regarding noise and social events, or undergraduate research opportunities?

    5. Are student learning experiences designed to complement the educational purposes of the institution?

E. Are multiple subcommunities celebrated, encouraged, and empowered? A subcommunity is a separate and distinctive living unit or subculture organized around themes consistent with the mission, such as academic interests, cultural or ethnic background, gender, and life-style orientation.

    1. To what extent are members of historically underrepresented groups successful in and valued by the institutional community?

        a. What leadership roles in campus affairs are held by faculty, administrators, and students of color? What is their impact on the institution?

        b. To what extent are students of color encouraged to understand, celebrate, and share their heritage?

        c. What institutional policies and practices support or inhibit people of color?

    2. To what extent are women students successful

in and valued by the institutional community?

    a.   What leadership roles in campus affairs
are held by female faculty, administrators,
and students? What is their impact?

    b.   To what extent are women encouraged to
understand and celebrate themselves as
women?

    c.   What institutional policies and practices
support or inhibit women?

3.   To what extent is recognizing, becoming comfortable with, and learning from differences a
priority for the institution? What evidence exists
that this is a priority? What policies and practices facilitate or inhibit realizing this aspiration?

4.   In what ways are students encouraged and enabled to explore issues of identity, such as race,
gender, ethnicity, cultural background, sexual
orientation, or physical ability?

5.   In what ways are subcommunities based on
ethnicity, race, sex, or life-style orientation encouraged and enabled?

6.   To what extent are subcommunities acknowledged and incorporated into the educational
purposes of the institution?

7.   Are subcommunities encouraged and enabled
to communicate and interact with one another?

8.   If the institution has Greek organizations, do
they (individually and as a system) operate in
ways consistent with the institution's educational purposes?

9.   In what ways does the institution capitalize on
the differences that exist among students and
student groups?

10.   In what ways is the institution moving toward
becoming a multicultural community?

F.   Does the institution put its money where its MIND is?

1.   Are institutional resources allocated according
to expressed educational priorities?

2. How are resource allocation decisions made?
3. Are trade-offs in the use and allocation of resources acknowledged and debated?
4. Are students given — and do they take — responsibility for determining how their resources will be used? Are processes of resource acquisition and allocation public, open, and accessible to all groups?

V. Institutional Agents
  A. Academic Administrators
    1. What does the president (or campus CEO) know about student life? How does she or he learn this?
    2. What does the president say and do regarding student life and student involvement?
      a. Where do students and the quality of their life appear on the president's agenda?
      b. How do students, faculty, and administrators describe the president's attitude about students and student life?
      c. What messages does the president send to external audiences about the importance of students and student life?
      d. What does the president do to symbolize and emphasize the importance of students?
      e. How visible is the president to students?
      f. What is the relationship between the president and the chief student affairs officer (CSAO)? Does this relationship positively influence the president's understanding of and commitment to students and the collegiate experience?
      g. What messages does the president send to faculty about how they should be involved with students?
    3. What do other academic administrators say and do regarding the out-of-class experiences of students?

      a.   Where do students and the quality of student life appear on the agenda of the chief academic officer (CAO) and other academic administrators?

      b.   How do the CAO and other academic administrators describe the contributions of nonacademic experiences to the institution's educational purposes?

      c.   What is the nature of the relationship between the CAO and the CSAO? Does this relationship influence the CAO's understanding of and commitment to student life? Do they find or create opportunities to cooperate with each other?

      d.   What messages do the CAO and other academic administrators send to faculty about their involvement with students and student life?

      e.   How do students, faculty, and administrators describe the attitudes of the CAO and other academic administrators about students and their learning?

B.   Student Affairs Administrators

    1.   Where do students and the quality of their learning environments appear on the CSAO's agenda?

    2.   What is the relationship between student affairs and academic affairs?

      a.   Is student affairs perceived to be a partner in achieving the institution's educational purposes?

      b.   Do faculty and student affairs staff have a shared vision of the enterprise?

    3.   To what extent do student affairs staff and their activities complement the institution's educational purposes and promote student learning?

    4.   Where, when, and how do student affairs staff work with students?

      a. In what ways do they challenge students to examine assumptions and community norms, assume personal responsibility, and so forth?

      b. Do they help students connect with others on the campus?

5. Are student affairs staff the campus experts on students?

      a. Are student affairs staff well informed about student characteristics, student needs and desires, and student concerns?

      b. How and with whom do they share this information?

6. To what extent and in what ways do student affairs staff serve as an "early warning system" for students with problems and collaborate with others to provide "safety nets" for students in trouble?

7. Are student affairs staff called upon to bridge the gap between academic programs and out-of-class life? To what extent do they expect themselves to do so?

8. How do students and faculty describe the roles and activities of student affairs staff?

C. Faculty

1. To what extent do students perceive that faculty members are (and/or should be) available and personally involved in their learning?

2. What is the nature of student contact with faculty outside the classroom?

      a. Are out-of-class contacts usually initiated by students in order to extend or question points made during class discussions?

      b. Does student interaction with faculty tend to relate to academic matters?

3. In what settings does informal faculty-student interaction occur?

4. What are the characteristics of those faculty

members who are involved with students outside the classroom? Is the number of such
faculty decreasing, stable, or increasing?

5. To what extent are changes (if any) in reward
systems and promotion and tenure criteria influencing faculty involvement with students beyond the classroom and laboratory? To what
extent are these changes consistent with the institutional mission and philosophy?

6. How do students and administrators (including student affairs staff) describe the roles and
activities of faculty?

D. Students

1. Why did students choose this institution? Did
they find what they expected? Why or why not?
Would they make the same choice again? Why
or why not?

   a. To what extent do students feel they "belong"?

   b. What do students describe as the highlights and disappointments of their collegiate experiences?

   c. If students could change anything they
   wanted about the institution, what would
   they change *and* what would they *not* change?

   d. What words do students use to describe
   student life? What values and experiences
   do those words reflect?

   e. What words do students use to describe
   other students? Faculty? Administrators?
   The institution as a whole? What values
   and experiences do those words reflect?

2. How do students spend their free time?

3. How do students, faculty, and others describe
student life (in and out of class) at the institution?

   a. In what ways, if any, are these descriptions similar or dissimilar?

          b.   To what extent do these descriptions portray student life that is compatible with the institution's mission, values, and educational purposes?

    4.   In what ways do student subcultures encourage or discourage educationally purposeful learning experiences? Do student subcultures support institutional values and expectations for student behavior?

    5.   In what ways do student subcultures perpetuate or inhibit positive traditions of participation in community life?

          a.   In what ways do older students "teach" younger students about these traditions?

          b.   Do students encourage other students to "get involved"?

          c.   To what extent do student subcultures facilitate or inhibit movement toward a multicultural learning community?

E.   What roles do other members of the campus community, such as trustees, maintenance personnel, secretaries, graduates, and parents play in encouraging high-quality learning experiences for students?

F.   What other context-specific questions should be asked to discover more about student learning?

References

Adelman, C. (ed.). *Assessment in American Higher Education: Issues and Contexts.* Washington, D.C.: U.S. Department of Education, Office of Educational Research and Improvement, 1986.

Allison, G. T. *Essence of Decision: Explaining the Cuban Missile Crisis.* Boston: Little, Brown, 1971.

American Council on Education. *The New Agenda of Women for Higher Education: A Report of the ACE Commission on Women in Higher Education.* Washington, D.C.: American Council on Education, 1987.

Argyris, C., and Schön, D. A. *Organizational Learning: A Theory of Action Perspective.* Reading, Mass.: Addison-Wesley, 1978.

Association of American Colleges. *Integrity in the Curriculum.* Washington, D.C.: Association of American Colleges, 1985.

Astin, A. W. *Four Critical Years: Effects of College on Beliefs, Attitudes, and Knowledge.* San Francisco: Jossey-Bass, 1977.

Astin, A. W. *Minorities in American Higher Education: Recent Trends, Current Prospects, and Recommendations.* San Francisco: Jossey-Bass, 1982.

Astin, A. W. "Student Involvement: A Developmental Theory for Higher Education." *Journal of College Student Personnel,* 1984, *25,* 297–308.

Astin, A. W. *Achieving Educational Excellence: A Critical Assessment of Priorities and Practices in Higher Education.* San Francisco: Jossey-Bass, 1985.

Astin, A. W., and Holland, J. L. "The Environmental Assessment Technique: A Way to Measure College Environments." *Journal of Educational Psychology,* 1961, *52,* 308–316.

419

Astin, H. S., and Kent, L. "Gender Roles in Transition: Research and Policy Implications for Higher Education." *Journal of Higher Education*, 1983, *54*, 309–324.

AT&T Human Resources Study Group. *College Experiences and Managerial Performance.* New York: AT&T, 1984.

Austin, A. E., and Gamson, Z. F. *Academic Workplace: New Demands, Heightened Tensions.* ASHE-ERIC Higher Education Research Report, no. 10. Washington, D.C.: Association for the Study of Higher Education, 1983.

Baird, L. L. "Big School, Small School: A Critical Examination of the Hypothesis." *Journal of Educational Psychology,* 1969, *60*, 253–260.

Baird, L. L. "The College Environment Revisited: A Review of Research and Theory." In J. C. Smart (ed.), *Higher Education: Handbook of Theory and Research.* Vol. 4. New York: Agathon, 1988.

Baird, L. L. "Comments on Involving Colleges: Factors and Conditions Associated with Student Out-of-Class Learning Experiences." Paper presented to the Association for the Study of Higher Education, Atlanta, Ga., Nov. 1989.

Baird, L. L., and Hartnett, R. T. *Understanding Student and Faculty Life.* San Francisco: Jossey-Bass, 1980.

Baldridge, J. V., Curtis, D. V., Ecker, G. P., and Riley, G. L. "Alternative Models of Governance in Higher Education." In J. V. Baldridge and T. Deal (eds.), *Governing Academic Organizations,* pp. 2–25. Berkeley, Calif.: McCutchan, 1977.

Banaka, W. H. *Training for In-Depth Interviewing.* New York: Harper & Row, 1973.

Banning, J. H. (ed.). *Campus Ecology: A Perspective for Student Affairs.* Portland, Oreg.: National Association of Student Personnel Administrators, 1975.

Barker, R. G. *Ecological Psychology: Concepts and Methods for Studying the Environment of Human Behavior.* Stanford, Calif.: Stanford University Press, 1968.

Barker, R. G., and Gump, P. V. (eds.). *Big School, Small School.* Stanford, Calif.: Stanford University Press, 1964.

Bean, J. P. "Interaction Effects Based on Class Level in an Explanatory Model of College Student Dropout Syndrome." *American Educational Research Journal,* 1985, *22*, 35–64.

Bean, J. P., and Creswell, J. W. "Student Attrition Among Women at a Liberal Arts College." *Journal of College Student Personnel*, 1980, *21*, 320–327.

Becker, H. S., Geer, B., Hughes, E. C., and Strauss, A. L. *Boys in White.* Chicago: University of Chicago Press, 1961.

Belenky, M. F., Clinchy, B. M., Goldberger, N. R., and Tarule, J. M. *Woman's Ways of Knowing: The Development of Self, Voice, and Mind.* New York: Basic Books, 1986.

Berger, P. L., and Luckmann, T. *The Social Construction of Reality: Treatise in the Sociology of Knowledge.* Garden City, N.Y.: Anchor Books, 1966.

Betz, B. L., Klingensmith, J. B., and Menne, J. W. "The Measurement and Analysis of College Student Satisfaction." *Measurement and Evaluation in Guidance*, 1970, *3*, 110–118.

Bickman, L., and others. "Dormitory Density and Helping Behavior." *Environment and Behavior*, 1973, *5*, 465–490.

Blocher, D. H. "Campus Learning Environments and the Ecology of Student Development." In J. Banning (ed.), *Campus Ecology: A Perspective for Student Affairs.* Cincinnati, Ohio: National Association of Student Personnel Administrators, 1978.

Bolton, C. D., and Kammeyer, K. C. W. "Campus Cultures, Role Orientations, and Social Types." In K. Feldman (ed.), *College and Student: Selected Readings in the Social Psychology of Higher Education*, pp. 377–392. New York: Pergamon Press, 1972.

Bourassa, D. M. "Programming Interventions to Address Racism." In J. H. Schuh (ed.), *Educational Programming in College and University Residence Halls*, pp. 108–121. Columbus, Ohio: Association of College and University Housing Officers, 1989.

Bowen, H. R. *Investment in Learning: The Individual and Social Value of American Higher Education.* San Francisco: Jossey-Bass, 1977.

Bowen, H. R., and Schuster, J. H. *American Professors: A National Resource Imperiled.* New York: Oxford University Press, 1986.

Boyer, E. L. *College: The Undergraduate Experience in America.* Princeton, N.J.: Carnegie Foundation for the Advancement of Teaching, 1987.

Boyer, E. L. "In Search of Community." Paper presented at annual meeting of the American Council on Education, Washington, D.C., Jan. 1990.

Bragg, A. K. *The Socialization Process in Higher Education.* ERIC Higher Education Research Report, no. 7. Washington, D.C.: American Association for Higher Education, 1976.

Bresler, W. "The Concern About Community." *Educational Record,* 1989, *70* (3/4), 5.

Brubacher, J. S., and Rudy, W. *Higher Education in Transition.* New York: Harper & Row, 1976.

Campbell, J. (with B. Moyers). *The Power of Myth.* New York: Doubleday, 1988.

Carmody, D. "Trying To Make Campuses Civil (and Safe) Again." *New York Times,* Nov. 22, 1989, p. 23.

Carnegie Foundation for the Advancement of Teaching. *Campus Life: In Search of Community.* Princeton, N.J.: Princeton University Press, 1990.

Chaffee, E. E., and Tierney, W. G. *Collegiate Cultures.* New York: American Council on Education/Macmillan, 1988.

Chapman, D. W., and Pascarella, E. T. "Predictors of Academic and Social Integration of College Students." *Research in Higher Education,* 1983, *19,* 295–322.

Chickering, A. W. *Education and Identity.* San Francisco: Jossey-Bass, 1969.

Chickering, A. W. *Commuting Versus Resident Students: Overcoming Educational Inequities of Living Off Campus.* San Francisco: Jossey-Bass, 1974.

Clark, B. R. (1963). "Faculty Culture." In M. Finkelstein (ed.), *ASHE Reader on Faculty and Faculty Issues in Colleges and Universities,* pp. 129–142. Washington, D.C.: Association for the Study of Higher Education, 1985.

Clark, B. R. *The Distinctive College: Antioch, Reed and Swarthmore.* Chicago: Aldine, 1970.

Clark, B. R. "The Organizational Saga in Higher Education." *Administrative Science Quarterly,* 1972, *17* (2), 178–184.

Clark, B. R. "The Academic Life: Small Worlds, Different Worlds." *Educational Researcher,* 1989, *18* (5), 4–8.

Clark, B. R., and Trow, M. A. "The Organizational Context." In T. M. Newcomb and E. K. Wilson (eds.), *College Peer Groups: Problems and Prospects for Research.* Chicago: Aldine, 1966.

Clark, B. R., and others. *Students and Colleges: Interaction and Change.* Berkeley, Calif.: Center for Research and Development in Higher Education, University of California, 1972.

Cohen, M. D., and March, J. G. *Leadership and Ambiguity: The American College President.* New York: McGraw-Hill, 1974.

Corbally, J. E. "Preserving a Quality Environment for Learning." In C. Gerber (ed.), *Preserving a Quality Environment for Learning: Second International Symposium,* pp. 5–9. Columbus: Ohio State University Press, 1989.

Cross, K. P. *Accent on Learning: Improving Instruction and Reshaping the Curriculum.* San Francisco: Jossey-Bass, 1976.

Crowson, R. L. "Qualitative Research Methods in Higher Education." In J. C. Smart (ed.), *Higher Education: Handbook of Theory and Research.* Vol. 3, pp. 1–55. New York: Agathon Press, 1987.

Dannells, M., and Kuh, G. D. "Orientation." In W. Packwood (ed.), *College Student Personnel Services,* pp. 102–124. Springfield, Ill.: Thomas, 1977.

Davies, G. K. "The Importance of Being General: Philosophy, Politics, and Institutional Mission Statements." In J. C. Smart (ed.), *Higher Education: Handbook of Theory and Research.* Vol. 2, pp. 85–102. New York: Agathon Press, 1986.

Dewey, J. *Democracy and Education.* New York: Macmillan, 1916.

Dill, D. D. "The Management of Academic Culture: Notes on the Management of Meaning and Social Integration." *Higher Education,* 1982, *11,* 303–320.

Dobbert, M. L. *Ethnographic Research: Theory and Application for Modern Schools and Societies.* New York: Praeger, 1984.

Ehrhart, J. K., and Sandler, B. R. *Campus Gang Rape: Party Games?* Report of the Project on the Status of Women. Washington, D.C.: Association of American Colleges, 1985.

El-Khawas, E. "Ways to Improve Campus Life: What the President Suggests." *Educational Record,* 1989, *70* (3/4), 10–11.

The Evergreen State College. "Constancy and Change — Self-Study Report Prepared by The Evergreen State College for the Northwest Association of Schools and Colleges, the Commission on Colleges." Unpublished document, Aug. 1989.

Ewell, P. T. *The Self-Regarding Institution: Information for Excellence.*

Boulder, Colo.: National Center for Higher Education Management Systems, 1984.

Ewell, P. T. "Assessment: What's It All About." *Change,* 1985, *17* (6), 32–36.

Ewell, P. T. "Assessment: Where Are We?" *Change,* 1987, *19* (1), 23–28.

Feldman, K. A., and Newcomb, T. M. *The Impact of College on Students.* San Francisco: Jossey-Bass, 1969.

Fiske, E. B. *Selective Guide To Colleges.* (4th rev. ed.) New York: Times Books, 1988.

Fleming, J. *Blacks in College: A Comparative Study of Students' Success in Black and in White Institutions.* San Francisco: Jossey-Bass, 1984.

Forrest, L., Hotelling, K., and Kuk, L. "The Elimination of Sexism in the University Environment." Paper presented at the Student Development Through Campus Ecology Second Annual Symposium, Pingree Park, Colo., July 1984. (ED 267 348)

Gaff, J. G. "General Education at Decade's End: The Need for a Second Wave of Reform." *Change,* 1989, *21,* 11–19.

Gaff, J. G., and Gaff, S. S. "Student-Faculty Relationships." In A. W. Chickering and Associates, *The Modern American College: Responding to the New Realities of Diverse Students and a Changing Society.* San Francisco: Jossey-Bass, 1981.

Gardner, J. "The Freshman Year Experience." *College and University,* 1986, *61,* 261–274.

Gardner, J. W. "Building Community." *Kettering Review,* Fall 1989, 73–81.

Gardner, J. W. *On Leadership.* New York: Free Press, 1990.

Geertz, C. *The Interpretation of Cultures.* New York: Basic Books, 1973.

Gerard, S. L. "Providing an Ambience for Excellence." In C. Gerber (ed.), *Preserving a Quality Environment for Learning: Second International Symposium,* pp. 17–20. Columbus: Ohio State University, 1989.

Gerber, C. (ed.). *Preserving a Quality Environment for Learning: Second International Symposium.* Columbus: Ohio State University, 1989.

Gilligan, C. *In a Different Voice: Psychological Theory and Women's Development.* Cambridge, Mass.: Harvard University Press, 1982.

Glaser, G. B., and Strauss, A. L. *The Discovery of Grounded Theory: Strategies for Qualitative Research.* Chicago: Aldine, 1967.

Goetz, J. P., and LeCompte, M. D. *Ethnography and Qualitative Design in Educational Research.* Orlando, Fla.: Academic Press, 1984.

Grant, G., and Riesman, D. *The Perpetual Dream: Reform and Experiment in the American College.* Chicago: University of Chicago Press, 1978.

Green, M. F. *Minorities on Campus: A Handbook for Enhancing Diversity.* Washington, D.C.: American Council on Education, 1989.

Green, M. F. (ed.). *Leaders for a New Era: Strategies for Higher Education.* New York: American Council on Education/Macmillan, 1988.

Grobman, A. B. *Urban State Universities: An Unfinished Agenda.* New York: Praeger, 1988.

Hafner, A. L. "The 'Traditional' Undergraduate Woman in the Mid-1980s: A Changing Profile." In C. S. Pearson, D. L. Shavlik, and J. G. Touchton (eds.), *Educating the Majority: Women Challenge Tradition in Higher Education,* pp. 32–46. New York: American Council on Education/Macmillan, 1989.

Hall, E. T. *The Hidden Dimension.* New York: Doubleday, 1966.

Hall, R. M., and Sandler, B. R. *Out of the Classroom: A Chilly Campus Climate for Women?* Report of the Project on the Status of Women. Washington, D.C.: Association of American Colleges, 1984.

Hanks, M., and Eckland, B. "Athletics and Social Participation in the Educational Attainment Process." *Sociology of Education,* 1976, *49,* 271–294.

Hanson, G. R. "Response to *The Involving College Inventory:* A Guide for Assessing Campus Environments." Paper presented at the Fourth National Assessment Forum, Atlanta, Ga., June 1989.

Hartnett, R. T. "Involvement in Extracurricular Activities as a Factor in Academic Performance." *Journal of College Student Personnel,* 1965, *6,* 272–274.

Hawley, K. T., and Kuh, G. D. "The Small College as a Developmentally Powerful Learning Environment." In G. Kuh and A. McAleenan (eds.), *Private Dreams, Shared Visions: Student Affairs Work in Small Colleges,* pp. 11–28. Cincinnati, Ohio: National Association of Student Personnel Administrators, 1986.

Heath, D. H. *Growing Up in College: Liberal Education and Authority.* San Francisco: Jossey-Bass, 1968.

Heath, D. H. "A College's Ethos: A Neglected Key to Effectiveness and Survival." *Liberal Education,* 1981, *67,* 89–111.

Heller, S. "General Education Reform Should Stress How Students Learn, Report Says." *Chronicle of Higher Education,* A14, 1988.

Hodgkinson, H. L. *All One System: Demographics of Education, Kindergarten Through Graduate School.* Washington, D.C.: Institute for Educational Leadership, 1985.

Holsti, D. R. *Content Analysis for the Social Sciences and Humanities.* Reading, Mass.: Addison-Wesley, 1969.

Hood, A. B. *Student Development: Does Participation Affect Growth?* Bloomington, Ind.: Association of College Unions–International, 1984. (ED 255 105)

Horowitz, H. L. *Alma Mater.* Boston: Beacon Press, 1984.

Horowitz, H. L. "The 1960s and the Transformation of Campus Cultures." *History of Education Quarterly,* 1986, *26,* 1–38.

Horowitz, H. L. *Campus Life: Undergraduate Cultures from the End of the Eighteenth Century to the Present.* New York: Knopf, 1987.

Hossler, D. *Enrollment Management.* New York: College Board, 1984.

Hsia, J., and Hirano-Nakanishi, M. "The Demographics of Diversity: Asian Americans and Higher Education." *Change,* Nov./Dec. 1989, 20–27.

Huebner, L. A. (ed.). *Redesigning Campus Environments.* New Directions for Student Services, no. 6. San Francisco: Jossey-Bass, 1979.

Huebner, L. A. "Interaction of Student and Campus." In U. Delworth and G. Hanson (eds.), *Student Services: A Handbook for the Profession.* (Rev. ed.) San Francisco: Jossey-Bass, 1989.

Hunt, D., and Sullivan, E. *Between Psychology and Education.* Hinsdale, Ill.: Dryden, 1974.

Hyman, H. H., Wright, C. R., and Reed, J. S. *The Enduring Effects of Education.* Chicago: University of Chicago Press, 1975.

Jackson, R. D., and Kleberg, J. R. (eds.). *The Best-Laid Plans: Components of Quality Campus Environments.* Columbus: Ohio State University, 1987.

Jackson, R. D., and Kleberg, J. R. "Introduction." In C. Gerber (ed.), *Preserving a Quality Environment for Learning: Second International Symposium,* p. 4. Columbus: Ohio State University, 1989.

Jacoby, B. *The Student as Commuter: Developing a Comprehensive Institutional Response.* ASHE-ERIC Higher Education Report No. 7. Washington, D.C.: School of Education and Human Development, the George Washington University, 1989.

Jencks, C., and Riesman, D. "Patterns of Residential Education: A Case Study." In N. Sanford (ed.), *The American College,* pp. 731–773. New York: Wiley, 1962.

Johnson, D. W., and Johnson, R. T. *Learning Together and Alone: Cooperation, Competition and Individualization.* Englewood Cliffs, N.J.: Prentice-Hall, 1975.

Jones, J. D., and Damron, J. *Student Affairs Programs at Universities in Urban Settings.* Washington, D.C.: National Association of State Colleges and Universities, n.d.

Kamens, D. H. "The College 'Charter' and College Size: Effects on Occupational Choice and College Attrition." *Sociology of Education,* 1971, *44,* 270–296.

Kapp, G. J. *College Extracurricular Activities: Who Participates and What Are the Benefits?* Doctoral dissertation, University of California, Los Angeles, 1979. (University Microfilms no. 80–01, 378)

Keeton, M. T. *Models and Mavericks.* New York: McGraw-Hill, 1971.

Kegan, D. L. "The Quality of Student Life and Financial Costs: The Cost of Social Isolation." *Journal of College Student Personnel,* 1978, *19,* 55–58.

Keller, G. *Academic Strategy: The Management Revolution in American Higher Education.* Baltimore, Md.: Johns Hopkins University Press, 1983.

Kerr, C. *Presidents Make a Difference: Strengthening Leadership in Col-*

References

leges and Universities. Washington, D.C.: Association of Governing Boards of Universities and Colleges, 1984.

Kerr, C., and Gade, M. *The Many Lives of Academic Presidents.* Washington, D.C.: Association of Governing Boards of Universities and Colleges, 1986.

Kohn, A. *No contest: The Case Against Competition.* Boston: Houghton Mifflin, 1986.

Kroeber, A. L., and Kluckhohn, C. *Culture: A Critical Review of Concepts and Definitions.* Cambridge, Mass.: Harvard University Press, 1952.

Krumboltz, J. "The Relation of Extracurricular Participation in Leadership Criteria." *Personnel and Guidance Journal,* 1957, *35,* 307–313.

Kuh, G. D. *Indices of Quality in the Undergraduate Experience.* AAHE-ERIC/Higher Education Research Report, no. 4. Washington, D.C.: American Association for Higher Education, 1981.

Kuh, G. D. (ed.). *Understanding Student Affairs Organizations.* New Directions for Student Services, no. 23. San Francisco: Jossey-Bass, 1983.

Kuh, G. D. "A Framework for Understanding Student Affairs Work." *Journal of College Student Personnel,* 1984, *25,* 25–31.

Kuh, G. D., Krehbiel, L. E., and MacKay, K. A. *Personal Development and the College Student Experience.* Trenton, N.J.: Department of Higher Education College Outcomes Project, 1988.

Kuh, G. D., Schuh, J. H., and Thomas, R. O. "Suggestions for Encouraging Student-Faculty Interaction in a Residence Hall." *National Association of Student Personnel Administrators Journal,* 1985, *22* (3), 29–37.

Kuh, G. D., Shedd, J. D., and Whitt, E. J. "Student Affairs and Liberal Education: Unrecognized Common Law Partners." *Journal of College Student Personnel,* 1987, *28,* 252–260.

Kuh, G. D., and Wallman, G. H. "Outcomes-Oriented Marketing." In D. Hossler (ed.), *Managing College Enrollments,* pp. 63–72. San Francisco: Jossey-Bass, 1986.

Kuh, G. D., and Whitt, E. J. *The Invisible Tapestry: Culture in American Colleges and Universities.* AAHE-ERIC/Higher Education Research Report, no. 1. Washington, D.C.: American Association for Higher Education, 1988.

Kuh, G. D., Whitt, E. J., and Shedd, J. D. *Student Affairs, 2001: A Paradigmatic Odyssey.* ACPA Media Publication no. 42. Alexandria, Va.: American College Personnel Association, 1987.

Lincoln, Y. S., and Guba, E. *Naturalistic Inquiry.* Beverly Hills, Calif.: Sage, 1985.

Louis, M. R. "An Investigator's Guide to Workplace Culture." In P. Frost and Associates, *Organizational Culture,* pp. 73–93. Beverly Hills, Calif.: Sage, 1985.

Mabry, M. "Black and Blue, Class of '89: Racism on Campus." *Newsweek,* Sept. 25, 1989, pp. 50–51.

McHugh, B., Dalton, J., Henley, B., and Buckner, D. *Racial Discrimination on Campus: Strategies for Awareness and Action.* DeKalb: Northern Illinois University, 1988.

McKnight, J. L. "Regenerating Community." *Kettering Review,* 1989 (Fall), 40–51.

Manning, K. *Campus Rituals and Cultural Meaning.* Unpublished doctoral dissertation, Indiana University, Bloomington, 1989.

Marchese, T. J. "Assessment Update: Third Down, Ten Years to Go." *AAHE Bulletin,* 1987, *40* (4), 2–4.

Marchese, T. J. "A New Conversation About Undergraduate Teaching: An Interview with Prof. Richard J. Light, Convener of the Harvard Assessment Seminars." *AAHE Bulletin,* 1990, *42* (9), 3–8.

Martin, J., and Siehl, C. "Organizational Culture and Counterculture: An Uneasy Symbiosis." *Organizational Dynamics,* 1983, *12* (2), 52–64.

Masland, A. T. "Organizational Culture in the Study of Higher Education." *Review of Higher Education,* 1985, *8* (2), 157–168.

Mathews, D. " . . . afterthoughts." *Kettering Review,* 1989 (Fall), 82–84.

Merriam, S. B. *Case Study Research in Education: A Qualitative Approach.* San Francisco: Jossey-Bass, 1988.

Merton, R. K., Fisk, M., and Kendall, P. L. *The Focused Interview.* New York: Free Press, 1956.

Messick, S., and Associates. *Individuality in Learning: Implications of Cognitive Styles and Creativity for Human Development.* San Francisco: Jossey-Bass, 1976.

Miles, M. B., and Huberman, A. M. *Qualitative Data Analysis: A Sourcebook of New Methods.* Beverly Hills, Calif.: Sage, 1984.

Moffatt, M. *Coming of Age in New Jersey: College and American Culture.* New Brunswick, N.J.: Rutgers University Press, 1988.

Moore, K. M. "Women's Access and Opportunity in Higher Education: Toward the Twenty-First Century." *Comparative Education,* 1987, 23 (1), 23–34.

Moos, R. H. *The Human Context: Environmental Determinants of Behavior.* San Francisco: Jossey-Bass, 1976.

Moos, R. H. *Evaluating Educational Environments: Procedures, Measures, Findings, and Policy Implications.* San Francisco: Jossey-Bass, 1979.

Morgan, G. *Images of Organization.* Beverly Hills, Calif.: Sage, 1986.

Moses, Y. T. *Black Women in Academe: Issues and Strategies.* Washington, D.C.: Association of American Colleges Project on the Status and Education of Women, 1989.

Naisbitt, J. *Megatrends: Ten New Directions Transforming Our Lives.* New York: Warner Books, 1982.

National Association of Student Personnel Administrators. *A Perspective on Student Affairs.* Iowa City, Iowa: American College Testing Program, 1987.

Nelson, T. *A Comparison of Selected Undergraduate Experiences of Alumni Who Financially Support Their Alma Mater.* Unpublished doctoral dissertation, Indiana University, Bloomington, 1984.

Newcomb, T. M. "Student Peer-Group Influence." In N. Sanford (ed.), *The American College,* pp. 469–488. New York: Wiley, 1962.

Ory, J. C., and Braskamp, L. A. "Involvement and Growth of Students in Three Academic Programs." *Research in Higher Education,* 1988, *28,* 116–129.

Pace, C. R. *Demise of Diversity: A Comparative Profile of Eight Types of Institutions.* New York: McGraw-Hill, 1974.

Pace, C. R. *Measuring Outcomes of College: Fifty Years of Findings and Recommendations for the Future.* San Francisco: Jossey-Bass, 1979.

Pace, C. R. "Measuring the Quality of Student Effort: On Improving Teaching and Institutional Quality." *1980 Current Issues in Higher Education,* no. 1, pp. 10–16. Washington, D.C.: American Association for Higher Education, 1980.

Pace, C. R. *Achievement and the Quality of Student Effort.* Los Angeles: Higher Education Research Institute, University of California, 1982.

Pace, C. R. *Measuring the Quality of College Student Experiences.* Los Angeles: Higher Education Research Institute, University of California, 1984a.

Pace, C. R. *Student Effort: A New Key to Assessing Quality.* Project on the Study of Quality in Undergraduate Education. Los Angeles: Higher Education Research Institute, University of California, 1984b.

Pace, C. R. *The College Curriculum: Where's the Content?* Project on the Study of Quality in Undergraduate Education. Los Angeles: Higher Education Research Institute, University of California, 1985.

Pace, C. R. *Separate Paths to Separate Places.* Project on the Study of Quality in Undergraduate Education. Los Angeles: Higher Education Research Institute, University of California, 1986.

Pace, C. R. *Good Things Go Together.* Project on the Study of Quality in Undergraduate Education. Los Angeles: Higher Education Research Institute, University of California, 1987.

Palmer, P. "Community, Conflict, and Ways of Knowing: Ways to Deepen Our Educational Agenda." *Change,* 1987, *19,* 20–25.

Pascarella, E. T. "Student-Faculty Informal Contact and College Outcomes." *Review of Educational Research,* 1980, *50,* 545–595.

Pascarella, E. T. "Reassessing the Effects of Living On-Campus Versus Commuting to College: A Causal Modeling Approach." *Review of Higher Education,* 1984, *7,* 247–260.

Pascarella, E. T. "College Environmental Influences on Learning and Cognitive Development." In J. C. Smart (ed.), *Higher Education: Handbook of Theory and Research.* Vol 1. New York: Agathon, 1985.

Pascarella, E. T., Duby, P., Terenzini, P., and Iverson, B. A. "Student-Faculty Relationships and Freshman Year Intellectual and Personal Growth in a Non-residential Setting." *Journal of College Student Personnel,* 1983, *24,* 395–402.

Pascarella, E. T., Ethington, C. A., and Smart, J. C. "The Influence of College on Humanitarian/Civic Involvement Values." *Journal of Higher Education,* 1988, *59,* 412–437.

Pascarella, E. T., and Terenzini, P. "Student-Faculty Informal Interaction Beyond the Classroom and Voluntary Freshman Attrition." *Journal of Higher Education,* 1977, *48,* 540–542.

Pascarella, E. T., and Terenzini, P. "Predicting Voluntary Freshman-Year Persistence/Withdrawal Behavior in a Residential University: A Path Analytic Validation of Tinto's Model." *Journal of Educational Psychology,* 1983, *75,* 215–226.

Pascarella, E. T., Terenzini, P., and Wolfle, L. "Orientation to College and Freshman-Year Persistence and Withdrawal Decisions." *Journal of Higher Education,* 1986, *57,* 155–175.

Patton, M. Q. *Qualitative Evaluation Methods.* Beverly Hills, Calif.: Sage, 1980.

Pearson, C. S., Shavlik, D. L., and Touchton, J. G. (eds.). *Educating the Majority: Women Challenge Tradition in Higher Education.* New York: American Council on Education, 1989.

Peters, T. *Thriving on Chaos: Handbook for a Management Revolution.* New York: Harper & Row, 1987.

Peterson, M. W., and others. *The Organizational Context for Teaching and Learning: A Review of the Research Literature.* Ann Arbor, Mich.: National Center for Research to Improve Postsecondary Teaching and Learning, 1986.

Polkinghorne, D. *Methodology for the Human Sciences: Systems of Inquiry.* Albany: State University of New York Press, 1983.

Power-Ross, S. K. "Co-curricular Activities Validated Through Research." *Student Activities Programming,* 1980, *13,* 46–48.

Prins, D. J. "Student Services and Policies: An Outdated Privilege Or a Necessary Part of Higher Education?" *International Journal of Institutional Management in Higher Education,* 1983, *7,* 149–156.

Rapoport, A. *The Meaning of Built Environments: A Non-verbal Communication Approach.* Beverly Hills, Calif.: Sage, 1982.

Reinert, P. C. "Building the University District." In C. Gerber (ed.), *Preserving a Quality Environment for Learning: Second International Symposium,* pp. 11–16. Columbus: Ohio State University, 1989.

Rhatigan, J. J. "Developing a Campus Profile of Commuting Students." *NASPA Journal,* 1986, *24* (1), 4–10.

Richardson, R. C., Jr., and Bender, L. W. *Fostering Minority Access and Achievement in Higher Education: The Role of Urban Community Colleges and Universities.* San Francisco: Jossey-Bass, 1987.

Richardson, R. C., Jr., and Doucette, D. S. "An Empirical Model for Formulating Operational Missions of Community Colleges." Paper presented at the meeting of the American Educational Research Association, New Orleans, Apr. 1984.

Richardson, R. C., Jr., Simmons, H., and de los Santos, A. "Graduating Minority Students." *Change,* 1987, *19* (3), 20–27.

Riesman, D., and Jencks, C. "The Viability of the American College." In N. Sanford (ed.), *The American College,* pp. 74–192. New York: Wiley, 1962.

Riesman, D., and Jencks, C. *The Academic Revolution.* New York: Wiley, 1969.

Rowe, M. P. "What Actually Works: The One-to-One Approach." In C. S. Pearson, D. L. Shavlik, and J. G. Touchton (eds.), *Educating the Majority: Women Challenge Tradition in Higher Education,* pp. 375–383. New York: American Council on Education/Macmillan, 1989.

Sanford, N. "The Developmental Status of the Freshman." In N. Sanford (ed.), *The American College,* pp. 253–282. New York: Wiley, 1962.

Schein, E. H. *Organizational Culture and Leadership: A Dynamic view.* San Francisco: Jossey-Bass, 1985.

Schlossberg, N. K., Lynch, A. Q., and Chickering, A. W. *Improving Higher Education Environments for Adults: Responsive Programs and Services from Entry to Departure.* San Francisco: Jossey-Bass, 1989.

Schroeder, C. S. "Territoriality: An Imperative for Personal Development and Residence Education." In D. DeCoster and P. Mable (eds.), *Personal Education and Community Development.* Washington, D.C.: American College Personnel Association, 1980.

Schroeder, C. S. "Student Development Through Environmental Management." In G. Blimling and J. Schuh (eds.), *Increasing the Educational Role of Residence Halls.* New Directions for Student Services, no. 13. San Francisco: Jossey-Bass, 1981.

Schuh, J. H., and Laverty, M. "The Perceived Long Term Effect of Holding a Significant Student Leadership Position." *Journal of College Student Personnel,* 1983, *24,* 28–32.

Sergiovanni, T. J. "Cultural and Competing Perspectives in Administrative Theory and Practice." In T. Sergiovanni and J. Corbally (eds.), *Leadership and Organizational Culture,* pp. 1–11. Urbana: University of Illinois Press, 1984a.

Sergiovanni, T. J. "Developing a Relevant Theory of Administration." In T. Sergiovanni and J. Corbally (eds.), *Leadership and Organizational Culture,* pp. 275–291. Urbana: University of Illinois Press, 1984b.

Sergiovanni, T. J. "Leadership as Cultural Expression." In T. Sergiovanni and J. Corbally (eds.), *Leadership and Organizational Culture,* pp. 105–114. Urbana: University of Illinois Press, 1984c.

Shriberg, A. (ed.). *Providing Student Services for the Adult Learner.* New Directions for Student Services, no. 11. San Francisco: Jossey-Bass, 1980.

Skinner, B. F. *Science and Human Behavior.* New York: Macmillan, 1953.

Skinner, E. F., and Richardson, R. C., Jr. "Resolving Access/Quality Tensions: Minority Participation and Achievement in Higher Education." Paper presented at the meeting of the Association for the Study of Higher Education, St. Louis, Mo., Nov. 1988.

Smith, D. G. *The Challenge of Diversity: Involvement or Alienation in the Academy.* ASHE-ERIC Higher Education Report, no. 5. Washington, D.C.: School of Education and Human Development, George Washington University, 1989.

Snyder, B. R. *The Hidden Curriculum.* New York: Knopf, 1971.

Solmon, L. C. *The Definition and Impact of College Quality.* New York: National Bureau of Economic Research, 1973. (ED 065 080)

Solomon, B. M. *In the Company of Educated Women: A History of Women and Higher Education in America.* New Haven, Conn.: Yale University Press, 1985.

Spradley, J. *The Ethnographic Interview*. New York: Holt, 1979.

Spradley, J. *Participant Observation*. New York: Holt, 1980.

Steele, S. "The Recoloring of Campus Life." *Harper's*, Feb. 1989, 47–55.

Stern, G. G. *People in Context*. New York: Wiley, 1970.

Stern, R. *Pride of Place: Building the American Dream*. Boston: Houghton Mifflin, 1986.

Stewart, S. S. (ed.). *Commuter Students: Enhancing Their Educational Experiences*. New Directions for Student Services, no. 24. San Francisco: Jossey-Bass, 1983.

The Study Group on the Conditions of Excellence in American Higher Education. *Involvement in Learning*. Washington, D.C.: U.S. Department of Education, 1984.

Sturner, W. F. "Environmental Code: Creating a Sense of Place on the College Campus." *Journal of Higher Education*, 1972, *43*, 97–103.

Tewksbury, D. G. *The Founding of American Colleges and Universities Before the Civil War*. New York: Archon Books, 1965.

Thelin, J. R. "Postscript to the 'Importance of Being General,'" by Gordon K. Davies—"The Campus As Chameleon: Rethinking Organizational Behavior and Public Policy." In J. Smart (ed.), *Higher Education: Handbook of Theory and Research*. Vol. 2, pp. 103–108. New York: Agathon, 1986.

Thelin, J. R., and Yankovich, J. "Bricks and Mortar: Architecture and the Study of Higher Education." In J. Smart (ed.), *Higher Education: Handbook of Theory and Research*. Vol. 3, pp. 57–83. New York: Agathon, 1987.

Tidball, M. E. "Women's Colleges: Exceptional Conditions, Not Exceptional Talent, Produce High Achievers." In C. S. Pearson, D. L. Shavlik, and J. G. Touchton (eds.), *Educating the Majority: Women Challenge Traditions in Higher Education*, pp. 157–171. New York: American Council on Education/Macmillan, 1989.

Tierney, W. G. "Organizational Culture in Higher Education: Defining the Essentials." *Journal of Higher Education*, 1988, *59*, 2–21.

Tinto, V. "Theories of Student Departure Revisited." In J. Smart (ed.), *Higher Education: Handbook of Theory and Research*. Vol. 1. New York: Agathon, 1986.

Tinto, V. *Leaving College.* Chicago: University of Chicago Press, 1987.

Toffler, A. *The Third Wave.* New York: Bantam Books, 1981.

Trice, H., and Beyer, J. "Studying Organizational Cultures Through Rites and Ceremonials." *Academy of Management Review,* 1984, *9,* 653–669.

Turner, P. V. "Growth and Development of the Campus." In C. Gerber (ed.), *Preserving a Quality Environment for Learning: Second International Symposium,* pp. 39–48. Columbus: Ohio State University, 1989.

U.S. News & World Report. "Testing for Eight Skills." October 26, 1987, *103* (17), 62.

Upcraft, M. L., Gardner, J., and Associates. *The Freshman Year Experience: Helping Students Survive and Succeed in College.* San Francisco: Jossey-Bass, 1989.

Vaill, P. B. "The Purposing of High-Performing Systems." In T. Sergiovanni and J. Corbally (eds.), *Leadership and Organizational Culture,* pp. 85–104. Urbana: University of Illinois Press, 1984.

Van Gennep, A. *The Rites of Passage.* Chicago: University of Chicago Press, 1960.

Van Maanen, J. "Reclaiming Qualitative Methods for Organizational Research: A Preface." *Administrative Science Quarterly,* 1979a, *24,* 520–526.

Van Maanen, J. "The Fact of Fiction in Organizational Ethnography." *Administrative Science Quarterly,* 1979b, *24,* 539–550.

Van Maanen, J. "Doing Old Things in New Ways: The Chains of Socialization." In J. Bess (ed.), *College and University Organization: Insights from the Behavioral Sciences,* pp. 211–247. New York: New York University Press, 1984.

Van Maanen, J. *Tales of the Field: On Writing Ethnography.* Chicago: University of Chicago Press, 1988.

Walsh, W. B. *Theories of Person-Environment Interaction: Implications for the College Student.* Iowa City, Iowa: American College Testing Program, 1973.

Walsh, W. B. "Person-Environment Interaction." In J. Banning (ed.), *Campus Ecology: A Perspective for Student Affairs,* pp. 6–16. Cincinnati, Ohio: National Association for Student Personnel Administrators, 1978.

Washington, V., and Harvey, W. *Affirmative Rhetoric, Negative Action: African-American and Hispanic Faculty at Predominantly White Institutions.* ASHE-ERIC Higher Education Report, no. 2. Washington, D.C.: School of Education and Human Development, George Washington University, 1989.

Weick, K. E. *The Social Psychology of Organizing.* (2nd ed.) Reading, Mass.: Addison-Wesley, 1979.

Welzenbach, L. F. (ed.). *College and University Business Administration.* Washington, D.C.: National Association for College and University Business Officers, 1982.

Werth, B. "Why Is College So Expensive? Maybe America Wants It That Way." *Change,* 1988, *20* (2), 13–25.

Western Interstate Commission for Higher Education. *The Ecosystem Model: Designing Campus Environments.* Boulder, Colo.: Western Interstate Commission for Higher Education, 1973.

Whitla, D. K. *Value Added and Other Related Matters.* Washington, D.C.: National Commission on Excellence in Education, 1981. (ED 228 245)

Whitt, E. J. "Hit the Ground Running: Experiences of New Faculty in the School of Education at a Research University." *Review of Higher Education,* in press.

Whitt, E. J. "Making the Familiar Strange: Discovering Culture." In G. D. Kuh (ed.), *Using Cultural Perspectives in Student Affairs Work.* Alexandria, Va.: ACPA Media, forthcoming.

Whitt, E. J., and Kuh, G. D. "Qualitative Methods in Higher Education Research: A Team Approach to Multiple Site Investigation." Paper presented at annual meeting of the Association for the Study of Higher Education, Atlanta, Ga., 1989.

Wildavsky, A. *The Politics of Budgetary Process.* Boston: Little, Brown, 1974.

Wilder, D., and others. "Greek Affiliation and Attitude Change in College Students." *Journal of College Student Personnel,* 1986, *27,* 510–519.

Wilder, M. A., and Kellams, S. E. "Commitment to College and Student Involvement." Paper presented at annual meeting of American Educational Research Association, Washington, D.C., 1987.

Wilkerson, M. B. "Majority, Minority, and the Numbers Game."

In C. S. Pearson, D. L. Shavlik, and J. G. Touchton (eds.), *Educating the Majority: Women Challenge Traditions in Higher Education,* pp. 25–31. New York: American Council on Education/Macmillan, 1989.

Wilkins, A. L. *Developing Corporate Character: How to Successfully Change an Organization Without Destroying It.* San Francisco: Jossey-Bass, 1989.

Wilson, E. K. "The Entering Student: Attributes and Agents of Change." In T. M. Newcomb and E. K. Wilson (eds.), *College Peer Groups,* pp. 71–106. Chicago: Aldine, 1966.

Wilson, R. C., and others. *College Professors and Their Impact on Students.* New York: Wiley, 1975.

Yankelovich, D. *New Rules: Searching for Self-Fulfillment in a World Turned Upside Down.* New York: Random House, 1981.

Yin, R. K. *Case Study Research: Design and Methods.* Beverly Hills, Calif.: Sage, 1984.

Young, R. B. "Notes on Student Affairs Administration in the Small College." In G. Kuh and A. McAleenan (eds.), *Private Dreams, Shared Visions: Student Affairs Work in Small Colleges,* pp. 71–82. Cincinnati, Ohio: National Association of Student Personnel Administrators, 1986.

Zammuto, R. F. "Managing Decline in American Higher Education." In J. Smart (ed.), *Higher Education: Handbook of Theory and Research.* Vol. 2, pp. 43–84. New York: Agathon, 1986.

Index

439